T0257875

Internet of Things

Internet of Things

Edited by **Anthony Rocus**

New Jersey

Published by Clanrye International,
55 Van Reypen Street,
Jersey City, NJ 07306, USA
www.clanryeinternational.com

Internet of Things
Edited by Anthony Rocus

© 2015 Clanrye International

International Standard Book Number: 978-1-63240-321-6 (Hardback)

This book contains information obtained from authentic and highly regarded sources. Copyright for all individual chapters remain with the respective authors as indicated. A wide variety of references are listed. Permission and sources are indicated; for detailed attributions, please refer to the permissions page. Reasonable efforts have been made to publish reliable data and information, but the authors, editors and publisher cannot assume any responsibility for the validity of all materials or the consequences of their use.

The publisher's policy is to use permanent paper from mills that operate a sustainable forestry policy. Furthermore, the publisher ensures that the text paper and cover boards used have met acceptable environmental accreditation standards.

Trademark Notice: Registered trademark of products or corporate names are used only for explanation and identification without intent to infringe.

Printed in the United States of America.

Contents

Preface

The term Internet of Things was first proposed by Kevin Ashton in 1999 and then became popular through the Auto-ID Centre at MIT. A thing, in the Internet of Things, can refer to any natural or man-made object, which can be assigned an IP address and provided with the ability to transfer data over a network. Thus, at a very basic level, Internet of Things refers to uniquely identifiable objects and their virtual representations in an Internet-like structure. From a farm animal with a biochip transponder to a patient with a heart monitor implant, any object can be classified as Internet of Things.

The concept of Internet of Things has evolved from the convergence of wireless technologies, micro-electromechanical systems (MEMS) and most importantly, the Internet. It involves converting networks on proprietary protocols to IP-based networks. Internet of Things has provided humans with the facility of automatically transferring data over a network without any human-to-human or human-to-computer interaction. Thus, Internet of Things represents the advanced connectivity of devices and systems that goes beyond the conventional machine-to-machine.

In other words, with the progress of technology, humans can easily assign an IP address to every "thing" which exists on this planet. When an object can represent itself digitally, it can be controlled from anywhere. This implies an increase in both the generation of the amount of upstream data and the number of smart nodes. This means data can be gathered from a lot of locations, thereby raising new concerns about data privacy and security.

Editor

1

Learning Based Falling Detection Using Multiple Doppler Sensors

Shoichiro Tomii, Tomoaki Ohtsuki
Graduate School of Science and Technology, Keio University, Yokohama, Japan

ABSTRACT

Automated falling detection is one of the important tasks in this ageing society. Such systems are supposed to have little interference on daily life. Doppler sensors have come to the front as useful devices to detect human activity without using any wearable sensors. The conventional Doppler sensor based falling detection mechanism uses the features of only one sensor. This paper presents falling detection using multiple Doppler sensors. The resulting data from sensors are combined or selected to find out the falling event. The combination method, using three sensors, shows 95.5% accuracy of falling detection. Moreover, this method compensates the drawbacks of mono Doppler sensor which encounters problems when detecting movement orthogonal to irradiation directions.

Keywords: Falling Detection; Doppler Sensor; Cepstrum Analysis; SVM; k-NN

1. Introduction

In these days, the elderly population has been growing thanks to advances in the medical field. Healthy, safe and secure life is important particularly for the elderly. However, we are faced with problem of increasing the old-age dependency ratio. The old-age dependency ratio is the ratio of the sum of the population aged 65 years or over to the population aged 20 - 64. The ratio is presented as the number of dependents per 100 persons of working age (20 - 64). According to estimates of the United Nations, for about 30 countries, this ratio is projected to reach 30% in 2020 [1]. In particular, it is expected to reach 52% in Japan. There is an urgent need to develop automated health care systems to detect some accidents for the elderly.

Falling detection is one of the most important tasks to prevent the elderly from having crucial accidents. Yu [2] and Hijaz *et al.* [3] classified falling detection systems into three groups, wearable device approach, ambient sensors approach, and cameras approach. Wearable devices are easy to set up and operate. Devices can be attached to chest, waist, armpit, and the back [4]. The shortcomings of these devices are that they are easily broken, and that they are intrusive. Furthermore, the older we become, the more forgetful we become. Therefore, no matter how sophisticated the algorithm implemented on wearable devices is, there is no meaning if they fail to wear them. On the other hand, ambient sensors such as pressure and acoustic sensors can also be used. These sensors are cheap and non-intrusive. Moreover, they are not prone to privacy issues. However, pressure sensors cannot discern whether pressure is from the user's weight, while acoustic sensors show high false alarm rate in a situation of loud noise [5]. Cameras enable remote visual verification, and multiple persons can be monitored using a single setup. However, in private spaces such as bath and restroom, cameras are prohibited. Also in living room, many people do not want to be monitored by cameras.

Doppler sensor is an inexpensive, palm-sized device. It is capable of detecting moving targets like humans. Using this sensor, we can construct passive, non-intrusive, and noise tolerant systems. Activity recognition using Doppler sensor has been actively studied recently. Kim *et al.* proposed classification of seven different activities based on micro-Doppler signature characterized by arms and legs with periodic and active motion [7]. Subjects act toward sensor. An accuracy performance above 90% is achieved by using support vector machine (SVM). Tivive *et al.* [8] classified three types of motion, free arm-motion, partial arm-motion, and no arm-motion. Based on arm-motion, they describe human activity status. Liu *et al.* [9] show automatic falling detection. They use two sensors, which are positioned 1.8 m and 3.7 m away from the point of falling. The data of each sensor is independently processed. Subjects act forward, back, left-side, and right-side fall. The directions of activities include between two sensors, toward a sensor, and away from a sensor.

Doppler sensor is sensitive to the objects moving along irradiation directions; however, less sensitive to movements orthogonal to irradiation directions. For the practical use of Doppler sensors, we propose falling detection using multiple Doppler sensors to alleviate the moving direction dependency. By using sensors that have different irradiation directions, each sensor complements less sensitive directions of the other sensors. Sensor data are processed by feature combination or selection methods. In the combination method, features of multiple sensors are simply combined. In the selection method, the sensor is selected based on the power spectral density of the particular bandwidth, which characterizes the falling activity. After the process of each method, features are classified by using SVM or k-nearest neighbors (k-NN). We evaluate both methods in terms of the number of features, the number of sensors, and the type of classifier. We also discuss the accuracy of each activity direction and the viability of these methods for the practical use.

The remainder of this paper is organized as follows. In Section 2, we introduce basic Doppler sensor system, how we can determine target velocity from Doppler shift. In Section 3, we explain about flow of the proposed falling detection algorithm using multiple Doppler sensors. In Section 4, the sensor setup of the proposed method and the type of tested activities are explained. Our methods are evaluated by comparing them to the one sensor method. We discuss the accuracy of falling detection for each activity direction, and the viability of the proposed feature combination and selection methods in terms of the practical use. In Section 5, we draw conclusion.

2. Doppler Sensor

In this section, we discuss the basic information about Doppler sensor. Doppler sensor transmits a continuous wave and receives the reflected wave which has its frequency shifted the moving object. The Doppler shift is defined as

$$f_d = \frac{2f_c}{c - v} \cdot v \tag{1}$$

where v is the target velocity, c is the light velocity, and f_c is the carrier frequency. In Equation (1), since $c \gg v$, the target velocity is represented as c

$$v = \frac{c}{2f_c} \cdot f_d \tag{2}$$

f_c and c are the given values. Only by observing the Doppler shift f_d, we can determine the target velocity v.

3. Falling Detection Algorithm Using Multiple Doppler Sensors

In this section, we show the proposed falling detection algorithm using multiple Doppler sensors. **Figure 1** depicts the algorithm of falling detection. Our approach involves four phases: 1) Decision of extraction time range, 2) Feature extraction, 3) Feature combination/selection, 4)Training and classification.

3.1. Decision of Extraction Time Range

This process is aimed at deciding the timing for extracting 4 second features from the voltage data of the sensors. Firstly, we compute spectrogram by using short time Fourier transform (STFT). It is reported that 25 - 50 Hz bandwidth features are suitable to distinguish falling and non-falling when the carrier frequency is 5 GHz [9]. As shown in Equation (2), Doppler shift is proportional to carrier frequency on the condition of the same target velocity. Our experiment uses 24 GHz carrier frequency so that bandwidth should be expanded by 4.8 times, *i.e.* to within 120 - 240 Hz. On each time bin, which is decided by discrete Fourier transform (DFT) points and window overlap, we calculate the power spectral density (PSD) of 120 - 240 Hz. t_{max}, the time that the PSD of 120 - 240 Hz becomes maximum in 12 second experiment duration, indicates the time that remarkable event happens. Remarkable events mean activities involving a sudden quick movement using whole body. We specify the 4 second voltage data centered at t_{max}, and then extract features. **Figures 2** and **3** show STFT spectrogram and PSD of 120 - 240 Hz of experienced activities, respectively. Subjects act at about time 7 second.

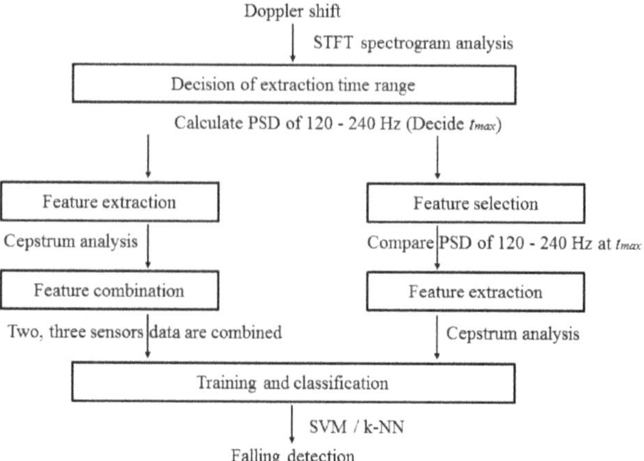

Figure 1. The proposed falling detection.

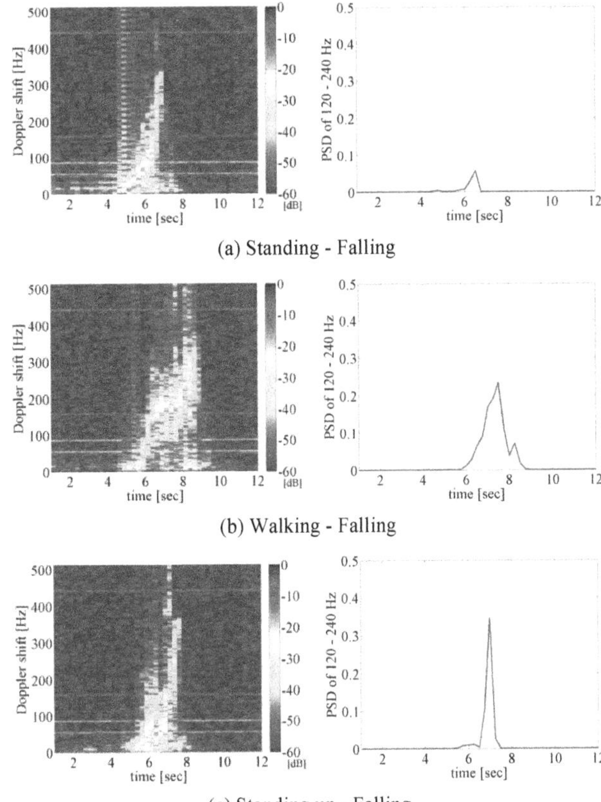

(a) Standing - Falling

(b) Walking - Falling

(c) Standing up - Falling

Figure 2. Spectrogram (left) and PSD of 120 Hz - 240 Hz (right) of Falling.

3.2. Feature Extraction

Using the 4 second voltage data centered at t_{max}, we compute cepstral coefficients. Mel-frequency cepstral coefficients (MFCC) are applied in [9]. Mel-frequency is the scale definition that emphasizes lower frequency 0 - 1000 Hz and compresses higher frequency. MFCC is basically applied to the analysis of voice up to about 16 kHz. On sensing falling motion, we found empirically that up to 500 Hz is enough to observe human activities on condition of 24 GHz carrier frequency. To compute MFCC, 0 - 1000 Hz frequency band is divided into linearly spaced blocks, which are called filter banks. Sampling frequency is 1024 Hz so that there is almost no process to compress higher frequency. Strictly speaking, instead of MFCC, cepstral coefficients analysis is applied. To calculate cepstral coefficients, we use the Auditory Toolbox [10]. The method is as follows.

1) Divide amplitude spectrogram into 13 linearly spaced filter banks.

2) Compute fast Fourier transform (FFT) of amplitude spectrum of each filter bank.

3) Compute discrete cosine transform (DCT) of the obtained data above. The result is called cepstrum.

4) We use C_1-C_6 coefficients, where C_0 is direct-current component. C_7-C_{12} come from latter half of 0 - 1024 Hz, which is not focused on to observe human activity.

Cepstral coefficient features are computed for each set of 256 DFT points which is called window. The window update frequency is defined as frame rate. As the frame rate becomes higher, the number of features increases.

3.3. Feature Combination/Selection

In our proposal, at most three sensors are used. We employ two methods to make features using multiple Doppler sensors, a combination method and a selection method. In the combination method, cepstral coefficients of the sensors are simply associated. **Figure 4(a)** shows the example of feature structure using two sensors. "label" represents the type of activity. In the selection method, the PSD of 120 - 240 Hz at t_{max} are compared among sensors before computing cepstral coefficients.

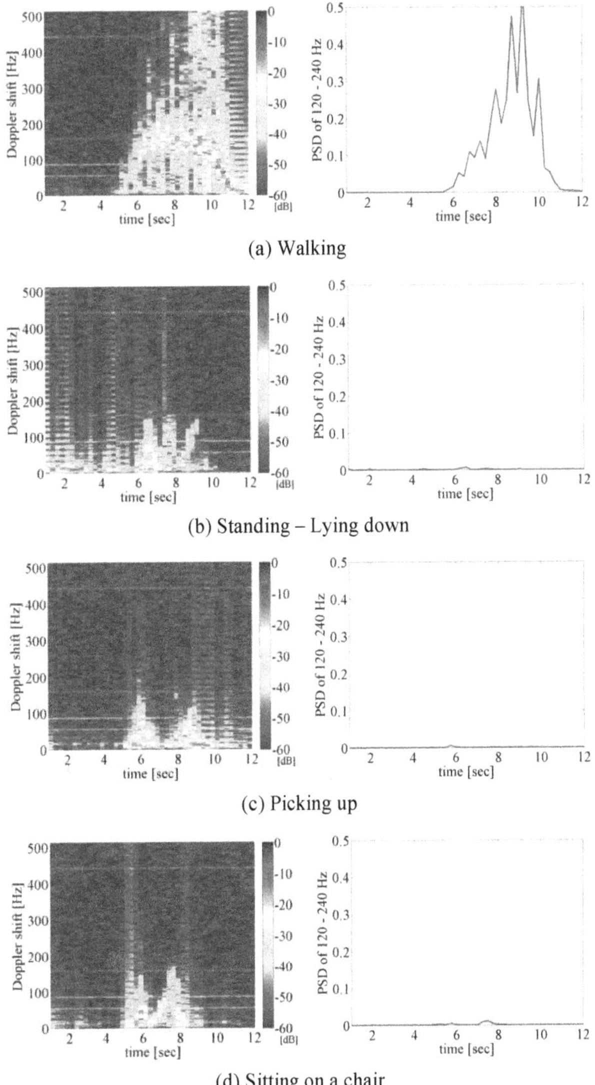

(a) Walking

(b) Standing – Lying down

(c) Picking up

(d) Sitting on a chair

Figure 3. Spectrogram (left) and PSD of 120 Hz - 240 Hz (right) of Falling.

The sensor that has the largest PSD of 120 - 240 Hz at t_{max} is selected for feature extraction. The selected sensor is assumed to catch human motion better than the other sensors.

3.4. Training and Classification

To train and classify the features, we use SVM and k-NN. For classification by using SVM on MATLAB, LIBSVM [11] is available. SVM has a kernel function that decides boundaries of groups. As a kernel function, linear, polynomial, radial basis function (RBF), and sigmoid are able to be used on LIBSVM. We exploit the RBF kernel. A linear kernel is the special case of RBF [12], and sigmoid kernel behaves like RBF with some parameters [13]. Polynomial kernel has numerical difficulty [14] so that RBF is the most suitable kernel in general. Kernel has several parameters and they should be tuned by changing each parameter. When we classify by using k-NN, Euclidean distance between the features is used.

We use four persons (A, B, C, D), who are men from 20's to 30's, as training and test subjects as shown in **Table 1**, and apply cross validation. This process generalizes the results of SVM and k-NN. In addition, features are normalized to prevent the greater values from having stronger effect on the results than the others.

4. Performance Evaluation

Figure 5 shows contents of the multiple Doppler sensors. They include client units, a base unit, and a PC. Client units receive reflected microwave at Doppler module and CPU (MSP430F2618, Texas Instruments) outputs data to base unit. The connection between base unit and each client unit is connected by LAN cable. The collected data of each Doppler sensor are sent to PC through USB port. The data are processed MATLAB.

Figure 6 shows how multiple sensors are deployed in the proposed methods. The room is rectangular, and its longer side is 10.5 m and shorter side is 7 m. In the middle of the each longer side, there is pillar. A dozen desks are placed in the rear. The angle between positions X and Y is 135°, and that between positions Y and Z is 90°. We used three sensors that transmit continuous wave whose frequency band is 24 GHz. Each sensor uses a slightly different transmit frequency to prevent interference among the sensors. Sampling frequency is 1024 Hz. Sensors are 1 m high from floor as shown in **Figure 7**, because strength of signal reflected from the torso is higher than that from any other parts of human body, and reflection on the floor cannot be negligible if they are deployed too close to the floor.

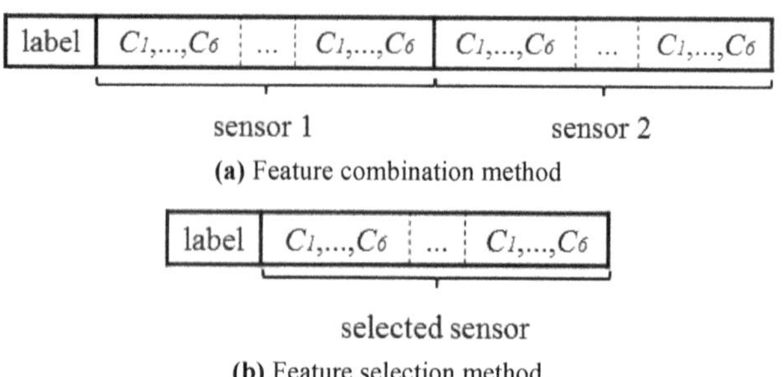

Figure 4. Feature structure. C_i is the *i*th cepstral coefficient.

Table 1. Training and testing subject patterns.

Training subjects	Test subject
A, B, C	D
A, B, D	C
A, C, D	B
B, C, D	A

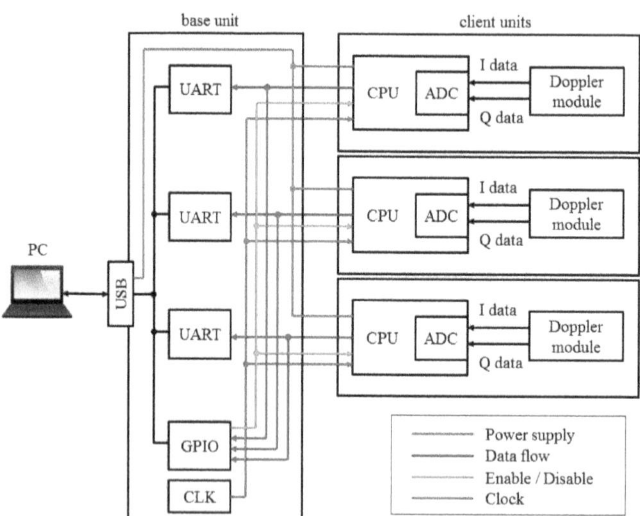

Figure 5. The diagram of sensing system of multiple Doppler sensors.

For evaluation of falling detection, subjects took seven activities listed in **Table 2**. Activities are roughly divided into two categories, "Falling" and "Non-Falling." Falling includes three following activities.

- Standing-Falling: Keep standing for seconds, then fall down toward each direction at the center, shown as circle in **Figure 8**.
- Walking-Falling: Walk from a distance of 2.5 m from the center, then fall down at the center.
- Standing up-Falling: Stand up, then fall down toward each direction at the center. This simulates lightheadedness.

Non-Falling includes four following activities.

- Walking: Walk from a distance of 2.5 m from the center, across the center, toward each activity direction. Totally 5 m walk.

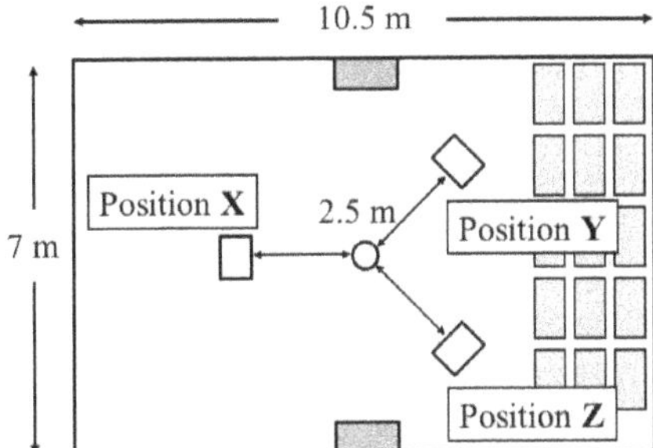

Figure 6. The deployment of multiple Doppler sensors.

Figure 7. The image of a Doppler sensor.

Table 2. Falling and Non-Falling activity.

Falling	Standing - Falling
	Walking - Falling
	Standing up - Falling
Non-Falling	Walking
	Standing - Lying down
	Picking up
	Sitting on a chair

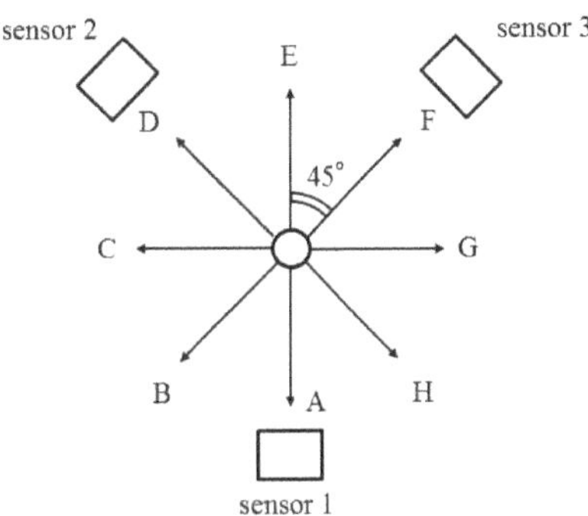

Figure 8. Deployment of multiple sensors.

- Standing-Lying down: Keep standing for seconds, then lie down on the floor toward each direction.
- Picking up: Pick up a pen on the floor. It is put about 30 cm apart from the center toward activity direction.
- Sitting on a chair: the back of a chair is toward activity direction.

These seven activities are tested in eight directions (A-H) as shown in **Figure 8**.

The accuracy of falling detection is defined as

$$\text{Accuracy} = \frac{TP + TN}{TP + TN + FP + FN} \times 100\ [\%] \qquad (3)$$

Each variable has the following meaning.

- *TP* (True Positive): Subject acts falling, and classified as falling.
- *TN* (True Negative): Subject acts non-falling, and classified as non-falling.
- *FP* (False Positive): Subject acts non-falling, and classified as falling.
- *FN* (False Negative): Subjects acts falling, and classified as non-falling.

4.1. Frame Rate

Frame rate is the number of window updates per second. The higher the frame rate becomes, the larger the number of features becomes. **Tables 3-5** show the relation between frame rate and accuracy of falling detection. The results of one sensor method and the combination and selection methods using three sensors are shown for comparison.

When we choose k-NN as a classifier, the accuracy increases until frame rate reaches 8 windows/second. When frame rate is higher than 16 windows/second, the degree of increase in accuracy becomes moderate or stable for all methods.

Referring the results using k-NN, we decide to set frame rate at 16 windows/second. We note that frame rate should not be too high because it increases the computation load. On the other hand, the low frame rate, which means lack of the features, causes the low accuracy because the k-NN classifier generally suffers from the problem of high variance in the case of limited sampling [15].

When SVM is chosen as a classifier, the best accuracy for falling detection occurs when the frame rate is 4 windows/second in all the methods. Unlike the case classified by k-NN, accuracy does not increase monotonically as frame rate increases. SVM is available to classify linearly non-separable features [13] so that it is generally thought to be able to separate complicated features. This result indicates that the optimum number of features should be found when SVM is applied. Based on these results, we use the optimum frame rate 4 windows/second on SVM.

Table 3. Relation between frame rate and accuracy of falling detection (one sensor method).

		Accuracy [%]			
		SVM	*k*-NN		
			k = 2	*k* = 3	*k* = 4
Frame rate [window(s)/second]	1	76.8	71.0	73.2	73.2
	2	87.1	87.5	87.1	86.6
	4	88.8	89.3	88.8	88.4
	8	87.9	90.6	89.3	89.3
	16	88.8	90.6	89.3	89.3

Table 4. Relation between frame rate and accuracy of falling detection (combination method, three sensors).

		Accuracy [%]			
		SVM	*k*-NN		
			k = 2	*k* = 3	*k* = 4
Frame rate [window(s)/second]	1	86.6	86.6	88.4	83.5
	2	90.2	92.4	93.8	91.5
	4	93.8	92.4	93.8	93.3
	8	90.6	94.2	94.2	94.1
	16	86.6	94.6	93.8	95.5

Table 5. Relation between frame rate and accuracy of falling detection (selsection method, three sensors).

		Accuracy [%]			
		SVM	*k*-NN		
			k = 2	*k* = 3	*k* = 4
Frame rate [window(s)/second]	1	77.7	83.0	80.4	80.8
	2	87.5	87.9	90.2	88.4
	4	91.5	90.6	90.2	89.7
	8	90.2	90.6	92.4	91.5
	16	90.6	90.6	92.4	93.3

4.2. One Sensor Method

Table 6 shows accuracy of falling detection using one sensor. The result of each sensor is classified by SVM and k-NN. The best accuracy of 90.6 % is achieved on sensor 1 using k-NN (k = 2). As shown in **Figure 6**, there are three positions, X, Y, and Z. We use three sensors, No. 1, 2, and 3. **Table 7** shows the position of each sensor in six deployments. The result shown in **Table 6** is for deployment type i. There are differences in accuracy based on sensor No.

Figures 9-14 show the spectrogram when no subject is moving. The color shows the strength of PSD in dB. The spectrogram should be characterized, in principle, by a lack of partiality of PSD on each Doppler shift. However, several spectrograms show strong PSD in specific Doppler shift, such as for deployment type ii, position Y (the middle of **Figure 10**, at 100 Hz, or deployment type iv, position X (the left of **Figure 12**), at 60, 90, 160, and 440 Hz. To find out the factor of this strong PSD, six different types of deployments are tested. When comparing six types of deployment, on each position, the strong PSD occurs on the similar Doppler shift. For instance, in position Y, a strong PSD appears on 100 Hz Doppler shift regardless of deployment type. Accordingly, the strong PSD did not occur because of device impairments, but by the effect of environment.

Table 6. Accuracy of falling detection using one sensor.

Sensor No.	Accuracy [%]			
	SVM	*k*-NN		
		k = 2	*k* = 3	*k* = 4
1	88.8	90.6	89.3	89.3
2	86.6	85.3	86.2	85.3
3	81.3	86.6	87.1	86.2

Table 7. Relation between position and sensor No.

		Position		
		X	Y	Z
Deployment type	i	1	2	3
	ii	1	3	2
	iii	2	1	3
	iv	2	3	1
	v	3	1	2
	vi	3	2	1

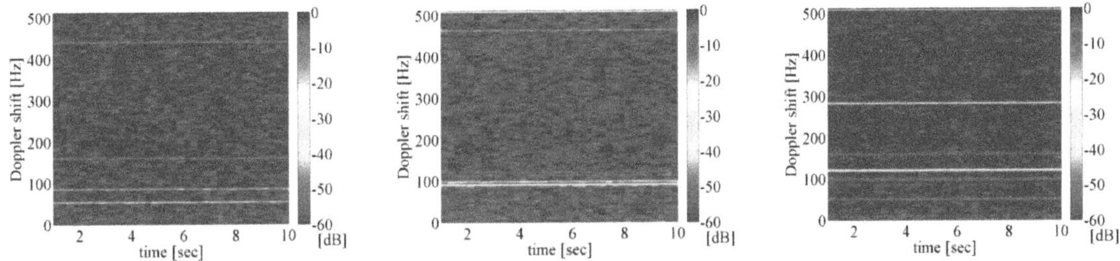

Figure 9. Spectrogram when no subject is moving in deployment type i. (left: Pos. X, middle: Pos. Y, right: Pos. Z).

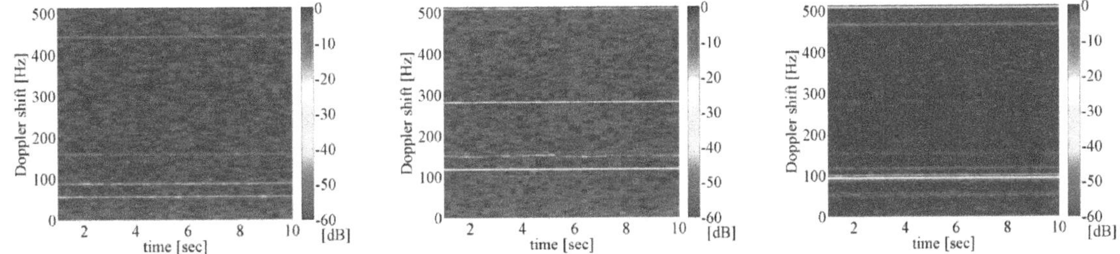

Figure 10. Spectrogram when no subject is moving in deployment type ii. (left: Pos. X, middle: Pos. Y, right: Pos. Z).

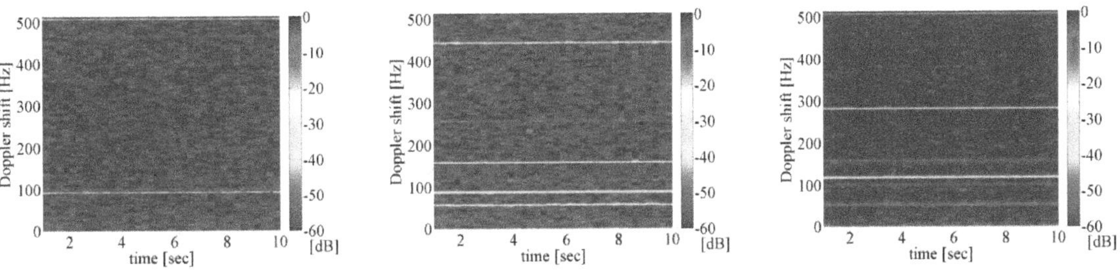

Figure 11. Spectrogram when no subject is moving in deployment type iii. (left: Pos. X, middle: Pos. Y, right: Pos. Z).

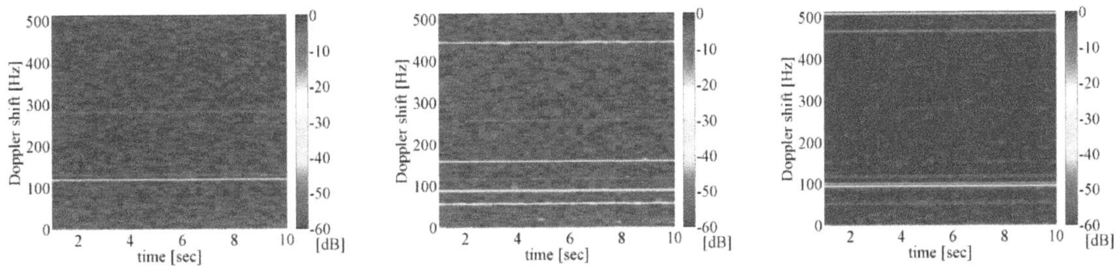

Figure 12. Spectrogram when no subject is moving in deployment type iv. (left: Pos. X, middle: Pos. Y, right: Pos. Z).

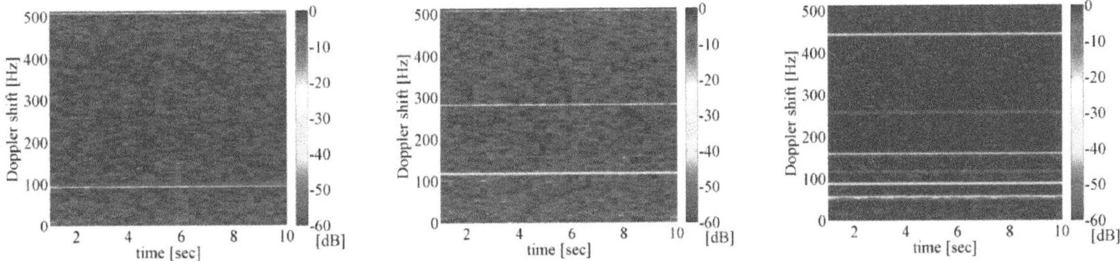

Figure 13. Spectrogram when no subject is moving in deployment type v. (left: Pos. X, middle: Pos. Y, right: Pos. Z).

In [6,7], a similar type of constant strong PSD at particular Doppler shift is reported when the Doppler sensor is used through the wall. This appears only on 60 Hz of Doppler shift, namely the strong PSD is caused by the alternate current (AC). The transmitted microwave is attenuated through the wall, and the strong PSD becomes non-negligible. On the other hand, the strong PSD on the result of our experiment appears on several Doppler shifts. This means that it is not caused by AC component. It is considered that the strong PSD comes from the reflection on the wall.

Table 8 shows the accuracy of falling detection for activity directions. Direction A-H corresponds to 8 directions in **Figure 8**. The relative position as seen from each sensor, in the same row in **Table 8**, is the same. For instance, direction A relative to sensor 1 is the same as direction D relative to sensor 2. Regardless of sensor No., the accuracy decreases in direction orthogonal to irradiation direction, that is, directions C and G for sensor 1, directions B and F for sensor 2, and directions D and H for sensor 3. This comes from the characteristics that Doppler sensor can figure out the activity through irradiation directions. The direction against the sensor also shows low accuracy. It is considered that the environmental noise, which comes from reflection on the wall, cannot be negligible. When the subject moves far from the sensor, the strength of microwave, which reflects on the body, decreases.

4.3. Feature Combination Method

Table 9 shows the accuracy of falling detection using the combination method. We test with two or three sensors. In particular, when we use two sensors, three types of sensor combinations are tested. In case of two sensors, 92.9% accuracy is achieved when k-NN is used with k set to 4. Just like the result of one sensor method, in **Table 6**, accuracy depends on the position in which the sensor is set. For instance, when sensors 2 and 3, or 1 and 3 are used, accuracy of falling detection is about 88%. On the other hand, when sensors 1 and 2 are used, an accuracy of 92.9% is achieved using k-NN ($k = 4$).

By using three sensors, 95.5% accuracy is performed and this is 4.9% higher than the best accuracy of the method using one sensor. In the combination method, three sensors are appropriate for the stable accuracy of falling detection.

Table 11 shows the relation between activity direction and accuracy of falling detection. We use k-NN (k = 4) as a classifier and deployment type is i in **Table 7**. As seen from sensor 1, B and H, C and G, D and F, are the same directions relative to the sensor.

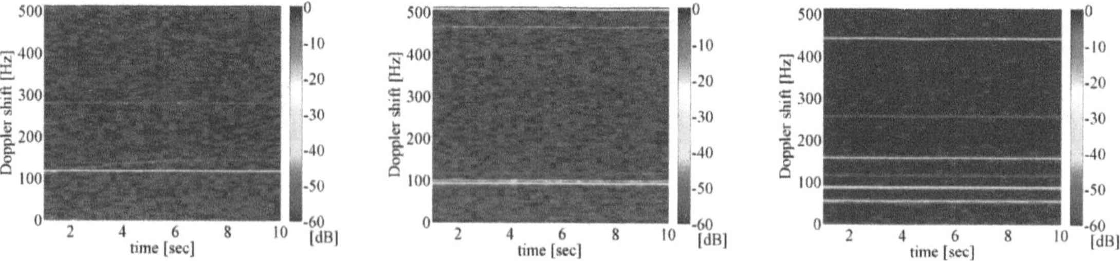

Figure 14. Spectrogram when no subject is moving in deployment type vi. (left: Pos. X, middle: Pos. Y, right: Pos. Z).

Table 8. Relation between activity directions and accuracy of falling detection (one sensor method).

Sensor 1		Sensor 2		Sensor 3	
Direction	Accuracy [%]	Direction	Accuracy [%]	Direction	Accuracy [%]
A	96.4	D	92.9	F	89.3
B, H	96.4	C, E	87.5	E, G	87.5
C, G	75.0	B, F	73.2	D, H	80.4
D, F	94.6	A, G	94.6	C, A	89.3
E	85.7	H	78.6	B	85.7

Table 9. Accuracy of falling detection using the combination method.

Number of sensors	Accuracy [%]			
	SVM	k-NN		
		$k = 2$	$k = 3$	$k = 4$
two (sensors 1 & 2)	92.0	92.0	92.0	92.9
two (sensors 2 & 3)	92.4	88.8	88.8	88.4
two (sensors 1 & 3)	88.4	91.1	89.7	88.8
three	93.8	94.6	93.8	95.5

Table 10. Accuracy of falling detection using the selection method.

Number of sensors	Accuracy [%]			
	SVM	k-NN		
		$k = 2$	$k = 3$	$k = 4$
two (sensors 1 & 2)	93.8	92.4	92.4	95.5
two (sensors 2 & 3)	90.2	87.1	87.9	89.7
two (sensors 1 & 3)	89.3	90.6	88.4	91.1
three	91.5	90.6	92.4	93.3

The accuracy of directions C and G in one sensor method is 75.0%. This is 21.4% lower than the direction A, which is the direction that the subject acts toward the sensor. In the combination method using three sensors, the accuracy of directions C and G is 94.6%. This result indicates that the combination method compensates the drawback of Doppler sensor. When using two sensors, the accuracy of directions C and G is improved compared to that of one sensor method. However, the accuracy depends on the deployment. Thus, three sensors are needed for high accuracy of falling detection and less dependency on deployment in our experiment.

4.4. Feature Selection Method

Table 10 shows the accuracy of falling detection using the selection method. The highest accuracy of falling detection is 95.5%, which occurs when two sensors (1 & 2) are used, and the features are classified by k-NN. However, as mentioned in the one sensor method and the combination method, the difference in accuracy appears in the feature selection methods using two sensors. To alleviate the effect of sensor dependency, we choose three sensor method. Accordingly, the best accuracy in the selection methods is 93.3%, which is in the three sensor method and classified by k-NN ($k = 4$).

The relation between activity direction and accuracy is shown in **Table 11**. Compared to one sensor method, the accuracy in the direction orthogonal to irradiation direction is improved. However, it is still relatively low in comparison with the other directions. This is caused by the algorithm to select feature from only one sensor.

In the view of the robustness in the direction orthogonal to irradiation direction, the combination method outperforms the selection method. However, that may not be always the case in practical situations. Consider, for example, the case that we are using multiple sensors, and one of them is obstructed by fallen objects such as furniture or plants. Without line of sight between the target and the sensor, the obstructed sensor cannot receive the Doppler information related to the target motion. The features of the combination method are constructed using features obtained from all the sensors. Thus, the obstructed sensor produces features that are different from the training data. This means that the system that simply combines the features is not tolerant to a situation that the sensors are obstructed by some objects.

Alternatively, the selection method has an advantage in the situation that a part of the sensors is obstructed. Even if one of the multiple sensors is obstructed by some objects, the selection method excludes the data of the obstructed sensor. This is because the decision of which sensor to choose is based on the selection of the largest PSD of 120 - 240 Hz at t_{max}. The data of the obstructed sensor is like the data in the environment that there are no targets moving around. Thus, the PSD of 120 - 240 Hz becomes smaller than that of the sensor that is not obstructed. Therefore, the selection method is more suitable for practical use.

4.5. True Positive Rate and False Positive Rate

When analyzing systems of falling detection, true positive rate (TPR) and false positive rate (FPR) are often used. TPR and FPR are calculated as follows.

$$TPR = \frac{TP}{TP + FN}, \quad FPR = \frac{FP}{FP + TN} \tag{4}$$

when FN becomes 0, TPR is equal to 1. Considering that FN is critical on falling detection system, TPR should be near 1. On the other hand, FPR should be near 0 because FP indicates over care. However, there sometimes exists trade-off between TPR and FPR. For practical systems, it is ideal that TPR reaches 1 and FPR reaches 0.

Figure 15 shows FPR and 1-TPR in each method. Both values should be near 0. Abbreviations "NoS," "mtd = s," and "mtd = c" in this figure means "Number of sensors," "method = selection," and "method = combination," respectively. Comparing to the conventional method using individual Doppler sensor data, in the proposed method using multiple Doppler sensor data, FPR and 1-TPR decrease.

Table 11. Relation between activity directions and accuracy of falling detection.

Direction	One sensor method	Combination method			Selection method		
	Sensor 1	Two sensors (sensors 1 & 2)	Two sensors (sensors 1 & 3)	Three sensors	Two sensors (sensors 1 & 2)	Two sensors (sensors 1 & 3)	Three sensors
A	96.4	96.4	89.3	96.4	96.4	96.4	92.9
B, H	96.4	91.1	89.3	94.6	94.6	94.6	91.1
C, G	75.0	89.3	87.5	94.6	91.1	80.4	89.3
D, F	94.6	98.2	89.3	98.2	98.2	96.4	96.4
E	85.7	89.3	89.3	92.9	100	89.3	100

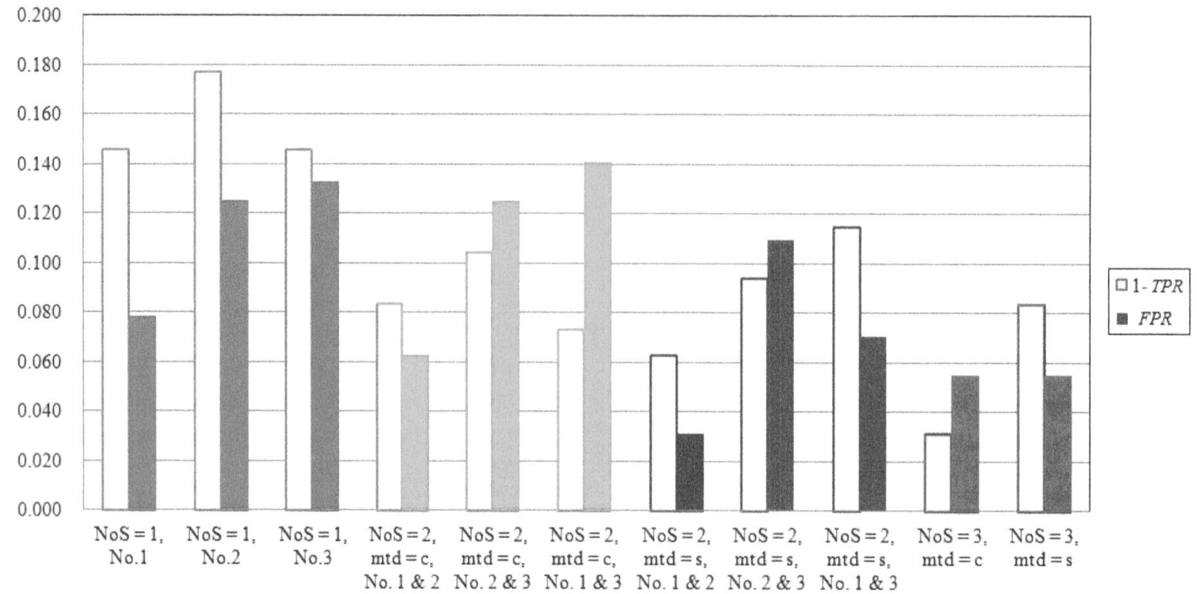

Figure 15. Results of False positive rate and True positive rate on each method.

5. Conclusion

This paper proposes falling detection using multiple Doppler sensors. We propose the combination and selection methods to extract features. The combination method achieves 95.5% accuracy of falling detection using k-NN (k = 4). In this method, three sensors are used. Doppler sensors are less sensitive to the direction orthogonal to the irradiation direction than the other directions. However, the combination method compensates this drawback of Doppler sensor and shows the high accuracy in each direction. The selection method achieves 93.3% accuracy using k-NN (k = 4). In this method, three sensors are used. This method also improves the accuracy of the direction orthogonal to the irradiation direction. However, the accuracy of the direction is still relatively low compared to the other directions. Although the selection method does not outperform the combination method in the view of the robustness of activity direction, we consider the idea of selection method to be useful for the practical use. The selection method excludes data of the echoless sensor such as accidentally obstructed by furniture or plants. Our future work is to construct the hybrid method between the combination and selection method.

REFERENCES

[1] Department of Economic and Social Affairs, "Population Division: World Population Prospects: The 2010 Revision," United Nations, Department of Economic and Social Affairs, 2011.

[2] X. Yu, "Approaches and Principles of Fall Detection for Elderly Andpatient," *Proceedings of the* 10*th International Conference of the IEEE HealthCom*, Singapore, 7-9 July 2008, pp. 42-47.

[3] F. Hijaz, N. Afzal, T. Ahmad and O. Hasan, "Survey of Fall Detectionand Daily Activity Monitoring Techniques," *Proceedings of International Conference on Information and Emerging Technologies*, *ICIET*, Pakistan, 14-16 June 2010, pp. 1-6.

[4] N. Noury, A. Fleury, P. Rumeau, A. Bourke, G. Laighin, V. Rialle and J. Lundy, "Fall Detection-Principles and Methods," *Proceedings of the* 29*th Annual International Conference of the IEEE EMBS*, Paris, 22-26 August 2007, pp. 1663-1666.

[5] J. Perry, S. Kellog, S. Vaidya, J. H. Youn, H. Ali and H. Sharif, "Surveyand Evaluation of Real-Time Fall Detection Approaches," *Proceedings of the* 6*th International Symposium of HONET*, Egypt, 28-30 December 2009, pp. 158-164.

[6] S. Ram, C. Christianson, Y. Kim and H. Ling, "Simulation and Analysis of Human Micro-Dopplers in through-Wall Environments," *IEEE Transactions on Geoscience and Remote Sensing*, Vol. 48, No. 4, 2010, pp. 2015-2023.

[7] Y. Kim and H. Ling, "Human Activity Classification Based on Microdopplersignatures Using a Support Vector Machine," *IEEE Transactions on Geoscience and Remote Sensing*, Vol. 47, No. 5, 2009, pp. 1328-1337.

[8] F. Tivive, A. Bouzerdoum and M. Amin, "Automatic Human Motion Classification from Doppler Spectrograms," *Proceedings of the* 2*nd International Workshop of CIP*, Elba Island, 14-16 June 2010, pp. 237-242.

[9] L. Liu, M. Popescu, M. Skubic, M. Rantz, T. Yardibi and P. Cuddihy, "Automatic Fall Detection Based on Doppler Radar Motion Signature," *Proceedings of the* 5*th International Conference of Pervasive Health*, Dublin, 23-26 May 2011, pp. 222-225.

[10] M. Slaney, "Auditory Toolbox Version 2".

https://engineering.purdue.edu/~malcolm/interval/1998-010/

[11] C. Chang and C. Lin, "LIBSVM: A Library for Support Vector Machines." http://www.csie.ntu.edu.tw/~cjlin/libsvm/

[12] S. S. Keerthi and C.-J. Lin, "Asymptotic Behaviors of Support Vector Machines with Gaussian Kernel," *MIT Press Journals*, Vol. 15, No. 7, 2003, pp. 1667-1689.

[13] C. J. Burges, "A Tutorial on Support Vector Machines for Pattern Recognition," *Data Mining and Knowledge Discovery*, Vol. 2, No. 2, 1998, pp. 121-167.

[14] V. N. Vapnik, "The Nature of Statistical Learning Theory," 2nd Edition, Springer, New York, 1999.

[15] H. Zhang, A. Berg, M. Maire and J. Malik, "SVM-KNN: Discriminative Nearest Neighbor Classification for Visual Category Recognition," *Proceedings of the IEEE Conference of CVPR*, New York, 17-22 June 2006, pp. 2126-2136.

2

Prospects for Mobile Health in Pakistan and Other Developing Countries

Aqil Burney[1,2], Zain Abbas[1], Nadeem Mahmood[1], Qamar-ul Arifeen[1]
[1]Department of Computer Science, University of Karachi, Karachi, Pakistan
[2]Institute of Business Management, College of Computer Science and Information Systems, Karachi, Pakistan

ABSTRACT

Pakistan is a developing country with more than half of its population located in rural areas. These areas neither have sufficient health care facilities nor a strong infrastructure that can address the health needs of the people. The expansion of Information and Communication Technology (ICT) around the globe has set up an unprecedented opportunity for delivery of healthcare facilities and infrastructure in these rural areas of Pakistan as well as in other developing countries. Mobile Health (mHealth)—the provision of health care services through mobile telephony—will revolutionize the way health care is delivered. From messaging campaigns to remote monitoring, mobile technology will impact every aspect of health systems. This paper highlights the growth of ICT sector and status of health care facilities in the developing countries, and explores prospects of mHealth as a transformer for health systems and service delivery especially in the remote rural areas.

Keywords: Mobile Health; Telemedicine; eHealth; mHealth; ICT; Heath Care in Pakistan

1. Introduction

The use of Information and Communication Technologies in health care is generally referred as eHealth, telehealth or telemedicine. Simply put telemedicine is provisioning of healthcare services at a distance using ICT. eHealth not only refers to the role of ICT in healthcare, but also to a way of thinking, a state of mind, and a commitment to improve the standard of health care being provided worldwide by using the ICT industry [1]. eHealth is the intersection of Information Sciences, Computer Science, Information Technology and Healthcare. It deals with various approaches used in storage, retrieval, and transfer of information in healthcare and biomedicine. It includes computers as well as clinical guidelines, formal medical terminologies, and information and communication systems [2].

Telehealth is transforming the systems of care throughout the world. It provides greater access to medical facilities and consultation, as well as sharing knowledge, experience, and training. Leap-frogging over prior barriers, ICT also has the potential to offer greater access to these services in developing countries [3]. The use of telehealth must be put in context of the critical health needs in each country, communication infrastructure, and likelihood for sustainability. Furthermore, it should be aimed at improving the indigenous capacity in providing health services and blending into the country's health care system [4].

Telemedicine is primarily used to provide health care to the inaccessible and underprivileged areas. It has a strong affect in developing countries since it allows remote locations to get access to medical care and create local knowledge. It is more efficacious and have big influence especially in areas where experts are rare, distances are large and/or infrastructure is limited [5]. The history of telemedicine dates back to 1950, when it was first used at the National Bureau of Standards, United States [6].

The rapid progress in ICT over the past few decades has brought about substantial advances in the quality of medical services provided to the patients. Developed countries are spending a lot of resources towards the integration of ICT with health care systems [2]. However, there are financial constraints in the developing countries that hamper their progress in telehealth [7]. They require technology transfer and capacity building sponsored by developed nations. Apart from financial constraints, the other important thing is the reforms in healthcare policy and a change of attitude towards eHealth [2].

The expansion of mobile and wireless technologies around the world has set up an unprecedented opportunity for global health delivery. The International Telecommunication Union estimates that total mobile cellular subscriptions reached almost 6 billion by the year 2012, corresponding to a global penetration of 86% [8], with more than 70% of them residing in developing countries. Mobile phone networks cover at least 90% of the world's population, including over 80% of those living in rural areas [9].

Mobile health, now commonly referred to as mHealth capitalizes on the successes of the mobile telephony to deliver health information and care in an efficient and improved manner. This paper highlights the prospects for mHealth in Pakistan and other developing countries of the region. The rest of the paper is organized as follows: Sections 2 and 3 illustrate the ICT growth and healthcare facilities in the region respectively. Section 4 presents a detailed discussion on mHealth, its conceptual model, applications and projects. Section 5 highlights the future steps needed to be undertaken to make mHealth benefits far reaching. Concluding remarks are provided in Section 6 which is followed by references.

2. ICT Growth in Developing Countries

Information and Communication Technologies have served as perfect accelerator for social, economic and Industrial progress. The speed at which ICT is diffusing in the society has taken everybody by surprise. More interesting is the fact that developing countries have left the developed countries behind in terms of the increase in use of communications such as the mobile telephone subscriptions. **Figures 1-4** show the ICT services subscriptions [8,10-12] in the developing countries of South East Asian region.

This surge in the usage of internet, broadband, mobile phones, smart phones and related technologies can be effectively used to provide health services at a low cost.

The penetration can also help the health care services in reaching the remote areas where such facilities, infrastructure and services are patchy [13].

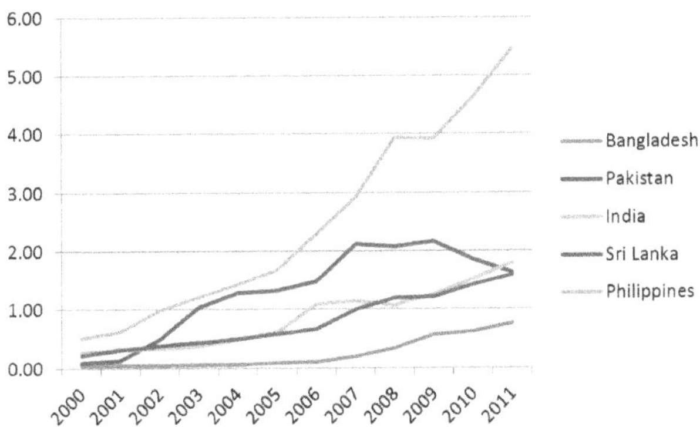

Figure 1. Fixed wired internet subscriptions per 100 inhabitants.

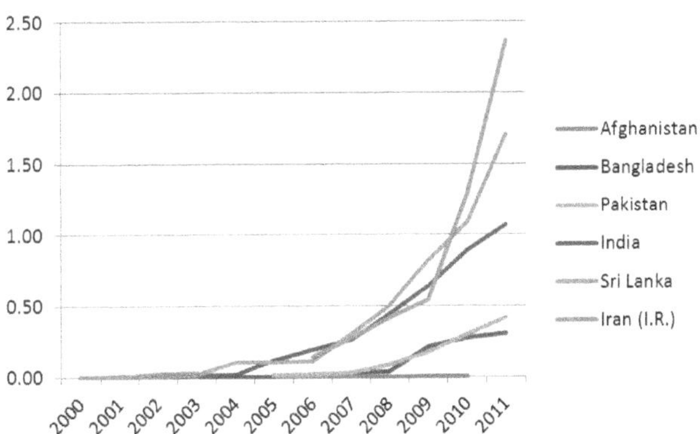

Figure 2. Fixed wired broadband subscriptions per 100 inhabitants.

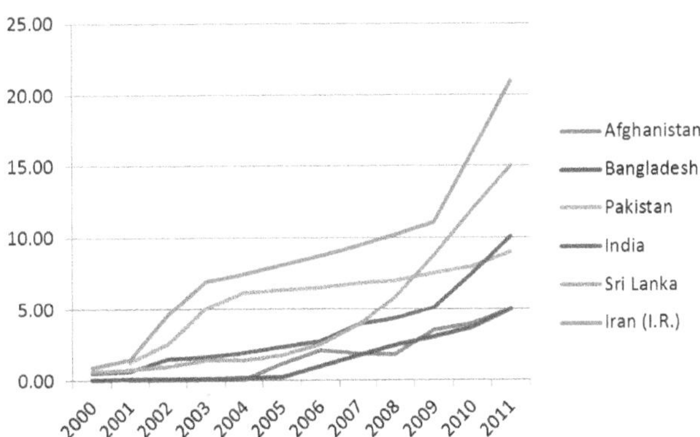

Figure 3. Percentage of Individuals using the Internet.

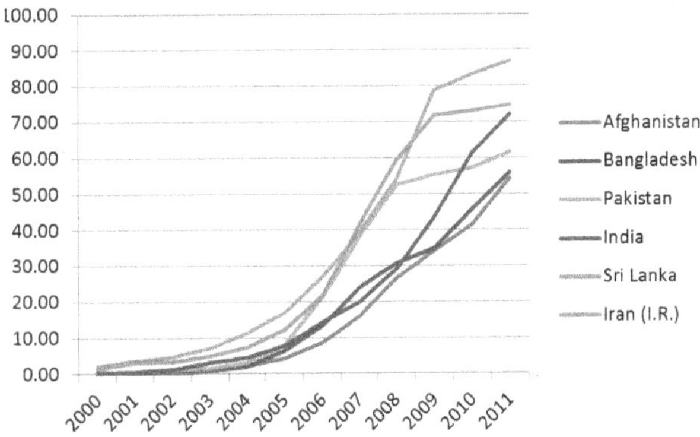

Figure 4. Mobile cellular subscriptions per 100 inhabitants.

3. Health Care Facilities in Pakistan

Many developing countries have inadequate health care services and suffer from a dearth of doctors and other trained health care professionals. The inappropriate distribution of doctors, scratchy infrastructure of health care facilities, roads and transport make it even more difficult to provide health care in remote and rural areas. Moreover, where clinics and hospitals exist, they are often ill-equipped or beyond reach [14]. **Figures 5** and **6** show the statistics pertaining to the physician density and hospital beds in developing countries of the region. Pakistan being a developing country lack even basic health care infrastructure. A brief summary of the core health indicators in the country is shown in **Tables 1** and **2**.

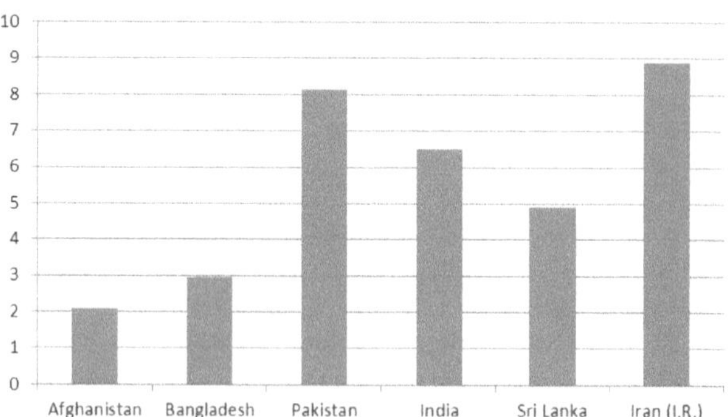

Figure 5. Physician density per 10, 000 population [15].

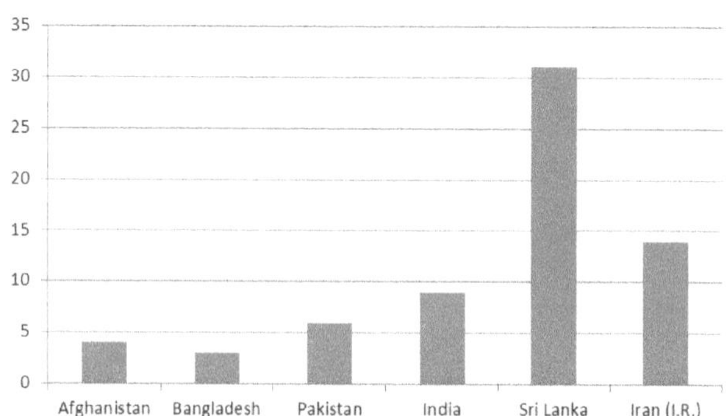

Figure 6. Hospital beds per 10, 000 population [15].

Table 1. Heath service facilities in Pakistan (2011-12) [16].

Facility	Quantity	Population/Facility
Hospitals	972	185,235/Hosp
Dispensaries	4842	37,185/Disp.
Basic Health Units	5374	33,504/BHU
Maternity Child Health Center	909	198,073/MCHC
TB Centers	304	592,264/TBC
First Aid Centers	1080	166,711/FAC
Beds in Hospitals	108137	1,665/Bed

Table 2. Registered Human Resources in Pakistan (2011-12) [16].

Human Resource	Quantity	Population/HR
Doctors	149201	1,207/Dr.
Specialists	19623	9,175/Sp. Dr.
Dentists	10958	16,431/Dentist
Dental Specialist	433	415,815/D.Sp.
Nurses	76244	2,361/Nurse
Midwives	27153	6,631/MW
Lady Health Visitors	11510	15,643/LHV

4. mHealth

The advancements in ICT and related services have paved way for availability of cost effective facilities to the people around the globe [17]. As already pointed out, the accelerated penetration of electronic devices into new markets has fuelled interest in eHealth, *i.e.* the storage, transmission, and retrieval of digital data using electronic means to support health care at local and distant sites [18]. The use of wireless technologies with eHealth services is termed as mHealth. In general terms, mHealth is the application of mobile computing, medical sensors, and communication technologies for healthcare. They are created as a synergy of emerging mobile medical computing, medical sensor technologies, and communication technologies [19].

Mobile technology promises a wide range of functions through the use of intelligent handsets called Smartphones. The functions include remote diagnostic monitoring, data collection, information dissemination, and public education and alerts systems [20]. Some key uses of smartphones are shown in **Figure** 7. Several platforms have been proposed to provide easy to use and cost effective solutions for remote patient doctor interaction over a cellular network [21,22]. Moreover, several specifications have been put forth to conceptualize patient data management for hospitals and other type of health care facilities [23-25].

MHealth has the potential to help developing countries combat many diseases. This includes communicable diseases such as tuberculosis. Messages and reminders can be sent to patients regarding their pills using mobile phones. Similarly, infant and maternal mortality can be reduced by delivering advice through SMS pregnant mothers and health information to community health workers [20].

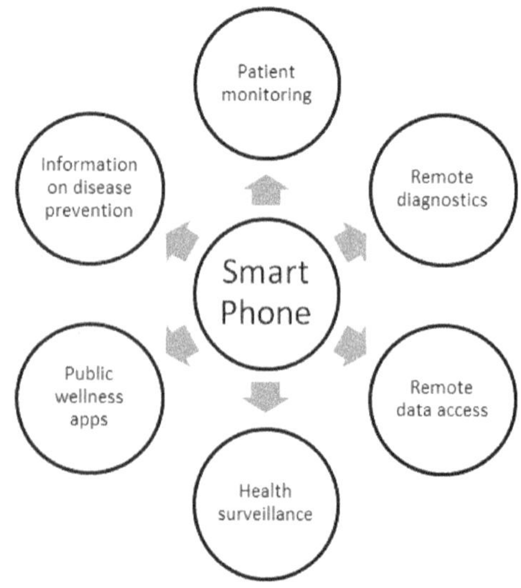

Figure 7. Mobile key to solving health challenges [20].

4.1. Conceptual Model of mHealth System

Figure 8 shows conceptual model of a mHealth system [17]. The model highlights that a mobile phone, laptop, or PDA can be used to connect to the health system through GSM network or Internet. Using the internet, the web portal of the health system can be accessed which can be used to access patient record database maintained at health care facility. On the other hand, GSM network may link a user with the 24 × 7 support center that can provide emergency medical response or medical advice using tele-triage mode.

These mHealth systems can be particularly beneficial in the areas that lack appropriate health care facilities and infrastructure. As indicated in earlier sections, such remote areas generally have access to ICT systems through a basic infrastructure. The availability these ICT facilities may be used to get medical advice from health care providers at remote locations through the support centers working round the clock.

These support centers have access to patient records as well as the health care providers and as a result, they can provide personalized health care advice to the patients.

4.2. mHealth Beneficiaries and Advantages

Many stakeholders can benefit from the advances in mHealth. These include individuals, government, health organizations, NGOs, employers, and suppliers. It has the potential to reduce per capita cost of healthcare while increasing or at least maintaining care quality.

Messages can enhance disease and epidemic awareness as well as the education of health service workers. All in all mHealth has a role to play in improving new "gross national happiness" indicators by producing a happier, healthier populace, and has the potential to transform health service delivery [20].

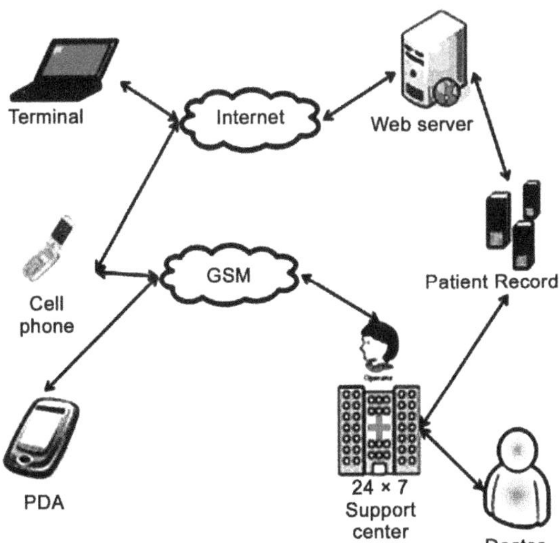

Figure 8. Conceptual model of mHealth System [17].

4.3. mHealth Applications

A number of mHealth applications are available in the market. Health service providers, whether public or private, are embracing the new technological solutions. An account of variety of such applications [9] follows:

4.3.1. Diagnostic Support and Data Collection

These tools help with disease surveillance, treatment as well as in collection of data for disease tracking. They are also used to collect and store patient data. Some examples include EpiSurveyor, ChildCount+, and Pesinet.

4.3.2. Reminders on Treatment and Appointments

These tools provide messages and reminders to the patient regarding treatment or appointments. WelTel, TxtAlert etc. are examples of such applications.

4.3.3. Emergency Medical Response

Call-in or SMS services are available to request ambulances or emergency response teams or personnel. Examples include the 1020 or 1021 helplines in Karachi, Pakistan.

4.3.4. Health/Medical Call Centers

These facilities provide access to medical advice, counseling, information using tele-triage mode. Telenor Teledoctor is an example of such application.

4.3.5. Healthcare Supply Chain Management

These tools help in tracking of medical goods in supply chains using mobile recording. Examples include Pedigree, PharmaSecure, and Stop Stock-outs.

4.3.6. Health Information and Promotion

These applications propagate text and voice messages to distribute health information to subscribers. The information may relate to epidemic, disease prevention, child care, maternal health etc. for instance, Texttochange, text4baby, and YoungAfricaLive.

4.3.7. Training and Support for Healthcare Workers

These are mobile device applications that are used to train, test, supervise, and support healthcare workers. They include FrontlineSMS, AMREF, and eMOCHA.

4.3.8. Healthcare Payments and Insurance

These are mobile device applications that link mobile money platforms to smart-cards, vouchers and insurance companies. Changamka and Arogya Raksha Yojana are such applications.

4.4. mHealth Projects

Many mHealth project case studies have been organized

by a number of organizations throughout the world. These studies include application areas from least specialized (education and awareness) to most specialized (diagnostic and treatment support). Some of these are categorized here by their more specialized function. A detailed description of these projects is available in [26].

4.4.1. Education and Awareness

- Freedom HIV/AIDS Project, India
- Learning about Living, Nigeria
- Project Masiluleke, South Africa
- Text to Change (TTC)—HIV Prevention through SMS Quiz, Uganda

4.4.2. Remote Data Collection

- Cell-PREVEN, Peru
- Dokoza System, South Africa
- EpiHandy, Uganda, Zambia, Burkina Faso
- Phones for Health, Rwanda

4.4.3. Remote Monitoring

- Cell-Life Project, South Africa
- Colecta-PALM, Peru
- Virtual Health Pet, Brazil

4.4.4. Training for Healthcare Workers

- HealthLine, Pakistan
- Mobile HIV/AIDS Support, Uganda
- Uganda Health Information Network, Uganda

4.4.5. Disease and Epidemic Outbreak Tracking

- Alerta DISAMAR, Peru
- FrontlineSMS, Worldwide
- GATHER, Uganda
- Handhelds for Health, India

4.4.6. Diagnostic and Treatment Support

- Ericsson and Apollo Hospitals Initiative, India
- HIV Mobile Decision Support, South Africa
- Mobile E-IMCI, Tanzania
- Nacer, Peru

5. Future Steps

5.1. Public-Private Partnerships

Public-private partnerships have demonstrated to be the cornerstone of successful mHealth initiatives. Private sector has remarkable capacity to produce state-of-the-art solutions for public health challenges. Governments have access to existing infrastructure and networks, making them an essential entity in successful integration of mHealth frameworks into existing health systems. Furthermore, an active role must be taken in scaling up the existing pilot projects to full-fledged healthcare platforms [18].

5.2. Health System Strengthening

Although mobile telecommunication devices will ease the burden on limited health care resources, thus making them available to more people than ever before but in order to tap the real potential of mHealth projects, their access to those seeking benefit must be ensured. This can on only be achieved by strengthening the health systems. A user centric framework is crucial to the success of these initiatives [18].

5.3. Adopt a Systematic Approach [9]

A systematic approach is needed for exploring worthy opportunities and developing solutions. The approach must identify the real needs of the masses and design standards, platforms and models that address them. The approach should be tied to the national health strategy, in particular for developing healthcare human resources.

5.4. Encouraging Developers and Innovations

The variety of mHealth applications presented in earlier sections indicates that the impact of these applications has been significant. Hence, it is imperative that technological innovations to mobile phone products offer exciting new prospects for future mHealth projects, and developers must be encouraged to develop more innovative products [18].

5.5. Aim for Scale [9]

The goals for mHealth projects must be ambitious and the focus should be on quick deployment of the most promising innovations and emphasis must be laid on pilot projects that have the ability to be scaled quickly.

5.6. Evaluations

mHealth is an emerging field with little experience or guidance on evaluation frameworks for implementations. Therefore the initiatives must be synthesized and information must be shared to ensure the availability of diverse resources on various aspects of project design, implementation, and management. The availability of practical information on mHealth implementation and evaluation can dramatically accelerate and ease the adoption of mobile technologies by groups working in health care sector [18].

6. Conclusions

The field of mHealth is growing rapidly. It has proven to be beneficial through dozens of successfully implemented projects round the globe. Moreover, technological innovations will bring about enhanced benefits in the years to come.

Health needs in developing countries have grown at alarming pace and now include chronic diseases to go with communicable diseases. mHealth is well positioned to counter these challenges using current trends in ICT. Emerging technologies will also be an asset in tackling health needs of today and tomorrow.

Careful thought must also be put in creating incentives that encourage all stake holders to contribute in the development of mHealth. The long-term goal underlying all these efforts must be to ensure that mHealth programs have a significant and lasting influence on level health care across the globe particularly in the developing countries.

REFERENCES

[1] Z. Ahmad, "mHealth: A Paradigm Shift in Delivery of Healthcare," *PIMA Biennial Convention*, 2012.

[2] A. Burney, N. Mahmood and Z. Abbas, "Information and Communication Technology in Healthcare Management Systems: Prospects for Developing Countries," *International Journal of Computer Applications*, Vol. 4, No. 2, 2010, pp. 27-32.

[3] R. Wootton, N. G. Patil, R. E. Scott and K. Ho, "Telehealth in the Developing World," Royal Society of Medicine Press, IDRC, 2009. ISBN 978-1-85315-784

[4] D. C. Alverson, L. R. Swinfen, L.P. Swinfen, K. Rheuban, C. Sable, A. C. Smith, *et al.*, "Transforming Systems of Care for Children in the Global Community," *Pediatric Annals Article on International Pediatric Telehealth*, Vol. 38, No. 10, 2009, pp. 579-585.

[5] R. Wootton, "Telemedicine," *British Medical Journal*, Vol. 323, 2001, pp. 557-560.

[6] N. Ullah, P. Khan, N. Sultana and K. S. Kwak, "A Telemedicine Network Model for Health Applications in Pakistan: Current Status and Future Prospects," *International Journal of Digital Content Technology and Its Applications*, Vol. 3, No. 3, 2009, pp. 149-155.

[7] C. C. Missen and T. M. Cook, "Appropriate Information-Communications Technologies for Developing Countries," *World Health Organization Bulletin*, Vol. 85, No. 4, 2007, p. 248.

[8] International Telecommunication Union (ITU), "Key Statistical Highlights: ITU Data Release June 2012," 2012. http://www.itu.int/ITU-D/ict/statistics/material/pdf/2011%20Statistical%20highlights_June_2012.pdf

[9] "MHealth Education: Harnessing the Mobile Revolution to Bridge the Health Education & Training Gap in Developing Countries," *MHealthEd*, Irish Global Health Education Innovation Institute (IHEED), June 2011. http://www.mobileactive.org/files/file_uploads/iheed_report_updates.pdf

[10] UNCTAD, "Information Economy Report 2012: The Software Industry and Developing Countries," United Nations Publication. http://unctad.org/en/PublicationsLibrary/ier2012_en.pdf

[11] UNCTAD, "Information Economy Report 2011: ICTs as an Enabler for Private Sector Development," United Nations Publication. http://unctad.org/en/PublicationsLibrary/ier2011_en.pdf

[12] UNCTAD, "Information Economy Report 2009: Trends and Outlook in Turbulent Times," United Nations Publication. http://www.unctad.org/en/docs/ier2009_en.pdf

[13] A. Burney, N. Mahmood, Z. Abbas and Z. Bashir, "Healthcare Management System and Information and Communication Technology: Prospects for Pakistan," *First International eHealth Conference*, AKUH Karachi, 2010.

[14] E. Z. A. Junejo, "SUPARCO Telemedicine Pilot Project." http://www.isnet.org.pk/downloadables/telemedicine_paper.pdf

[15] World Health Organization (WHO), "Global Health Observatory Data Repository." http://apps.who.int/gho/data/node.main.475

[16] "Economic Survey 2011-12," Ministry of Finance, Government of Pakistan. http://www.finance.gov.pk/survey_1112.html

[17] N. Mahmood, A. Burney, Z. Abbas and K. Rizwan, "Data and Knowledge Management in Designing Healthcare Information Systems," *International Journal of Computer Applications*, Vol. 50, No. 2, 2012, pp. 34-39.

[18] "Interactive Research and Development," MHealth to Improve TB Care, Version 1.0, 2012. http://irdresearch.org/wp-content/uploads/2012/05/mHealth-to-Improve-TB-Care.pdf

[19] R. S. H. Istepanian, E. Jovanov and Y. T. Zhang, "Guest Editorial Introduction to the Special Section on M-Health: Beyond Seamless Mobility and Global Wireless Health-Care Connectivity," *IEEE Transactions on Information Technology in Biomedicine*, Vol. 8, No. 4, 2004, pp. 405-414.

[20] The Boston Consulting Group & Telenor Group, "The Socio-Economic Impact of Mobile Health," April 2012.

[21] A. Holopainen, F. Galbiati and K. Takizawa, "Health Gateway Mobile Phone Technology Offers Easy-to-Use and Cost-Effective Telemedicine Services for Rural and Remote Areas," *Journal of eHealth Technology and Application*, Vol. 5, No. 3, 2008, pp. 261-266.

[22] E. Jovanov, A. Milenkovic, C. Otto and P. C. Groen, "A Wireless Body Area Network of Intelligent Motion Sensors for Computer Assisted Physical Rehabilitation," *Journal of Neuro Engineering and Rehabilitation*, Vol. 2, No. 6, 2005.

[23] N. Mahmood and A. Burney, "Temporal and Fuzzy Relational Databases," Lambert Academic Publisher, Germany, 2011.

[24] A. Burney, N. Mahmood and Z. Abbas, "Advances in Fuzzy Rough Temporal Databases," *Proceeding of 11th WSEAS International Conference on AIKED*, University of Cambridge, 22-24 February 2012, pp. 237-242.

[25] A. Burney, Z. Abbas, N. Mahmood and Q. Arifeen, "Application of Fuzzy Rough Temporal approach in Patient Data Management (FRT-PDM)," *International Journal of Computers*, Vol.6, No. 3, 2012, pp. 149-157.

[26] UN Foundation, "mHealth for Development: The Opportunity of Mobile Technology for Healthcare in the Developing World," 2009. http://unpan1.un.org/intradoc/groups/public/documents/unpan/unpan037268.pdf

3

Improving the Patient Discharge Planning Process through Knowledge Management by Using the Internet of Things

Nitya Ahilandam Kamalanathan, Alan Eardley, Caroline Chibelushi, Tim Collins
Faculty of Computing Engineering and Sciences, Staffordshire University, Stafford, UK

ABSTRACT

The UK National Health Service (NHS) is faced with problems of managing patient discharge and preventing the problems that result from it such as frequent readmissions, delayed discharge, long waiting lists, bed blocking and other such consequences. The problem is exacerbated by the growth in size, complexity and the number of chronic diseases in the NHS. In addition, there is an increase in demand for high quality care, processes and planning. Effective Discharge Planning (DP) requires practitioners to have appropriate, patient personalised and updated knowledge in order to be able to make informed and holistic decisions about a patients' discharge. This paper examines the role of Knowledge Management (KM) in both sharing knowledge and using tacit knowledge to create appropriate patient discharge pathways. The paper details the factors resulting in inadequate DP, and demonstrates the use of Internet of Things (IoT) and Machine2Machine (M2M) as candidate technologies and possible solutions which can help reduce the problem. The use of devices that a patient can take home and devices which are perused in the hospital generate information, which can serve useful when presented to the right person at the right time, thus harvesting knowledge. The knowledge when fed back can support practitioners in making holistic decisions with regards to a patients' discharge.

Keywords: National Health Service (NHS); Knowledge Management (KM); Discharge Planning (DP); Internet of Things (IoT); Machine2Machine (M2M)

1. Introduction

The NHS, a publicly funded organisation, provides healthcare for all UK citizens (currently more than 62 million people) [1]. The NHS is divided into primary and secondary care [1]. Patients requiring further attention are usually transferred from Primary care (PC) to Secondary care (SC). Both PC and SC have links between one another and cannot exist without the other [1]. The sharing of information about a patient between a PC and SC is therefore important. The NHS, like any other healthcare system and other systems, is made up of subsystems which have conventional components such as inputs, processes and outputs. These systems and subsystems are interdependent and inter-related. It is therefore important to understand healthcare subsystems in order to gain a deeper insight into the functioning of the system [2,3]. The research project that this paper describes therefore focuses on analysing the hospital system in terms of its structure and process in terms of:

- The components themselves (e.g. patients, nurses) and their roles in the system;
- The relationship between the components and their interaction (e.g. nurses care for patients);
- The boundaries of the system or its extent and scope (e.g. where an admission ward hands over to an operating theatre) or where patients are discharged;
- How the system deals with and adapts to changes within the organisation (e.g. emergency admission or an outbreak of an infection);
- How the system deals with its internal factors (e.g. changes in management, targets, IT systems etc.);
- The relationship of the system to external systems whose services are vital to a patients convalescence (e.g. social care systems);
- The knowledge flow within the system and subsystems.

With sound understanding of the system and subsystems, the practitioner is able to understand the knowledge required, the knowledge which currently exists and can be updated to make informed decisions in processes such as DP. Patient discharge can be considered to be the beginning of convalescence. Careful planning of post-treatment care is essential to a patient's complete healthcare pathway, which is an essential component of DP. Careful planning and a clear decision-making framework are vital to the smooth flow of patients from admission to discharge at the end of the treatment period. The NHS has grown, since it was launched in 1948 and is continuously growing in size and complexity [1]. This growth in size, complexity and the number of chronic diseases (e.g. obesity, diabetes) in the NHS causes an increase in demands, processes and planning [1]. A consequence of the complexity, increasing size and demands on the NHS is a disarray of processes that affect functions such as DP. DP is a key part of the overall process and is not an isolated or final event [1]. It is important to include what happens to a patient after discharge, to prevent unwanted readmissions, delayed discharged, bed blocking, cancellations in procedures and long waiting lists. It has implications for the provision of resources in the healthcare, social care and other support service sectors and warrants this research to improve its efficiency and effectiveness. A smooth DP process facilitates patients moving from one healthcare setting to another, or going home. It begins on admission and is a multidisciplinary process involving physicians, nurses, social workers, and possibly other health professionals [4]. The aim of DP is therefore to enhance the continuity of care and can have significant implications for a patient's wellbeing and recovery, the efficient use of medical resources and streamlined interconnecting processes within the hospital setting.

The complexity of the discharge process implies that careful planning is needed to make it more effective [5]. Recent years have witnessed significant advances in medical informatics to increase productivity and efficiency in healthcare [6]. Some parts of the NHS are currently faced with the problem of "islands of information"[1] related to the existence of organisational "silos"[2]. In some cases, it is suggested that very little knowledge is shared between these silos. This leads to the foundation of this paper, which is to examine the role of KM in an integrated "cross-silo" approach to use shared knowledge and tacit knowledge to create appropriate patient discharge pathways. The tacit knowledge of Doctors and Nurses is yet to be exploited to its full potential along with the knowledge of patients and carers. According to [7] patients, carers and information are the most underutilised resources the NHS has. It is the patients who are facing the symptom, and the carers who look after the patient, the knowledge they have is most valuable to making decisions, which unfortunately is currently overlooked. Each patient has a unique problem and personalising the discharge process will reduce the current problems faced with DP. KM therefore forms a bridge between these "islands of information" [8].

2. The Current Discharge Planning Dilemma in the NHS

Discharge is defined when an in-patient leaves an acute hospital to return home, or is transferred to a rehabilitation facility or an after-care nursing centre [9]. DP should commence as early as possible in order to facilitate a smooth discharge process. Discharge guidelines have been prescribed by the Department of Health (DH) and different trusts implement discharge pathways or process maps following these guidelines. Several DP improvement attempts have been made and reasonable improvements have been noticed. Several methods by which DP takes place have been identified in the primary research in two UK hospital trusts and include the following:

- DP commences on admission;
- Patient and carer are involved in the decision making process;
- A clinical management plan where an expected date of discharge is predicted based on actual performance in the ward or, on benchmarking information from past cases;
- Multidisciplinary teams make a decision based on experience during their meetings.

A bed management system stores information on beds occupied and a weekly meeting are held to decide the discharge date for patients. All of these methods involve KM. From the Primary research carried out, it is seen that, a rough DP is currently drafted for patients upon entry to hospital according to their diagnosis, and a tentative discharge date is provided in line with recommendations. Changes are made over the course of the patient's stay and records are manually updated by nurses, upon instruction by the doctors. This sometimes results in confusion and even disagreement on discharge dates by different doctors (e.g. when treating the patient for different symptoms) and nurses (e.g. when a change of shift occurs). This research proposes that Patient DP requires viewing the whole system and not as isolated units. In the discharge plan the patient and care giver involvement needs to be considered, however very little indication has been provided on these. To date, based on the primary research, clear guidelines are not present on what information needs to be collected, stored and reused on patients. The UK NHS is facing problems of managing patient discharges while having to meet waiting time, treatment time and bed usage targets [10]. Patient dis-

[1]IT applications that were originally developed to solve localised problems, but which do not communicate with other applications in the same IT infrastructure.

[2]Parts of the organisation (e.g. departments, functions) that are separate in terms of processes, communication and policies.

charge is currently being driven by quantitative measures such as targets (e.g. to reduce "bed-blocking") and problems resulting from this situation has received a great deal of popular press attention recently and political capital has been made from this [10]. Targets are prioritized while compromising patient's after-care quality.

Being target-driven (rather than knowledge driven) implies that the healthcare system fails to consider the factors that affect the effective recovery of a patient after treatment and discharge [11]. Hospitals focus on accomplishing and achieving internal targets, resulting in compromised patient safety and well-being after discharge. The exact situation with regard to patient discharge and readmissions is not really well established, as there are variations in discharge methods between trusts, as identified in the primary research. However, it is reported in the popular press that doctors have to make quick decisions about patients just to "get the clock to stop ticking" [12] resulting in deteriorating trust between doctors and patients. More reliably, doctors find themselves torn between meeting targets and providing their sick patients with the best treatment. These claims in the assorted news media have been reaffirmed by Andrew Lansley the Secretary of State for Health in the UK Government who in a speech in December 2011 stated that:

> "The NHS is full of processes and targets, of performance-management and tariffs, originally, all designed to deliver better patient care, but somewhere along the line, they gained a momentum of their own, increasingly divorced from the patients who should have been at their centre."
>
> (Guardian 7 December 2012)

Several factors result in the current inadequate DP. These factors are internal and external to the NHS along with psychosocial factors of the patient and family [13]. It is important to understand the factors behind inadequate DP to be able to analyse and diagnose the factors causing the problem systematically. A comparison can then be made between the factors along with the results obtained from the primary research, followed by a catalogue of possible solutions underpinned by KM. This will then lead to making a diagnosis *i.e.* the proposed KM model. A root cause analysis [14] highlighted the factors contributing to inadequate DP as represented in **Figure 1**.

Figure 1 demonstrates the discharge of a patient as a complex process, with various inter-related factors. A

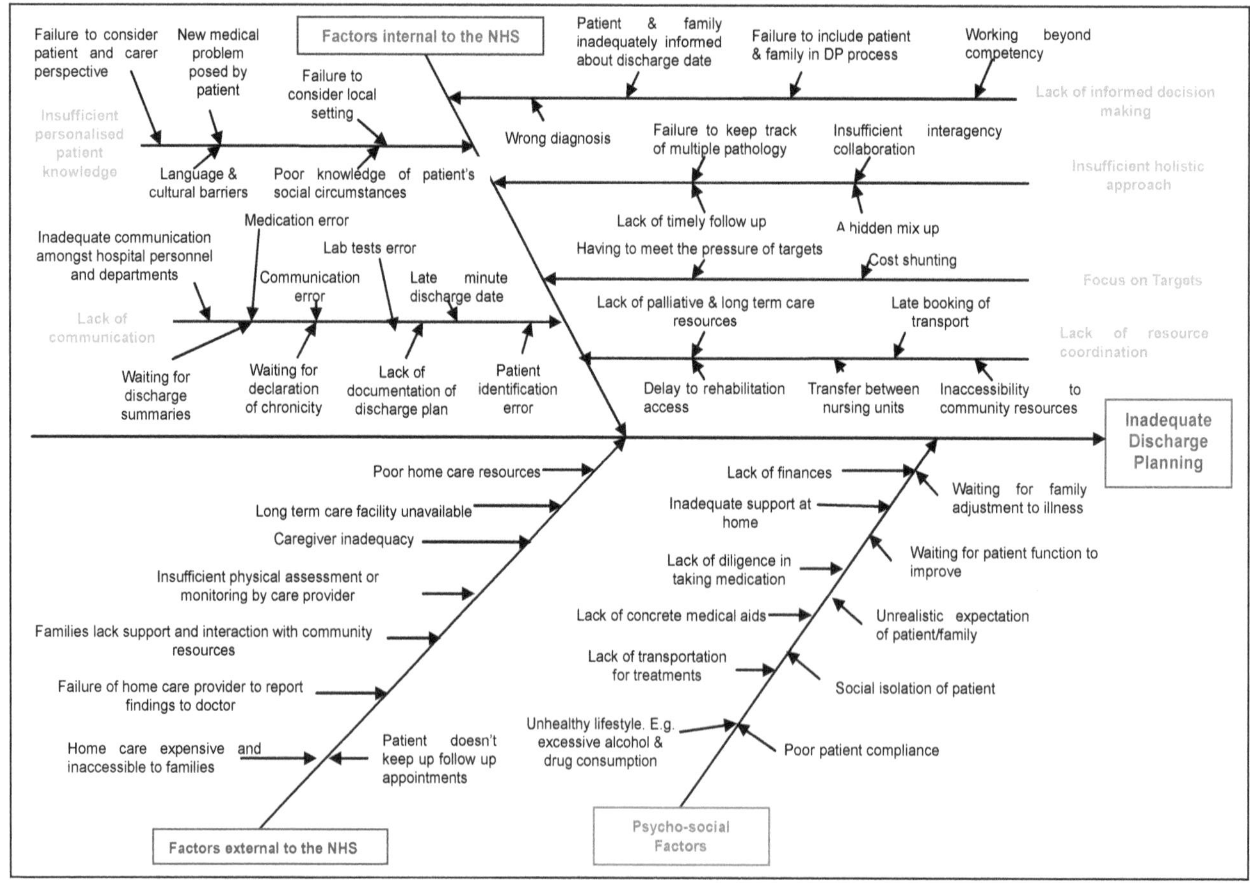

Figure 1. Root Cause Analysis of factors resulting in inadequate DP [12].

carefully designed discharge plan supported by KM can ensure more efficient utilisation of hospital resources and will encourage better inter-department communication to ensure that tacit knowledge makes more informed decisions about patient discharge. It is believed that this in turn will allow for better coordination of the external factors and will give hospital personnel more time to inform patients and their families, thus addressing the psychosocial factors. At discharge, preventable and undetected errors can occur. These can be reduced by knowledge sharing among hospital staff and having patient centric discharge pathway leading to improved DP. Patient participation and understanding in discharge process will help reduce potential readmissions and delayed discharge. Patient participation in the discharge process is a legally stated right in the United Kingdom and therefore more active participation of patients is encouraged [15]. The failure to assess a patient's care needs correctly can result in a disproportionate delay in patients being discharged [16]. The problems caused by inadequate DP have been identified in the secondary and primary research and are summarized succinctly in **Figure 2**.

The number of patients readmitted to hospitals through Accident and Emergency (A&E) departments within 28 days of being discharged has risen steadily from 359,719 in 1998 to 546,354 in 2008 [17]. While in 2010 more than 660,000 patients were re-admitted to hospital within 28 days of discharge [18]. According to statistics provided by the Department of Health, in England in 2010-2011 the total number of patients who were readmitted was 561,291. According to the statistics, readmission rates in England have been rising since 2001-2002 to 2010-2011. **Figure 3** follows the increasing trend of the percentage of patients readmitted for treatment to UK acute hospitals within 30 days of discharge and a "line of best fit" shows the regularity (and therefore the predictability) of the rise.

The problem of inadequate DP does not just concern readmissions, however. "Bed-blocking" due to delayed discharge has equivalent negative implications. It is reported by the NHS confederation that one in four patients are occupying beds when they could be recovering at home [16], which results in longer waiting lists, loss of confidence in the NHS and escalating expenditure. The average number of patients and days of delayed discharge per month in England for the year 2012 according to the Department of Health was 3997 patients and 114,386 days respectively.

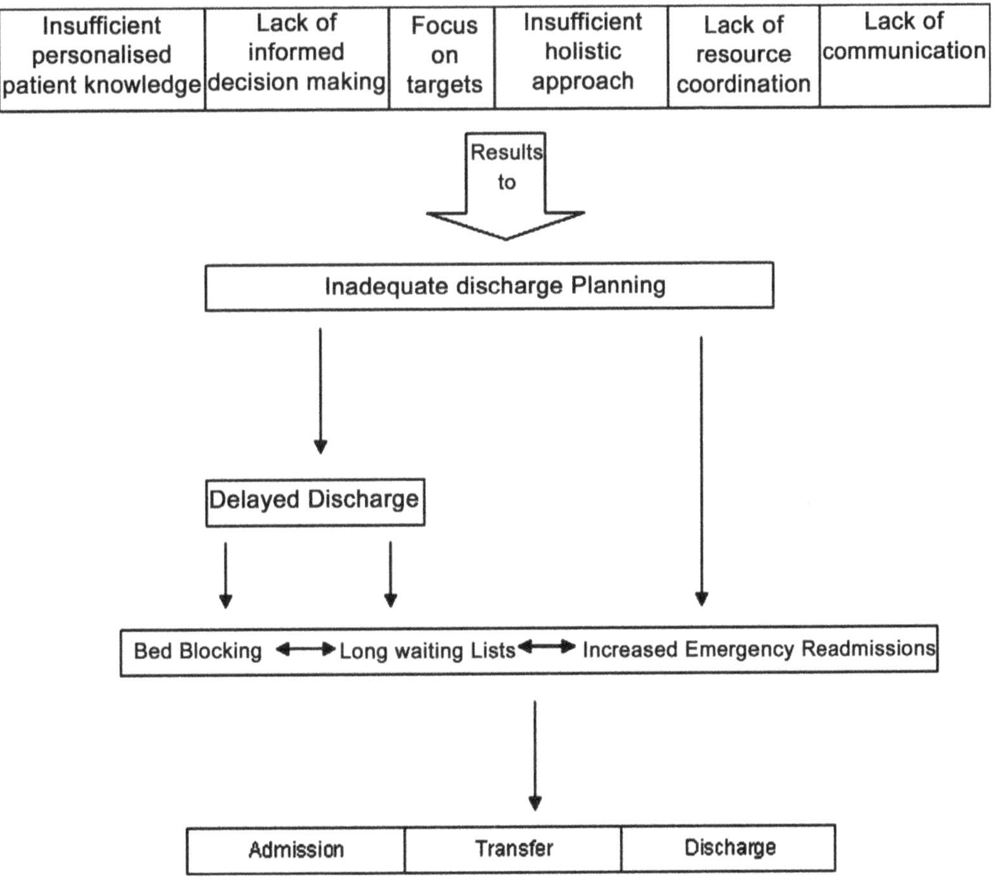

Figure 2. Problems resulting from inadequate discharge planning [12].

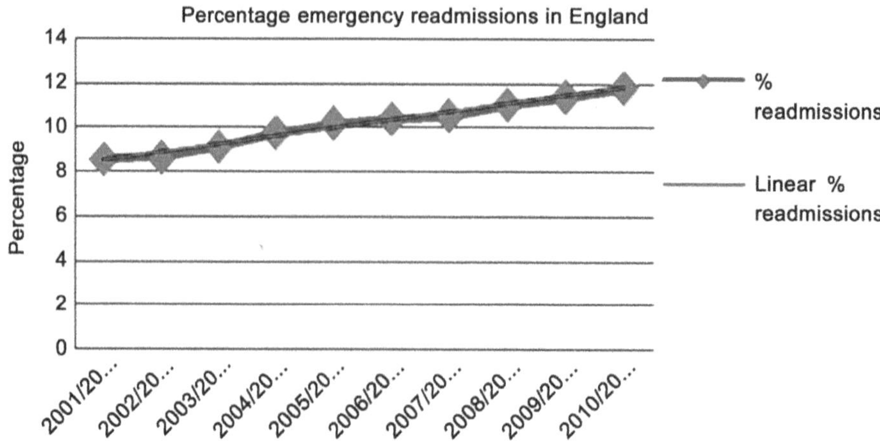

Figure 3. Emergency readmissions in England as a percentage of admissions [12].

Approximately £250m was spent on "delayed discharges" between August 2010 and the end of 2011, amounting to £550,000 a day [17]. Apart from the financial implications the delay in discharge is clearly disadvantageous to the well-being of patients, the morale of their relatives and wastes valuable hospital resources. The King's Fund reports that if it was better organised the NHS could reduce the number of overnight stays by 2.3 million, freeing up 7000 beds and saving the NHS nearly £500m a year [18]. Mike Farrar, the Chief Executive of the NHS Confederation indicates that these problems are the result of an "outdated hospital model of care" [19] while a breakdown in communication may also be a possible contributory cause [17]. Many older patients face the brunt of delayed discharge [12] as due to a lack of communication between the NHS and social care homes, they are forced to stay in hospital, causing longer waiting lists for other patients who are seeking urgent treatment [20]. The reasons for the dilemma as described in the previous section are clearly a result of inadequate support for DP among NHS staff, including physicians, nurses, social workers, and possibly other health professionals [12].

3. Knowledge Management

Knowledge is a multifaceted concept with multi-layered meanings [12]. Due to this nature, it has become important to manage knowledge in order to drive performance by ensuring that relevant knowledge is delivered "to the relevant person in the right place in a timely fashion" [12] (or simply put right knowledge is delivered to the right person at the right place at the right time). Apart from existing in the human mind (*i.e.* tacit knowledge), knowledge can exist in physical records (*i.e.* explicit knowledge), such as patient records and medical notes, which needs to be accessed more readily in paper or in computerised form. The major focus of KM in healthcare is to create environments for "knowledge workers" to develop, leverage and share knowledge. For this to happen effectively KM requires deep-rooted strategic and behavioural change. From this point of view KM represents an evolution towards greater personal and intellectual freedom [21] empowering individuals to engage more actively in their work by sharing ideas, thoughts and experiences [10]. Once knowledge has been discovered, storing it, reusing it and generating new knowledge from it, is important to "adding value" to data to create shared knowledge.

Continued progress in technology makes sharing knowledge easier, and the Internet with collective portals makes knowledge accessible to a wider range of audience [21]. The rise of networked computers has made it easier and cheaper to codify, store and share knowledge [22]. There is no shortage of technologies to aid in managing knowledge in a healthcare environment [10]; rather the prevalence of such technologies can create confusion. The goal of KM is to enhance the performance of a process (e.g. DP) by providing efficient access to knowledge and communities of healthcare professionals. It aims to combine the information from different sources (tacit, implicit and explicit) and provide it on a platform which allows applications to be built on it. It aims to prioritise, share, consolidate and provide consistent and accurate information and performance indicators to help with efficient decision making processes. As workers in a "knowledge intensive environment", healthcare professionals inevitably hold a considerable amount of experiential knowledge, which can be used to solve day to day problems related to decisions on patient discharge. It is important that knowledge used to solve such problems is captured, shared and reused in order to prevent the lack of "nourishment" (*i.e.* update and replenishment) of that knowledge [23] and to improve "knowledge of context". The "knowledge process" in a healthcare environment can be used to increase collaboration among clinicians, nursing staff with social service agencies for purposes of innovation and process improvement. Updating of knowledge assets cultivates the collective knowledge in a healthcare environment, enriching effective management, smoothening the flow of knowledge to enable better problem solving [23,24] and increase "knowledge potential".

KM when applied effectively can result in increased efficiency, responsiveness, competency and innovation [6] which results in superior performance in potentially critical applications [5] such as patient discharge. The challenge is therefore to create a KM system that can acquire, conserve, organise, retrieve, display and distribute what is available in a manner that informs, educates and facilitates the discovery of new knowledge to contribute [9] to the benefit of the organisations. KM can therefore be viewed as an integrator that offers a framework for balancing the technologies and approaches to provide valuable decision making actions [25]. It integrates into a seamless whole by aligning organisational information and practices with the organisation's objectives. This fits into an employee's daily work activities, manages content effectively, and encourages the potential opportunities of knowledge sharing with external agents [6].

4. Knowledge Management in Healthcare

The healthcare industry has been called "data rich while knowledge poor" [24] as its functions hold large amounts of data (e.g. patient records, outcomes of surgery and medical procedures, clinical trial data etc.) and yet the knowledge potential of many actions is yet to be fully exploited because much of the data is not translated into knowledge (*i.e.* there is low added value) in order to provide a wider context, a deeper understanding and to help with strategic decision making [26]. Knowledge appears to be underutilised at the point of care and need [26]. This limits the ability of experienced personnel to "harvest" knowledge and provide a clearer understanding of the involved process and factors by providing "a window on the internal dynamics of the healthcare enterprise" [27]. Multidisciplinary healthcare teams harvest personal expertise essential for patient safety, learn from it, adapt it to local situations and individual patients, then distribute it via reliable networks to care givers to improve care quality. The healthcare application with a "high value form of information" that allows sharing of the lessons learned from past experiences [27] (e.g. knowing what factors to take into account when planning the discharge of a patient) improves the context of knowledge potential processes in future.

A fundamental challenge faced by clinical practitioners and healthcare institutions is in the ability to interpret clinical information to make potentially lifesaving decisions while dealing with large amounts of data [10]. Clinical practise is quantitative and very much qualitative too. The tacit knowledge acquired by clinicians and nurses over the years, mainly through experience represents a valuable form of clinical knowledge [19]. KM in Healthcare involves understanding diseases, hospital systems and most importantly patients [19]. [9] argues that clinical methods exist for understanding diseases and illnesses but clinical methods or models are not so readily available for understanding patients. When quantitative and qualitative methods complement each other, and when various modalities of knowledge are used, a holistic view of a situation is best obtained thus leading to efficient decision making [9]. KM strategies can be broadly classified into codification (where knowledge is identified, captured, indexed and made available) and personalisation, where tacit knowledge is shared by means of discussion, effective communication through a multidisciplinary approach, allowing for creative problem solving [9]. In Healthcare, the use of both strategies of understanding diseases and patients is according to the different scenarios. When dealing with routine cases, the codification strategy can be applied and when dealing with a situation where a more creative solution is required, the personalisation strategy can be applied [9]. This approach, however, usually only works when the required knowledge is shared (*i.e.* processed) successfully. For example the National Institute for Clinical Excellence (NICE), in framing its guidelines, has noted a lack of willingness to share knowledge on the part of doctors who could potentially contribute to the guidance it gives [28].

5. Knowledge Management for Discharge Planning

A hospital is a dynamic environment, with changes taking place rapidly as patients move from one ward to another and treatments are carried out over time. Similarly, DP involves changes from a stable temporal state to another with an element of unpredictability of what is going to happen next [23]. In this context the past experiential knowledge of doctors and nurses is useful in assessing situations and deciding on plans. This enables making critical decisions, as their knowledge can be reconfigured and extended to fit the new situation and provide a personalised approach in assessing patients' journey along codified guidelines [23]. KM may have the potential to remove bottlenecks to improve the DP process mapping and identify possible improvement opportunities [12]. Understanding the relevant knowledge for a given situational decision is crucial to this process and a decision can never be completely separated from the context in which it is made [6]. This implies that in a hospital setting when looking at DP the interrelated factors need to be considered in the context of knowledge process [12]. Clearly, monitoring and understanding a patient's condition after discharge is a key part of successful DP and this requires the support of appropriate sensing and monitoring technologies.

6. The Internet of Things

This section of the paper examines the Internet of Things (IoT) as a possible solution to some of the problems of knowledge sharing in a healthcare environment. The IoT is an abstract concept in which physical objects are identified and connected to each other and have the ability to communicate with and to interact with their surroundings, providing some intelligence in their functionality. "IoT" is concerned with the network of smart embedded devices that communicate with each other and with cloud based applications in order to provide a better quality of life [29]. The term "IoT" refers to the idea of implementing networked RFID technologies with a view to providing a better quality of life and increasing knowledge sharing [29]. The implementation of the IoT may drive advancements in all areas of human life by extracting knowledge from the raw data provided, with the possibilities of solving many socio-technical interaction problems. [30] goes on to discuss the benefits and applications that have already been made by similar systems and suggests that the function of the IoT is to make tasks simpler, quicker and more efficient, providing results to a higher quality than is possible with purely human intervention.

The aim of the IoT in relation to healthcare is therefore to create a better quality of life by connecting "Things", which can be people (e.g. patients and medical staff), objects (e.g. medical equipment) and systems (e.g. patient monitoring systems) and integrating them seamlessly into network using a world-wide web (WWW) technology and connectivity [31]. For instance, healthcare systems could remotely monitor the vital signs of a patient and homes could be re-designed to help with the complex lifestyles many now live by recognising the preferences of its inhabitants. This information could be remotely monitored after patient discharge and the consequent improvement in home care would reduce the incidence of readmission. The integration, evolution and adaptation of emerging biomedical technologies will therefore provide a basic foundation for the IoT [31]. In 2008, the number of Things connected to the Internet already exceeded the number of people on earth, and it is possible that 50 billion Things will be interconnected by the year 2020. A technological evolution of tele-medicine has taken place in which healthcare professionals can now monitor a patient's vital signs remotely and continuously. In addition, the technology supports personalisation, in which patients with chronic conditions are able to live independently in their own homes or secure housing (*i.e.* a non-hospital setting) using IoT technology to support their lifestyles. Such devices include Lifeline Home Units, Personal Pendants, Wandering Client Alarms, PIR Movement Detectors, Fall Detectors, Bed Occupancy Sensors, Temperature Extreme Sensors, Automatic Medicine/Pill Reminders and Dispensers, Talking Colour Detectors for blind and partially-sighted people and assisted GPS/GSM technologies which recognise when the user goes outside the chosen safety zone [32]. The number of such devices and their applications is increasing daily [32].

6.1. An Analogy of IoT

To better understand and explain the IoT concept, [33] uses the human body as an analogy for the IoT, describing parts to sense, connect and control the networks. The "brain" is necessary to recall, process and to provide intelligence to react to the data it receives. The "nervous system", provides a network of sensor signals to and from the "brain", allowing interaction with other parts of the network. "Senses and muscles" provide raw data to the "brain" to understand and react to, allowing response to its environment. By considering the "brain" to be the servers for processing, the "nervous system" to be the communication networks and the "senses and muscles" to be instruments for data capture and actuation, it is understandable how these systems could be considered "intelligent".

6.2. The Senses & Muscles

Machine-to-Machine communications (M2M) is a domain of computing which is essential for the development of the IoT. It deals directly with the physical objects and provides a means of capturing and returning data to a central controller for processing, analysis, correlation and reaction, which may include alerting users, changing attributes of a Thing or communicating with another system. The major difference between the M2M and IoT concepts concerns the "interconnectedness" of their supporting systems. The IoT concept suggests a ubiquitous ecosystem made up of a matrix of services and sub-systems working collectively, whereas M2M systems simply represent sub-systems of the IoT. Protocols for IoT communications, processing and storage are vital, all of which must be highly scalable, versatile and adaptable for changing environments and requirements. The purpose is to provide an entire system (from sensor to software) to capture, analyse and act upon information passing among Things in the network. Various sensors can be deployed, depending on the requirements and the attributes that require monitoring.

Sensors and actuators require interfaces to the network infrastructure, known as a gateway, which manages connections to and from the base station, sending the digital values to be processed by control systems. Gateways deal with initial data processing, validation, caching, remote management of devices and security. They must be configured to understand the specific protocol of each sensor, which often causes issues due to the lack of standards between sensors and protocols. One of the biggest difficulties for M2M systems currently is developing an open standardised framework for sensors to connect to gateways allowing mobility and flexibility between systems and ultimately supporting the heterogeneity for IoT. With sensors and actuators connected to a network interface, monitoring applications can be developed to operate in domestic and medical environments [34].

Although sensors, actuators and gateways can be combined in to one unit they are often separated and connected via wired or wireless technologies.

Sensors, actuators and gateways can be deployed in various styles to maximise scalability, utilisation and manageability, including star, mesh, bus and other common network topologies. To deal with communications between sensor-to-sensor, sensor-to-gateway and gateway-to-network various methods are used, including Ethernet, 3G, 4G, satellite communications, Wi-Fi, ZigBee, etc. A basic requirement for the IoT is mobility and flexibility of Things and to achieve this Wireless Sensor Networks (WSN) are designed to allow flexibility and redundancy. In order to manage devices remotely, to handle various protocols and to control low level architectures, embedded frameworks allow developers to focus on functional logic rather than protocol specifics which speeds deployment. If open standards are not adopted progress in M2M and IoT systems will be limited, so to provide communications between gateways and base stations a client/server paradigm is most commonly used. Hyper Text Transfer Protocol (HTTP) drives the Internet and IoT gateways use HTTP to make requests and receive data, although for this purpose HTTP is considered to be extremely demanding, requiring high overheads to maintain and ensure efficient communications.

6.3. The Nervous System

For M2M systems to function and expand a reliable open network is a major requirement. The Internet provides a suitable backbone for transferring data anywhere and between virtually anything. Both Cloud Computing and M2M will evolve into components supporting the IoT. To provide an accessible universal network the Internet, or the "Cloud" as it has aptly been named, is evolving into such a network. This will provide a suitable solution meeting the requirements of the IoT. The Cloud can support connectivity anywhere, between anything, at any time and adapt to its environment [35]. The cloud is essentially a modern day metaphor for the efficient use of the internet, the next stage in the internet's evolution, encourage resource optimisation to develop flexible services consisting of remote assets lowering responsibility and cost for the user. Cloud computing refers specifically to the architecture that supports the Cloud. That is the hardware, networks, hypervisors, operating systems, middleware and databases which software and applications rely on. Receiving them as a service reduces management, maintenance and investment. The need for private infrastructure, software licencing, training and many other costly responsibilities are less of a burden compared to traditional "on-premise" solutions. Cloud service providers generally hold all liability, but public infrastructure must be taken into account due to the associated risks with regards to security [35]. Compared to traditional models for distributed applications which often vary in type, style, complexity and interoperability, cloud services provide a cost effective, adaptable and reusable way of deploying services [36].

By optimising existing systems to provide services capable of multi-tenancy supporting adaptability, redundancy, transparency and ubiquitous functionality, which has become a major driving force for Cloud Computing. These characteristics allow quality systems to be developed with minimal resources and investment required, in turn reducing IT costs by maximising hardware utilisation, efficiently provisioning resources and improving user experience [37]. By consolidating resource pools, costs are reduced by between 50% - 70% due to improved management, control and utilisation. VMware also states that return on investment is met in less than one year providing profits fast. A study by PwC also shows that the most important use of the cloud is to deploy IT solutions faster than in-house options by utilising external service providers and lowering costs due to the superior technical skills required to satisfy new requirements.

6.4. The Brain

To assist in deploying, managing and controlling remote devices various management and host functions would be required to deal with the vast amounts of data and connectivity to and from other systems. Typical M2M systems specifically require a base station with the following components:

- Databases for storage, retrieval and access;
- API functionality to provide logic and to develop custom programs for reusability, connectivity and

data access;

- Web services to provide access to API's via the internet to again reuse business logic and maximise use;
- Web applications providing business logic and functionality dealing with data input, processing and output;
- Interfaces for user access which provide enhanced interaction, control, flexibility and feedback;
- Flexible programming languages are required to retrieve information and allow access to the system. Lightweight and efficient protocols are preferred to minimise bandwidth and speed software development;

These components provide the tools to develop and manage M2M systems. By suitably deploying each component data can be stored appropriately and communicated via a number of different methods which supports openness by allowing numerous interfaces for connectivity. This is essentially the "brains" of an M2M system providing logic and control. To counterpart the base station of an M2M system, deploying embedded devices integrated into Things can provide a suitable way for constant and reliable services, access and enhanced functionality, especially when network connections are limited. Pervasive computing concerns the integration of micro-computers in a less obvious fashion, to be indistinguishable in everyday tasks operating without human interaction. The aims of pervasive computing are to improve human experiences and quality of life by implementing technologies in a less evasive way [38]. The impact of pervasive computing on M2M technologies can allow for complex computational programs on smaller and less demanding devices, such as are suitable for comfortable patient monitoring in an aftercare situation. This allows for sensors and gateway devices to be enhanced, adding additional functionality and reducing cost. When combined with the Cloud and M2M technologies, applications allow for pervasive systems to infuse stationary and passive objects with mobility and dynamism allowing them to act and react to their environment, ultimately providing the self-aware environment for the IoT [38].

By empowering inanimate objects with sensors, actuators, computing power and a communication interface it allows the object to become an interactive part of the environment in which it resides. Embedding such technology into an object allows for programs to run on the object and for complex systems to manage and analyse objects in a group. Common characteristics of pervasive computing include heterogeneity, automation, transparency, mobility, scalability and security, all of which align with the aims of the IoT. The IoT will depend on pervasive computing in order to empower, control and manage the sensor and actuator networks and to provide enhanced interfaces to the cloud. The ability of a device to react to its environment suggests it possesses intelligent characteristics which have produced the term "Smart device", referring to a device with a range of functional capabilities allowing it to react to other smart devices or systems. To enhance mobility and lower evasiveness objects may connect to more powerful devices in their surroundings, providing the same smart nature without the resources embedded in an object [39]. In isolation these devices may not be considered "smart" as the same tasks which depend on the infrastructure and communications provided by more powerful devices [39]. "Intelligent environments" describes a group of smart devices communicate in order to benefit the user. This is a step towards the IoT and a major achievement for pervasive computing. Personal Area Networks (PAN) provides methods of interlinking such devices to react to data sources specified by user.

The term "smart" became prevalent due to "smart phones", referring to mobile telephones with features allowing them to react to data automatically. Smart devices allow for custom software to be installed and allow data to be stored, processed and sent to network services without user interaction. RFID, barcode and other similar identifying technologies require dedicated systems to instil intelligence therefore it cannot be a smart device. Other authors also argue that smart devices should be capable of acquiring and applying knowledge autonomously and automatically to its environment, adapting to inhabitants' preferences and requirements [40]. Smart devices can be categorised by size, form factor, technology and purpose. [41] classifies six types including tabs, pads, boards, dust, skin and clay. Each device can also be classified as passive or active. Passive refers to relying on infrastructure and on-object memory such as barcodes or passive RFID. Active devices typically consist of computational power and do not rely completely on sensor networks and applications to hold state information. A repeating theme with regards to M2M, Cloud and the IoT is taxonomy and RTLS (Real time Location-based Services) which allow the physical location of an object to be communicated (e.g. the location of a nurse or doctor within a hospital or an at-risk patient within their home. [42] describes how the following methods for RTLS may be implemented:

- Geographical—Using spatial information to map location;
- Special—Identify the item by the size of its surrounding;
- Proximity—Detect distance from other devices and sensors;
- Transitional—Recognised by referenced fixed receivers.

This is a vital component for environments to react as the presence of an object or device which can imply that a human has entered a room, an object has left a specific zone or a new device can be utilised in an environment. Trends in pervasive computing have focused on miniaturisation and embedded frameworks to support web services, APIs and artificial intelligence. Artificial intelligence would allow a device, or environment, to adapt and learn a hosts habits and preferences to customise operations to their needs. Similarly this logic relates to the current use of internet data being tailor for targeted advertising and product services to the user [43]. In a healthcare setting therefore, as vast amounts of data and information is generated, the ability of "smart" devices to feed knowledge back into the system to help make more informed and personalised decisions with regards to DP and other areas would be of significant importance.

6.5. Conclusion

This paper has examined the problem of patient readmission into hospitals. It has suggested ways of reducing the number of patient readmissions through improved DP. The study suggests that KM may be a way of reducing readmissions and improving DP through improved knowledge of the patient's aftercare environment and medical situation. The Internet of Things (IoT) is suggested as a way of monitoring patients continuously and effectively once they have left hospital (e.g. in their own homes after discharge or in other healthcare situations).

The IoT is discussed in this paper because it is a candidate technology which will enforce knowledge sharing. The Smart environment will allow information to be generated by Things and will automatically been sent and stored in a cloud. Through the use of Artificial Intelligence techniques, data will be analysed and categorised accordingly. The role of KM is to use this information to inform the design of DP upon a patient's admission in hospital. The proposed KM Model will consider factors, internal to a healthcare setting, external to a healthcare setting and psychosocial factors of patients in order to make informed decisions, thus resulting in effective and personalised DP.

REFERENCES

[1] NHS, "About the NHS," 2012. http://www.nhs.uk/NHSEngland/thenhs/about/Pages/overview.aspx

[2] P. Ashmos and P. Huber, "The Systems Paradigm in Organization Theory: Correcting the Record and Suggesting the Future," *JSTOR*: *The Academy of Management Review*, Vol. 12, No. 4, 1987, pp. 607-621. http://jaylee.business.ku.edu/MGMT916/PDF/AshmosHuber 1987 AMR.pdf

[3] L. Ervin, "The Systems View of the World," Hampton Press, New Jersey, 1996.

[4] A. D. Chetty, V. K. Kartha, A. McKenna, K. DePaoli, M. R. B. Jack, "Re-Engineering the Hospital Discharge: An Example of a Multifaceted Process Evaluation," *Advances in Patient Safety*: *From Research to Implementation*, Vol. 1-4, Agency for Healthcare Research and Quality, Rockville, 2005. http://www.ahrq.gov/qual/advances/

[5] I. Reychav and J. Weisberg, "Bridging Intention and Behaviour of Knowledge Sharing," *Journal of Knowledge Management*, Vol. 14, No. 2, 2010, pp. 285-300. http://www.emeraldinsight.com/10.1108/13673271011032418.

[6] M. Fontaine and E. Lesser, "Challenges in Managing Organizational Knowledge," 2002. http://www-935.ibm.com/services/us/imc/pdf/g510-3234-00-esr-managing-organizational-knowledge.pdf

[7] A. Hannan, "Opportunities and Challenges of Using Electronic Health Records to Enhance Patient Care," 2010. http://www.bcs.org/upload/pdf/assist-140910-ahannan.pdf

[8] M. Polanyi, "Tacit Knowing," In: M. Polanyi, Ed., *The Tacit Dimension*, Doubleday & Company, New York, 1966, pp. 3-25.

[9] H. J. Levenstein, C. E. McCracken, M. R. Ian, A. M. Stewart and B. J. Brown, "The Patient-Centred Clinical Method," *Family Practice*, Vol. 3, No. 1, 1986, pp. 24-30. http://fampra.oxfordjournals.org/content/3/1/24.full.pdf+html

[10] A. Eardley and A. Czerwinski, "Knowledge Management for Primary Healthcare Services," In: R. Bali and A. Dwivedi, Eds., *Knowledge Management*: *Issues*, *Advances and Successes*, Springer Science + Business Media, New York, 2007.

[11] R. K. Bali, A. Dwivedi, A. E. James, R. N. G. Naguib and D. Johnston, "Towards a Holistic Knowledge Management Framework for Healthcare Institutions," *Proceedings of the Second Joint EMBSBMES Conference*, Houston, 2002, pp. 1894-1895. http://ieeexplore.ieee.org/stamp/stamp.jsp?arnumber=01053081

[12] N. Kamalanathan, A. Eardley, C. Chibelushi and P. Kingston, "The Discharge Planning Dilemma in the UK NHS: The Role of Knowledge Management," In: G. Huang, *et al*., Ed., *Health Informations Systems*, Springer-Verlag, Berlin Heidelberg, 2013, pp. 172-185.

[13] Sg2 Healthcare Intelligence, "Reducing 30-Day Emergency Readmissions," 2011, pp. 1-28. http://www.hsj.co.uk/Journals/2/Files/2011/6/15/Sg2_Service Kit_Reducing30-DayReadmissions.pdf

[14] K. Ishikawa, "Introduction to Quality Control," 3A Corporation, Tokyo, 1990.

[15] Social Care Institute for Excellence, "SCIE Research Briefing 12: Involving Individual Older Patients and Their Carers in the Discharge Process from Acute to Community Care: Implications for Intermediate Care." http://www.scie.org.uk/publications/briefings/briefing12

[16] Institute for Healthcare Improvement, "Improving Patient Flow at Bon Secours Venice Hospital," 2011. http://www.ihi.org/knowledge/Pages/ImprovementStories

/ImprovingPatientFlowBonSecoursVeniceHospital.aspx

[17] N. Triggle, "Organise Urgent Care Better, NHS Told," *BBC News*, 2012. http://www.bbc.co.uk/news/health-19181905

[18] R. Ramesh, "One in Four Hospital Patients Could Be Recovering at Home," *The Guardian*, 2011. http://www.guardian.co.uk/society/2011/dec/29/hospital-patients-discharge-bed-blocking

[19] S. Adams, "'Intolerable' Bed-Blocking Crisis Threatens NHS," *The Telegraph*, 2011. http://www.telegraph.co.uk/health/healthnews/8343879/Intolerable-bed-blocking-crisis-threatens-NHS.html

[20] R. Winnett, "Scandal of NHS 'Production Line' as Readmissions Soar," *The Telegraph*, 2011. http://www.telegraph.co.uk/health/healthnews/8983505/Scandal-of-NHS-production-line-as-readmissions-soar.html

[21] T. Chunsheng, "The Research on Knowledge Management and Knowledge Portal Framework Based on Agent Mechanism," *IEEE* (Vol. 00, pp. 263-267), Hefei, China. *3rd World Congress on Intelligent Control and Automation.* http://ieeexplore.ieee.org/stamp/stamp.jsp?tp=&arnumber=859962

[22] T. M. Hansen, N. Nohria and T. Tierney, "What's Your Strategy for Managing Knowledge?" *Harvard Business Review*, 1999, pp. 1-11. http://consulting-ideas.com/wp-content/uploads/Whats-your-strat-art.pdf

[23] S. Liao, "Problem Solving and Knowledge Inertia," *Expert Systems with Applications*, Vol. 22, No. 1, 2002, pp. 21-31. http://linkinghub.elsevier.com/retrieve/pii/S095741740100046X

[24] A. M. Mills and T. A. Smith, "Knowledge Management and Organizational Performance: A Decomposed View," *Journal of Knowledge Management*, Vol. 15, No. 1, 2011, pp. 156-171. http://www.emeraldinsight.com/10.1108/13673271111108756

[25] P. J. Sharp, W. A. Eardley and H. Shah, "Visual Tools within MakE: A Knowledge Management Method, Electronic," *Journal of Knowledge Management*, Vol. 1, No. 2, 2003, pp. 177-186.

[26] A. Copper, "We Haven't Got a Plan, So What Can Go Wrong? Where Is the NHS Coming from?" In: R. K. Bali and A. Dwivedi, Eds., *Healthcare Knowledge Management*, Springer Science + Business Media, New York, 2007, pp. 221-232.

[27] S. Shepperd, J. McClaran, C. Phillips, N. Lannin, L. Clemson, A. McCluskey, I. Cameron and S. Barras, "Discharge Planning from Hospital to Home," The Cochrane Library, Vol. 1, 2010, pp. 1-75. http://onlinelibrary.wiley.com/doi/10.1002/14651858.CD000313.pub3/pdf

[28] NHS, "Leaving Hospital," 2012. http://www.nhs.uk/nhsengland/aboutnhsservices/nhshospitals/pages/leaving-hospital.aspx

[29] Theinternetofthings.eu, "Russian Research Center on the Internet of Things Is Official Partner for the Internet of Thing Council: The Internet of Things." http://theinternetofthings.eu/russian-research-center-internet-things-official-partner-internet-thing-council

[30] D. Evans, "The Internet of Things: How the Next Evolution of the Internet Is Changing Everything," 2012. http://www.cisco.com/web/about/ac79/docs/innov/IoT_IBSG_0411FINAL.pdf

[31] C. Pfister, "Getting Started with the Internet of Things," O'Reilly Media, Inc., Sebastapool, 2011.

[32] M. R. McGee-Lennon and P. D. Gray, "Including Stakeholders in the Design of Home Care Systems: Identification and Categorization of Complex User Requirements," *INCLUDE Conference*, London, April 2007.

[33] H. Ning, "Future Internet of Things Architecture: Like Mankind Neural System or Social Organization Framework?" *IEEE Communications Letters*, Vol. 15, No. 4, 2011, pp. 461-463.

[34] I. F. Akyilidiz, T. Melodia and K. Chowdhury, "A Survey on Wireless Multimedia Sensor Networks," *Journal of Computer Networks*, Vol. 51, No. 4, 2007, pp. 921-960.

[35] J. Hurwitz, "Cloud Computing for Dummies," Wiley Publication. Hoboken, 2010.

[36] Exelanz, "Cloud vs. Traditional Hosting," 2012. http://www.exelanz.com/cloud-vs-traditional-hosting/

[37] Fasthosts, "The Myth behind the Extinction of IT Departments," 2012. http://blogs.fasthosts.co.uk/cloud-computing/the-myth-behind-the-extinction-of-it-departments/?goback=%2Egde_45151_member_191264989

[38] D. B. Lange and M. Oshimma, "Ten Good Reasons for Mobile Agents," *Communications of the ACM*, Vol. 42, No. 3, 1998, pp. 88-89.

[39] M. Satyanarayanan, "Pervasive Computing: Vision and Challenges," *IEEE Personal Communications*, Vol. 8, No. 4, 2001, pp. 10-17. http://www.cs.cmu.edu/~aura/docdir/pcs01.pdf

[40] D. J. Cook, M. M. Youngblood, E. O. Heiermann, K. Gopalratnam, S. Rao, A. Litvin and F. Khawaja, "Mavhome: An Agent-Bqased Smart Home," *Proceedings of the First IEEE International Conference on Pervasive Computing and Communications*, Fort Worth, 26 March 2003, pp. 521-524.

[41] S. Poslad, "Ubiquitous Computing: Smart Devices, Environments and Interactions," John Wiley and Sons, London, 2011.

[42] K. M. Dombroviak and R. Ramnath, "A Taxonomy of Mobile and Pervasive Applications," *Proceedings of the* 2007 *ACM Symposium on Applied Computing*, Seoul, 11-15 March 2007, pp. 1609-1615.

[43] D. Chaffey, "Internet Marketing: Strategy, Implementation, and Practice," Financial Times, Prentice Hall, Harlow, 2000.

4

MAEB: Routing Protocol for IoT Healthcare

Haoru Su[1], Zhiliang Wang[1], Sunshin An[2*]
[1]School of Computer and Communication Engineering, University of Science and Technology, Beijing, China
[2]Department of Electrical Engineering, Korea University, Seoul, Korea

ABSTRACT

Healthcare is one of the most promising applications of Internet of Things. This paper describes a prototype for the IoT healthcare systems. We propose the Movement-Aided Energy-Balance (MAEB) routing protocol. The movement and energy information of the neighbor Coordinators are collected and stored in the neighbor discovery procedure. The MAEB forwarding is used to select the most suitable neighbor to forward the data. The simulation results show that the proposed protocol has better performance than the other three routing protocols.

Keywords: IoT; Healthcare; Routing

1. Introduction

Healthcare needs a major shift toward more scalable and more affordable solutions. Restructuring healthcare systems toward proactive managing of wellness rather than illness, and focusing on prevention and early detection of disease emerge as the answers to these problems [1]. In the last few years, the Internet of Things in healthcare applications has gained the attention of various researchers in order to cope with the rising healthcare costs. An important task of such a system is to collect physiological parameters like the heartbeat and body temperature. Wireless Body Area Network (WBAN) [2] is one of the most suitable technologies for building unobtrusive, scalable, and robust IoT healthcare systems. A WBAN is composed of structured sensor nodes. These sensors are placed in clothes, directly on the body or under the skin of a person. The sensors are equipped with a wireless interface. Similar to the traditional wireless sensor networks, body sensors collect information about the environment (the human body), that is subsequently correlated for monitoring and/or actuation purposes [1].

Since the wireless sensor nodes are energy constrained, it is necessary to find an energy-efficient routing protocol to deliver the data [3]. The authors of [4] give a survey of energy-efficient routing protocols which can be applied in IoT healthcare systems. However, most of the protocols are designed for the general wireless sensor networks. They did not consider the feature of WBANs. Actually, there are few existing routing protocols for WBANs specially [5].

In this paper, we present architecture for the IoT healthcare systems. It is composed of the WBANs, and a broader telemedicine system. A WBAN consists of multiple sensor nodes, each capable of sampling, processing, and communicating biotic signals. The communication of the WBAN can be supported by IEEE 802.15.6 [2]. All the data packets are delivered to the Access Gateway (AG) by the Coordinators. The AG transmits the information to the medical server through which the medical personnel can get it. In the IoT healthcare systems, the sensor nodes placed on the people move along with them.

We propose the Movement-Aided Energy-Balance (MAEB) routing protocol for the IoT healthcare systems. The first step of MAEB is neighbor discovery. After this step, local Coordinators have the movement and energy information of their reachable Coordinators. And then, according to this information, the Coordinator calculates which neighbor is most suitable to forward the data packet. The MAEB forwarding considers the distance and velocity towards AG, as well as the remaining energy. In the simulation, we compare the performance of MAEB with three other routing protocols: PAOLSR [6], EOLSR [7], and MMPR [8]. We evaluate the performance according to four metrics: latency, energy consumption, packet delivery ratio, and throughput. The simulation results show that the MAEB has the better performance than the other three routing protocols.

*Corresponding author.

The remainder of this paper is organized as follows. In Section 2, we describe the architecture of the IoT healthcare systems. Section 3 introduces the group mobility model and the MAEB routing protocol. Section 4 presents the performance evaluation of our protocol. Finally, Section 5 concludes this paper.

2. Architecture of IoT Healthcare Systems

Recent technological advances in wireless networking, microelectronics integration and miniaturization, sensors, and the Internet allow us to fundamentally modernize and change the way healthcare services are deployed and delivered. The IoT healthcare systems have gained the attention of various researchers. WBANs are one of the most suitable technologies for building unobtrusive, scalable, and robust IoT healthcare systems. They allow an individual to closely monitor changes in user's vital signs and provide feedback to help maintain an optimal health status.

The architecture of the IoT healthcare systems is illustrated in **Figure 1**. It is composed of the WBANs and a broader telemedicine system. It services hundreds or thousands of individual users. Each user wears a number of body sensor nodes that are placed on or in the human body, each capable of sampling, processing, and communicating one or more vital signs such as heart rate, blood pressure, oxygen saturation, etc. Typically, these sensors are placed strategically on the human body as tiny patches or hidden in users' clothes. For example, the heart sensor monitors heart activity. It has a single-channel bio amplifier for three-lead ECG. This sensor is capable of sending either row ECG signal (signal is filtered) or R-peak events recognized by the on-sensor feature extraction software modules. The activity sensor attached to the user's belt, an ankle, a knee or the trunk can be used to differentiate user activity states such as sitting, walking, running and lying.

The communication within the WBAN is supported by IEEE 802.15.6 protocol stacks. The beacon-enabled cluster-tree topology is used. For each user, the Coordinator (C), which has more energy and computing ability, organizes the whole network on one human. It collects data from the sensor nodes on or in the human body. In this IoT healthcare system, there is no personal server such as PDA or PC. It can reduce the expenditure of each user. The collected data of Coordinator delivers data to the Access Gateway (AG) through other Coordinators using multiple hop routing. AG may be plugged into either a hospital server or a wired or wireless network appliance. The AG and Coordinators transmit periodic beacon frames to synchronize nodes in the network. The AG also transmits the data to the medical server through Internet. If a user moves out of the communication range (there's no neighbor user), the Coordinator automatically begin buffering data locally. When the user returns, the route link is reestablished. The Coordinator automatically uploads stored sensor and event data.

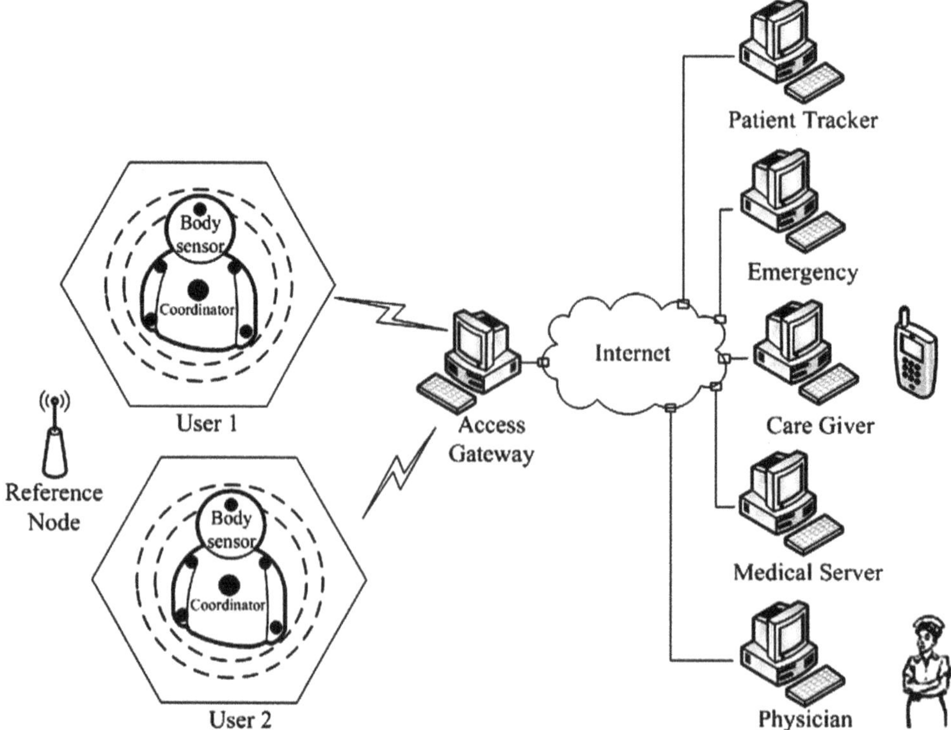

Figure 1. Architecture of the IoT healthcare systems.

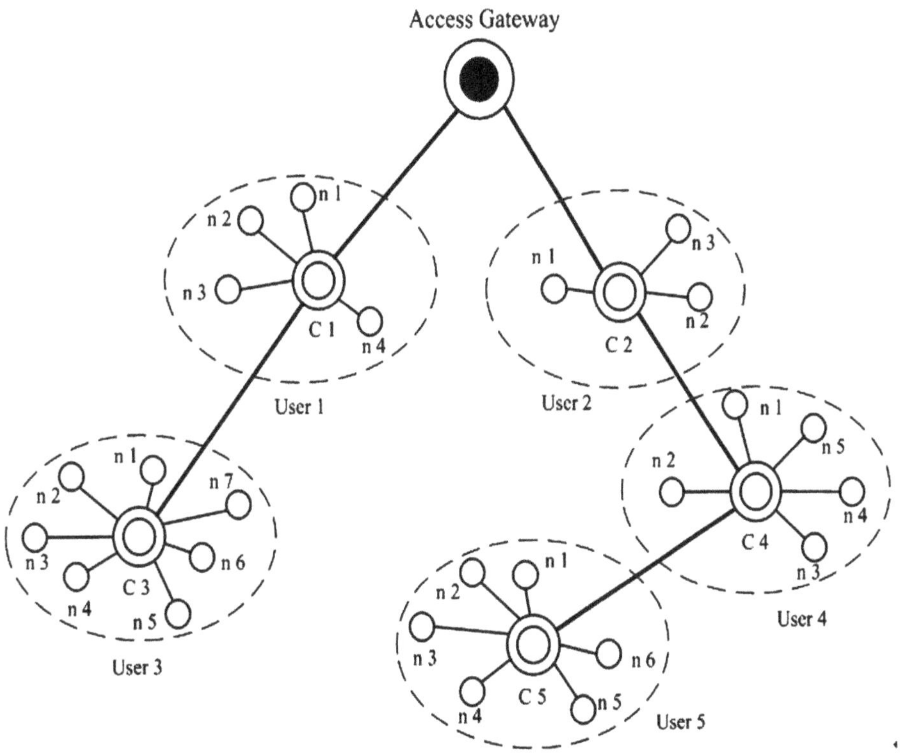

Figure 2. An illustration of the communication structure of the IoT healthcare systems.

Since the users' location information is also essential in the IoT healthcare system, localization scheme is used. There are some Reference Nodes (RNs) around. They are GPS equipped or preprogramming nodes with their locations. The Coordinators can get their own locations from the signal of RNs and the localization algorithm. The medical provider can analyze the patients' information and provide medical services. The medical server stores the information of the users and their health information. There is an expert system to diagnose the simple disease. If the situation of the patient is serious, the experts in the hospital can make a diagnosis according to the data of the patient [1]. Through Internet, experts from different places can perform a consultation or collaboration. If the patient needs an ambulance in an emergency, the system can send the instruction to the nearest ambulance on the way. An illustration of the communication structure of the IoT healthcare systems is shown in **Figure 2**.

3. MAEB Routing Protocol

Routing protocols for the IoT healthcare systems can be divided in intra-body communication and extra-body communication ones. The first controls the information handling between the body sensor nodes and Coordinator. The latter ensures communication from Coordinator to the Access Gateway. In this paper, we just consider the extra-body routing since the intra-body WBAN is star structure. After the body sensors send their data to the Coordinator, there are two kinds of methods to deliver the data from the Coordinator to AG. The first one is single-hop delivery, which means that Coordinator transmits data directly to AG. Another method is multi-hop delivery, which means that other Coordinators forward data to AG. The multi-hop routing method can obtain larger network coverage.

In this section, we will introduce the Movement-Aided Energy-Balance (MAEB) routing protocol. The first step of the MAEB is neighbor discovery procedure which conducts by the Coordinators. After the Coordinators get information of their neighbor Coordinators, they send their packet data to the Access Gateway following a forwarding rule, in which the distance and velocity to the AG and the remaining energy is considered to select the neighbor Coordinator.

3.1. Neighbor Discovery Procedure

Before communication with the AG, the sensor nodes have to complete the association procedure to form the star topology. After that, the Coordinators perform the neighbor discovery procedure. The aim of the neighbor discovery is to establish the neighbor table of Coordinators which get information to decide the route in the following steps. One Coordinator scans the strength of the receiving signals and finds the neighbors in its transmission range. Then one Coordinator establishes a neighbor table to store the information of the neighbors. **Figure 3** exhibits an example of neighbor discovery.

The neighbor discovery flow chart is shown in **Figure 4**. At the beginning of neighbor discovery procedure, the Coordinator establishes a neighbor table to store the information of the neighbor Coordinators. Then it sets a timer to 0. The Coordinator sends a broadcast message to find the neighbors. The Coordinator which receives this message sends a response message containing its information including ID (e.g., address), location, velocity, and remaining energy. We encode location as two four-byte floating-point quantities, for x and y coordinate values. Before the timer increase to 5, if the Coordinator receives the response from the neighbor Coordinators, it examines it is a duplicate. If its ID is unique, the responding Coordinator will be added to the neighbor table. After the neighbor discovery procedure, the Coordinators

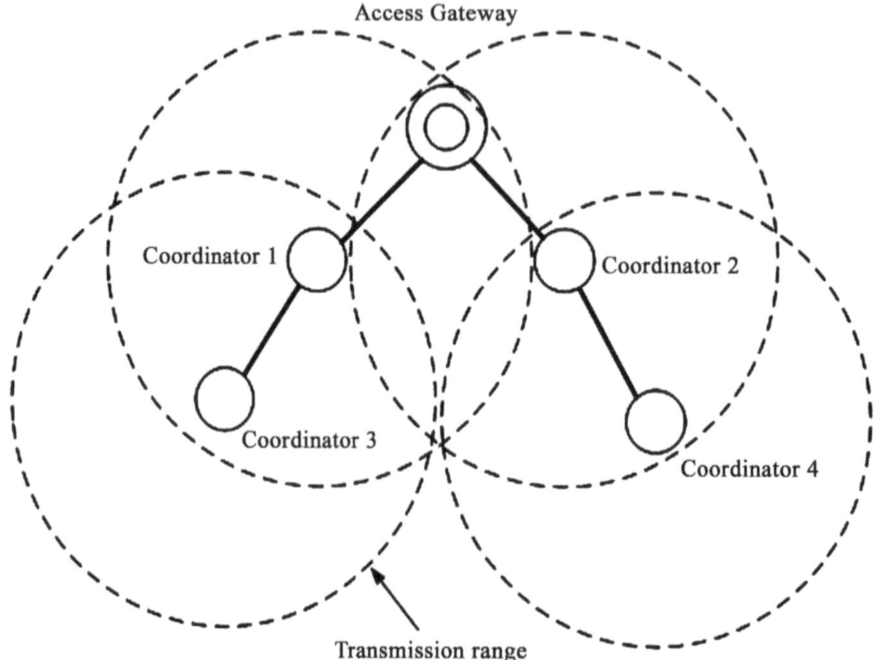

Figure 3. An example of neighbor discovery.

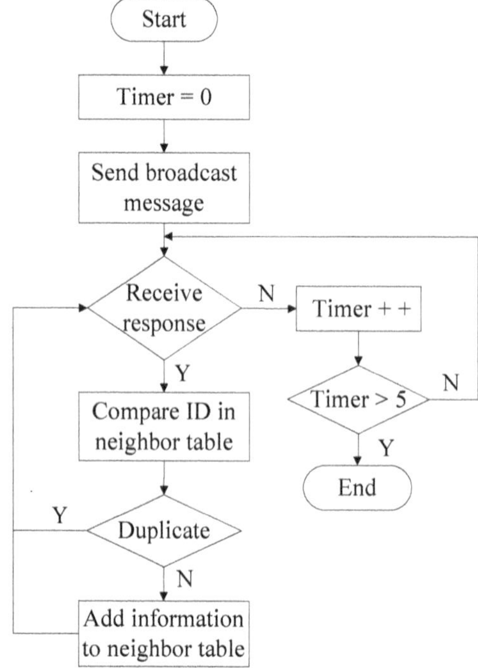

Figure 4. Flow chart of neighbor discovery.

have the information of reachable Coordinators. The neighbor discovery procedure is repeated every period of time to update the neighbor table. The correct choice of update interval depends on the rate of mobility in the network and range of Coordinators' radios.

3.2. MAEB Forwarding

After the system setting, location information of the AG is stored in every Coordinator of the network. After the procedure of neighbor discovery, the Coordinators have the information of reachable Coordinators, including the movement (location and velocity) and remaining energy. Each Coordinator collects the data packets from its sensor nodes. The destination of these data packets is the AG. When the AG is in the transmission range of the Coordinator, it transmits the data to the AG directly. Otherwise, it sends the data to one of its neighbor Coordinators. The mechanism of the neighbor selection impacts on the packet delay and energy consumption of the whole network.

Firstly, the distance from a neighbor Coordinator to AG is considered. Less distance can reduce the average packet delay, as well as the number of hops. Secondly, the relative velocity is concerned. If a neighbor Coordinator is moving towards AG rapidly, it can take the packet close to AG. Thirdly, to balance the energy consumption and prolong the network lifetime, the residual energy of the Coordinator is also took into account. We tend to choose the Coordinator which has more residual energy. A parameter *k* is defined to indicate which Coordinator neighbor is most suitable to forward the data packet, which can be calculated by

$$k = a\frac{D_N}{D_S} + b\frac{V_N}{V_S} + c\frac{E_T}{E_R} \quad (1)$$

where D_N is the distance between the neighbor Coordinator and AG. D_S is the distance from Coordinator itself to AG. V_N is the relative velocity of the neighbor Coordinator and AG. It is the projection of the velocity vector on the interlink from Coordinator to AG. V_S denotes the relative velocity of Coordinator itself and AG. E_T is the data packet transmission energy. E_R denotes the residual energy of the neighbor Coordinator. There are three weighting parameters *a*, *b*, and *c*, which are between 0 and 1. They can be adjusted according to the application scenario.

The pseudocode of MAEB forwarding is shown in **Figure 5**. Suppose the address of AG is *g.a*. The location of AG is *g.l*. Each C has a neighbor table (N), each of whose entries contain the information of a neighbor Coordinator: address (*a*), location (*l*), velocity (*v*), and remain energy (*e*). We denote the own address and location of a Coordinator by *self.a* and *self.l*. Equation (3) is used to calculate the variable *k*. *k* is calculated by *l*, *v*, and *e*. The initial k_{best} is set to 1. If there is one neighbor Coordinator which has smaller *k*, k_{best} is substituted by this value. After one loop, n_{best} represents the neighbor Coordinator which has the smallest *k*. This neighbor Coordinator is the most suitable one to forward the data packet. After transmitting data to neighbor Coordinator, next step forwarding begins. This forwarding repeats until the data packet reaches AG.

Figure 6 gives an illustration of MAEB forwarding. In this example, the Coordinator of user 1 has a data packet aim to transmit to the AG. There are four other users in this system, user 2, 3, 4, and 5. The Coordinator of user 4 is not in the transmission range of Coordinator 1 (C1). C1 has three neighbor Coordinators: C2, C3, and C5. The distance from C2 to the AG is shorter than other two Coordinators. Also, based on its velocity and remaining energy, the parameter k of C2 is smaller than C3 and C5. Therefore, C1 forwards the data packet to C2.

```
n_best = self.a
  k_best = 1.0
  for each (a,l,v,e) in N
    do k = k (l,v,e)
    if (a = g.a) or (k < k_best)
      then n_best = a
        k_best = k
        if a = g.a
          then break
        end if
    end if
  end for
  if n_best = self.a
    then return forwarding failure
    else forward p to n_best
      return forwarding success
  end if
```

Figure 5. Pseudocode of MAEB forwarding.

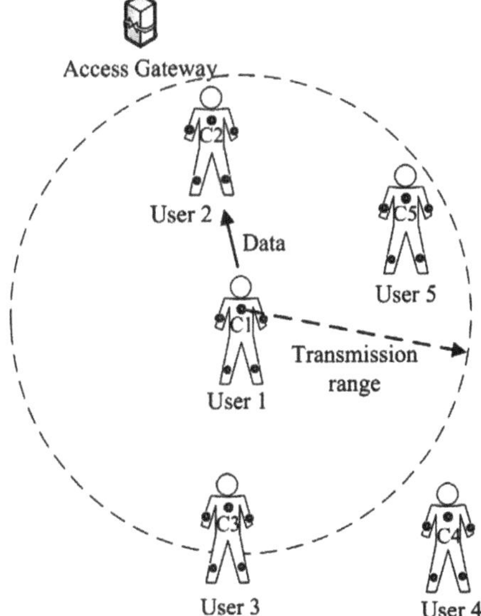

Figure 6. An illustration of MAEB forwarding.

4. Performance Evaluation

To evaluate the performance of the proposed protocol, we did a series of simulations. 100 sensor nodes and 10 Coordinators were deployed in a 10 m × 10 m field. The basic parameters used in the simulation are tabulated in **Table 1**. The application traffic was a constant distribution with the fixed data rate of 2kbps. All nodes generated their first data frame randomly in one cycle. The data frame had the fixed payload length. The sensor node energy consumptions of the transmission, reception, idle, and sleep were set to 36.5 mW, 41.4 mW, 41.4 mW, and 42 μW, respectively. Each Coordinator starts the simulation by remaining stationary for pause time seconds and moves at a speed distributed uniformly between 0 and 1.5 m/s. The velocity of the sensor node had a differential from its Coordinator, which was a random variable uniformly distributed in the interval [0, 0.5 m/s]. The reason why the speed of mobile node limits is that the body area network not corresponds to the extremely high speed environment. The parameters *a*, *b*, and *c* were set to 1/3. All simulations were run independently and their results averaged fewer than 1000 seeds. The simulation held on for 1000 seconds.

We compared MAEB with PAOLSR [6], EOLSR [7], and MMPR [8] in terms of the latency, energy consumption, packet delivery ratio, and throughput. Firstly, the latency is defined as the average time taken for a data packet from the sensor to the Coordinator. Secondly, the energy consumption denotes the average amount of energy consumed by the sensor nodes. Thirdly, the packet delivery ratio is the ratio between the number of data packets originated by source mobile node and the number of data packets reached by Access Gateway. Fourthly, the throughput is a measure of the average amount of data transmitted from the sensor nodes in a unit period of time (second).

The simulation results of the latency of the routing protocols are shown in **Figure** 7. With the traffic load increases, the latency increases gradually. When the traffic load is larger than 3pkts/s, the latency of the MAEB is less than that of the other three routing protocols. The MAEB has better performance than the other protocols. The latency of the MMPR is better than that of the EOLSR. The latency of PAOLSR is mostly larger than EOLSR.

The simulation results of the energy consumption are displayed in **Figure 8**. As the figure shows, the energy consumption also increases gradually with the increase of the traffic load. The energy consumption of the MAEB is considerably reduced compared to the other three routing protocols. The EOLSR consumes less energy than the MMPR. PAOLSR consumes more energy than MMPR. PAOLSR has worse performance than the other three protocols. The differences between the energy consumption of the protocols rise as the traffic load increases.

Table 1. Basic simulation parameters.

Parameter	Default Value
Radio propagation range of body sensor node	2 m
Radio propagation range of Coordinator	25 m
Frequency band	2400 - 2483.5 MHz
Channel rate	250 kbps
Simulation start time	1 sec
Simulation end time	1000 sec
Payload size	10 byte
MAC header	27 byte
Maximum packet size	127 byte

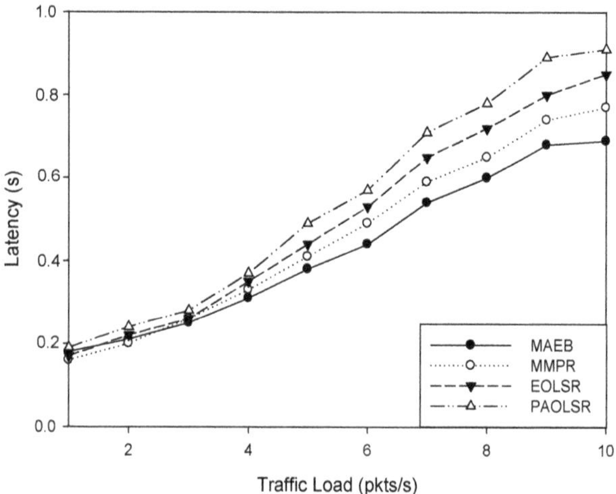

Figure 7. Latency varying with the traffic load.

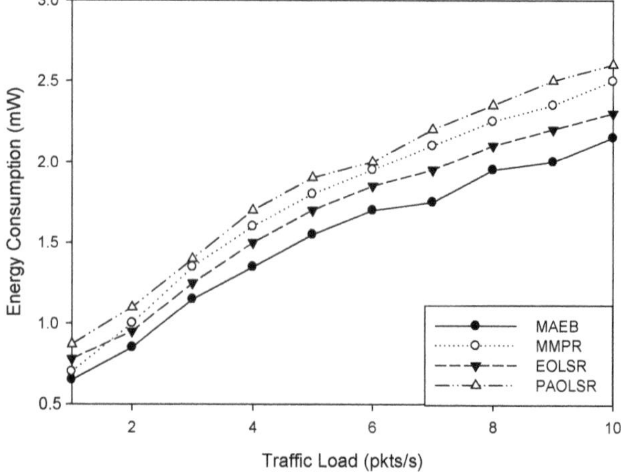

Figure 8. Energy consumption varying with the traffic load.

Figure 9 depicts the simulation results of packet delivery ratio varying with the traffic load. We can see that with the increase of traffic load, the packet delivery ratio decreases gradually. The reason for this is that packets are frequently dropped and the number of backoffs is increased with the higher traffic load. As we know, the requirements of quality of service (QoS) always depend on the application. The packet delivery ratio is thought as one of the measures of the network dependability. In ideal condition, packet delivery ratio equals to 1. In general, the delivery ratio of MAEB is greater than that of the other three routing protocols.

Figure 10 demonstrates the throughput varying with the traffic load. The throughput is an important metric that directly presents the system performance. As the figure shows, the system throughput also increases with the increase of the traffic load. MAEB has better throughput than the other three protocols.

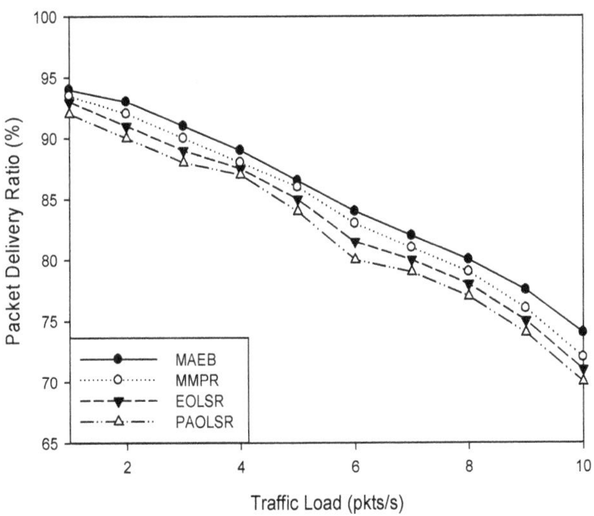

Figure 9. Packet delivery ratio varying with the traffic load.

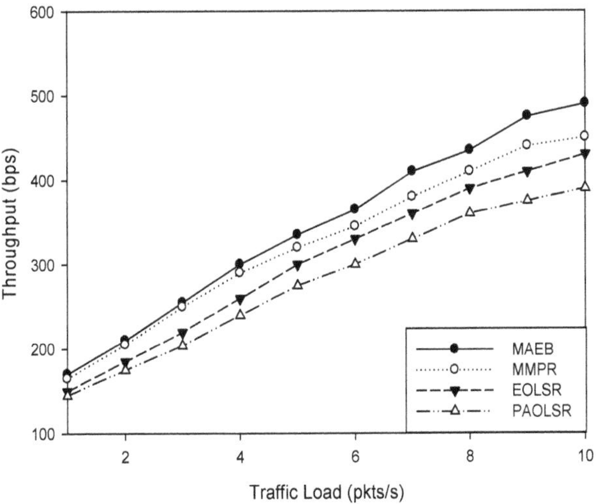

Figure 10. Throughput varying with the traffic load.

5. Conclusion

In this paper we introduce the architecture of an ambulatory IoT healthcare system including Wireless Body Area Networks (WBANs) and a broader telemedicine system. A WBAN consists of multiple sensor nodes. They can collect the vital signs of the user. The information is delivered to the AG through Coordinators. The AG transmits the information to the Internet, where the broad telemedicine system can get it. According to the group mobility character of the WBAN, we use the group mobility model to define body sensor nodes behavior. Using this model, the movement of the body sensor nodes of one user can be represented by their Coordinators. The Coordinators get the movement and energy information of their neighbors in the neighbor discovery procedure. Using the MAEB forwarding, the Coordinator selects the most suitable Coordinator to forward the data. According to the simulation results, MAEB has the better performance than the other three routing protocols.

6. Acknowledgements

This work is jointly supported by National Science and Technology Major Project under Grant No. 2010ZX-07102-006, National Natural Science Foundation of China under Grant No. 61170117, and Central College Basic Research Foundation under Grant No. 2302013-FRF-TP-13-016A.

REFERENCES

[1] M. Chen, *et al.*, "Body Area Networks: A Survey," *Mobile Networks and Applications*, Vol. 16, No. 2, 2011, pp. 171-193.

[2] IEEE Standards Association, "IEEE Standard for Local and Metropolitan Area Networks-Part 15.6: Wireless Body Area Networks," *IEEE Standard for Information Technology*, *IEEE* 802.15.6 *Standards*, 2012, pp. 1-271.

[3] S. Ullah and K. S. Kwak, "Throughput and Delay Limits of IEEE 802.15.6," *Proceedings of IEEE Wireless Communications and Networking Conference* (*WCNC*), Quintana-Roo, Mexico, 28-31 March 2011, pp. 174-178.

[4] N. A. Pantazis, S. A. Nikolidakis and D. D. Vergados, "Energy-Efficient Routing Protocols in Wireless Sensor Networks for Health Communication Systems," *Proceedings of the* 2nd *International Conference on PErvasive Technologies Related to Assistive Environments*, Corfu, 9-13 June 2009, pp. 1-8.

[5] M. A. Razzaque, C. S. Hong, *et al.*, "Data-Centric Multi-objective QoS-Aware Routing Protocol for Body Sensor Networks," *Sensors*, Vol. 11, No. 1, 2011, pp. 917-937.

[6] Z. Guo and B. Malakooti, "Energy Aware Proactive MANET Routing with Prediction on Energy Consumption," *Proceedings of the* 2007 *International Conference on Wireless Algorithms, Systems and Applications*, Chi-

cago, 1-3 August 2007, pp. 287-293.

[7] S. Mahfoudh and P. Minet, "EOLSR: An Energy Efficient Routing Protocol in Wireless Ad hoc Sensor Networks," *Journal of Interconnection Networks*, Vol. 9, No. 4, 2008, pp. 389-408.

[8] T. Kunz and R. Alhalimi, "Energy-Efficient Proactive Routing in MANET: Energy Metrics Accuracy," *Ad Hoc Networks*, Vol. 11, No. 7, 2010, pp. 755-766.

5

Motion-Sensing Based Management System for Smart Context-Awareness Rehabilitation Healthcare

Tung-Hung Lu, Hsing-Chen Lin, Rong-Rong Chen, Ya-Ling Chen
Service Systems Technology Center, Industrial Technology Research Institute, Hsinchu, Taiwan

ABSTRACT

In this paper, a motion-sensing based management system for smart context-awareness rehabilitation healthcare including various balance exercise is built by the integration of the physiological sensing and feedback coaching. The home-end system can not only provide the exercise coaching instruction, the balance stability analysis, and the motion similarity analysis in real-time, but also simultaneously transmit the user image, exercise skeleton streaming, center of pressure (COP), center of gravity (COG) and physiological information to the telecare-end center. According to the combination of the home-end and the telecare-end as well as the real-time care management of one-to-multiple personal balance exercise monitor, this system can provide user various personalized balance exercise prescription and cardiac rehabilitation coaching in an effectiveness rehabilitation exercise environment. Therefore, via this tele-system, the spinocerebellar ataxia (SCA) patients in balance rehabilitation stage not only can be monitored execution status of the rehabilitation exercise prescription, but also can be long-term monitored and evaluated the predicted goal of the rehabilitation exercise balance stability in order to improve patient's compliance.

Keywords: Motion-sensing Rehabilitation Exercise System; Care Service Platform; Balance Rehabilitation

1. Introduction

The cerebellum is a crucial part of the central nervous system, coordinating our movements, regulating the muscle tension, and controlling posture and gait. Various symptoms of uncoordinated movement and imbalance—indicative of spinocerebellar atrophy appear when pathological changes occur in the cerebellum. The official term for this disorder proposed by the Department of Health, Taiwan is spinocerebellar ataxia (SCA). Following onset, patients with SCA walk unsteadily (similar to a penguin); therefore, they are also termed "penguin family". SCA, which is among a group of genetic disorders, is primarily characterized by progressive incoordination of gait, and associated with poor coordination of hands, speech, and eye movements. One study indicated that Tai Chi helps improve the unsteady gait of patients with Parkinson's disease [1]. Hence, one of the hospitals in Taiwan attempted to improve the unsteady gait of SCA patients using medicine along with Tai Chi. Each week, volunteer professional instructors provided Tai Chi lessons to these patients at the hospital, allowing the patients to relieve emotional stress and simultaneously increase interaction between patients.

Based on this example, physical therapists may develop personalized home-based Balance Tai Chi rehabilitation exercise programs. By implementing Balance Tai Chi exercise prescriptions, patients are enabled to understand the effect that this exercise has on their physiological conditions and, with sufficient awareness, continue this exercise at home by themselves. Currently, tracking of patients prescribed with home-based balance exercises occurs weekly when they return to the hospital to practice the exercises. Thus, no objective and instant information is available as a basis for the hospital to evaluate the patients' balance status.

Under the rehabilitation model described previously, the existing traditional balance rehabilitation training must continue at the hospital under the supervision of a professional case manager. The rehabilitation exercises are constantly repeated, which become dull. Therefore, it is difficult for many patients to practice rehabilitation exercises according to the instructions of the Tai Chi coach at home, apart from problems regarding the correctness of the posture and the control of exercise duration and intensity. Patients are required to return to the hospital for rehabilitation follow-up once a week; however, transportation and caregivers' availability is another issue. In addition, the amount of time that the case managers are available may also be limited, because they can only assist 1 - 2 patients concurrently. These factors affect the patients' willingness to continue and comply with their exercise prescriptions, often causing a deterioration of their symptoms that forces them to be re-admitted; consequently, medical resource utilization and burdens on the patients and their families increase [2].

Many existing studies have suggested introducing technology to improve patients' willingness to undergo rehabilitation. Videogames can be leveraged as a telehealth technology [3]. Telehealth technology is gaining attention as a promising strategy for acquiring accurate, reliable, and time-critical health marker data, reducing health care costs, empowering patients, and promoting disease self-management with resultant improved healthcare outcomes. Although telehealth technologies provide opportunities, several barriers relating to the acceptance and use by patient, caregiver, clinical support networks include problems in use of technology among older adults, lack of adequate training or support, lack of consensus on the value of the technology, and absence of adequate technology infrastructure [4].

To overcome these barriers, it will be important for designers of telehealth technologies to work closely with specific patients throughout the design and development process in order to learn how their capabilities relate to technology adoption and long-term use [3,5]. Videogames have already been proven to improve cognitive abilities, displaying a feasible alternative to more traditional aerobic exercise for middle-aged and older adults, and can be used to train stepping ability in older adults to reduce the risk of falls [6]. The use of Wii Sports and Wii Fit has been reported in an increasing number of studies involving people with motor deficits resulting from other causes such as balance and mobility in people with some diseases [7,8].

Spinocerebellar ataxia (SCA) is a progressive, degenerative, genetic disease with multiple types. The signs and symptoms of an ataxia is one of a group of genetic disorders characterized by slowly progressive in coordination of gait and is often associated with poor coordination of hands, speech, and eye movements. With progression of the disease, patients lose postural stability and have gait dysfunction, difficulty in managing activities of daily living, and frequent falls. Although some motor dysfunctions may be alleviated with drug therapy, characteristics such as postural instability are less responsive to medication and require alternative approaches. The relevance of this study is timely; technology developments within the videogame sector are continually enhancing and pushing the boundaries to bring innovative and exciting modes of interaction to consumers. With this knowledge, maximizing the utility of such technologies into health services can offer methods for delivery of rehabilitation and training services.

In this paper, a motion-sensing based management system for smart context-awareness rehabilitation care was developed, consisting of a home-end motion-sensing rehabilitation exercise system and a remote care service platform. The home-end motion-sensing rehabilitation exercise system is equipped with various balance rehabilitation exercise models. The users' whole-body image is captured using a motion-sensing camera and projected into virtual exercise scenarios. The users' compliance is computed instantly through a motion analysis technology to provide exercise coaching instructions. The balance status of the users during exercise is subject to a real-time cross-analysis: the center of gravity (COG) trace is calculated using a depth image captured by a motion-sensing camera; and the center of pressure (COP) trace is calculated using a pressure array sensor. In addition, the physiological information is incorporated to analyze physiological changes before, during, and after exercise. Through VoIP and streaming data integration technology, this system provides a real-time, one-to-multiple remote care service platform for exercise monitoring and interactive instructions.

2. System Framework

Figure 1 shows the motion-sensing based management system for smart context-awareness rehabilitation care, which is a home-end interactive motion-sensing rehabilitation exercise system that assists users in their balance rehabilitation exercises using several real-time sensors (motion-sensing camera, webcam, biomedical sensor, and pressure array sensor) through the wire/wireless connection (*i.e.*, similar to the internet of things (IoT) model for physiological monitoring using motion-sensing rehabilitation). This system allows users to maintain their optimum exercise tolerance benchmark (that they reached in the hospital) within a certain range, and to enhance their compliance with the rehabilitation exercise and their balance function. Through physiological data that are detected automatically by a wireless physiological measuring device, this system au-to-computes the risks of patients encountering danger when exercising by themselves. Through a motion-sensing camera (e.g., Microsoft Kinect or ASUS Xtion PRO), the correctness of the users' movements is automatically analyzed. Their balance status is cross-analyzed using a pressure array sensor and a motion-sensing camera. The remote care service platform integrates the VoIP, motion image analysis, exercise skeleton streaming, balance analysis, and physiological information convergence technologies to construct a personal health management platform server, enabling care managers to simultaneously and remotely supervise the actual conditions and physiological changes of several users during exercise. This system automatically alerts the telecare managers when the users' physiological measurement or balance data are abnormal or when the system calculated risk is higher than usual. By using the data transmitted by the rehabilitation exercise system, the care managers can understand the problem and address it through VoIP or real-time video-conferencing to the patient's home. In the following section, we introduce the home-end motion-sensing rehabilitation exercise system, the remote care service platform, and the clinical decision support system (CDSS) of the motion-sensing based management system for smart context-awareness rehabilitation care.

2.1. Motion-Sensing Rehabilitation Exercise System

The framework of the motion-sensing rehabilitation exercise system, as shown in **Figure 2**, consists of an exercise template database and modules for motion feature analysis, rehabilitation coaching, vital sign fusion, balance analysis, care service platform interface, and back-end rehabilitation CDSS. The various balance re-habilitation exercises, which were designed by physicians and led in the system by a virtual exercise coach, are recorded through a professional motion-capture system and stored in the exercise template database, allowing users to execute rehabilitation exercises by following the virtual coach's instructions. If user movements do not meet the system standards, the skeleton motion trace of the users is captured by the motion-sensing camera and the motion feature analysis module. Movements and gestures of the users can then be interpreted by comparing them instantly with the standard skeleton exercise trace of the

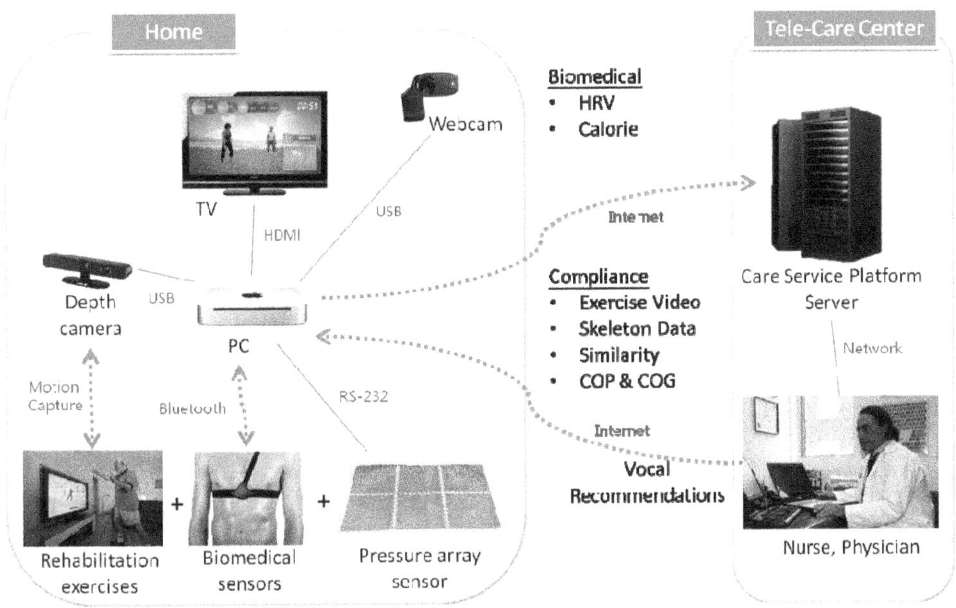

Figure 1. System framework.

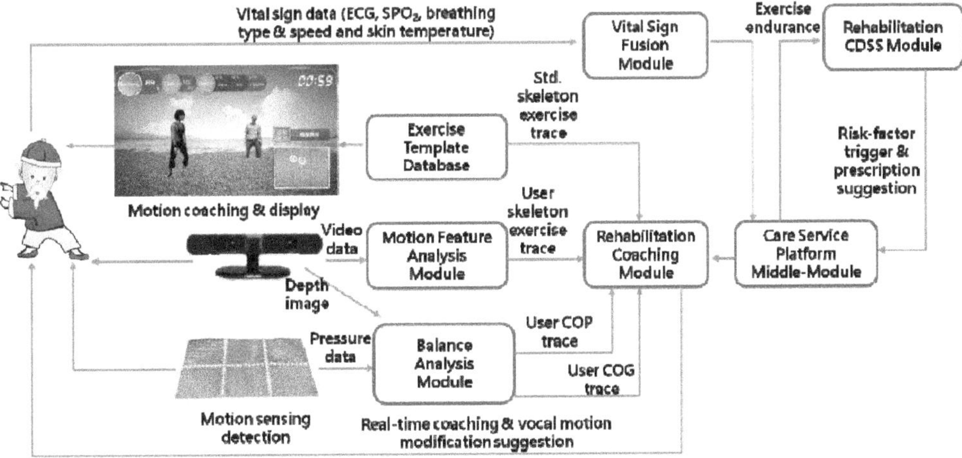

Figure 2. Framework of the motion-sensing rehabilitation exercise system.

exercise template database. In addition, the balance status of the users during exercise can be analyzed instantly through the depth image of the users captured by a motion-sensing camera, the foot pressure measured by a pressure array sensor, and the COG and COP computed by the balance analysis module. The system provides an instant voice feedback to correct the users' movements through statistics of balance analysis and motion similarity comparison received by the rehabilitation coaching module. With an appropriate wireless physiological measuring device and a sensor, information about the physiological status during exercise can be collected and monitored using a vital sign collection module. The back-end rehabilitation CDSS module and the interfaced personal care service platform module are immediately triggered if an abnormal balance or physiological status of the users is detected. The system then automatically alerts the telecare case managers to ensure the users' exercise safety.

In addition, this system provides virtual game scenarios, as shown in **Figure 3**, which incorporates the users' RGB image into virtual scenarios; it also allows for exercising with a virtual coach to promote the patients' enjoyment for rehabilitation. In addition, the system employs sensing devices and a 3D motion-sensing camera to accurately understand the users' exercise progress, including calories burned, heart rate variability (HRV; including LF%, HF%, and LF/HF), real-time COP, and exercise compliance represented by motion similarity [2, 9-12].

2.2. Care Service Platform

Through integration of the home-end motion-sensing rehabilitation exercise system, various sensing devices, and VoIP, the remote personal care service platform is a back-end monitoring platform for caregivers, allowing simultaneous 30 monitoring online users practicing different rehabilitation exercises using the motion-sensing rehabilitation exercise system. The care managers can supervise the exercise conditions of six users simultaneously. Through both the physiological data and COP, which are respectively detected by a wireless physiological measuring device and a pressure array sensor, this system auto-computes the exercise risk of the patients.

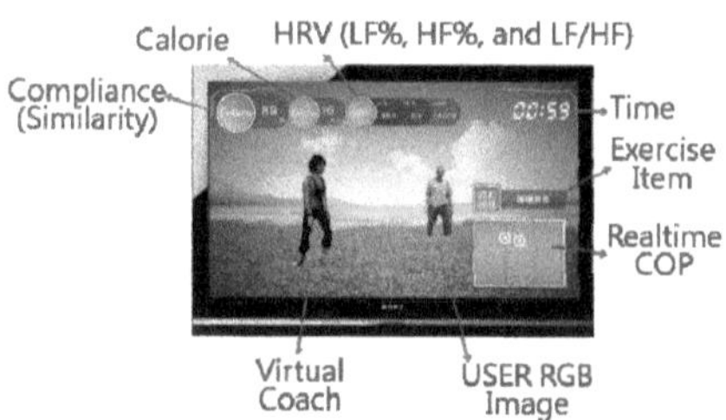

Figure 3. The virtual game interface for motion-sensing rehabilitation exercise scenarios.

The system automatically alerts the telecare case managers when the physiological measurement is abnormal or when the system calculated risk is higher than usual. Using the data received by the rehabilitation exercise system, the case managers can understand and address the problem through VoIP or real-time videoconferencing to the patients' home.

The real-time exercise information that is transmitted to the care service platform from the home-end motion-sensing rehabilitation exercise system consists of physiological information (*i.e.*, heart rate, exercise intensity, and HRV) and monitored exercise information (*i.e.*, motion similarity, skeleton node, COP, and COG). Specifically, 60 data entries per second are received from the electrocardiogram, with a data rate of 1204 bps. Fifteen nodes are allocated to a skeleton, each consisting of an x-axis, a y-axis, and a z-axis. Thirty entries of skeleton data are obtained per second, with approximately 1 K data received per second. Compliance is denoted by an integer representing the percentage of motion similarity.

The framework of the care service platform, as shown in **Figure 4**, consists of application, computing, repository, and integration service layers. Through the interface between the Super Socket series integrated service module and the home-end motion-sensing rehabilitation exercise system, the care service platform receives a variety of physiological data and exercise monitoring information from the home-end system. The platform then instantly computes and statistically analyzes the data transmission frequency (times/second), the data quantity (total bytes), and the transmission quantity (bytes/s) through the skeleton, HRV, heart rate, exercise intensity, COP, and COG processing modules in the computing services. The received raw data and the computed results obtained through the computing services can be stored in the repository services to provide the case managers with anytime access to the users' exercise history. The application services, comprising the videoconferencing, exercise instruction, compliance display, and motion and vital sign display modules, can display the exercise conditions of several online users on the monitor interface, as shown in **Figure 5** (including skeleton streaming, an audio/visual interface for videoconferencing, and the vital signs of multiple online users). The case managers can immediately understand and address issues through videoconferencing if the users' compliance declines, as shown in **Figure 6**.

2.3. Clinical Decision Support System

The medical profession has developed from general practice in the past to specialty-based practice in the present. Currently, the development of each specialty emphasizes further specialization. Therefore, when treating patients who require cross-disciplinary integrated care,

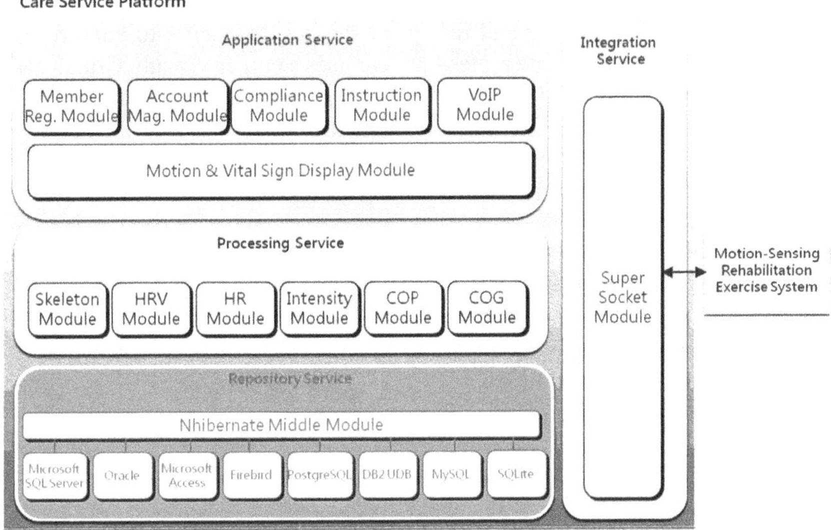

Figure 4. Framework of the care service platform.

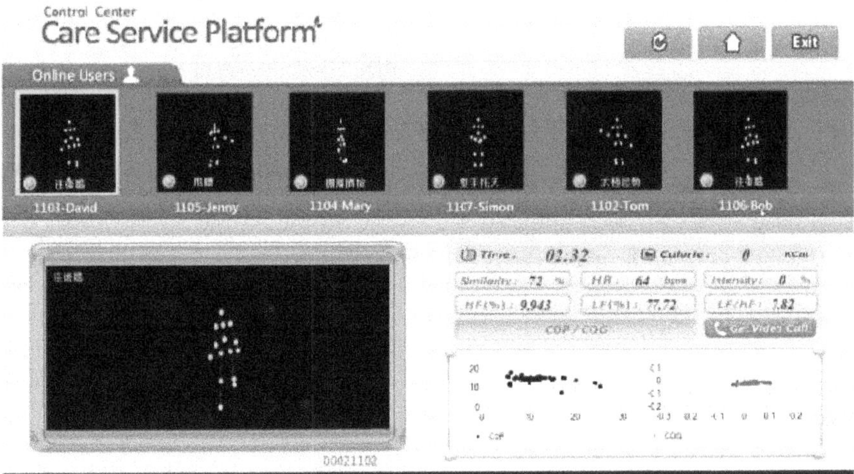

Figure 5. The exercise monitoring interface for six patients.

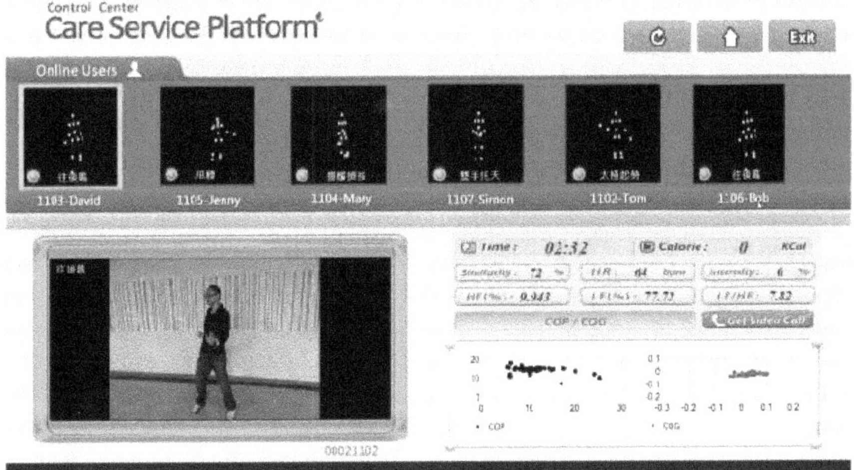

Figure 6. The audio/visual interface for videoconferencing.

specialized physicians are often unable to fully address patients' complaint, resulting in time-consuming and repeated visits. The CDSS can simultaneously provide professional cross-disciplinary decision support for medical personnel, solve the problem of insufficient interdisciplinary knowledge, enhance diagnosis and service performance, and lower the professional threshold for providing rehabilitation care to patients with SCA.

The framework of the CDSS, as shown in **Figure 7**, is designed based on the execution engine of a core clinical pathway, providing different user interfaces for relevant medical personnel to access various decision support information. Through a back-end management function, medical experts can also maintain information related to multiple clinical pathways and rules to adjust existing information regarding contexts applicable to various clinical decisions. The CDSS, comprising a process control engine and professional medical knowledge rules, allows medical personnel to better understand the patients' status and provide personalized care services.

3. Pilot Verification

This motion-sensing based management system for smart context-awareness rehabilitation healthcare now is being tested in clinical settings of one hospital in Taiwan. The conditions of the test target users group are: ages from 20 to 80 years old; diagnosis of SCA confirmation; gait ≤ 7 or stance ≤ 5 in the scale for the assessment and rating of ataxia (SARA scale).

These group exercise testing at hospital once a week for five weeks, supervised by lots of the motion-sensing based management systems for smart context-awareness rehabilitation healthcare. Participants will be instructed by virtual coach to maintain their usual exercise via motion-sensing based Balance Tai Chi rehabilitation exercise program. COP and COG matching are measured by pressure array sensor during the intervention mainly for assessment standing balance data (e.g., center shift degree in x-/y-axis and center shift trace distance etc). In addition, motion compliance (or motion similarity) is one of the key indicators to analyze the patients motion accuracies compared with virtual coach. Case manager in front of care service platform also can monitor the rehabilitation status via this back-end system for patients safe exercise in terms of rehabilitation CDSS. Therefore, pilot verification can evaluate the balance status of the patients with SCA via this motion-sensing based management systems for smart context-awareness rehabilitation healthcare in terms of the COP, COG matching, and motion similarity.

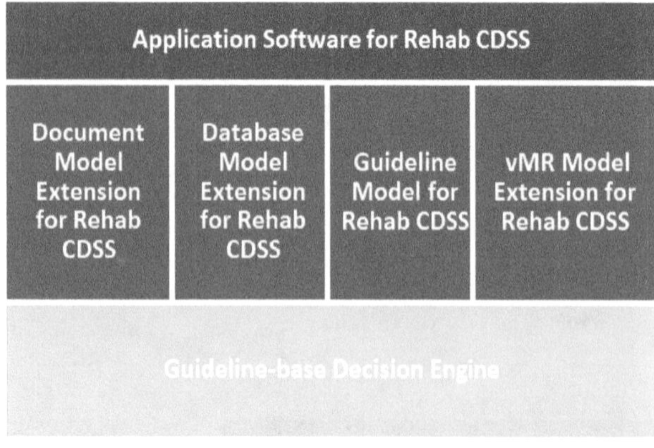

Figure 7. Framework of the clinical decision support system.

4. Conclusion

A system was designed to develop a set of balance rehabilitation exercises for patients with SCA for continuous and safe practice at home through information and communication technology. By integrating physiological monitoring and feedback coaching with a telecare center that enables real-time one-to-multiple personal exercise monitoring by case managers, this home-end rehabilitation exercise system provides users with diverse personalized balance exercise prescriptions and rehabilitation exercise coaching in an effective home exercise environment. Consequently, patients are enabled to maintain their optimum exercise tolerance benchmark that they achieved in the hospital.

REFERENCES

[1] F. Li, P. Harmer, K. Fitzgerald, E. Eckstrom, R. Stock, J. Galver, G. Maddalozzo and S. S. Batya, "Tai Chi and Postural Stability in Patients with Parkinson's Disease," *New England Journal of Medicine*, Vol. 366, No. 6, 2012, pp. 511-519.

[2] T. H. Lu, H. C. Lin, Y. H. Lee, R. R. Chen, H. L. Chen, S. Y. Chang, J. D. Chen, B. R. Wu and T. H. Wu, "A Motion-Sensing Enabled Personalized Exercise System for Cardiac Rehabilitation," *IEEE 14th International Conference on e-Health Networking, Applications and Services*, Beijing, 10-13 October 2012, pp. 167-171.

[3] H. R. Marston and S. T. Smith, "Interactive Videogame Technologies to Support Independence in the Elderly: A Narrative Review," *Game for Health*, Vol. 1, No. 2, 2012, pp. 139-152.

[4] S. Mattke, L. Klautzer, T. Mengistu, J. Garnett, J. Hu and H. Wu, "Health and Well-Being in the Home: A Global Analysis of Needs, Expectations, and Priorities for Home Health Care Technology," RAND Corporation, Santa Monica, 2010.

[5] G. Demris, N. Charness, E. Krupinski, D. Ben-Arieh, K. Washington, J. Wu and B. Farberow, "The Role of Human Factors in Telehealth," *Telemedicine and E-Health*, Vol. 16, No. 4, 2010, pp. 446-453.

[6] B. Guderian, L. A. Borreson and L. E. Sletten, "The Cardiovascular and Metabolic Responses to Wii Fit Video

Game Playing in Middle-Aged and Older Adults," *Journal of Sport Medicine and Physical Fitness*, Vol. 50, No. 4, 2010, pp. 436-442.

[7] J. E. Deutsch, D. Robbins, J. Morrison and P. G. Bowlby, "Wii-Based Compared to Standard of Care Balance and Mobility Rehabilitation for Two Individuals Post-Stroke," *Virtual Rehabilitation International Conference*, Deutsch, Haifa, 2 June 2009, pp. 117-120.

[8] E. Bainbridge, S. Bevans, B. Keeley and K. Oriel, "The Effects of the Nintendo Wii Fit on Community-Dwelling Older Adults with Perceived Balance Deficits: A Pilot Study," *Physical & Occupational Therapy in Geriatrics*, Vol. 29, No. 2, 2011, pp. 126-135.

[9] G. Burdea, "Virtual Rehabilitation-Benefits and Challenges," *International Medical Informatics Association Yearbook of Medical Informatics*, International Medical Informatics Association, Geneva, 2003.

[10] R. A. Clark, Y. H. Pua, K. Fortin, C. Ritchie, K. E. Webster, L. Denehy and A. L. Bryant, "Validity of the Microsoft Kinect for Assessment of Postural Control," *Gait Posture*, Vol. 36, No. 3, 2012, pp. 372-377.

[11] A. Ramchandani, K. Carroll, R. Buenaventura, J. Douglas and J. Liu, "Wii-Habilitation Increases Participation in Therapy," *IEEE Conference of Virtual Rehabilitation*, Vancouver, 25-27 August 2008, p. 69.

[12] C. Watters, S. Oore, M. Shepherd, A. Abouzied, A. Cox, M. Kellar, H. Kharrazi, F. Liu and A. Otley, "Extending the Use of Games in Health Care," 39*th Annual Hawaii International Conference on System Sciences*, Kauai, Hawaii, 4-7 January 2006.

Evaluation of Microblog Users' Influence Based on PageRank and Users Behavior Analysis

Lijuan Huang, Yeming Xiong
School of Economics and Management, Xidian University, Xi'an, China

ABSTRACT

This paper explores the uses' influences on microblog. At first, according to the social network theory, we present an analysis of information transmitting network structure based on the relationship of following and followed phenomenon of microblog users. Informed by the microblog user behavior analysis, the paper also addresses a model for calculating weights of users' influence. It proposes a U-R model, using which we can evaluate users' influence based on PageRank algorithms and analyzes user behaviors. In the U-R model, the effect of user behaviors is explored and PageRank is applied to evaluate the importance and the influence of every user in a microblog network by repeatedly iterating their own U-R value. The users' influences in a microblog network can be ranked by the U-R value. Finally, the validity of U-R model is proved with a real-life numerical example.

Keywords: Social Network; Microblog Users Behavior; PageRank Algorithms; U-R Model; Influence

1. Introduction

Microblog, is a platform based on user relationships for sharing, transmitting and acquiring information, on which users can establish individual communities, update information with around 140 characters and achieve real-time sharing via WEB, WAP and a variety of clients [1]. As the development of WEB2.0, microblog, which is a booming information communicating platform, develops rapidly. Since there are a large number of active users and hotspot information, the influence of microblog on information transmitting, the change of living habits, *et al.*, cannot be ignored. While microblog users' influence refers to as a user's influence in the microblog community. The greater the influence is, the more attention the netizens pay to, and then impact on network will become remarkable. So microblog possesses vast potential for future development theoretically and practically, especially in the field of word of mouth marketing, information mining, public opinion controlling and so on.

2. Reviews

At present, many scholars have started to pay attention to and study the microblog or twitter (in China, microblog is ordinarily called, so in the context "microblog" is used) all over the world. Also, the hot areas of these researches include the motivation and behaviors of microblog users, besides microblog social network structure. The evaluation of microblog users' influence (microblog influence) has also become a new research focus in the analysis of the social network. Foreign studies mainly discuss Twitter, which is considered as the pioneer prototype of microblog. In addition, AKSHAYJAVA *et al.* (2007) [2] studied the data sets of Twitter from 1st April 2007 to 30th May 2007 and found that the main types of user intentions are: daily chatter, conversations, sharing information and reporting news. Then, they analyzed the microblog network on the growth, degree distribution, geographical distribution of Twitter users, and so on. Besides, TEUTTE (2010) [3] analyzed Twitter from network dynamics, including the description of the microblog network's changes by the growth of in degree and out degree, network density, betweenness and so forth. KRISHNAMURTHY *et al.* (2008) [4] explored the structural characteristics of microblog network, and identified distinct classes of microblog users and their behaviors. Meanwhile, Chinese scholars mainly apply their minds to hotspot discovery in microblog network, propagation mechanism and user behavior characteristics. Caishuqin, Zhangjing (2012) [5] designed some metadata models for micro-blogging content through the structured metadata acquired from open APIs. And the hotspot discovery process was regarded as a value-added process of the original materials to clusters of hot products. Finally, a complete production and processing model was established.

However, there are a few academic researches on microblog users' influence presently. GABRIEL W (1994) [6] made an evaluation of Twitter users' influence learning from PageRank algorithm and considered the number of friends to be an important indicator of users' influence. In other words, it means that the more the friends are, the bigger influence it has, and the more easily it has effects on others. Furthermore, the basic equations are consistent with PageRank algorithms. However, when taking into account the situation in China that a large number of microblog fans are traded, the model is not fully applicable. In fact, YUTO Y (2010) [7] proposed TU Rank (Twitter User Rank) based on User-Tweet Graph to rank the users, which laid a lot of emphasis on the quality of the content, while the influence of fans' retreating was ignored. KLOUT [8], a famous assessment service on the influence of social network sites, uses the relationship among Facebook, LinkedIn and Twitter, and the user behavior (initiating a session, comments, forwarding, etc.) data. Assessing the users' influence by Klout algorithm, Klout believes everyone has influence on the era of social media. Also, Klout measures your influence in the social networks, and give the insight into whom you do effect on and on what topics you are affected. Klout measures your influence index on a scale of 0 - 100. Kang (2011) [9] advanced a new algorithm to evaluate the influence of nodes in microblog social network through the users' behavior and relationship based on the SINA microblog. They considered the frequency of posting microblogs as a factor to evaluate the users' activity and presented Behavior-Relationship Rank algorithm after combining the users' activity with PageRank. But they only took into account the frequency of posting microblogs as a factor to evaluate the users' activity without referring to interaction behaviors such as the users' mentioning friends, commenting, and forwarding microblogs etc., which also have effects on users' influence.

In this paper, on the basis of previous studies, we learn from the PageRank algorithm which is used to evaluate the page of search engine. Then, considering the factors that include users' activity represented by the frequency of posting microblogs and interactive positiveness, we propose a U-R model, which is an algorithm for evaluating users' influence based on PageRank and microblog users' behavior analysis. And this model could cover some shortages of above models.

3. U-R Model

3.1. Hypotheses

In microblog networks, the description of friend relationship varies with service providers. For instance, when we use SINA microblog, the relationship is "follow and followed", while using Tencent microblog, it is "listen and listened". In this paper, we adopt the "follow and followed", shown in **Figure 1**. For example, if user A follows user B, A is a Follower to B, whereas B is a Followee to A.

According to the characteristics of microblog, combining with social network analysis theory, we propose the following definitions:

- Node: every user is a node in a microblog network, such as user A and user B (See **Figure 1**).
- Edge: that is the relationship of "follow and followed" among microblog users, between which the edge has directionality.
- In degree and Out degree: the number of Followee is the out degree of user nodes, instead, the number of Follower is the in degree.

Additionally, PageRank algorithm is based on the following two assumptions [10]:

- If a page is referenced for multiple times, it may be very important. In spite of a webpage isn't referenced frequently, if it is referenced by important webpages, it still may be important. The importance of a webpage is transmitted averagely to the pages referenced.
- Assume that at the beginning, access to a page of a webpage collection randomly, then continue to browse the pages following the current page links, and the PageRank value is the probability to browse the next page.

In other words, if a webpage is linked by many significant webpages, it means that the content of this page has been recognized and trusted largely. Moreover, the content has high authority and should have a higher ranking. Therefore, the equation [10] that calculates the PageRank value of the webpage is:

$$PR(u) = \sum_{v \in M(u)} \frac{PR(v)}{N(v)} \quad (1)$$

where

$PR(X)$ is the PageRank value of webpage X;

$N(X)$ is the out degree (the number of the links from this webpage to other webpages);

$M(X)$ is the page collection that points to webpage X.

This is a recursive equation, and the PageRank value

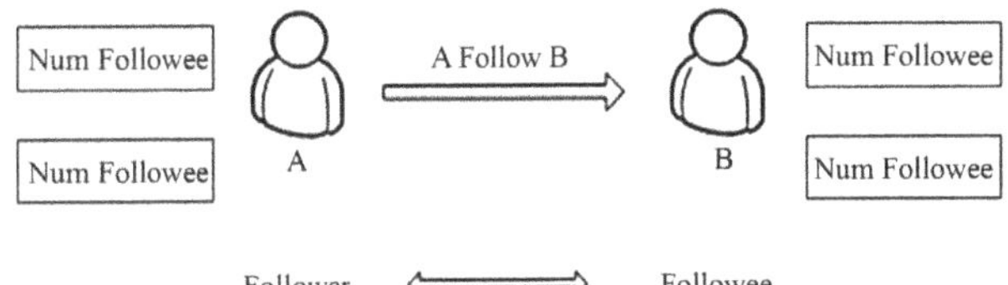

Figure 1. The description of microblog network relationship.

of a webpage will be evenly distributed to each forward link. In addition, PageRank value is a rank value about the indicator of the importance of a webpage and the value is generated by the hyperlink structure of the network. Then PageRank value of any webpage can be calculated by other pages' and the specific number of hyperlinks. In other words, as for each webpage linked into, the PageRank value is divided by the respective number of links out. Next, sum up them. In the calculation, we make simple modification to Equation (1) by adding damping coefficient [11] p which means that after browsing a webpage, the user will continue to browse a webpage linking out in the probability $1 - p$ and the probability to select a random page to browse is p. Namely,

$$PR(u) = p + (1-p) \sum_{v \in M(u)} \frac{PR(v)}{N(v)} \tag{2}$$

According to empirical analysis, the p is always set as 0.85, so that the result is convergent.

Hence, we propose two assumptions of U-R model drawing on PageRank algorithms:

- If a microblog is forwarded and commented for multiple times, it may be very important. On the other hand, although the microblog isn't forwarded and commented frequently, if it is forwarded and commented by important microblog users, it still may be important. The influence of a user is distributed equally to the other users he/she follows.
- Assume that at the beginning, access to a user in the microblog user collection randomly, then continue to browse microblogs following the current user's following, forwarding and comments, the U-R value is the probability to browse the next user.

3.2. Model Establishment

In the microblog network, if user A follows user B, A is a follower of B. Then, A can see the microblog posted by B, but B cannot see the microblog posted by A. The flow of information in the microblog network is completed by follow and followed. Actually, the structure of microblog network is similar to the link model of webpages. A follows B is equal to A votes B. Hence, we are able to rank influence of microblog users at the basis of PageRank.

The more Followers a user has, the greater influence of information transmitting he has in the microblog network. And the microblog he has posted will appear on webpages of tens of thousands of Followers; therefore, he has bigger weight in the process of calculating his authority. On the other side, the vote has bigger weight if he follows other users. That is to say, the influence which belongs to the user he has voted will become bigger. Cite an instance, if user A has 100,000 Followers and follows user B, A will see the content posted by B. As a result of A's forwarding, this microblog is presented to 100,000 Followers. In this way, A is like an amplifier to enlarge the effects of information forwarding. Consequently, B is highly authoritative in microblog network. However, a condition relative to B's authority is whether A will forward the B's microblog, the probability of which is similar to damping coefficient [9] in PageRank. Thus, this paper proposes a U-R model, which combines mind of PageRank with user behavior, to evaluate microblog users' influence in a new way. This model synthetically considers the user behavior and microblog network structure and identifies the most influential network node by iterative calculation of each node's UR value.

Additionally, in PageRank, UR value of a webpage is evenly transmitted to the pages linking out of it, then, as a result of this, we will overlook the importance of the page itself. When PageRank algorithm is applied to the analysis process of microblog network, the weight ratio of user behavior is a standard to distribute PageRank value. Under this standard, the user with higher weight will accordingly obtain higher PageRank value and the PageRank transmitting is nonuniform. Eventually, active users will have more authority than inactive users in the network. The shortage, merely relying on the relationship of follow and followed to evaluate the influence, will be overcome by above process and the model can better reflect the objective reality. At last, based on the above analysis and combining the user behavior analysis, we advance a new U-R model to evaluate microblog users' influence.

$$UR(u) = p + (1-p) \sum_{v \in M(u)} A_{(v,u)} UR(v) \tag{3}$$

where

$UR(u)$ and $UR(v)$ represent the influence evaluation value of microblog user u and user v;

p is the probability for v to forward u's microblog, and here p is set as 0.5;

$M(u)$ is the collection of u's Followers;

$A_{(v,u)}$ is user u's UR value ratio assigned by user v, which is determined by the ratio that the u's weight account for of the total behavior weights of v's entire Followees. The equation is

$$A_{(v,u)} = \frac{W_u}{\sum_{i=1}^{N_u} W_i} \tag{4}$$

In Equation (4), W_u is user u's microblog behavior weight. N_v represents the number of Followees of u (node u's out degree).

3.3. Weight of User Behavior Influence

According to the description of microblog user behavior, microblog behavior is a major factor of microblog's influence, such as the frequency of updating microblog, interaction with other users, and so on. At the same time, we need to consider the users' active degree and the enthusiasm to participate in interaction. So the higher active degree and interactive positiveness the user has the greater influence he will generate. In order to facilitate the subsequent analysis, a model on the weight of user behavior influence is defined to describe the active degree of microblog users and interactive positiveness. The model is shown in **Figure 2**.

If W represents the weight of user influence, then

$$W_i = a \cdot X_i + b \cdot Y_i \quad (5)$$

where

X_i is the user's positiveness;

Y_i is the user's interactive positiveness;

a and b are both weighting coefficients.

Then, the users' active degree is defined as the frequency of updating microblogs under a unified time scale. Meanwhile, the definition for interactive positiveness is the state of users' mentioning, commenting and forwarding under a unified time scale. That is

$$X_i = \frac{Q_i}{T} \quad (6)$$

$$Y_i = c \cdot \frac{A_i}{T} + d \cdot \frac{R_i}{T} + e \cdot \frac{C_i}{T} \quad (7)$$

Among above equations, T is a unified time scale. In order to objectively characterize users' active degree and positiveness indicators, we unify the T time. Also, the number of microblogs that users have posted is Q. A represents the amount of "@", and the number of comments is shown by C. The number of forwarding is R. In addition, c, d, e are all weighting coefficients. Since the impact on a user's weight varies with the user behaviors, weighting coefficients can be given different values. Then, after calculating the user's weights on active degree and interactive positiveness, then we can get the weight on user behaviors.

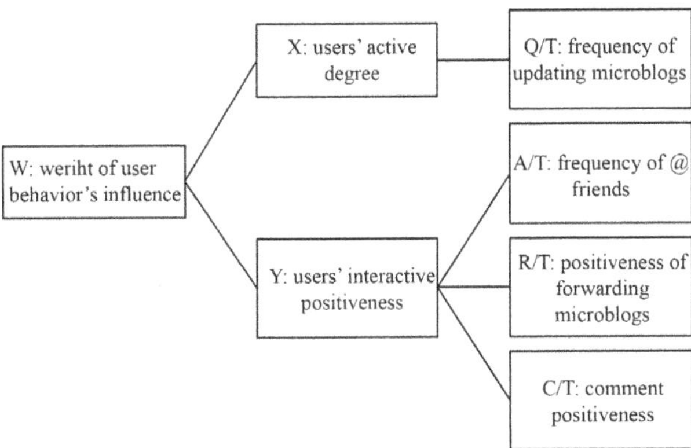

Figure 2. The weight model of user influence.

3.4. Example of U-R Model

The microblog data set [12] used in this paper, which we have preprocessed, is based on the Tencent Weibo provided by KDD Cup 2012. In order to obtain accurate analytical results, the abnormal data such as whose Tweet is less than 10 etc. is removed. At last, the effective sample size is 809,732. And the data structure of the sample is presented in **Table 1**.

Due to the large user group of microblog network, in this paper, only 10 nodes are selected from the data set as a sub-network of the entire microblog social network. We use these nodes to achieve the U-R model calculations and explore the information transmitting and nodes' influence. Next, the relationship (follow and followed) among nodes is shown in the form of adjacency matrix.

If $H_{ij} = \begin{cases} 1, & \text{if } i \text{ Follow } j \\ 0, & \text{otherwise} \end{cases}$ exists, the adjacency matrix is

$$\boldsymbol{H} = \begin{bmatrix} 0 & 0 & 1 & 0 & 0 & 1 & 0 & 0 & 1 & 0 \\ 0 & 0 & 0 & 0 & 1 & 1 & 0 & 1 & 0 & 1 \\ 0 & 0 & 0 & 0 & 1 & 0 & 1 & 1 & 1 & 0 \\ 1 & 1 & 1 & 0 & 1 & 1 & 0 & 0 & 1 & 0 \\ 0 & 0 & 0 & 1 & 0 & 0 & 0 & 1 & 0 & 1 \\ 0 & 1 & 0 & 0 & 0 & 0 & 0 & 0 & 0 & 0 \\ 0 & 0 & 0 & 0 & 0 & 0 & 0 & 1 & 0 & 0 \\ 0 & 1 & 0 & 0 & 0 & 1 & 0 & 0 & 1 & 0 \\ 0 & 0 & 1 & 0 & 0 & 0 & 0 & 0 & 0 & 0 \\ 1 & 0 & 0 & 1 & 0 & 0 & 0 & 1 & 0 & 0 \end{bmatrix}$$

According to the above weight setting model and attribute analysis in the samples, we make the following settings, $a = 0.4$, $b = 0.6$, $c = 0.5$, $d = 0.3$, $e = 0.2$, $T = 100$. The network attributes and user weights of the sample are presented in **Table 2**.

At the basis of the relationship among nodes and Equation (3), the iterative equation is as follows:

Table 1. Data structure of the microblog sample.

UserID	User ID
Birth	Year of Birth
Gender	Gender
Num_Followee	Number of Followee
Num_Follower	Number of Follower
FlollowerID	Flollower ID
Num_Tweet	Number of Tweet
Num_At	Number of "@"
Num_Retweet	Number of Retweet
Num_Comment	Number of Comment
Num_Action	Number of Interactive Friends

$$
\begin{aligned}
UR(1) &= 0.5 + 0.5\left(A_{(4,1)}UR(4) + A_{(10,1)}UR(10)\right) \\
UR(2) &= 0.5 + 0.5\left(A_{(4,2)}UR(4) + A_{(6,2)}UR(6)\right. \\
&\quad \left. + A_{(8,2)}UR(8)\right) \\
&\vdots \\
UR(9) &= 0.5 + 0.5\left(A_{(1,9)}UR(1) + A_{(3,9)}UR(3)\right. \\
&\quad \left. + A_{(4,9)}UR(4) + A_{(8,9)}UR(8)\right) \\
UR(10) &= 0.5 + 0.5\left(A_{(2,10)}UR(2) + A_{(5,10)}UR(5)\right)
\end{aligned} \tag{8}
$$

Then, the user's weight proportion assigned to the node is then calculated in accordance with Equation (4). For instance, node 4's following nodes are 1, 2, 3, 5, 6, 9, node 1's weight proportion assigned by node 4 is

$$A_{(4,1)} = \frac{W_1}{W_1 + W_2 + W_3 + W_5 + W_6 + W_9}$$

Similarly, node 10's following nodes are 1, 4, 8, and the user's weight proportion assigned to node 1 is

$$A_{(10,1)} = \frac{W_1}{W_1 + W_4 + W_8}$$

Each node's initial value is 1. Next, each node's value is iteratively calculated based on Equation (8) until the result is converged. The iterative process is the iterative process table of U-R model example shown in Appendix. Eventually, after calculated, the *UR* values presented in **Table 3** in proper order are

$$
\begin{aligned}
& UR(2) > UR(8) > UR(5) > UR(3) > UR(6) \\
& > UR(4) > UR(1) > UR(7) > UR(9) > UR(10)
\end{aligned}
$$

It can be concluded from the calculations of 10 nodes selected that there isn't a positive correlation between the number of Follower and the user's influence. For example, although node 8's number of Follower (in degree) is more than node 2, node 8's microblogs posted by users themselves and interactive positiveness is less and the influence is smaller. In this way, U-R model covers some shortages of the algorithm model proposed by GABRIEL W [6] and makes up for PageRank shortcoming, simply relying on network relationship. With combining users' weight model with PageRank, the model can evaluate the users' influence and better reflect the objective reality.

4. Conclusions

Currently, microblog is the most popular online social network, for it has not only the characteristics of the social network, but also clear ones of media, it is also

Table 2. U-R model calculation example.

Node	In Degree	Follower Node	Out Degree	Following Node	User's Weight *W*
1	2	4, 10	3	3, 6, 9	13.319
2	3	4, 6, 8	4	5, 6, 8, 10	8.9796
3	3	1, 4, 9	4	5, 7, 8, 9	7.214
4	2	5, 10	6	1, 2, 3, 5, 6, 9	5.8512
5	3	2, 3, 4	3	4, 8, 10	5.3948
6	4	1, 2, 4, 8	1	2	3.5828
7	1	3	1	8	3.577
8	5	2, 3, 4, 5, 7, 10	3	2, 6, 9	3.2604
9	4	1, 3, 4, 8	1	3	0.6426
10	2	2, 5	3	1, 4, 8	0.5228

Table 3. U-R model calculations.

Node	In Degree	Follower Node	Out Degree	Following Node	User's Weight	UR Value
2	3	4, 6, 8	4	5, 6, 8, 10	8.9796	1.792067
8	5	2, 3, 4, 5, 7, 10	3	2, 6, 9	3.2604	1.480926
5	3	2, 3, 4	3	4, 8, 10	5.3948	1.179344
3	3	1, 4, 9	4	5, 7, 8, 9	7.214	1.144562
6	4	1, 2, 4, 8	1	2	3.5828	1.122385
4	2	5, 10	6	1, 2, 3, 5, 6, 9	5.8512	0.932253
1	2	4, 10	3	3, 6, 9	13.319	0.827392
7	1	3	1	8	3.577	0.658997
9	4	1, 3, 4, 8	1	3	0.6426	0.59549
10	2	2, 5	3	1, 4, 8	0.5228	0.568366

called "social media". This paper can reflect the influence of microblog users veritably through the UR algorithm which is simple and clear, and that can be helpful for marketing, public opinion control etc.

However, how to set the values of the damping coefficient p in U-R algorithm and the weighting coefficients a, b, c, d, e in weight model is a hypothesis, which is necessary to make specific judgment based on the actual situation. Additionally, the U-R model doesn't accurately reflect the quality of microblog content, while in a microblog network, it is easy for the higher quality content to be spread in a viral way and these microblogs tend to have an impact on other users. These two problems remain to be studied further.

5. Acknowledgements

This paper is supported by the fundamental research funds for the central universities under grant No. 72115096.

REFERENCES

[1] Baidu Encyclopedia, "MicroBlog," 2012. http://baike.baidu.com/view/1567099.html

[2] A. Java, X. Song, T. Finin and B. Tseng, "Why We Twitter: Understanding Microblogging Usage and Communities," *Proceedings of the* 9*th WebKDD and* 1*st SNA-KDD* 2007 *Workshop on Web Mining and Social Network Analysis*, San Jose, 12-15 August 2007, pp. 56-65.

[3] A. R. M. Teutle, "Twitter: Network Properties Analysis," *20th International Conference on Electronics Communications and Computer*, Cholula, 2010, pp. 80-186.

[4] B. Krishnamurthy, P. Gill and M. Arlitt, "A Few Chirps about Twitter," *Proceedings of the* 1*st Workshop on Online Social Networks*, Seattle, 2008, pp.19-24.

[5] S. Cai and J. Zhang, "Method of Micro-Blogging Hotspot Discovery Based on Centralization," *Chinese Journal of Management*, Vol. 9, No. 6, 2012, pp. 874-879.

[6] G. Weimann, "The Influentials: People Who Influence People," State University of New York Press, Albany, 1994, pp. 468-470.

[7] Y. Yamaguchi, "TURank: Twitter User Ranking Based on User-Tweet Graph Analysis," *Web Information Systems Engineering*, Vol. 6488, 2010, pp. 240-253.

[8] Klout, 2012. http://klout.com

[9] S. Kang, "Evaluation of the Social Network's Nodes Influence Based on Users' Behavior and Relationship—Take Microblogging for Instance," Master Thesis, Beijing University of Posts and Telecommunications, Beijing, 2011.

[10] J. Cao, "Technique Analysis of Page Rank in Google," *Journal of Information*, Vol. 19, No. 10, 2002, pp. 15-18.

[11] W. Ma, "Study on Web Information Credibility Evaluation Method Based on Improved Page Rank," Master Thesis, Hebei University, Baoding, 2011.

[12] "Tencent Microblog Data Source," 2012. http://www.Kddcup2012.Org/c/kddcup 2012-track1

APPENDIX

U-R model iterative process

Iterative times	UR(1)	UR(2)	UR(3)	UR(4)	UR(5)	UR(6)	UR(7)	UR(8)	UR(9)	UR(10)
0	1	1	1	1	1	1	1	1	1	1
1	0.967070465	1.666181665	1.407487058	0.934090846	0.98785515	0.977114684	0.638914779	1.536723699	0.585585061	0.54742603
2	0.821487964	1.731456977	1.183821388	0.871374162	1.208193613	1.134403921	0.695520754	1.454397859	0.607347549	0.560616064
3	0.814731067	1.764395842	1.143017665	0.940002916	1.170680061	1.106644754	0.664450287	1.498270412	0.595158752	0.567918978
4	0.828578286	1.791280175	1.141118463	0.929563992	1.173759724	1.119261113	0.658782047	1.478779636	0.595581653	0.567569626
5	0.826698101	1.788822279	1.144733942	0.930453603	1.178272276	1.122046578	0.658518219	1.479168429	0.595363234	0.568198776
6	0.827036283	1.790707408	1.144113883	0.931905952	1.178576353	1.121503773	0.659020463	1.480029564	0.595417416	0.56827133
7	0.82730498	1.791285194	1.144381475	0.932007752	1.178941329	1.122002217	0.658934327	1.480557987	0.595444318	0.568317837
8	0.827336112	1.791687628	1.144489033	0.932124647	1.179125407	1.122200999	0.6589715	1.480691305	0.595472236	0.568339465
9	0.827362426	1.791868179	1.144523583	0.932183366	1.179240275	1.122285281	0.658986441	1.480812032	0.595479998	0.568352627
10	0.827376326	1.791961849	1.144541173	0.932219963	1.179289372	1.122333578	0.658991241	1.480869568	0.595485019	0.568359407
11	0.827384567	1.79201457	1.14455144	0.932235756	1.179315196	1.122358263	0.658993684	1.480896375	0.595487549	0.56836264
12	0.827388215	1.792039638	1.144556759	0.93224402	1.179329476	1.122371245	0.658995111	1.480910831	0.595488818	0.568364411
13	0.827390147	1.792052873	1.144559306	0.932248587	1.179336409	1.122377642	0.65899585	1.48091828	0.595489473	0.568365307
14	0.82739119	1.792059691	1.144560663	0.932250809	1.179340029	1.122381005	0.658996203	1.480922075	0.59548981	0.568365764
15	0.827391704	1.792063168	1.144561365	0.932251968	1.179341895	1.122382733	0.658996392	1.480924025	0.595489983	0.568366
16	0.827391971	1.792064963	1.144561721	0.932252566	1.17934285	1.122383615	0.658996489	1.48092503	0.595490072	0.568366122
17	0.827392109	1.792065883	1.144561905	0.932252871	1.179343341	1.12238407	0.658996539	1.480925546	0.595490118	0.568366184
18	0.82739218	1.792066356	1.144561999	0.932253029	1.179343594	1.122384303	0.658996564	1.480925811	0.595490142	0.568366216
19	0.827392216	1.792066599	1.144562048	0.93225311	1.179343723	1.122384423	0.658996578	1.480925947	0.595490154	0.568366232
20	0.827392234	1.792066724	1.144562073	0.932253151	1.17934379	1.122384485	0.658996584	1.480926017	0.59549016	0.568366241
21	0.827392244	1.792066788	1.144562086	0.932253172	1.179343824	1.122384517	0.658996588	1.480926053	0.595490163	0.568366245
22	0.827392249	1.792066821	1.144562092	0.932253183	1.179343842	1.122384533	0.658996589	1.480926071	0.595490165	0.568366247
23	0.827392251	1.792066838	1.144562096	0.932253189	1.179343851	1.122384541	0.65899659	1.480926081	0.595490166	0.568366249
24	0.827392253	1.792066847	1.144562097	0.932253192	1.179343856	1.122384546	0.658996591	1.480926086	0.595490166	0.568366249
25	0.827392253	1.792066851	1.144562098	0.932253193	1.179343858	1.122384548	0.658996591	1.480926088	0.595490166	0.568366249
26	0.827392254	1.792066854	1.144562099	0.932253194	1.179343859	1.122384549	0.658996591	1.48092609	0.595490166	0.56836625
27	0.827392254	1.792066855	1.144562099	0.932253195	1.17934386	1.12238455	0.658996591	1.48092609	0.595490166	0.56836625
28	0.827392254	1.792066856	1.144562099	0.932253195	1.17934386	1.12238455	0.658996591	1.480926091	0.595490166	0.56836625
29	0.827392254	1.792066856	1.144562099	0.932253195	1.17934386	1.12238455	0.658996591	1.480926091	0.595490166	0.56836625

7

Integrating RFID Technology with Intelligent Classifiers for Meaningful Prediction Knowledge

Peter Darcy, Steven Tucker, Bela Stantic
School of Information and Communication Technology, Griffith University, Gold Coast, Australia

ABSTRACT

Radio Frequency Identification (RFID) is a wireless technology that has been designed to automatically identify tagged objects using a reader. Several applications of this technology have been introduced in past literature such as pet identification and luggage tracking which have increased the efficiency and effectiveness of each environment into which it was integrated. However, due to the ambiguous nature of the captured information with the existence of missing, wrong and duplicate readings, the wide-scale adoption of the architecture is limited to commercial sectors where the integrity of the observations can tolerate ambiguity. In this work, we propose an application of RFID to take the reporting of class attendance and to integrate a predictive classifier to extract high level meaningful information that can be used in diverse areas such as scheduling and low student retention. We conclude by providing an analysis of the core strengths and opportunities that exist for this concept and how we might extend it in future research.

Keywords: Radio Frequency Identification; Classifier; Prediction; Neural Network; Bayesian Network

1. Introduction

Radio Frequency Identification (RFID) has become an integral part of a wide array of business applications ranging from pet identification to stock tracking at retail stores. The architecture involves attaching a large group of items which is intended to be tracked by the user with a unique identifying tag. This tag is then read wirelessly within certain proximity by a reader to determine which items are within the vicinity of the device. The observations captured in this process are then passed from the device into a middleware system that will filter out any anomalies detected at this stage. The middleware will then pass the information onto the data warehouse where the observations will be stored for later use such as data mining.

Some potential problems that occur due to RFID include anomalous readings and meaningless low-level observations. Anomalies that persist include false-negatives, readings that are meant to be present but are not false-positives, readings that exist in the data warehouse but are not meant to be present. Regarding the observations, due to the nature of the records being the tag identification number, reader identification and timestamp, without high level transformations performed on the data, the data cannot provide the user with meaningful context-specific information that can be used in business processes. For example, an observation of a tag at a specific time and location has little meaning but once it is known that it belongs to an employee taking a break from work, the information provides a higher level of meaningful information for the user. The problem of low-level information is compounded by the issues of false-negative and false-positive anomalies which reduces the overall integrity of the information.

In this research, we propose a concept that uses the information captured from tags used in a university lecture and various other instances of context-specific information to accurately predict the future attendance of students in the class. In particular, this system will not only provide lecturers with meaningful information not available from traditional attendance records, but will also be able to forecast the highest and lowest attended classes ahead of time thereby allowing lecturers to tailor their schedules accordingly. Finally, by incorporating a probabilistic approach in the system architecture, the anomalies that usually lower the overall integrity of the system will be countered to a certain degree. We have also identified two core opportunities that can enhance the system specifically by integrating the student's personal attendance history to further tailor the report on a case-by-case basis, and by integrating multiple-class averages to analyse the overall student year and to apply that to the prediction model.

The remainder of this paper is structured as follows: Section 2 will contain the relevant background information required for this research including a brief introduction to RFID, Bayesian and Neural Networks. Section 3 provides an analysis of already existing methodologies that use RFID Technology to find the attendance of people or objects. In Section 4, we introduce our core concept by discussing the motivation, architecture and assumptions. Section 5 contains our preliminary analysis of the system and we will conclude this paper by summarising the contents and suggesting future work we intend to pursue in Section 6.

2. Background

Wireless and automatic systems such as Radio Frequency Identification (RFID) allow users to effortlessly capture large amounts of data with relative ease. Unfortunately, the captured readings are not utilised to their full potential of applications due to anomalies such as false-positive/false-negatives and the low-level nature of the observations. To counter the negative issues associated with RFID-enabled environments, intelligent classifiers can be employed to reduce the ambiguity of the captured information. Two such intelligent approaches include Bayesian and Neural Networks that use probabilistic approaches to determine the conclusion which has the highest chance of being accurate.

2.1. Radio Frequency Identification

Radio Frequency Identification (RFID) refers to technology comprised of tags and readers to uniquely identify large quantities of items automatically and wirelessly [1]. As seen in **Figure 1**, a tag which is either Passive, Semi-Passive or Active [2,3] is attached to an object that is desired to be tracked. Wireless readers will then interrogate all tags within certain proximity and then transmit all found tags through the middleware. The middleware is used to filter out any found anomalies such as collisions on the air interface [4] so that the readings processed further have a higher level of integrity. All the collected data are then stored within a data warehouse which is then used for further analytical techniques such as data mining or event extraction [5].

2.2. Intelligent Classifiers

When given a large set of information extracted from real-world observations, the data are prone to being unreliable due to various factors making it difficult to discover meaningful information or to predict future trends.

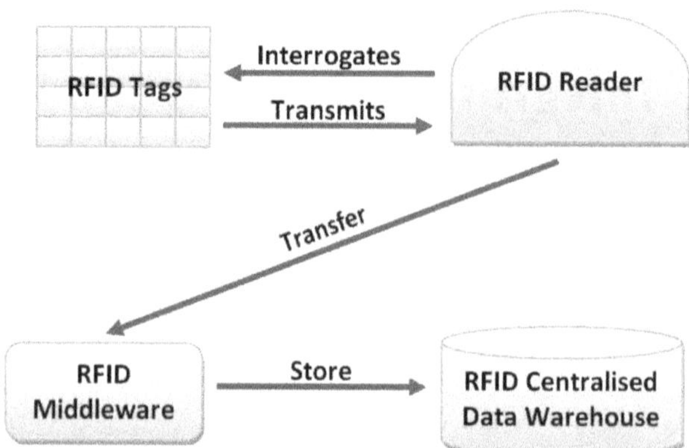

Figure 1. A high-level representation of the data transfer among the various components of the RFID system.

For example, in a RFID scenario, false negative or false positive [6] readings may occur due to the environment. To counter this consequence, intelligent and probabilistic techniques can be employed to correct certain anomalies [7] or to produce predictions which deterministic approaches may not be able to consider. Two such approaches include using a Bayesian Network which examines the probability of all inputs or using a Neural Network which operates similarly to the human brain.

2.2.1. Bayesian Networks

Bayesian Networks refer to a network designed to find the highest probable solution to any given problem. This is usually performed by determining the product of evidence found in a situation and comparing it with other possible causes until the greatest probable outcome has been discovered. The mathematical equation is a formula designed to express the process utilised in determining the percentage of likelihood of a cause being true. As seen in Equation (1), the probability from X_1 to X_n is equal to all the products on which X_i is dependent [8].

$$P(X_1,\cdots,X_n)=\prod_{i=1}^{n}P(X_i\mid X_1,\cdots,X_{i-1}) \quad (1)$$

When representing a naïve Bayesian Network in a program, the probabilities are stored in a table structure containing the percentage or weight of the conclusion being correct when an observation is found to either be true or false. For each conclusion, a percentage of likelyhood is found from multiplying the weights in the cells that match up with the observations with the highest achieving conclusion being returned. The weights of the Bayesian Network can be created in a static table or dynamically such as having the network trained with a genetic algorithm to find the optimal weights of the system [9].

2.2.2. Neural Networks

As seen in **Figure 2**, an Artificial Neural Network is a

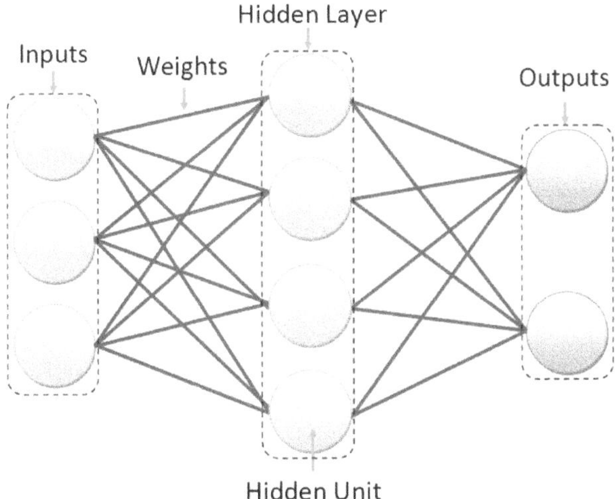

Figure 2. A high-level interpretation of how a neural network is designed with its three main layers: the input, hidden and output layers.

classifier designed to emulate the learning behaviour of the brain. It does this by creating a fixed amount of Neurons which are trained to deliver a certain output when fed various inputs. The Artificial Neural Network consists of three main layers: the Input Layer, Hidden Layer(s) and the Output Layer [10]. The processes include receiving inputs which are modified at a central sum area. The Neuron will then apply an activation function such as the hard limiter or sigmoidal functions.

When attempting to configure the Neural Network weights, one method that exists is to utilise training algorithms. Two dominant training algorithms that have been proven to excel in network training are the Back-Propagation Algorithm [11,12] and the Evolutionary Neural Network [13,14]. Back-Propagation relies on the concept of training the network by propagating error back through the network via modifying the weights after the output has been calculated. Evolutionary Neural Network training algorithm in contrast to Back-Propagation utilises the theory of genetic evolution to train the network weights. Similar to the genetic algorithm process of training a Bayesian Network, all the weights are added into a chromosome as genes to be manipulated according to the fittest output obtained.

3. Related Work

In previous studies and system architectures, Radio Frequency Identification technology has been integrated into various applications to track the attendance of people in an enclosed environment. These include hardware integrations in Schools [15,16], Asset Tracking [17] and bus tours [18]. None of these studies however have utilised the captured data to accurately predict the current or future presence of missing items. We believe that within a scenario where it is crucial to know the amount of students attending a class, the ability to predict an estimate attendance count can greatly benefit the user.

4. Proposed Methodology

The following section will introduce the core concepts of the proposed methodology. We will do this by first discussing the motivation behind the development of the concept. This will be followed by an in-depth analysis of the various components of our approach including the physical hardware, inputs, processes and outputs of the system. Finally, we will then discuss any assumptions we identified to ensure that the system is used in its intended environment.

4.1. Motivation

The primary motivation behind this research is finding an effective use of information captured from the average attendance of university classes. This has leaded us to considering a way of extracting the data to improve retention of students in classes across the university semester. A common problem with university classes are students who are not retained for the entirety of the university year. We believe that providing a predictive model that can highlight the trend of the class attendance will significantly help instructors to tailor their teaching approach to those lectures.

Additionally, by providing the students with the tags, student engagement and interaction will be encouraged as they will have a common event they can discuss with each other. Furthermore, by optionally having their name displayed on the screen and projector as they scan their tag, it may act as an ice-breaker for the class allowing students to determine each other's names. Although this activity may not be applicable to students in second year classes and above who have already worked together for a year, we believe that first year students will benefit greatly from this. Furthermore, as the interaction between students increase, it should improve the retention rate as we believe that students encourage each other throughout the semester.

4.2. Architecture

As seen in **Figure 3**, the architecture of our concept contains four distinct core components. The first component is the physical hardware that includes the RFID tags used by the students to scan into the readers which are used by the lecturers. The reader will then transmit the information to the website used to record the information. The website will then store the information in the centralised database which will then be accessed by the intelligent classifiers. The Bayesian and Neural Networks will ex-

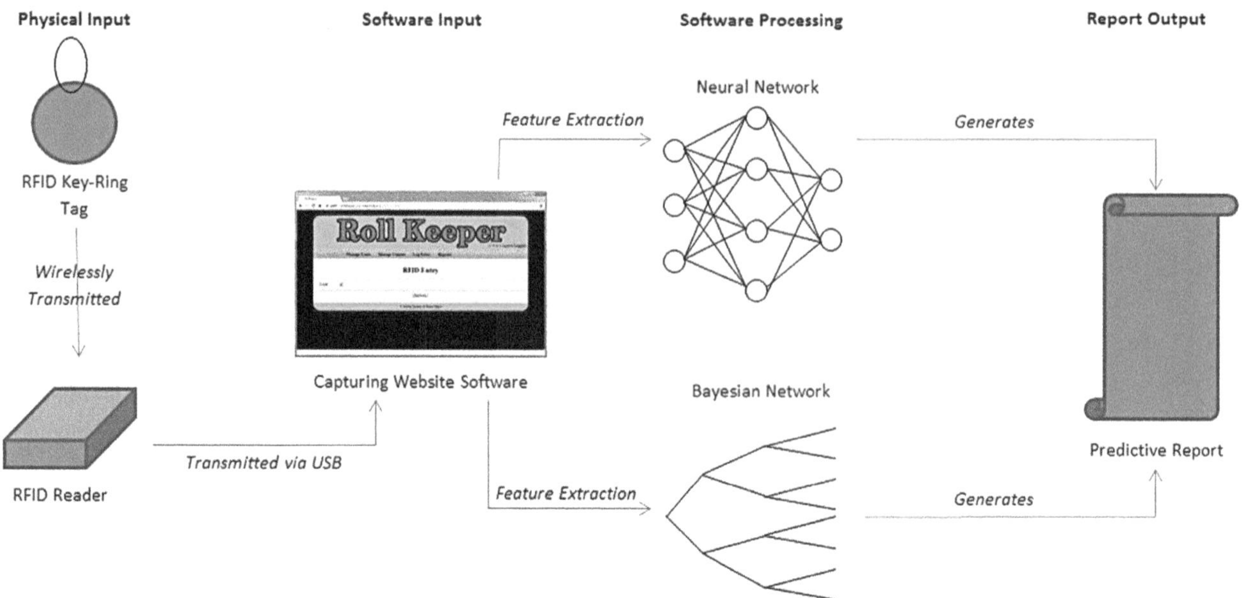

Figure 3. A high-level diagram describing the data flow of the information in the proposed concept.

tract a feature set from the database including various pieces of information gained from the system. This information can then be processed to generate a predictive report based on the likelihood of the amount of people present in the future week's classes or if a specific person will be present during a particular week.

4.2.1. Physical Hardware

The physical hardware involved in this system includes many RFID tag keyrings which are distributed to each individual student and a RFID reader to capture these reading. The student's tags will have a unique identification number that will align to their respective name and university student number stored on a centralised database. During the class, lecturers would have the students lining up to scan in as being present in the class with the Low-Frequency USB-powered reader. From our preliminary testing of the system, we have found that the scanning process takes less than one minute on average to record the attendance of approximately 20 students. Alternatively, other means of tag technology could be used instead of the keyring such as swipe cards which allow for the possibility in financial cost reduction.

4.2.2. Capturing Software

The capturing software consists of a website which interacts with the RFID reader to pass the identifier of the tag and current timestamp into the data warehouse. This requires the lecturer to select the correct subject and week at which point the system will then have a single form element for the identification number and a button on the site to process the data. Being that the reader automatically returns the tag id and then "enter" from the keyboard, the system will run seamlessly as the individuals walk up and swipe their tags over it. It will then store all the information entered (current timestamp, tag id, lecture, week) into their respective places in the data warehouse for further analytical processing.

4.2.3. Feature Extraction

The Feature Set Extraction will consist of the software capturing relevant information we believe will determine if the student will be present in the coming week. This includes:

- **The week number:** From our previous observations, we have found that there is a trend in student absences for most classes following certain weeks, for example, the week directly after a semester break. We believe that due to this factor, the week number for the currently observed week should be included in the Feature Set.
- **The location of the class:** We believe that the physical location of the building where the class takes place may influence the decision to attend, for example, if the class was on one side of the campus and a class previous to this was on the opposite end of campus. Since the location will most likely not be changed throughout the semester, the location will be a static variable unless changed manually.
- **The size of the class:** With a large amount of people present in the class, individuals would not be noticed as being absent by the lecturer. In contrast, a smaller class of fewer than 15 people, it would be harder for the lecturer not to notice an absent student. While the class size may have minor variations throughout the semester (late enrolments or students dropping the

course), this variable will most likely be static throughout the semester.

- **The time of the class:** As some university classes are run at 8:00 am and the university is located close to the Central Business District of the city, we believe that issues such as traffic gridlock would play a significant role in discouraging students from attending class. Similarly to the previous two items, this value will be a static throughout the semester unless the class time is changed.
- **The average time the student stays:** In the given scenario, a student would have to scan twice to be considered attending that class. This would allow us to determine how long a student is present in the lecture each week. For example, a student may not stay for the entire duration of the class in the event they left early before a general class discussion towards the end or during a break. We could then capture each week's time and extrapolate an average time which may play a factor in the regular attendance. Similarly to the week number, this variable would change periodically.

Additionally, we have had thoughts of extending this input information to incorporate multiple-class data, for issues such as scheduling conflicts, and the historical information of the class and the individual students. Once this information has been obtained from the data warehouse, it is processed as the input nodes for the Bayesian and Neural Networks.

4.2.4. Intelligent Classifiers

Once the feature extraction has been performed, all of the extracted information will be passed directly into the Bayesian and Neural Networks. Using the weights that have already been trained by using Back-propagation a Genetic Algorithm, the system will return a set of outputs that will correspond with each individual student in the class. Therefore, the amount of returned values will be equal to the number of students in class which will then give the user an adequate estimate of the amount of students present within the class for that specific week. Eventually, we would like to modify the structure to incorporate historical information from other semesters and possibly the student's individual attendance record to predict the trend of attendance for the entire semester rather than the sequentially following week.

4.2.5. Predictive Reports Generated

Finally, the Bayesian and Neural Networks will return the information regarding the whole class or the individual to the user. This will be accessible as an option on the website to allow the lecturers to have access to the information dynamically and anywhere the user has access to an internet connection. Eventually, we would like to increase its user friendliness by adding various features such as highlighting the students the system predicts will not be present.

4.3. Assumptions

Regarding the practical use of the system, we have to make three core assumptions that need to be in place to ensure the predictive analysis reports provide the highest integrity. First, we have to assume that the readings obtained from the students are correct and truly reflect the people present at the lecture. For example, if one student brings in a friend's tag to scan for both of them, the system will count this second tag as being present for every week even though this will not be the case. Second, we assume that the data input by the convenor at the start of each semester to be factual and will be updated if any changes do occur. Without this information being accurate, the historical information of other lectures taking place at the same place or location will not be useful for later iterations of the course. The final assumption we make for this concept is that the information will be recorded each time class is run. This is important for the system to extrapolate linear regressive information from the data such as a consistent decline in students after a certain date such as the mid-semester exam.

5. Analysis

In the following section, we will provide all information regarding the implementation of the technology. This includes the environment of the system including the physical hardware needed and the software required to process the data. We will then provide the core strengths and opportunities the system has been found to possess from our preliminary implementation of the system.

5.1. Environment

The physical RFID reader we have been using for this research is a USB-powered low cost system that plugs-and-plays directly into the computer functioning in the same way a keyboard does. The tags and the reader both operate at 125 Khz making it necessary for students to be within approximately 5 cm of the device to be scanned and, concurrently, ensuring their privacy. The web-based system used to manage the input data has been successfully tested and runs on the Firefox and Chrome browsers. The application has been written and implemented on Linux, Apache, MySQL and PhP (Lamp) stack, Debian GNU/Linux distribution Release 6 "Wheezy" has been used as the Operating System. The client systems used in the process of capturing attendance has had Windows XP with Service Pack 3 as its Operating System. The prediction tool will be written in PhP and integrated into the current web application as an option to be chosen for the lecturers and convenors.

5.2. Concept's Strengths

The main strength of this concept is that the predictive analysis will provide intelligent information not originally considered by the lecturer of the course. As an example, if it is known that after a mid-semester break, a large amount of students will not likely attend class, the staff member can restructure that week's lecture to have crucial information for the course to retain students who are prone to being absent. Additionally, knowing the weeks that most students attend or miss a week in hindsight will allow the convenors to structure the course in such a way that would be tailored to most students, for example, introducing and discussing the assignment in an earlier week when the majority of the class is present. Finally, we believe that be incorporating a predictive model over traditional deterministic methodologies, a level of ambiguity crucial for the system to cope with false-negative and false-positive anomalies present in the observation data sets will be provided.

5.3. Concept's Opportunities

We have also discovered several opportunities which we would like to pursue in future work after the implementation of the system is complete. The two core opportunities include incorporating multiple-class information categorised by certain characteristics and using historical information relative to the students to further enhance the prediction of their attendance. By using the predictive analysis over multiple-classes, we could incorporate extra information for that specific category. This includes categorising the students based on the department or university, age group of the students or specific classes/ lecturers. Furthermore, we believe that, if this approach was run over long periods of time, a trend could emerge from a student's behaviour over their time at university. This could additionally be used on a case-by-case scenario to improve specific student retention. From the incorporation of this extra information not originally designed in the initial approach, we believe that the predictions determined by the classifiers will increase in accuracy thereby providing staff with greater opportunities to encourage and help students through their university tuition.

6. Conclusions

In this research, we have proposed an extension to a RFID-enabled attendance recording system that would provide lecturers and convenors information about students that was previously not possible. We believe that by using this information, the users can significantly enhance their teaching experience. The primary motivation of this concept was to take the observations from the automatic attendance system and incorporate intelligent approaches to turn the observations into high level meaningful predictive analysis information. This resulted in the presented concept outline in this research that incurporates the both Bayesian and Neural Networks. We have identified that the main strength of this concept include bringing information to the lecturers about the students not originally found from standard analysis of attendance records. Additionally, the system is able to identify the classes that students are most likely to attend or miss allowing lecturers to tailor the course around these constraints. Finally, by incorporating a probabilistic approach to predict the attendance, we believe that the system will be able to handle the ambiguity due to the anomalies present in the majority of RFID applications.

Regarding future work, we first intend to completely implement the concept described in this paper with the preliminary information we gained from the previous integration of the system. As discussed previously, we believe that the incorporation of average class information over multiple courses and personal histories of student attendance will enhance the integrity of the system. We would also like to incorporate other probabilistic classification techniques such as a Support Vector Machine or Hidden Markov Model and to investigate the potential of integrating deterministic approaches such as Non-Monotonic Reasoning into the classification approach as well.

Another possible future research area we would like to explore would involve integrating Near Field Communication (NFC) technology. This will not only allow the integration of NFC tags but also Smart Phones as the readers that may provide additional sensor readings. It would then be possible to extract sensor information regarding the environment such as the geographical location or temperature which can then be incorporated into the feature set input. For each class, we would also like to incorporate a second scan of the students as they leave the room therefore adding extra information to the intelligent classifiers. Coupled with the scan at the beginning of class, this will determine how long the students attend the class and if they only stay for a certain portion of the class. Finally, while we have applied this technology in an education environment for a local university, we do believe that this approach can be applied to a wide-array of domains that require large amounts of people to attend specific events.

REFERENCES

[1] S. S. Chawathe, V. Krishnamurthy, S. Ramachandran and

S. E. Sarma, "Managing RFID Data," *Proceedings of the Thirtieth International Conference on Very Large Data Bases*, Vol. 30, 2004, pp. 1189-1195.

[2] P. Darcy, B. Stantic and A. Sattar, "A Novel Integrated Classifier for Handling Data Warehouse Anomalies," *Advances in Databases and Information Systems* (*ADBIS* 2011), Vienna, 20-23 September 2011, pp. 98-110.

[3] R. Derakhshan, M. E. Orlowska and X. Li, "RFID Data Management: Challenges and Opportunities," *IEEE Conference on RFID*, Brisbane, 26-28 March 2007, pp. 175-182.

[4] P. Pupunwiwat and B. Stantic, "Resolving RFID Data Stream Collisions Using Set-Based Approach," *The Sixth International Conference on Intelligent Sensors, Sensor Networks and Information Processing* (*ISSNIP* 2010), Gold Coast, 7-10 December 2010, pp. 61-66.

[5] P. Darcy, P. Pupunwiwat and B. Stantic, "The Fusion of Pre/Post RFID Correction Techniques to Reduce Anomalies," *Intelligent Sensor Networks*: *Across Sensing, Signal Processing, and Machine Learning*, CRC Press, New York, 2012.

[6] P. Darcy, B. Stantic and A. Sattar, "Applying a Neural Network to Recover Missed RFID Readings," *Australasian Computer Science Conference* (*ACSC* 2010), Brisbane, 18-22 January 2010, pp. 133-142.

[7] P. Darcy, B. Stantic and A. Sattar, "X-CleLo: Intelligent Deterministic RFID Data and Event Transformer," *Journal of Personal and Ubiquitous Computing*, Vol. 16, No. 3, 2011, pp. 259-269.

[8] M. Singh and M. Valtorta, "Construction of Bayesian Network Structures from Data: A Brief Survey and an Efficient Algorithm," *International Journal of Approximate Reasoning*, 1995, pp. 259-265.

[9] P. Darcy, B. Stantic and A. Sattar, "Augmenting a Deferred Bayesian Network with a Genetic Algorithm to Correct Missed RFID Readings," *Malaysian Joint Conference on Artificial Intelligence* (*MJCAI* 2009), Kuala Lumpur, 14-16 July 2009, pp. 106-115.

[10] W. S. Mcculloch and W. Pitts, "A Logical Calculus of the IdeasImmanent in Nervous Activity," *Bulletin of Mathematical Biophysics*, Vol. 5, No. 4, 1943, pp. 115-133.

[11] D. Rumelhart, G. Hinton and R. Williams, "Learning Representations by Back-Propagating Errors," *Nature* (*London*), Vol. 323, 1986, pp. 533-536.

[12] M. Blumenstein, X. Y. Liu and B. Verma, "An Investigation of the Modified Direction Feature for Cursive Character Recognition," *Pattern Recognition*, Vol. 40, No. 2, 2007, pp. 376-388.

[13] J. Holland, "Adaptation in Natural and Artificial Systems," University of Michigan Press, Massachusetts, 1975.

[14] A. Rooij, R. Johnson and L. Jain, "Neural Network Training Using Genetic Algorithms," World Scientific Publishing Co., Inc, River Edge, 1996.

[15] AT&T, "RFID Tags Help Schools Keep Tabs," 2008. http://www.corp.att.com/edu/docs/k12rfid2.pdf

[16] C. Des Marais, "Texas School Uses RFID Badges to Track Student Locations," 2012. http://www.pcworld.com/article/2011352/texas-school-uses-rfidbadges-to-track-student-locations.html

[17] G. Bhanage, Y. Zhang, Y. Zhang, W. Trappe and R. Howard, "Roll Call: The Design for a Low-Cost and Power Efficient Active RFID Asset Tracking System," *The International Conference on Computer as a Tool*, Piscataway, 9-12 September 2007, pp. 2521-2528.

[18] W. Wang, C. Chang and C. Huang, "A Study on RFID Combined with Network Technology for Collective Management of Tour Bus Tourists," *Service Systems and Service Management* (*ICSSSM*), Shanghai, 2-4 July 2012, pp. 547-550.

8

Personal Perspectives: Individual Privacy in the IOT

Johanna Virkki[1], Liquan Chen[2]
[1]Department of Electronics and Communications Engineering, Tampere University of Technology, Tampere, Finland
[2]School of Information Science and Engineering, Southeast University, Nanjing, China

ABSTRACT

The Internet of Things (IOT) is the extension of the Internet to the next level, *i.e.*, bringing the Internet to the real physical world of things. In this research, 22 people working with different aspects of IOT development were interviewed in Finland and in China, in order to investigate their thoughts and personal opinions on the IOT and the individual privacy in the IOT. This paper presents the background of the IOT, interviews and collected answers, as well as highlights of collected free comments.

Keywords: China; Finland; Individual Privacy; Internet of Things; Interviews

1. Introduction

The Internet of Things (IOT) means connecting things and devices in order to create an omnipresent computing world. Things will exchange data and information about the environment, while reacting autonomously to different events, influencing the environment, and creating services with or without human intervention. The IOT is thus the extension of the Internet to the next level, *i.e.*, bringing the Internet to the real physical world of things. Possible applications of the IOT are versatile and some examples are presented next.

Health-related applications include e.g. assistance and monitoring of conditions of patients inside hospitals and old people at home. For example, a tiny, wearable device that can detect a person's vital signs and send an alert to a healthcare professional if a certain threshold is reached or if a person has fallen down. Also, when an accident occurs, the victim's medical journals are automatically made available to the ambulances to ensure that optimal treatment can be provided. Electronic tags can be used in drugs and drug boxes can carry information on adverse effects and optimal dosage, monitor the use, inform the pharmacist when new supply is needed, know incompatible drugs, and prevent overdoses. The IOT also offers many applications to home-environment, for example energy and water supply consumption monitoring in houses to save cost and resources, remotely armed home security system, control of temperature gauges, switching appliances on and off, controlling lightning, etc. Possible retail applications including e.g. payment processing based on location or duration in public transport allow customers to pay in department stores without using a cash desk, only by walking out with the products that have electronic tags, and advices in the point of sale according to customer habits, preferences, presence of allergic components, or expiring dates. The IOT has many potential applications in catastrophic prevention, for example, detection and warning of forest fires and earthquake and monitoring of vibrations and material conditions in buildings and bridges. In addition, smart cities and intelligent transportation are examples of potential future IOT applications [1].

The term "Internet of Things" was coined by Kevin Ashton, executive director of the Auto-ID Center, in 1999. Different definitions for the IOT have appeared and the term was evolving as the technology and implementation of the ideas move forward. A number of countries or districts have realized the importance of the IOT in the recovery of economic growth and sustainability. Amongst them, the European Union (EU), the United States, and China are prominent examples. Academia has a relatively long history of IOT research. The IOT research in China has a strong support from the government. Several research institutes have been, and currently are, involved in far-reaching, government-supported, projects. In Europe, the academic research work in the IOT has been largely performed in different EU-funded seventh Programme Framework (FP7) projects. To better utilize the research achievements and to provide a place to share expertise, in 2009, the European Research Cluster on the Internet of Things was founded. The industrial activities in the IOT started around the same time as the academia, though the corresponding products were very sparse the first several years [2]. Thus, a wide range of research and application projects have been set up in different application areas, the technical aspects of the future Internet are widely studied, and a lot of development work is done [2-5].

One of the most important challenges in convincing users to adopt this kind of all-around network is the protection of privacy [6-9]. Concerns over privacy can spread wide, particularly as wireless systems can track users' actions, behaviour and ongoing preferences. Invisible and constant data exchange between things and people, and between things and other things, will occur unknown to the owners and originators of such data. The sheer scale and capacity of the new technologies will magnify this problem and source suspect [10]. Privacy problems, nevertheless, are not caused by the technology alone, but primary through activities of people, businesses, and the government [11].

Severàl interesting survey studies have already been conducted. The results from an empirical study with 92 subjects indicated that the acceptance of IOT services is influenced by various contradicting factors, such as perceived privacy risks and personal interests. It was also assumed that legislation, data security and transparency of information influence the adoption behavior [12]. Also, a survey with 475 subjects, focusing on the activities and habits that people do at home that they would not want to be recorded, was conducted, and bedroom was found to be the most private place [13]. A study that investigated American, Chinese, and Indian social networking site users' privacy attitudes and practices, based on 924 responses, found the American respondents to be the most privacy concerned, followed by the Chinese and Indians, respectively [14].

While our work shares many similar objects to the work above, we focus only on the personal perspectives of the people who are working with different aspects of the development of the IOT, in two very different countries, in different parts of the world. In this research, people working with IOT research and development were interviewed in Finland (EU member) and in China, in order to investigate their personal feelings about the Internet and the individual privacy in the Internet today and in the future. In this study, the individual privacy refers to the evolving relationship between the technology and the legal right to, or public expectation of, privacy in the collection and sharing of data about one's self. This definition is used for both the Internet and the IOT.

2. Interviews

For this research, 22 people working with the research and development of the IOT, e.g. with wireless components/devices, wireless systems, Internet protocols, and mobile communications were interviewed. People of different age (the average age of the answerers was 28, the youngest answerer was 20 years old and the oldest answerer was 48 years old), of both gender (genders of the answerers can be seen in **Table 1**), and from different organizations (researchers of different universities in Finland and China, workers of companies on the field, and participants of an international conference) were chosen from Finland (11 people) and from China (11 people).

Personal interviews were conducted by an associate of the researcher, and they took place either at the answerers working facility or at a neutral, public place. Some of the interviews were done by private e-mails between the researcher and the answerer. All these interviews thus had more flexibility than only an anonymous paper survey as both the researcher and the answerer were able to ask for clarification. This study had 5 questions and a possibility for free comments. The idea of this research was not only to compare the answers from China and from Finland, but also to gather more versatile answers by making interviews in two very different countries. Questions are listed next.

Question 1: How much do you think a person can currently affect his/her own individual privacy in the Internet? Scale = 1 - 5, where

1 = A person can completely control his/her individual privacy;

5 = A person has no control over his/her individual privacy.

Question 2: How worried are you about individual privacy in the following Internet/IOT applications?

Scale = 1 - 5, where 1 = Not worried at all, 5 = Very worried.

- Personal health-related applications (e.g. your medical conditions, drugs, treatments);
- Personal finances-related applications (e.g. your account and credit information);
- Personal purchases-related applications (e.g. what did you buy, from where, how much did you spend);
- Personal communication-related applications (e.g. what did you communicate, when, with whom);

Table 1. Gender and nationality of the answerers.

	China	Finland	All
Female	7	6	13
Male	4	5	9
All	11	11	22

- Personal tracking-related applications (e.g. where are/ were you).

Question 3: Do you believe that the current Internet will grow into the IOT and this kind of all-around network will come to use? What will be the schedule?

- In the near future;
- During the following 10 years;
- During the following 20 years;
- Longer than 20 years;
- Never.

Question 4: If you think that the current Internet will grow into the IOT in the future, do you feel that the use of at least some IOT applications will be mandatory so that it is very hard to stay out?

- Yes;
- No;
- I don't know.

Question 5: How much do you think a person can affect his/her own individual privacy in the Internet/IOT after 10 years from now? Scale = 1 - 5, where 1 = A person can completely control his/her individual privacy, 5 = A person has no control over his/her individual privacy.

3. Results and Discussion

Questions 1 and 5 dealt with the opinions and feelings on how much people can currently and after 10 years affect their own individual privacy in the Internet. Results can be seen in **Figures 1** and **2**, respectively. As can be seen, the answerers from Finland are currently less worried about the individual privacy in the Internet than the answerers from China. This is an unexpected result, since traditionally Finland is more of an individualistic society and thus values individual privacy, where as China is more of a collective society. Since the explanation to this result cannot be found from this survey, more research is definitely needed. According to these answers, people from both countries believe that moving from the traditional Internet towards the IOT during the following 10

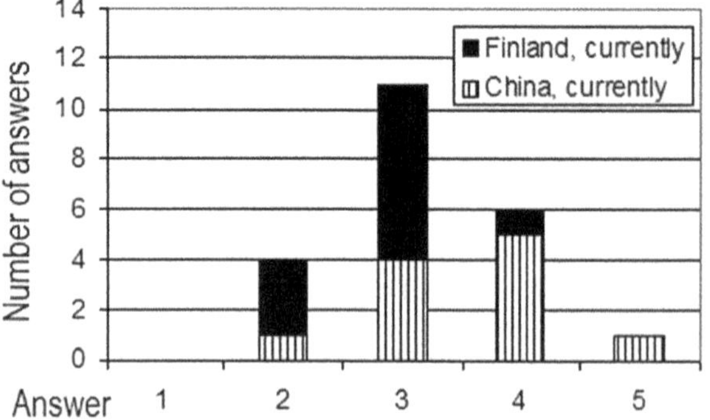

Figure 1. Results from Question 1. Opinions on how much people can currently affect their individual privacy in the Internet.

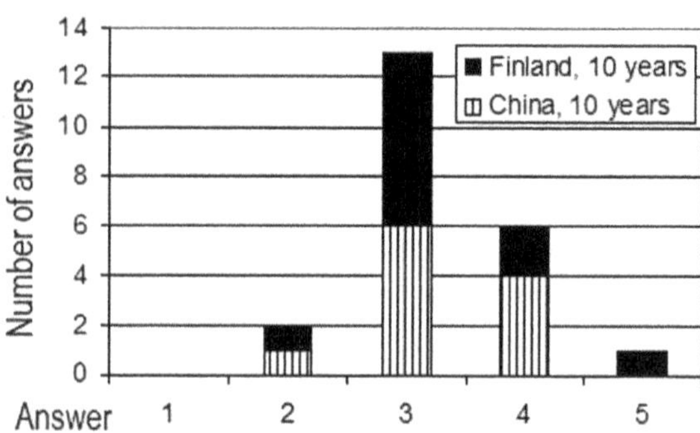

Figure 2. Results from Question 5. Opinions on how much people can affect their individual privacy in the Internet after 10 years.

years will not significantly affect how they can control their individual privacy in the Internet. Some answerers from Finland believe for a negative change, whereas some of the answerers from China believe that they might have even better control of their privacy in the Internet after 10 years. This is probably because a lot of work is currently done to improve the individual privacy in the Internet and also the awareness of people is rising. This was also seen in free comments from both countries:

"*New technology must strengthen, rather than undermine, the privacy of people.*"

"*Users should be able to monitor and control the security and privacy settings of all the devices that they own, some services should be accessible in an anonymous way, while others should require an explicit authentication or authorization of the user.*"

It is also probable that achieving this kind of high level individual privacy may first require some bad experiences:

"*Nowadays alertness of privacy issues and identity theft possibilities are increasing, regrettably, for the most part, by bad practice.*"

"*If we want to make good use of it (the IOT), we must make some strict policy to manage the use of it.*"

Question 2 inquired how worried the answerers are about individual privacy in different Internet/IOT applications. The application areas were chosen to be versatile areas from everyday life. Results from China and Finland can be seen in **Figures 3** and **4**, respectively. In China, personal finances related applications were clearly the ones that the answerers were most worried about. Salary and other aspects of personal finances are seen very private information in China and the future Internet applications must not affect this. Applications related to personal health were the least worrying ones and also the one and only lowest level of concern (1 = not worried at all) answer was nominated for this question. According to free comments from China, many applications were seen tempting, but safety must first be ensured. Also, it was questioned if the cost of applications in many areas

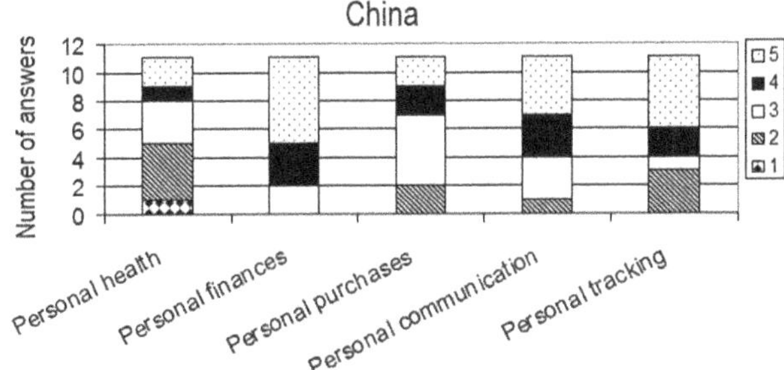

Figure 3. Results from Question 2. Opinions on individual privacy in different Internet/IOT applications in China.

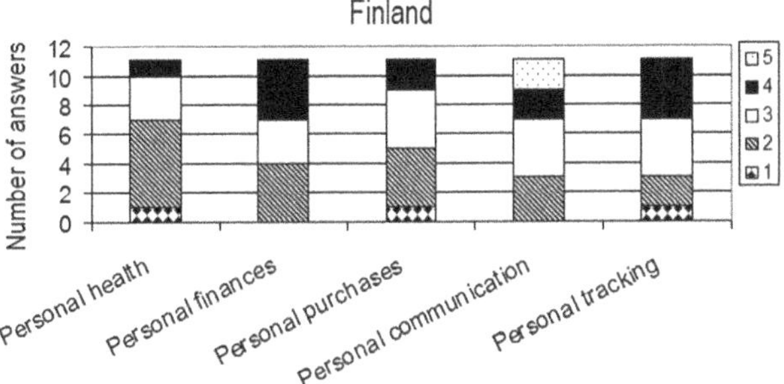

Figure 4. Results from Question 2. Opinions on individual privacy in different Internet/IOT applications in Finland.

will be too high.

"Insuring the individual privacy is obviously the key point of popularizing the IOT."

"Seeing it as a possibility for new applications but also a lot of work must be done to safely implement them."

"Until the devices and services will become both cheap and safe, I will not let this kind of applications (home automation) enter my life."

Again, unexpected results were achieved in this part, when the answerers from Finland were significantly less worried than the answerers from China. For example, in China, there were more than one nominations for the highest concern (5 = very worried) for all applications, whereas in Finland there were only two nominations for the highest concern at all, both in personal communication related applications. As in China, applications related to personal health were the least worrying ones also in Finland. It was stated in free comments that in healthcare, the most important thing is that all the vital information is available when needed. The future of the public healthcare is currently a hot topic in the Finnish media and thus also opposite opinions, pointing important issues, were presented in free comments. For example, in one comment from Finland, it was stated that there already are individual privacy problems related to personal health.

"There is not enough control, who can truly view your healthy records as the cases of misuse in publicity indicate."

"I want all my information to be available to anyone who needs it when they take care of me. I also think future applications can improve the privacy in the healthcare."

Thus, the effects of carefully designed and secured IOT applications to individual privacy in the future can also be positive. One important issue related to these different applications is the data aggregation (combining seemingly non-sensitive separate bits of information may well reveal additional, possibly sensitive, information) [15]. Similar effect can occur when data collected for one purpose is used for a different purpose without the person's approval. This was also made known in free comments:

"Giving a small piece of information there and something small somewhere else does not seem bad, but what if somebody combines all information? And will I even know about that?"

In Question 3, it was inquired what the answerers think will be the possible schedule for the current Internet to grow into the IOT and this kind of all-around network to come to use, if it will come to use. The answers to this question can be seen in **Figure 5**. According to these results, 41% of the answerers felt that this will happen during the following 10 years, 36% during the following 20 years, and 14% that it will take longer than 20 years. In addition, 9% of the answerers (all from Finland) felt that this growing into IOT will never happen. None of the answerers felt that this will happen in the near future. In free comments, the IOT was seen tempting but challenging. Also the necessity of versatile IOT applications was questioned in free comments.

"I am interested in living in world with IOT."

"It is useful, but it is difficult."

"Are ordinary people willing to pay for all these great applications that are invented?"

In Question 4, it was asked if the answerers feel that the use of at least some IOT applications will be mandatory in the future, so that it is very hard to stay out. The answers from China and Finland can be seen in **Figure 6**.

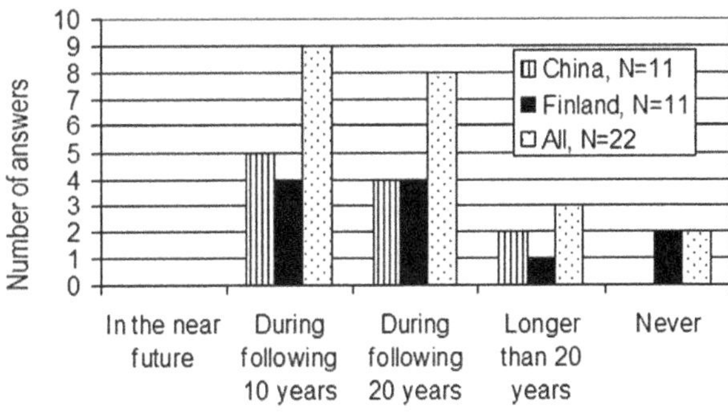

Figure 5. Results from Question 3. Opinions on the possible schedule for the current Internet to grow into IOT and this kind of all-around network to come to use.

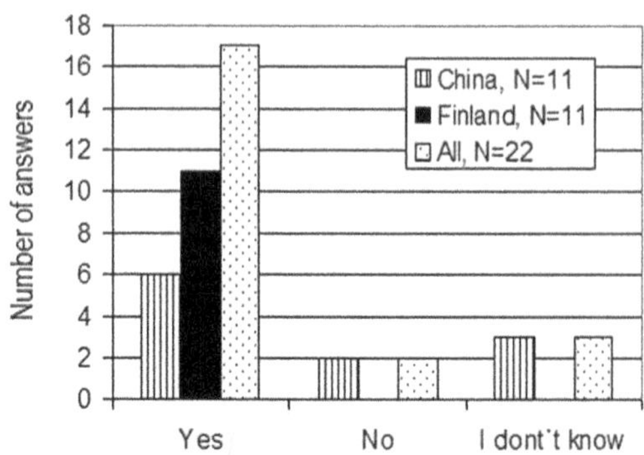

Figure 6. Results from Question 4. Opinions on if the use of at least some IOT applications will be mandatory in the future.

In China, 55% of the answerers felt that the IOT will be mandatory in some way. People in Finland were more concerted and all 11 answerers felt that the IOT will be mandatory in some way. It was also mentioned that the use of the Internet is already mandatory when living in Finland and thus this will also be the case in the future with the IOT. Also some feeling of helplessness was seen in free comments. Thus, unlike the people in Finland, some people in China feel that it is still possible to live without the Internet in China and this may also be possible in the future.

"*Living without Internet is already impossible in Finland*!"

"*It is also a matter of control. For example, I am not comfortable that anyone can track my personal contact details from my car's license number and I cannot do much about it.*" (in Finland)

4. Conclusion

In this study, 22 people working with different aspects of research and development of the IOT were interviewed in Finland and in China, related to the IOT and the individual privacy in the IOT. This paper presents and discusses the collected answers and highlights of free comments. We feel that this research study brings a new perspective to this interesting research area. Most of the answerers believed that we were heading towards the IOT and in the future it would be mandatory to be part of it somehow. According to answers, many future applications were seen tempting, but they contained great risks and thus individual privacy must first be ensured. Also individual privacy problems today were stated. In general, the answerers from Finland were less worried about the individual privacy in the IOT than the answerers from China. This was an unexpected result and the reasons for this definitely required more research work. Next step is also to compare these answers with answers collected from normal people. This future research also has to involve significantly more answerers in order to achieve more meaningful results.

5. Acknowledgements

J. Virkki would like to thank the Helsingin Sanomat Foundation.

REFERENCES

[1] Libelium, "50 Internet of Things Applications," 2012. http://www.libelium.com/top_50_iot_sensor_applications_ranking

[2] The Strategic Centre for Science, "Technology and Innovation in the Field of ICT, Internet of Things Strategic Research Agenda." http://www.Internetofthings.fi/

[3] Futuretech Alert, "Technology Convergence Leading to the Internet of Things," Frost & Sullivan, Mountain View, 2012.

[4] "The Internet of Things 2012—New Horizons-Cluster Book," 2012. http://www.Internet-of-things-research.eu/pdf/IERC_Cluster_Book_2012_WEB.pdf

[5] European Commission, Information Society and Media, "Internet of Things in 2020 Roadmap for the Future," 2008. http://www.iot-visitthefuture.eu/fileadmin/documents/researchforeurope/270808_IoT_in_2020_Workshop_Report_V1-1.pdf

[6] L. Wu and P. Shao, "Research on the Protection Algorithm and Model of Personal Privacy Information in Internet of Thing," *International Conference on E-Business and E-Government*, Guiyang, 6-8 May 2011, pp. 1-4.

[7] H. Feng and W. Fu, "Study of Recent Development about Privacy and Security of the Internet of Things," *International Conference on Web Information Systems and Mining*, Beijing, 23-24 October 2010, pp. 91-95.

[8] D. Gessner, A. Olivereau, A. S. Segura and A. Serbanati, "Trustworthy Infrastructure Services for a Secure and Privacy-Respecting Internet of Things," *International Conference on Trust, Security and Privacy in Computing and Communications*, Heidelberg, 25-27 June 2012, pp. 998-1003.

[9] V. Oleshchuk, "Internet of Things and Privacy Preserving Technologies," *International Conference on Wireless Communication, Vehicular Technology, Information Theory and Aerospace & Electronic Systems Technology*, Grimstad, 17-20 May 2009, pp. 336-340.

[10] International Telecommunication Union, "The Internet of Things, Executive Summary." http://www.itu.int/dms_pub/itu-s/opb/pol/S-POL-IR.IT-2005-SUM-PDF-E.pdf

[11] D. J. Solove, "A Taxonomy of Privacy," *University of Pennsylvania Law Review*, Vol. 154, No. 3, 2006, p. 477.

[12] T. Kowatsch and W. Maass, "Privacy Concerns and Acceptance of IoT Services," *Internet of Things Intitiative*, 2012, pp. 176-187.

[13] E. K. Choe, S. Consolvo, J. Jung, B. Harrison and J. A.

Kientz, "Living in a Glass House: A Survey of Private Moments in the Home," *Proceedings of the* 13*th International Conference on Ubiquitous Computing*, Beijing, 17-21 September 2011, pp. 41-44.

[14] Y. Wang, G. Norcie and L. F. Cranor "Who Is Concerned about What? A Study of American, Chinese and Indian Users Privacy Concerns on Social Network Sites," *International Conference on Trust & Trustworthy Computing*, Vol. 6740, 2011, pp. 146-153.

[15] D. J. Solove, "'I've Got Nothing to Hide' and Other Misunderstandings of Privacy," *San Diego Law Review*, Vol. 44, 2007, p. 745.

9

Comprehensive Study on the Basis of Eye Blink, Suggesting Length of Text Line, Considering Typographical Variables the Way How to Improve Reading from Computer Screen

Muzammil Khan[1], Khushdil[2]

[1]Department of Computer Science and Software Engineering, University of Swat, Saidu Sharif, Pakistan

[2]Institute of Business and Computer Mgt Sciences, Department of Computer Science, Agriculture University, Peshawar, Pakistan

ABSTRACT

The advent and extensive use of computer and increasing development of different technologies it is important to increase the awareness of issues related to the electronic text or text presentation on computer screen. The usage of web shows the importance of usability and readability of the web applications or sources provide by the web and web textual contents. Web application fails to encounter the user's requirements in effective manner specially related to textual information, because the designers are unaware from some of the important factors effecting readability, reading from the screen. In this regard, this study is the continuation of the previous work that has been done for the improvement of readability, to handle the readability issues on the basis of Eye Blink for male participants and female participants. To achieve general recommendations for suitable or optimum length of text line for all type of users on the bases of eye blink. Basically during reading from the computer screen focus losses at two positions, when eye blink in the middle of text line and when text line ends. The study specifies suitable length of text line on the basis of Eye Blink, assuming three typographical variables *i.e.* font style, font color, font size, and with white background, which improve the overall readability or reading from computer screen. The study also shows two important things the degree of understandability and the degree of attractive appearance of different combination.

Keywords: Readability; Text Line Length; Understandability; Appearance; Eye Blink; Typographical Variable; Reading from Screen

1. Introduction

Regarding reading from computer screen *i.e.* electronic text and reading from the paper, there exist two schools of thought. One school of thought firmly belief that paper based reading will never be replaced by any electronic text, and as an argument they mention different scenarios like reading news paper in the bus, on the beach, and reading magazine in the bed etc. Garland [1] summed up some of the potential uses of electronic text. The second school of thought really thinks that the electronic text has enormous potential to replace or to compete paper based reading. This thinking based on different perspective like ease of storage and retrieval, flexibility of structure and saving natural resources are key motivation and it is the matter of habit as well. Ted Nelson [2] arose a question, when and how we can present things on the screen, and how can we make it great. This article is not to present the dominancy of one medium over the other or replace electronic text by paper but a try to cover the question how we can make it great, easy and naturally perceivable, efficient for the readers when they are reading from the computer screen.

In present era of technology, plethora of information are available, in this fast and busy life people want and wish to get the desire information as easy as possible. The usage of computer and internet increases day by day, today online reading from computer systems become more common. According to Google data centre June 2006, about 900 million computer users exist in the world [3]. According to Internet World States, internet users in the world distributions in the world 2011 are 2,095,006,005, which are approximately 2100 million or 2 billions [4]. It means a large population use internet to get the desire information easily, cheaply, and accurately.

Though information readily available, and Internet is the source which provides information with comfort and almost with no cost, but these content is not up to the mark. As huge part of the information is consists of textual data, it is difficult and tedious to spend a lot of time in front of computer because user facing a lot of problems during reading from computer screen, can call as readability problems. During reading from the computer screen, usability of the web contents must be consider with significance and should not be ignored. Typography plays a major role in the web contents usability, many studies exist regarding typography, standards has been deduce after different studies for soft copy and hard copy. Web usability is an approach to make web sites easy to use for an end user, non specialized web user, without any specialized training, and without having any pre knowledge. Keep it in mind that huge amount of information are access through World Wide Web and Web browsers. There is an urgent need to increase our knowledge about the usability or readability factors influence reading from computer screen. Few problems create inefficiency and keep users away from online reading for long time. One of the main problem that act as a huddle in reading from computer screen is Eye Strain, focus loss during reading, brain fog, and headache etc. These problems are interrelated, the focus is to reduce the focus loss during reading and hence eye strain become less or to get large time to get tired. During reading from the screen users become tired after some time and get bored. It may involve many reasons but this study and the previous studies specifies suitable Length of Text Line with special relationship to Eye Blink on the basis of font style, font size, font color and background color. The study reduces the problem caused by reading and increase readability that will ultimately lead to efficiency and comfort.

The structure of the paper is as follow. First the document describes the focus area and importance. Second section describes how to deal with the problem and approach that solve the problem. Third section introduces related work. Next section includes methods and procedures, analysis, facts and figure about experiment, lastly conclude the whole work and future work.

2. Reading from Computer Screen

Reading from computer screen initiates many problems like eyestrain, a feeling of being unable to focus on the screen that is focus losses again and again, confusion, attention deficit/brain fog, irritability, headache, neck pain, dizziness (faintness), queasiness (vomiting), or an uncomfortable feeling down through the chest. These problems prevent users from online reading or reading from computer screen [5]. This list of problems is directly associated with eye, and why not, as eye is the main source of perceiving objects, images etc and also plays a vital role in reading from computer screen, paper pages or other readable materials. These problems are instigating as;

- Using computer at a fixed and set distance for a long continuous period of time. Even if a person has more than adequate focusing ability, focusing at a set distance continuously can fatigue the lens that cause many other problems.
- Reading or working at very close distances from the screen. This requires much more focusing and leads to more rapid fatigue or tiredness.

Actually eyestrain not damage eye or cause any vision loss. However, it can be very uncomfortable and lead to a loss of productivity when reading. Anyone who uses a computer can take measures to reduce eye discomfort [6]. Another important limitation is slow reading from computer screen as compare to reading from paper, in this regard A. V. Kak 1981, Muter *et al.* 1982, Wright *et al.* 1983, Gould *et al.* 1984, and Smedshammar *et al.* 1989 produced experimental findings during silent reading from screen and deduce that reading from the screen is significantly slower as compare to reading from the paper. Figures vary according to means of calculation and experimental design but the evidence suggests a performance discrepancy of 20% and 30% when reading from the screen [7,9]. The people don't like to read online because it is time consuming as compared to the reading from the paper. Reading from the paper is 25% slower than reading from the paper [10]. Among various issues regarding reading one of the major issues is focus loss during reading. During reading the human losses focus or concentration or accommodation at two positions that is when line breaks and when eye blink. When we are reading, during reading we blink our eye to make our eye relax (a natural process) then we loss the focus or concentration from the fix position (from the word we are reading) all the involve muscles relaxes from the contraction form. Then when we start reading again the muscles goes in contraction form to get focus. In same way when the line breaks and we sweep from the end of the line to the beginning of next line we lost our focus and the eye muscles goes from contraction to rest and then from rest to concentration. If this process happens as many times the eye become tired and then will cause many problems. 10% of the retina center is called the macula. This is responsible for your sharp vision, your reading vision. The peripheral retina is responsible for the peripheral vision [11]. During focus loss many eye muscles are involved, that discussed in detail in [12,13].

The main objective of the study is how to improve the reading capability or productivity during reading or electronic text from computer screen. This can be achieve by making the eye muscles less stress during reading, and make the text naturally perceivable for human eye. The main issue that is addressed in this study is focus, means the mentioned problems can be overcome up to some extent by decreasing the process of focus loss and focus gain during reading, that protect eye from stress and fatigue which lead to many other problems. As focuses loss at two positions *i.e.* when eye blinks & when line breaks, if the length of text line is so adjust that convert two focus losses to one, means that when human eye blink naturally then the line should be end which will lead to convert maximum focus losses to minimum focus losses. The reduction of focus losses will protect eyestrain and indirectly all other relevant problems, the efficiency and readability will increase. Blinking, function and anatomy of blinking discussed in detail in [12,13].

3. Related Work

Large volume of material accessible from the World Wide Web or through web browser, there is an urgent need to increase our knowledge of factors influencing reading from screen. Web usability is an approach to make web sites easy to use for an end-user, without any specialized training. For this purpose a lot of work has been done till now since 1880. Before the evolution of computer system these experiment been done on printed media, but afterwards the efforts transformed towards online reading or reading from computer screen as well. This section contained literature about length of text line, text layout, blinking and blink rate.

3.1. Line Length

Weber, 1881, suggested that an ideal line length is 4 inches *i.e.* 100 millimeters. The study investigates the influence of line length on the speed of reading prose text. He stated further that the maximum never should exceed 6 inches or 150 mm. The same year Javel (1881) reported that line lengths should be no longer than 3.6 inches or 90 mm [14]. These recommendations were for book, magazine and newspaper publishers, and assumed the use of 10-point black characters typeset on white paper.

Cohn, 1883, confirmed that 3.6 inches or 90 mm was the best length of text line, and that 4 inches or 102 mm was the longest tolerable line length for printed media and assumed 10-point black characters typeset on white paper [15].

Tinker & Paterson, 1929, found that line lengths between 3 inches and 3.5 inches or from 75 to 90 mm yielded the fastest reading performance Using 10-point black type on white paper. These recommendations were for Printed materials [16].

Spencer, 1968, proposed that the number of characters should not be exceeded from 70 characters per line, these recommendations also for printed materials or for hard copy. These recommendations had been analyzed on the bases of reading rate and comprehensions [17].

Jackson & McClelland, 1979, analyze and measure the reading rate for effective reading performance on the bases of users or readers comprehension. These authors multiplied reading rate by the comprehension score to produce their index. However, they do acknowledge that multiplication may not be the optimal formula, as sacrificing comprehension for very fast reading may exaggerate reading ability [18].

Duchnicky & Kolers, 1983, found an affect reading rate for reading from screen and suggested appropriate Line length for text line, and specified that line length should be about 75 characters per line. The study has been done on the base of studying different display technologies [19].

Masson, 1985, study says that the effect of line length on reading rate may be dependent upon the overall reading speed, means how fast a reader can read, as speeding up reading may result in different patterns of eye movements. Masson has reviewed research on the characteristics of naturally fast readers and found that "super readers" make fewer fixations during reading from the printed materials and also from the computer screen [20].

Rayner & Pollatsek, 1989, deduce that Tinker's work identified an optimal line length of 52 characters per line. The trade-off between two opposing factors that are: If line lengths are too long, the return sweeps to the beginning of the next line are difficult. If the lines are too short, readers cannot make use of much information in each fixation [21].

Dyson & Kipping, 1998, Kipping et al used different display technologies and suggest in their study that 4-inch line length of text line produced the slowest reading rate and the 7.3 inch line length produced the fastest but the user prefer 4 inch or 102 mm line length. These experiments are done with using 12-point type font size. The study further identifies the reading rate improves if characters per line increased [22].

Youngman & Scharff, 1999, according to Youngman and Scharff 8 inch line length of text line elicited the fastest speed as compare to the line of 4 inches or 6 inches text line lengths. They used 12-point type for font size [23].

DYSON & HASELGROVE, 2001, a medium line length of 55 characters per line appears to support effective reading at normal and fast speeds. The investigation was made on three effecting factors that are; comprehension, reading rate and scrolling patterns [24].

Bernard, Fernandez & Hull, 2002, had participants read 12 point prose text with line lengths of 9.6 inches or 245 mm, 5.7 inches or 145 mm and 3.3 inches or 85 mm. the study found no significant differences on average reading speed for the different line lengths. Their adult subjects preferred the two shorter line lengths [25].

Bob Bailey, 2002, users tend to read faster if the line lengths are longer up to 10 inches. If the line lengths are too short, means around 2.5 inches or less then it may impede rapid reading. Users prefer lines that are moderately long in length that is 4 to 5 inches [26].

Dawn Shaikh, 2005, presented a news article in 35, 55, 75, or 95 characters per line on a computer monitor and examined the longest line length of 95 characters per line or 10 inches resulted in the fastest reading speed [27].

MUZAMMIL & MUSHTAQ, 2010, 2012, suggested different text line lengths for three variables on the bases of eye blink during reading from computer screen in two different studies for male and female. The study concluded if the text for reading is provided in the given length it can reduce eye strain and enhance reading capabilities from the computer screen. The experimental set-up was explained *i.e.* equipment, participants, material for experiment, the collection of data procedures, and then explain three main major factors that's must be consider during reading. Previous study presents eight different combinations from the combination of three given variables for experiment, *i.e.* Font color, style and size. Understandability, appearance, and line length on the bases of eye blink were three major factors that were considered. According to Muzammil *et al.* combination "Verdana, 10, Black" and "Verdana, 10, Green" are best, when consider clarity and appearance. The experiment has been done for male participants only. Both of these studies [12,13] are compared, analyze and deduce overall conclusions in this article.

The following **Table 1** summarizes the literature that has been done regarding length of text line. Acronyms for **Table 1**; Characters per line: cpl, Inches: in, Millimeters: mm.

3.2. Text Layout

J. Nielsen, 2000, uses colors with high contrast between the text and the background. Optimal legibility requires black text on white background and so-called positive text. White text on a black background and called it as negative text. Negative text is considered to be equally good, but has no proof [10]. Richard and Hanna provide systematic approach to prove Nielsen statement [28]. Bradley Wilson, Times are the most popular body font that is 29%, then Palatino 13%, Garamond 8% and the rest fonts 50%. The font sizes that are normally used are, Average 9.99, Median 10, Largest 12 and Smallest 8.5 [29]. City of Seattle Web Presentation and Accessibility Standards Version 2.5 are; the minimum font size for basic page body text will be or appear equal to Verdana 10 points. All page body text will be black. All page body text will be presented in Verdana font [29]. Mushtaq Raza, 2007, Preliminary mean analysis of the fonts revealed that font type Time New Roman is the most readable, conveyed personality Business like and first preference of the participants as compared to Courier New, Arial and Bradley [30].

Table 1. Comparison of different studies.

Studies	Suggested length of text line	Units of measurement	Recommendations for		Recommendation basis
			Electronic materials	Printed materials	
Weber, 1881	4 in (100 mm)	Inches and millimeters	No	Yes	Speed of reading prose text
Cohn, 1883	3.6 in (90 mm)	Inches and millimeters	No	Yes	10-point black characters
Tinker & Paterson, 1929	3 to 3.5 in (75 to 90 mm)	Inches and millimeters	No	Yes	10-point black characters
Spencer, 1968	70 cpl	Character per line	No	Yes	Comprehensions
Duchnicky & Kolers, 1983	75 cpl	Character per line	Yes	No	Display technologies
Rayner & Pollatsek, 1989	52 cpl	Character per line	No	Yes	10-point black characters
Dyson & Kipping, 1998	100 cpl	Characters per line	NA	Yes	12-point characters
Youngman & Scharff, 1999	8 in	Inches	NA	Yes	12-point characters
DYSON & HASELGROVE, 2001	55 cpl	Characters per line	Yes	No	Reading rate, and comprehension
Bernard, Fernandez & Hull, 2002	9.6 in (245 mm), 5.7 in (145 mm) and 3.3 in (85 mm)	Inches and millimeters	Yes	No	12-point prose text reading speed for adults and children
Bob Bailey, **2002**	4 to 5 in	Inches	Yes	No	User preference
Dawn Shaikh, 2005	95 cpl (10 in)	Characters per line and inches	Yes	No	Arial font
Muzammil & Mushtaq, 2010	Suggested 8 different lengths	Characters per line with spaces, without spaces, & inches	Yes (for web browser)	No	Font size, style, & color of different standards for male
Muzammil & Mushtaq, 2012	Suggested 8 different lengths	Characters per line with spaces, without spaces, & inches	Yes (for web browser)	No	Font size, style, & color of different standards for female

3.3. Blinking and Blink Rate

The analysis of the eye movement in reading is blinks, when readers close their eyes. Blinking rate increases with increasing reading time, resulting in high data losses, especially for older adults or reading impaired subjects [31]. Spontaneous blink rate was significantly larger in women than in men (19 vs. 11 blinks per minute); older women blinked more frequently than younger women. Eyelid displacement was greater in young than in older subjects [32]. When eyes are focused on an object for an extended period of time, such as when reading, blinking rate decreases up to about 3 - 4 times per minute [33].

4. Methods and Procedures

4.1. Variables

There are many factors that can affect reading from computer screen. For example typographic aspects of text *i.e.* font size, font style, foreground color (font color), background color, reader reading speed, comprehension, display technology, user preferences etc. Consider individual factor for implementation from these factors may, may not be that beneficial for improving reading from computer screen. Therefore it will be more effective to consider maximum factors; likewise this study presumes at different steps.

4.2. Study Variables

As this study focus on length of text line on the bases of eye blink so analysis the factors those directly affects e.g. typographic related factors *i.e.* font size, font style, font color, and background color. The focus here on two type of standards that is standards for printed materials and web standards [34].

The study involves:

- Typographical Variable.
- Fonts size.
- 10 points.
- 12 points.

12 point and 10 point character size has been consider for experiments because being taken in different studies and 10 points size for Verdana font is Web Presentation and Accessibility Standard for web page body text [34, 35].

- Font face.
- Verdana.
- Time New Roman.

Verdana is Web Presentation and Accessibility Standards Version 2.5 [34], and Time New Roman showed promising results regarding readability, conveyed personality, business likeness and general preferences in [30].

- Color combination (foreground and background).
- Black and white.
- Green and white.

Black text is easily visible or readable on white background because this combination has high contrast and is called positive text [10], green text on white background is consider because human eye has natural tendency for green color and the rays are converges on retina without eye lens adjustment that may not cause eye fatigue [36].

- User.
- User between 20 to 40 years old.

The accessible population for the study is considered within the mention range.

- Medical Factors that affect reading from the screen.

This study is based on eye blink which is affected by different reasons, e.g. Environmental factors can indirectly affect eye blink such as humidity, temperature and pollutants etc., and cognitive factors such as speaking, memorizing, mental arithmetic, focused reading, concentration etc [33,37].

4.3. Equipment

A Intel(R) Core(TM)2 Duo CPU T5750 @ 2.00 GHz, 1995 MHz Laptop, model "Dell Studio 1535" has been use for the experiments and data collection, with the following properties.

Lid size	15.4"
Device Technology	Raster Display
Resolution	1280 × 800
Color Depth	32-bit
Color Planes	1
Font Resolution	96 dpi
Pixel Width/Height	36/36
Pixel Diagonal	51
Vertical Refresh Rate	60 z

4.4. Participants

Seventy Five (75) volunteers were considered for experiments, out of 75 participants, 43% or 57% were male and 32% or 43% were female participants. All the participants were having correct vision, means with no disabilities. Participant's categorization on the bases of age and education are summarized in the following **Table 2**.

4.5. Data Collection Environment

The data has been collected in the month of August. The temperature were around 30 degree centigrade (30°), weather were dry. All the data are taken in under normal room light and the users are sat 24 to 28 inches away

Table 2. Participants categorization on the bases of age and education.

	Male Participants	Female Participants
Age Ranges		
21 - 25	49%	56%
26 - 30	28%	28%
31 - 35	16%	13%
36 - 40	07%	03%
Education		
Postgraduates	72%	50%
Graduates	19%	31%
Professionals	09%	19%

from the screen, means that follow the safety precautions that should follow during using computer. The text provide for experiment in "Internet Explorer" web browser.

4.6. Experimental Material

Web page is designed with 8 different paragraphs with different typographical properties or each paragraph is a combination of different typographic parameters. The contents of the each paragraph is provided according to the comprehension (level of education) of each user, the length is so adjust that the users did not get bore during reading. The composition of each paragraph is given in the following passage.

Short hands: Font Style, Font Size, Font Color.

Paragraph 1: Time New Roman, 10, Black.

Paragraph 1 has 5 lines on average, and contains 41 words on average.

Paragraph 2: Time New Roman, 12, Black.

Paragraph 2 has 6 lines on average, and contains 36 words on average.

Paragraph 3: Verdana, 10, Black.

Paragraph 3 has 6 lines on average, and contains 33 words per line on average.

Paragraph 4: Verdana, 12, Black.

Paragraph 4 has 6 lines on average, and contains 27 words per line on average.

Paragraph 5: Time New Roman, 10, Green.

Paragraph 5 has 5 lines on average, and contains 40 words per line on average.

Paragraph 6: Time New Roman, 12, Green

Paragraph 6 has 6 lines on average, and contains 37 words per line on average.

Paragraph 7: Verdana, 10, Green.

Paragraph 7 has 6 lines on average, and contains 32 words per line on average.

Paragraph 8: Verdana, 12, Green.

Paragraph 8 has 6 lines on average, and contains 28 words per line on average.

In simple words each paragraph is around 5 to 6 lines and the length of each line is around 10.5 inches. The designed web page is presented to each user or participant. Each paragraph is the combination of different parameters, means that each paragraph has one parameter different than all other paragraphs. This textual material is provided in Internet Explorer Web browser.

4.7. Data Collection Procedure

Data collection is one of the tricky and important part of this study, because the identification of correct blink location is utmost significant in order to find out the correct length of text line for different combinations as mention in the previous section. So the process is advanced in the following stepwise manner.

- The reader is educated how to read the paragraphs and positioned in such a way that to collect data correctly.
- During reading video has been taken from the reader when he/she is reading from the computer screen, but they kept unaware from it in order to get natural blink of eye during reading and to analyze the video keenly.
- After the video has been taken, the process is explained to the reader, the purpose of the study being explained and why the paragraph being read by them with such constrains.
- Questioner has been conducted in order to collect information about the different combinations, information means usability, understandability and readability of different combinations.
- Questioner: A questioner contains of 16 questions, 8 about "to find out the degree of understandability or clarity of words in the paragraph based on fonts' style and size". And
- 8 about "to find out the degree of pleasant appearance or good-looks of the paragraph based on fonts' style and size".
- A thorough discussion has been done with the reader about each question, their feeling and view about each paragraph. Then conclusion was deduced.
- Each video analyzed carefully in order to find out the suitable length of Text Line on the bases of Eye blink for each combination, through which the maximum focus losses is replaced by fewer one.
- The values are put in EXCEL tool and the Results are deduced in the form of Charts and Tables to get better understanding.

5. Results and Analysis

The central purpose of this study is to suggest suitable length of text line on the basis of eye blink, but beside that the two most important factors are understandability of the textual material and how attractive these combinations are. This section explains these three things considering typographical variables.

5.1. Clarity and Understandability

The user is asked to rate the paragraph, on the basis of "the degree of understandability/clarity of words in the paragraph based on fonts' style and size". It is a subjective judgment which very difficult to formulize and empirically analyze, but thorough and hard work is done for the deduction of results.

Average perception that were deduce from the reader during discussion on each paragraph.

Paragraph 1 with combination "Time New Roman, 10, Black" is too small, looking to much condense, difficult to read and required to come closer to the computer screen.

Paragraph 2 with combination "Time New Roman, 12, Black" is a bit easier to read than the first combination but the words are looking attached to each other. The words are looking shaky, means unstable.

Paragraph 3 with combination "Verdana, 10, Black" is Clearer, Understandable and very much easier to read as compare to the previous two paragraphs.

Paragraph 4 with combination "Verdana, 12, Black" is also clear and easy to read but it is observe that the user lost correct line when the finish one and starting next line it may be because the lines are looking very close. During discussion it is observed that the readers get bored during reading such large font size of textual materials.

Paragraph 5 with combination "Time New Roman, 10, Green" is too much difficult to read because there is not high contrast between background and Text color, the words are too small and looking very condensed plus the green color font is looking very sharp with white background.

Paragraph 6 with "Time New Roman, 12, Green" combination is difficult to read because small, low contrast and looking unstable.

Paragraph 7 with "Verdana, 10, Green" combination is ok and is clear than the paragraph 5 and 6, observing that the readers have positive approach towards this combination.

Paragraph 8 with "Verdana, 12, Green" combination is ok but looking a bit larger, unattractive and same problem as in paragraph 4.

Table 3 *Description*: Column with column head "paragraph" represents the paragraph provided with different typographical combination.

Columns 2 & 3 represent the subjective judgment averages obtained in [7,8]. Where the Questionnaire is evaluated, then the user's data is converted from qualitative data into quantitative data for better understanding and comparison. For the conversion of qualitative measures into quantitative measure, Categories are assigned to some numeric values, that as Excellent = 0.6, V-Good = 0.5 … V-Bad = 0.1 and then each numeric value is multiplied by the number of user's chosen option respectively. That is;

$$0.6 \times X1 + 0.5 \times X2 + 0.4 \times X3 + 0.3 \times X4 + 0.2 \times X5 + 0.1 \times X6 = \text{Average}.$$

Where Xx is the number of user select the respective category/choice.

Average for male and average for female column are generated because the study involves different number of males and female participants in respective studies and needs to have same effects on the average of different combination text line for improve reading. The averages for columns 4-6 are calculated by standard mathematical formula.

The **Table 3** and **Figure 1** show the understandability and clarity for each combination, specified in each paragraph for both genders. The overall average in the **Table 3** shows the clarity of each combination and in chart the BAR height shows the clarity of each paragraph. Each

Table 3. Understandable measures.

Paragraphs	Subjective Judgment Average		Average for Male Participants	Average for Female Participants	Overall Average
	Male	Female			
Paragraph 1	15.3	11.2	0.3558	0.35	0.3529
Paragraph 2	20.7	17.5	0.4813	0.5468	0.5141
Paragraph 3	23.3	19.5	0.5418	0.6093	0.5756
Paragraph 4	20.7	15.4	0.4813	0.4812	0.4813
Paragraph 5	11.7	7.3	0.2720	0.2281	0.2501
Paragraph 6	19.5	15.3	0.4534	0.4781	0.4658
Paragraph 7	22.5	18.4	0.5232	0.575	0.5491
Paragraph 8	19.6	12.1	0.4558	0.3781	0.4169

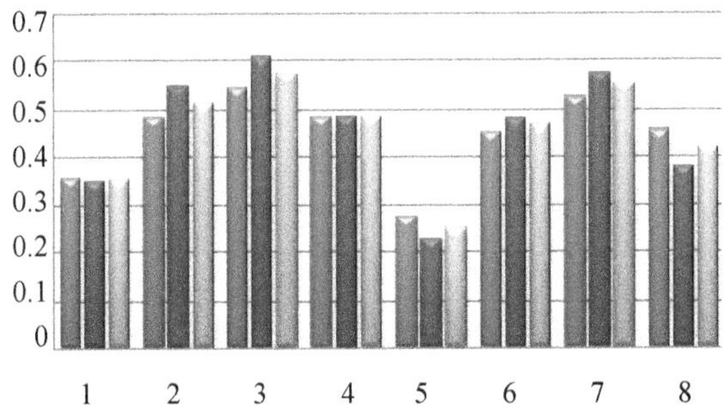

Figure 1. Graphical display of entries for understandability.

combination can be ranked in the order as paragraphs 3, 7, 2, 4, 6, 8, 1 & 5. The combination in paragraph 3 "Verdana, 10, Black" and paragraph 7 *i.e.* "Verdana, 10, Green" showed the most promising results in terms of understandability and clarity which is one of the essences of reading.

5.2. Look and Feel "Appearance"

Another very important measurement of reading from the screen is appearance or good look of the textual information that is to be presented. The analyses contain fifty percent of questions regarding appearance of each combination. The users were asked to rate the different combination on the basis of "the degree of pleasant appearance or good-looks of the paragraph based on fonts' style and size".

Average perception that were deduce from the reader during discussion on each paragraph.

Paragraph 1 with combination "Time New Roman, 10, Black" is looking very nice but not comfortable; the text is not easy to read.

Paragraph 2 with combination "Time New Roman, 12, Black" is looking very much nice and nice to read. Observed that the user like the chemistry of the font. Most of the users like the font style.

Paragraph 3 with combination "Verdana, 10, Black" is very much simple and very stable and much comfortable, enjoying reading.

Paragraph 4 with combination "Verdana, 12, Black" is looking boring, irritating, very simple and extra large.

Paragraph 5 with combination "Time New Roman, 10, Green" is appearing nice but too much uncomfortable, looking shaky and flashy because the white background has less contrast with green foreground, therefore reading this combination is more irritating.

Paragraph 6 with "Time New Roman, 12, Green" combination is very nice in appearance comparing to other combinations.

Paragraph 7 with "Verdana, 10, Green" combination is ok and fair enough.

Paragraph 8 with "Verdana, 12, Green" combination is ok but looking a bit larger, unattractive and boring.

Table 4 *Description*: **Table 4** shows facts and figures for attractiveness and good look of each combination. Column with column head "paragraph" represents the paragraph provided with different typographical combination. Columns 2 & 3 represent the subjective judgment averages obtained in [7,8]. Where the Questionnaire is evaluated, then the user's data is converted from qualitative data into quantitative data. For the conversion of qualitative measures into quantitative measure, Categories are assigned to some numeric values, that as Excellent = 0.6, V-Good = 0.5 ... V-Bad = 0.1 and then each numeric value is multiplied by the number of user's chosen option respectively. That is;

$0.6 \times X1 + 0.5 \times X2 + 0.4 \times X3 + 0.3 \times X4 + 0.2 \times X5 + 0.1 \times X6 = \text{Average}$.

Where Xx is the number of user select the respective category/choice.

Average for male and average for female column are generated because the study involves different number of males and female participants in respective studies and needs to have same effects on the average of different combination text line for improve reading. The averages for columns 4, 5 & 6 are calculated by standard mathematical formula.

The **Table 4** and **Figure 2** show the measures about the appearance or look and feel for each combination, specified in each paragraph for both genders. The overall average values in the **Table 4** and in chart the BAR height shows the attractiveness level of each combination. Each combination can be ranked in the order as paragraphs 2, 6, 7, 3, 4, 8, 1 & 5. The combination in paragraph 2 "Time New Roman, 12, Black" and paragraph 6 *i.e.* "Time New Roman, 12, Green" showed the most promising results for appearance.

Table 4. Measures for appearance.

Paragraphs	Subjective Judgment Average		Average for Male	Average for Female	Overall Average
	Male	Female			
Paragraph 1	16.7	12.7	0.3883	0.3968	0.3926
Paragraph 2	22	15.8	0.5116	0.4937	0.5026
Paragraph 3	22	15.3	0.5116	0.4781	0.4948
Paragraph 4	20.1	13.9	0.4674	0.4343	0.4509
Paragraph 5	14.7	12.5	0.3418	0.3906	0.3662
Paragraph 6	22.4	15.4	0.5209	0.4812	0.5010
Paragraph 7	21.7	15.8	0.5046	0.4937	0.4992
Paragraph 8	19.1	14	0.4441	0.4375	0.4408

5.3. Length of Text Line on the Bases of Eye Blink

The studies in [7,8] and the comparison presenting in this studies revolving around the concepts of length of text line on the based on eye blink during reading from computer screen, considering different typographical variables font size, style and color while some of the direct and indirect variable is considered as constant. The length of Text line was calculated for each Blink, average it for every paragraph for both the genders. The length is measured in three different units that are Characters per Line without spaces, Characters per line with spaces and length in Inches per line as shown in the subsequent **Table 5**.

The **Table 5** shows length of text line in three different measurable units which is explained below.

Character per line without spaces means that the number of spaces are not considered in suggested length of text line. The character per line with spaces means that the spaces are counted with characters where (±5 or ±7) means the number of spaces vary in range of 10 spaces per line that is 93 (±5) means 88 to 98 and 133 (±7) means 126 to 140. The length per line in C/L without spaces and Length per line in inches give us exact measure than the C/L with spaces.

Figure 3 shows length of line as Character per Line without spaces (spaces are not counted) for each combination of parameters. The paragraph 3 (Verdana, 10, Black) accommodate 116 characters per blink which is greater than all other combinations for both the genders and the overall result confirmed that the combination in paragraph 3 is most efficient. The combination in paragraph 7 and paragraph 2 accommodate 114 and 111 characters per blink respectively and so on.

Figure 4 shows the number of characters per line with spaces for one natural eye blink. The length is same as in above **Figure 4** but not precise and accurate like other units because the number of spaces varies up to ±5 or ±7 spaces per line and depends upon the words used.

Figure 5 shows length of text line of each combination in inches. As the length of paragraph 4 is longest one but it does not means that it is more efficient than other paragraphs because the number of words are less than from paragraphs 3, 7 & 2 because the size is bigger which increase the length of text line but accommodate less words.

6. Conclusions

Reading electronic text or textual material from computer screen considered more difficult than the paper text because of many reasons discus in Section 2. the crucial part is how to improve reading from the screen, the study suggest that the parameters involve in the text presentation must be use in a way which is easy and comfortable to the human eye naturally and according the human psyche. This study focus typographically parameters that closely related to the textual material *i.e.* Font size, style, color and background color in order to improve efficiency during reading while some of the parameters discus in the future work Sections 4.2 & 2.

The explanation for the legibility of moderate line

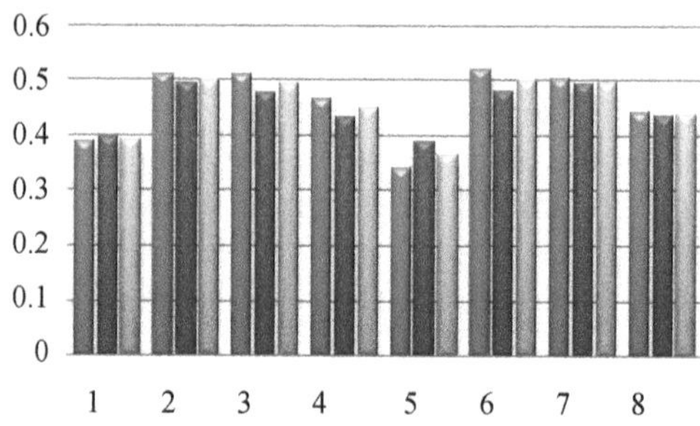

Figure 2. Graphical display of entries for appearance.

Table 1. Length of text line on the bases of eye blink for male, female and average.

Paragraphs	Character per Line without Spaces			Character per Line with Spaces			Character per Line in Inches		
	Male	Female	Average	Male	Female	Average	Male	Female	Average
Paragraph 1	77	71	74	93 (±5)	86 (±5)	89.5 (±5)	5.25	5.02	5.135
Paragraph 2	111	105	108	133 (±7)	122 (±7)	127.5 (±7)	9.13	9	9.065
Paragraph 3	116	110	113	141 (±7)	129 (±7)	134 (±7)	9.5	9.3	9.4
Paragraph 4	102	99	100.5	122 (±7)	117 (±7)	119.5 (±7)	10.74	10.5	10.62
Paragraph 5	74	72	73	87 (±5)	81 (±5)	84 (±5)	4.87	4.88	4.875
Paragraph 6	96	91	93.5	115 (±7)	109 (±7)	112 (±7)	8.13	8.03	8.08
Paragraph 7	114	108	111	134 (±7)	124 (±7)	129 (±7)	10	9.3	9.65
Paragraph 8	96	97	96.5	111 (±7)	110 (±7)	110.5 (±7)	10	10.02	10.01

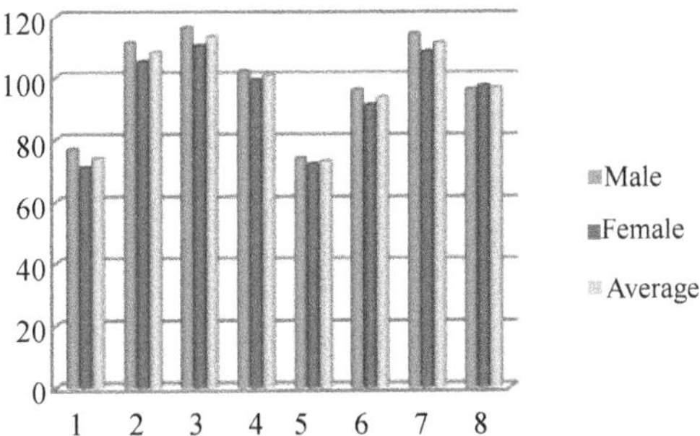

Figure 3. Length of text line based on eye blink character per line without space.

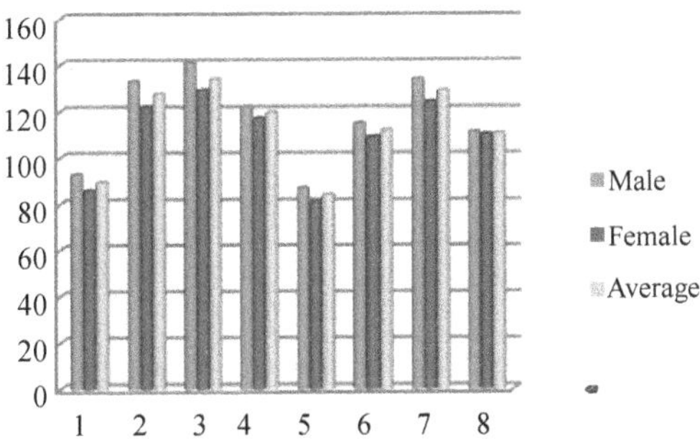

Figure 4. Length of text line based on eye blink character per line with spaces.

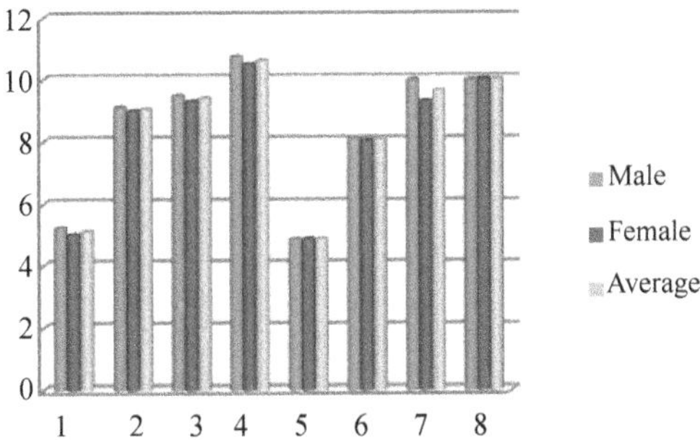

Figure 5. Length of text line based on eye blink character per line (in inches).

length is that it is the outcome of a trade-off between two opposing factors. One; if line lengths are too long, the return sweeps to the beginning of the next line are difficult. Second; if the lines are too short, readers cannot make use of much information in each fixation [22].

The study compare the studies in [12,13] done for both the "male and female" genders. Focus of the study is to suggest suitable length of text line for web page or online reading, while keeping Eye forefront. On the bases of eye blink suggest the suitable length of text line considering different typographical variables *i.e.* font style, font color, and font size with white background. This scrutinize illustrate three important things about various combination of standards. One; the length of text line on the bases of eye natural blink for female, second; understandability or clarity, third; the good attractive appearances of the combinations. The study suggested the Length of Text Line in three units of different standards combinations. Presenting these text materials for reading through internet or generally from computer screen in the suggested line length will deduce the problems of causing reading, by converting maximum focus losses to minimum ones. The study proves that "paragraph 3"; the combination "Verdana, 10, Black" shows overall promising results for efficient line length, understandings, and for attractiveness. The combinations in paragraph 2 and paragraph 7 are the competitive combinations showing good results in all three aspects. These recommendations serve materials that study online or from computer screen, for example Thesis, e books, research papers etc. In simple words, during designing electronic text for reading from computer screen, the recommendations should be considered for different combinations to achieve maximum efficiency.

7. Future Work

As computer technologies are improving so rapidly and the use of computer system is increasing in parallel. So it is the demand of present era to facilitate computer user with easy and comfortable web contents whether its images, layouts, or textual information. The main source of conveying knowledge to general user of computer is textual information through online reading or reading from computer screen.

Online reading is affected by different reasons.

Typographic variables.

These are the most influential factors that directly affect online reading (handle in this study).

Foreground and background text colors.

There are two type of text display *i.e.* Positive text; black text on white background and Negative text; white text on black background. Beside these two combinations there may be some more comfortable combination also exist but the selection of these combination should be on the bases of "which combination is naturally suitable to human eye and produce less eye strain and increase productivity and efficiency" during reading from computer screen. High contrast may not be the optimum criteria for the selection of these two colors.

Medical Factors that affect reading from the screen.

The study is based on eye blink which is affected by different reasons, e.g. Environmental factors can indirectly affect eye blink such as humidity, temperature and pollutants etc, and cognitive factors such as speaking, memorizing, mental arithmetic, focused reading, concentration.

In simple words in the selection of any solution the main source of human perception *i.e.* eye should be kept forefront, think which solution will naturally support human eye and psyche.

REFERENCES

[1] K. Garland and Associates, "Designers: 20 Years Work and Play 1962-82," Garland, 1982

[2] T. Nelson, "The Secret of Human Life," 1987.

[3] Google Data Center vs. Microsoft Infrastructure, 2006. http://dondodge.typepad.com/the_next_big_thing/2006/06/google_data_cen.htm

[4] Internet World States, "World Internet Users and Population Statistics," 2012. http://www.internetworldstats.com/stats.htm

[5] R. Conrad, "Computer Screens, TV's and Flicker Sensitivity," Subliminal Flicker Part I.

[6] Pasadena Eye Associates, "Frequently Asked Questions". www.pasadenaeye.com/faqs.html

[7] A. V. Kak, "Relationships between Readability of Printed and CRT-Displayed Text," *Proceeding of Human Factors Society*, *25th Annual Meeting*, Vol. 25, No. 1, 1981, pp. 137-140.

[8] R. S. Kruk and P. Muter, "Reading Continuous Text from Video Screen," *Proceeding of Human Factors*, Vol. 26, No. 3, 1984, pp. 339-3345.

[9] Smedshammar, *et al.*, "Why Is the Difference in Reading Speed When Reading from VDUs and from Paper Bigger for Fast Readers then for Slow Readers?" *WWDU* 1989, *2nd International Scientific Conference*, Montreal, 1-4 May 1989.

[10] J. Nielsen, "Designing Web Usability: The Practice of Simplicity," New Riders Publishing, Indianapolis, 2000, p. 420.

[11] Bradley Wilson Readability First at wilsonbrad@aol.com

[12] M. Khan, M. Raza and N. Rashid, "Appropriate Length of Text Line with Special Relationship to Eye Blink to Reduce Maximum Focus Loss," *International Conference on Internet Computing*, Las Vegas, 12-15 July 2010, pp. 97-102.

[13] M. Khan and M. Raza, "Suitable Length of Text Line on the Bases of Eye Blink for Reducing Maximum Focus Losses," *International Journal of Computer Applications*, Vol. 37, No. 8, 2012, pp. 15-21

[14] A. Weber, "Ueber die Augenuntersuchungen in Den Hoheren Schulen zu Darmstadt," Abtheilung fur Gesunheitspflege, Marz, 1881.

[15] H. Cohn, "Die Hygiene des Auges in den Schulen, Leipzig. [See Tinker and Paterson, 1929]," 1883.

[16] Tinker and D. G. Paterson, "Studies of Typographical Factors Influencing Speed of Reading: Length of Line," *The Journal of Applied Psychology*, Vol. 13, No. 3, 1929, p. 205.

[17] M. A. Tinker, "Legibility of Print," Iowa State University Press, Ames, 1968.

[18] M. D. Jackson and J. L. Mcclelland, "Processing Determinants of Reading Speed," *Journal of Experimental Psychology*, Vol. 108, No. 2, 1979, pp. 151-181.

[19] R. L. Duchanicky and P. A. Kolers, "Readability of Text Scrolled on Visual Display Terminals as a Function of Window Size," Vol. 25, No. 6, 1983, pp. 683-692.

[20] M. E. J. Masson, "Rapid Reading Processes and Skills," In: G. E. Mackinnon and T. G. Waller, Eds., *Advances in Theory and Practice*, Vol. 4, Academic Press, Orlando, 1985, pp. 183-230.

[21] K. Rayner and A. Pollatsek, "The Psychology of Reading," Lawrence Erlbaum, Hillsdale, 1989.

[22] M. Dyson and G. J. Kipping, "The Effects of Line Length and Method of Movement on Patterns of Reading from Screen," *Visible Languages*, Vol. 32, No. 2, 1998, pp. 150-181.

[23] M. Youngman and L. Scharff, "Text Width and Margin width Influences on Readability of GUIs," 1998.

[24] M. C. Dyson and M. Haselgrove, "The Influence of Reading Speed and Line Length on the Effectiveness of Reading from Screen," Department of Typography & Graphic Communication, The University of Reading, Reading, 2001.

[25] M. Beernard, M. Fernandez and S. Hull, "The Effects of Line Length on Children and Adults' Online Reading Performance," Usability News, 2002.

[26] B. Bailey, "Optimal Line Length: Research Supporting How Line Length Affects Usability," 2002.

[27] A. D. D. Shaikh, "The Effects of Line Length on Reading Online News," Usability News, 2005. http://psychology.wichita.edu/surl/usabilitynews/72/LineLength.htm

[28] R. Hall and P. Hanna, "The Impact of Web Page Text-Background Color Combinations on Readability, Retention, Aesthetics, and Behavioral Intention," *Behavior & Information Technology*, *Forthcoming*, Vol. 23, No. 3, 2004, pp. 183-195.

[29] City of Seattle Web Presentation and Accessibility Standards Version 2.5: Revised by Internet Board, Approved by the Technology Board, January 2009. Originally Approved 2003 by the Web Governance Board and the Business Management Council.

[30] M. Raza, SZABIST Islamabad Pakistan, "Perception of Participants about Font's Readability, Style, Youthfulness and Fun, Business Likeness and General Preference," *The* 2008 *International Conference on Semantic Web and Web Services*.

[31] "Reconstruction of Eye Movements during Blinks," Max-Planck-Institut für Physik Komplexer Systeme, Nöthnitzerst.

[32] Spontaneous Blinking in Healthy Persons, "An Optoelectronic Study of Eyelid Motion," Functional Anatomy Research Center (FARC), Università degli Studi, Milano.

[33] L. E. Ebite, T. C. Ozoko and A. O. Eweka, "Rate of Blinking among Medical Students in Delta State Nigeria: Is the Eyelid a Polygraph?" *The Internet Journal of Ophthalmology and Visual Science*, Vol. 6, No. 2, 2009.

[34] Standard font size. http://www.ixda.org/node/19341

[35] L. F. Bacher, "Factors Regulating Eye Blink Rate in Young Infants," *Optometry and Vision Science*, Vol. 87, No. 5, 2010, pp. 337-343.

[36] H. ur Rasheed, Eye Specialist, Saidu Medical College, Saidu.

[37] L. F. Bacher and P. S. William, "Spontaneous Eye Blinking in Human Infants: A Review," *Developmental Psychobiology*, Vol. 44, No. 2, 2004, pp. 95-102.

10

The Study and Application of the IoT in Pet Systems

Chung-Ming Own[1], Haw-Yun Shin[2], Chen-Ya Teng[3]

[1]Department of Computer and Communication Engineering, St. John's University, New Taipei City, Chinese Taipei
[2]Department of Computer Science and Engineering, National Taiwan Ocean University, Keelung City, Chinese Taipei
[3]Department of Computer Science and Information Engineering, Tamkang University, New Taipei City, Chinese Taipei

ABSTRACT

The interaction between human and physical devices and devices in the real world is gaining more attention, and requires a natural and intuitive methodology to employ. According to this idea and living well, life has been a growing demand. Thus, how to raise pets in an easy way has been the main issue recently. This study examines the ability of computation, communication, and control technologies to improve human interaction with pets by the technology of the Internet of Things. This work addresses the improvement through the pet application of the ability of location-awareness, and to help the pet owners raise their pet on the activity and eating control easily. Extensive experiment results demonstrate that our proposed system performs significantly help on the kidney disease and reduce the symptoms. Our study not only presents the key improvement of the pet monitor system involved in the ideas of the Internet of Things, but also meets the demands of pet owners, who are out for works without any trouble.

Keywords: Internet of Things; Wireless Sensor Network; Pet System

1. Introduction

Over the past half century, computers have exponentially increased in processing power and simultaneously decreased in both size and price. This rapid change indicates that computers participate in more daily activities in society. Computers are becoming smaller and cheaper, and the single-purpose computers with embedded sensors are practical from both economical and theoretical viewpoints. Wireless sensor networks have attracted increasing attention and play a vital role in connecting everything in our lives.

Today users are more and more immersed into a complex ubiquitous information. To capture handy information, make use of context information and interact directly with the physical object is the main request in our modern world with the mobile client. That's the main issue of the internet of things (IoT). The IoT provides a set of standards and methodologies to associate object in the real world. There are several approaches for the provision of applications that make such interactions as possible [1,2]. In 2000, the term IoT appears to have been coined by a member of the RFID developer, who referred as the discovering tag information corresponds to a particular RFID. Since that time, people have sized on the phrase "Internet of Things" to refer as the general connection of things, especially to those objects, that are readable, recognizable, locatable, addressable, and controllable via the Internet [3]. In [4], Kranz *et al.* developed various prototypes to explore novel ways for human computer interaction to realize the appliance of IoT. For example, they make some prototypes to demo the context-aware kitchen utilities, included an instrumented cutting board, vision and sound-based activity detection system, activity recognition using body-worn sensors, and a sensor-augmented knife net gets to infer the context and activities occurring in the kitchen. In addition, the intelligent environment can learn, recognize, and use behavior to provide a variety of novel services to household members. Besides, the authors used policy-aware object design to develop health and safety-aware smart objects as an appliance of IoT, which acts as a smart barrel with embedded storage rules for various chemicals. Depending on temperature, vibration, and barrels' relative proximity, it informs workers about safety violations and prompts them to take appropriate action [5]. Hence, by embedding computational capability's sin all kinds of objects and living objects, IoT will be possible to provide a qualitative and quantitative leap in several sectors: healthcare, logistics, education, entertainment, and so on. In fact, one of the most import elements in the IoT is wireless sensor networks (WSNs) and the extension of ubiquitous computing [6].

WSNs consist of a large number of unattended, self-organized microsensors, which are scattered in an area for a specific application. Each microsensor senses data from the environment, performs simple computations, and transmits the data over a wireless medium either directly to the command center or through a cluster gateway. Although WSNs are similar to networks, they differ from networks for their energy constraints, markedly larger density of sensor nodes, lower cost, and precise design for information-gathering [7]. The current trend is to move away from proprietary standard to embrace IP-based sensor networks using the 6LoWPAN/IPv6. This allows the peer connectivity between WSNs and Internet, which is enabling smart objects to participate to the IoT. This integrated factor plays a significant role in our study.

Because of the low birth rate in Taiwan, researchers should focus more on the rapid changes in lifestyle. Some studies indicate that when people go to a park on the weekend, more of them are walking dogs than carrying babies. According to a June 2006 report from Pet Care Services in the United States, America's pet care service generated approximately 363 million USD in revenue in 2005. The annual growth rate of this service should reach 6% in the future [8]. In addition, Eastern Europe and Asia will become potential markets for pet services. Meadows and Flint indicated that a low birth rate and weakening links between family members have increased the importance of pets [9], leading to a corresponding rise in pet services.

This study attempts to improve pet appliances with the ability of location-awareness, and to help pet owners raise their pets easily. Although numerous automatic pet monitoring systems exist, such as automatic pet doors and pet feeders, these systems cannot meet the needs of pet owners. For example, most pet care systems are based on infrared detector/recognition, which can be used to spot pets at the door, register their movements, and alert owners when pets enter areas where they are not allowed. This infrared detector design has some disadvantages because infrared detectors can be influenced easily by various factors. The detection cannot be correctly recognized. According to the author's previous study, own has built a prototype of the pet system with the cyber-physical-system idea [10]. Herein, the author implements the system with the IoT infrastructure and applied the case study on cat raising.

Accordingly, the organization of this paper is as follows. A brief review of pet products and WSN platforms are given in Section 2. The proposed system modeling is presented in Section 3 while the experiment and analysisare discussed in Section 4. Finally, the conclusion is presented in Section 5.

2. Preliminaries

2.1. Pet Care Solution

As Taiwanese society continues to have a low birth rate and an aging population, increasingly more people regard their pets as family members. This trend is reflected in pet-related products and activities. For example, some pet owners have started bringing their pets with them while traveling. A report from the 2010 Asia Pacific Pet Economic Conference mentioned that the pet industry has grown considerably in recent years [11]. They forecasted that the market would double in the following two years. Families in Taiwan raised 1,630,000 dogs than in 1999. The family average has 1.55% dogs in 2007. Conversely, only 195,000 cats were in families in 2001, and the total increased to 281,000 in 2006 [9]. This is an increase of 4.4% per family, and we concluded the average family has 1.6% cats. According to a report of the council for economic planning and development, more than 166,000 babies were born in Taiwan in 2009, representing a drop of more than 20,000 from the previous year [9]. Thus, Taiwan's birthrate has dropped to the world's lowest at 8.29%, with only under one baby born per woman over a lifetime. The average family has more pets than children. This means that the demand for pet products will grow quickly, and household spending on pets will exceed that for children. The pet industry and pet owners have gradually begun to realize the demand for automated raising devices.

Pet doors are one of the most common products in the market, and various types of pet doors are available for cats and dogs. Pet doors can be fitted in a lower portion of a wall or an existing full-sized door. A pet door may consist simply of a flap hung from a horizontal axis. This flap swings open, against the force of gravity, when pushed by an animal. A simple latch may hold the door in a closed position to prevent the movement of the door in either direction. The problem with this simple construction is that any animal small enough to fit through the opening may gain entry or egress, depending on the position of the latch. To prevent passage of unwanted stray animals, electronic pet doors have been designed with magnetically operable latches. In this type of design, any magnetic tag of adequate field strength can unlock the latch.

Pets face many of the same problems as humans, such as obesity, diabetes, and stomach problems. Automated feeding machines can provide for the care of such pets. Several automated pet feeders on the market are capable of dispensing kibbles, and some are capable of feeding canned food. Feeding kibbles prevent food spoilage, whereas feeding canned food does. Canned food cannot be left in a device for prolonged periods because it spoils. Besides, pets also tend to be restless when owners are not at home, and they become hyperactive when owners return. It is occasionally necessary for pet owners to reinforce pet behavior by providing food for certain behaviors they may want the pet to perform. Automated feeding machines is just invented for pet owners demand.

There are many automatic pet feeders for feeding pets at predetermined times during an owner's absence. This type of pet feeder comprises a base, a feeding bowl with pie-shaped divisions, a timer module, a bowl cover, and a locking mechanism to hold the entire unit in place. The timer provides programmed feeding schedules that determine the time the bowl cover closes or opens. This programming can be achieved through the timer interface or RF and IR remote controllers.

2.2. The Technology and Architecture of IoT

The "things" in the IoT not only be referred as "connected together", but also can be realized the functions of recognition, localization, tracing, management and so on. IoT requires all things must can be identified. Generally, the RFID technology is the "speaking technology" for these things on IoT. The RFID technology possessed an outstanding status in the IoT technology. A typical RFID system consists of RFID tag, reader and the application. An agreement from code data preserved in the RFID tag, it can mark objects uniquely. However, without the battery support, the serious disadvantage is the short communication distance of the passive HF RFID tag. Thus, in our study, for the purpose to extend the communication distance, we used the sensor network tags for instead.

To describe the IoT with a technical perspective, the relative study derived the IoT with three parts in the 2011 [12]. The first part is the hardware device layer or the sensing layer. This physical layer occupies less space, making it easier to connect practically anything, anywhere, anytime. The technology of WSN is an outstanding advantage of the IoT in this layer, not only can gain objects' environment information, but can also distinguish each object precisely.

The Second part is the infrastructure or the network layer. This layer consists of converged network formed by all kinds of communication network and internet. It has been widely accepted that this part is the maturest part. Besides, the IoT management center and information center are the parts of network layer. That is, the network layer not only has the ability of network operation, but also should improve the ability of information operation. Besides, with millions of devices connected to the Internet, 3G or LTE technology won't be able to work with. Although the 3G business is growing, the capacity of the mobile networks is acting as a bottleneck. Hence, to take advantage of these opportunities, the WSNs must be open to the wider public.

The third and last part consists of the applications and services that use the vast quantity of information created by the IoT, it's the application layer. The application layer combined with industry expertise to achieve a broad set of intelligent application solutions. This applications also involve creating new business models and very interesting business initiatives in terms of innovation. The main purpose of the IoT application layer is to provide the information services, and it mainly consisted of three parts, IoT client side, data storage module and data inquiry module.

In our study, we follow the IoT architecture to construct our pet monitor system. The hardware of the first part is based on the WSNs. These sensor nodes are varying in size and depend on the size because different sizes of sensor nodes work efficiently in different fields. In the present era, there are many technologies which use for monitoring are completely based on the wireless sensor networking. Some of the important applications are environmental monitoring, traffic control application, weather checking, and regularity checking of temperature [13]. Wireless sensor networks can also use for detecting the presence of vehicles such as motor cycles up to trains. In our system, the pet wears the collar with sensor tag as an identification. **Figure 1** is the example of collar design. Our proposed system can organize as the first pet monitoring system based on the WSN.

Besides, the system infrastructure of the second part is designed to meet the needs of the pet owner. General speaking, home is small and pet sets are messy, WSN is the best choice to build the network structure. Thus, the system is open to the wider public; the pet owner can connect to the gateway at home to control/schedule the pet activity. Furthermore, in the final part, our system supports the following services, the first one is the smart pet door, the pet owner can restrict the pet activity from the outdoor to indoor. The second service is the smart pet feeder, with this system help, the pet owner can schedule the open time of the eating bowl remotely. Thus, the pet can eat food on the health and efficiency control.

3. The Proposed Pet System

In our study, the first device of the pet monitor system is the smart pet door, which can help the pet owner to con-

Figure 1. The sensing tag on the collar.

trol the pet activity. The other device is the smart pet feeder. With the system help, the pet owner can schedule the pet eating bowl time remotely, and make the eating environment on the health and efficiency control.

3.1. The Smart Pet Door

Many families install a pet door for their pets. Pet doors are adapted to be fitted in the lower portion of a wall or existing full-sized door. Pet doors allow family pets to pass the door easily. **Figure 2(a)** shows the system diagram of the pet door. The pet door system consists of one control server, one smart pet door, several environment nodes, and the tag on collars. The pet wears a sensing tag on its collar, and the collar broadcasts the pet ID for every 20 seconds continuously. **Figure 1** shows the collar design. The pet door detects the pet's location and periodically requests the pet activity list from the server. Accordingly, when the device on the pet door receives the broadcast packet from the pet tag, the device will measure the estimated distance by the *RSSI* (Received Signal Strength Indicator) value between them, the measuring equation is listed as follows,

$$RSSI = -\left(10n\log_{10} d + A\right) \quad (1)$$

In (1), n is signal propagation constant or exponent, d is the distance from sender and A is the received signal strength at 1 meter distance [14].

In this study, the proposed system is based on the following rules:

- The pet tag broadcasts the pet ID for every 20 seconds continuously.
- An item identification can detect the animal seeking passage through the pet door. Because the node of WSN is the active tag, the sensing range is about from 1 m to 2 m. The pet door will unlock when the activity list is permitted.
- The pet owner can set the different passage permission for the different pets. Thus the specific pet, for example, the sick pet, can be forbidden to go outside. The passage permission will store in the control server.
- Aled light can indicate the pet owner where the pet is located. In this case, the pet owner doesn't need to whistle the pet for making sure the location; the led indicator can show the pet location. This indicator costs less power, but can gain more conveniently.
- The environment nodes can report the weather to the server for every 10 minutes, the pet owner can set the weather rules to control the curfew. For example, if it's raining outdoors, the pets must come home but get no permission to go outside.
- If there are more than one pets around the pet door, the pet door will arrange the pet priority by their RSSI values. Then check the activity list from the control server by their sequence.

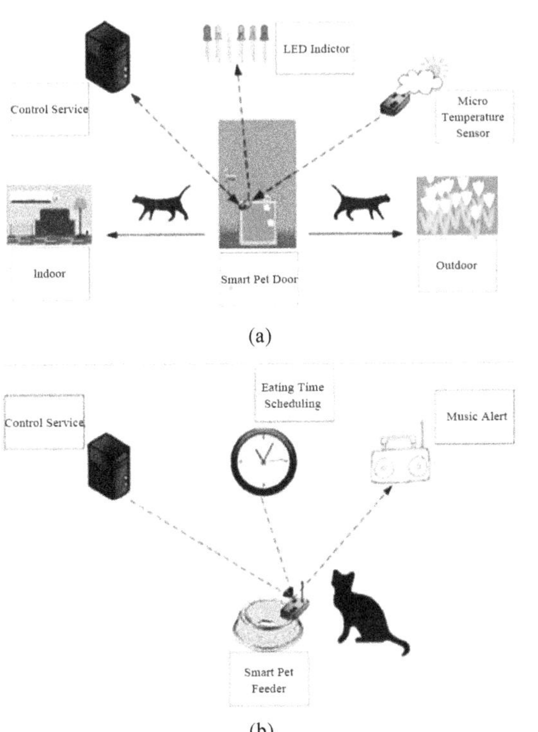

Figure 2. The diagram of pet system with (a) the smart pet door; (b) the smart pet feeder.

Figure 3 shows the interior design of the smart pet door. The WSN module is installed on the upper right of the pet door as the control and communication center, which is responsible for receiving the pet id and driving the control motors shown in **Figure 3(a)**. **Figures 3(b)** and **(c)** show the tow motors; the tow motors in **Figure 3(b)** is used to unlock the pet door, and the tow motor in **Figure 3(c)** controls the swing direction of the flap. **Figures 3(d)** and **(e)** show the light motion sensors installed on the top panel over the pet door. These sensors are used to detect the flap swing direction, and the system can use this data to trigger the LED at the top of the pet door, which can indicate the pet location to the pet owner. For example, a red LED indicates that the pet is indoors, whereas a green LED indicates that the pet is outdoors.

We compared the proposed system with the general product of Staywell [15], as shown in **Table 1**, to identify the differences between these systems. Because the Staywell product is based on magnetic tag sensing, the cost and power supply is lower than those in our smart pet door. However, according to previous discussions, our system is designed based on the support of pet owner demand. The power saving is another advantage of WSN. Hence, our system exhibits dominance.

3.2. The Smart Pet Feeder

Most pets eat dry food. Pet owners cannot leave out wet

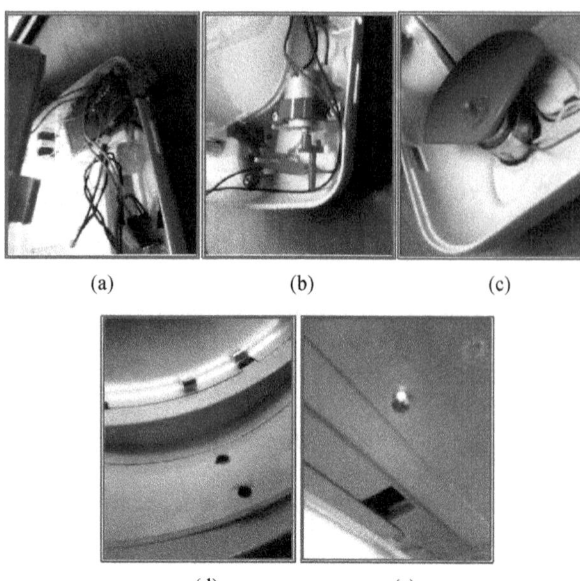

Figure 3. The outlook of the pet door, (a), (b) and (c) show the tow motors, (d) and (e) are the light motion sensors.

Table 1. The comparison between our proposed smart pet door and the general product.

	Smart Pet Door	General Pet Door [15]
Cost	Higher	Lower
Power Supply	Higher	Lower
Pet Tag	Sensor Tag	Magnetic Tag
Active Schedule	Support	No
Remotely Control	Support	No
Position Indicator	Support	No
Environment Control	Support	No
Pet Identification	Support	No

food because it spoils in the time the pet must eat it. Dry food feeders can keep dry food fresh to longer, and allow the owner to feed a pet automatically, even when outside the home. These feeders are nearly always placed on the floor next to an external wall where they are accessible to crawling insects, such as ants, which have a propensity to seek a supply of food. These insects not only contaminate the pet food, but are often intolerable to the pet owner.

Numerous attempts have been made to design a pet feeder that resolves the problem of crawling insects. Most of these efforts have produced feeders with a multiplicity of discrete components. These feeders must be disassembled for cleaning and then reassembled before further use. The pet feeder produced by the trading company has the general appearance of a conventional feeder, but has a moat-forming cavity surrounding the food bowl [16]. This pet feeder can keep the pet food and water clean until the pet is ready to eat. This pet feeder also has a bowl cover that opens and closes automatically. The bowl cover is actuated by an infrared proximity sensor and battery-operated electric motor. The sensor detects the presence of the pet and then opens the cover, enabling only the pet to have access to the food. When the pet is out of sensor range, the bowl cover closes automatically. This keeps dust, flies, and bugs from reaching the food and keeps the food fresh. The pet feeder system consists of on control server, one smart pet feeder, and the tag on collars.

In this study, our proposed smart pet feeder is based on the following design rules:

- The pet tag broadcasts the pet ID for every 20 seconds continuously.
- An item identification can detect the animal seeking passage through the pet feeder. Because the node of WSN is the active tag, the sensing range is about from 1 m to 2 m. The pet feeder will remove the bowl cover when the eating activity is permitted.
- The pet owner can set the eating permission for one pet to one feeder. Thus, only the granted pet can approach the feeder for food. Besides, most of the pets have deeply locality of animal behavior, share food is not common for them.
- The pet owner can schedule eating time remotely, and prevent the unwelcome insects by closing the bowl cover in the non-eating time.
- The pet owner can record the greeting voice to alert the eating time.
- During the eating time, the pet is free to approach for food.
- If there are more than one pets around the pet feeder, the pet feeder will arrange the pet priority by their RSSI values. Then check the eating activity list from the control server by their sequence.

Figure 4 shows the interior design of the smart pet feeder. **Figure 4(a)** shows the feeder device. This study referred to the feeder product, which has four bowls. **Figure 4(a)** also shows the embedded sound playback module, which is used to play the received playback command from the WSN module. **Figure 4(b)** shows the inside view of the smart pet feeder, in which the WSN module can drive the rotation gear in the middle of the feeder to remove the bowl cover, and is also responsible for receiving the signal of pet id, checking the RSSI value, controlling the voice greeting, and triggering the bowl cover to open or close.

The difference between our proposed smart pet feeder and the product from the Trading Company is shown in **Table 2** [14]. As shown in **Table 2**, our smart pet feeder has a higher cost and larger power supply because of the WSN module. Traditional feeders in the market do not support pet identity recognition, and do not require tags.

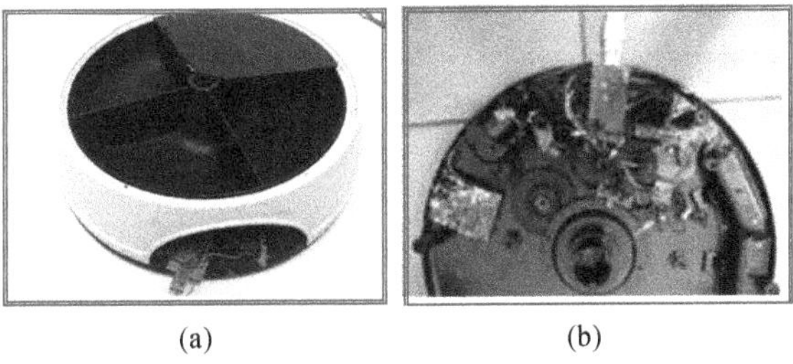

(a) (b)

Figure 4. The outlook of the pet feeder, (a) is the feeder device, (b) is the inside view of the feeder.

Table 2. The comparison between our proposed smart pet feeder and the general product.

	Smart Pet Feeder	General Pet Feeder [14]
Cost	Higher	Lower
Power Supply	Need	Need
Pet Tag	Need	No
Eating Schedule	Full Functional Support	Partly Support
Bowl Cover	Full Automatic Support	Partly Support
Remotely Control	Support	No
Pet Identification	Support	No
Voice Greeting	Support	No

With the function of identity recognition, our proposed system can fulfill the requirement of pet owners than traditional products. For example, the comparison product supports the setup of an eating schedule in the front panel; however, it lacks the convenience of our system. By contrast, our system enables the owner to set the eating schedule on web page remotely, which can help the pet to moderate its eating habits.

3.3. The Control Center

Figures 5(a) and **(b)** show the proposed management system of the control service. **Figure 5(a)** is the Window executed program, which can help the pet owner to execute on the PC. A php program can be remotely executed on the mobile device for the pet owner convenience in **Figure 5(b)**. In our management system, the pet owner can upload the pet image to the corresponding pet id. Furthermore, the micro temperature (temperature and humidity), pet activity permission, eating time schedule; all the user defined data can be defined in this software and stored at the control server.

4. Experiments and Analysis

Mrs. Lee, who lives in an apartment with a balcony in Taipei, Taiwan, was applied as our experimental case. She has two cats, one of which is young and energetic, and the other is old and has kidney disease. Generally, kidney disease or kidney failure is the most common medical problem experienced by older cats. Several cats with kidney disease can survive for months or years after diagnosis. However, kidney disease is not curable. The disease is chronic and progressive, and results in fatality in most cases.

The goal of treatment for kidney disease is to reduce the symptoms and slow the progression of the disease. The main forms of treatment are dietary change and fluid therapy, and dry food is not recommended. A low-protein diet was previously recommended to help to reduce the workload of the ailing kidneys. Thus, in the past, the old cat was isolated in a cage because of the distinct treatments for both cats. However, Mrs. Lee desired superior treatment for her cats. Therefore, we installed our system in her apartment as a one-month experiment.

Mrs. Lee previously installed a small pet door for her cats. We installed our smart pet door on the sliding door to the balcony. Our smart pet door enabled the cats to go to outdoors, and the activity schedule restricted the older

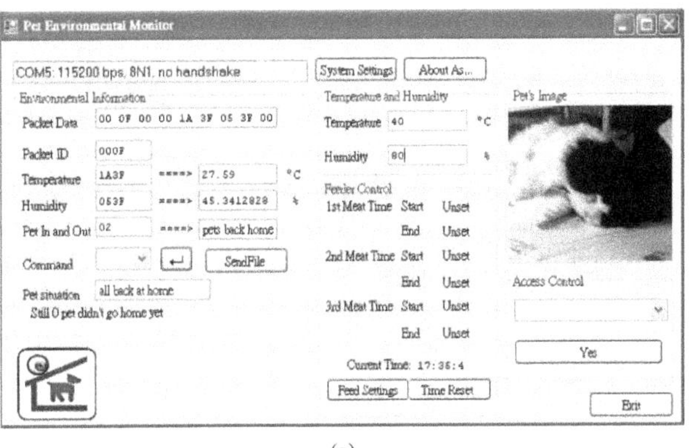

(a)

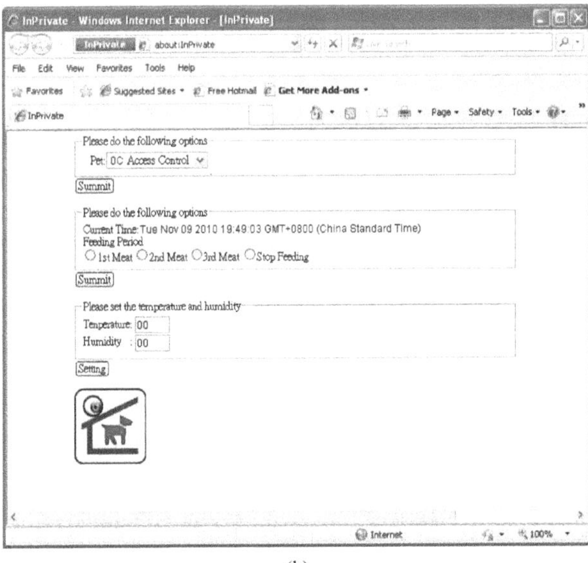

(b)

Figure 5. (a) The System management for windows; (b) The system management program for web.

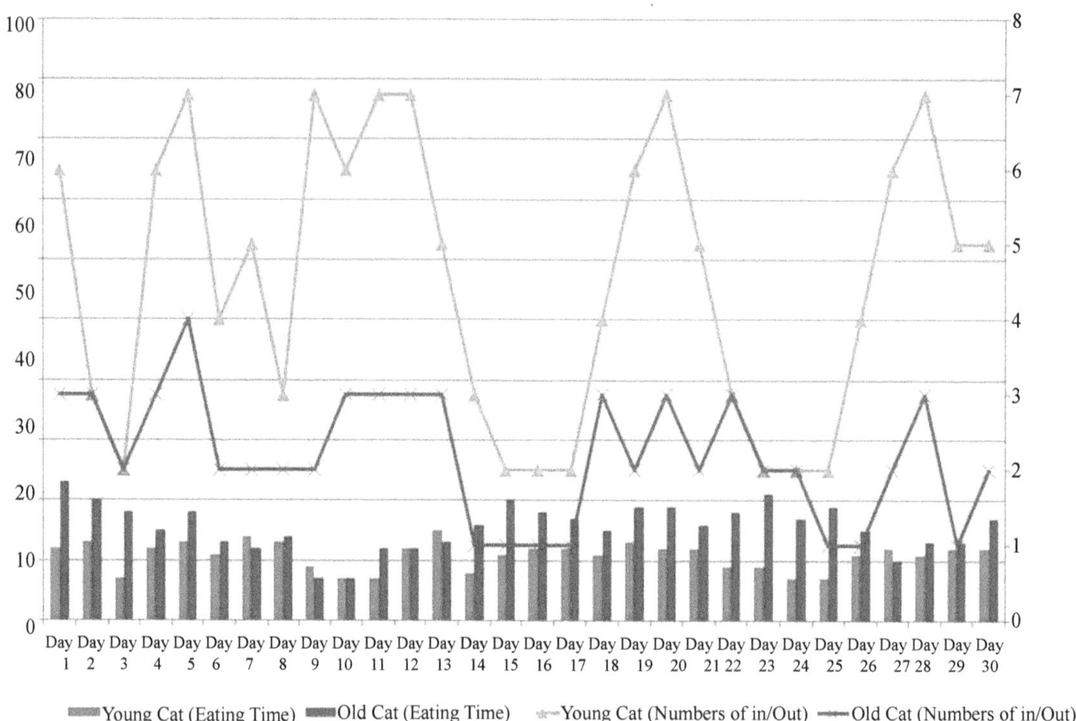

Figure 6. The experiment of two cats in the Mrs. Lee apartment.

cat from remaining on the balcony for long periods. Our system provided two smart pet feeders for both cats, which supplied them with different meals at each feeding time. We record the eating time for each cat as the illness tracking. The cats wore different pet tags for identity recognition.

Figure 6 shows the experimental results of the two cats in Mrs. Lee's apartment. With the help of the smart pet care system, we collected in and out numbers of the apartment and the eating times of the two meals for both cats. Because the old cat had kidney disease and was restricted to the balcony at night, the number of ins/outs was lower than those of the young cat (The average ins and outs were 4.6 per day for the young cat, and the average number was 2.2 for the old cat). The prescription food for the old cat was not as appealing as the normal food; therefore, the eating time was longer (The average eating time was 10.8 minutes per day for the young cat, and the eating time of the old cat was 15.5 minutes per day).

5. Conclusions and Future Work

The interaction between humans and physical devices and objects is attracting increasing attention. Many studies have attempted to provide a natural and intuitive approach to request services. The current trend of combining pet control and IoT technology offers exciting future developments. The proposed system is also referred on smart-home technology, including the smart pet door and pet feeder. The results not only present the key improvement of the pet monitor system involved in the IoT technology, but also meet the demand of pet owners.

The basic vision behind the IoT, it may have a new way of operational method, it may have a new method of connecting devices, and there might be the even complete clean-slate approach. As the full operational definition is not yet finalized, there are numerous research issues that can be worked on. As a next step, we will fully integrate the other pet care devices into our system, including litter boxes, pet cam, etc. With that, the diverse needs of the owners can be met, and the health, monitor, and entertainment topics for pets are all covered. Besides, standing as the cloud term, how to connect the numerous networking devices around the globe is the next issue. In the future, we will centralize on the study of the IoT gateway and long distance detection of the pets.

6. Acknowledgements

The author thanks the National Science Council of the Republic of China, Taiwan for partially supporting this research under Contract No. NSC 101-2221-E-129-014.

REFERENCES

[1] M. Rohs and B. Gfeller, "Using Camera-Equipped Mobile Phones for Interacting with Real-World Object," *Proceedings of Advances in Pervasive Computing*, April 2004, pp. 265-271.

http://catalog.hathitrust.org/Record/004761231

[2] C. Sammarco and A. Lera, "Improving Service Management in the Internet of Things," *Sensors*, Vol. 12, No. 9, 2012, pp. 11888-11909.

[3] H. Ning and H. Liu, "Cyber-Physicl-Social Based Security Architecture for Future Internet of Things," *Advanced in Internet of Things*, Vol. 2, No. 1, 2012, pp. 1-7.

[4] M. Kranz, P. Holleis and A. Schmidt, "Embedded Interaction Interacting with the Internet of Things," *IEEE Internet Computing*, Vol. 14, No. 2, 2010, pp. 46-53.

[5] G. Kortuen, F. Kawsar, D. Fitton and V. Sundramoorthy, "Smart Objects as Building Blocks for the Internet of Things," *IEEE Internet Computing*, Vol. 14, No. 1, 2010, pp. 44-51.

[6] I. F. Akyildiz, W. Su, Y. Sankarasubramaniam and E. Cayirci, "Wireless Sensor Networks: A Survey," *Computer Networks*, Vol. 38, No. 4, 2002, pp. 393-422.

[7] A. L. Bleda, A. J. Jara, R. Maestre, G. Santa and A. F. G. Skarmeta, "Evaluation of the Impact of Furniture on Communications Performance for Ubiquitous Deployment of Wireless Sensor Networks in Smart Homes," *Sensors*, Vol. 12, No. 5, 2012, pp. 6463-6496.

[8] APPEC, Asia Pacific Pet Economic Conference. http://www.2010appec.org

[9] Packaged Facts, "Pet Care Services in the US," 2nd Edition, 2006.

[10] C.-M. Own, "For the Pet Care Appliance of Location Aware Infrastructure on Cyber Physical System," *International Journal of Distributed Sensor Networks*, Vol. 2012, 2012, 8 Pages.

[11] Council for Economic Planning and Development 2009. http://www.cepd. gov.tw/

[12] G. Feller, "The Internet of Things: In a Connected World of Smart Objects," Accenture & Bankinter Foundation of Innovation, 2011.

[13] J. Yick, B. Mukherjee and D. Ghosal, "Wireless Sensor Network Survey," *Computer Networks*, Vol. 52, No. 12, 2008, pp. 2292-2330.

[14] Chipcon: CC2420 802.15.4 Compliant Radio. http://www.chipcon.com.

[15] The Staywell International. http://www.staywell.co.uk

[16] Automatic Pet Feeder. http://gadgets.softpedia.com/

11

Intelligent Video Surveillance System for Elderly People Living Alone Based on ODVS

Yiping Tang, Baoqing Ma, Hangchen Yan
Zhejiang University of Technology, Hangzhou, China

ABSTRACT

Intelligent video surveillance for elderly people living alone using Omni-directional Vision Sensor (ODVS) is an important application in the field of intelligent video surveillance. In this paper, an ODVS is utilized to provide a 360° panoramic image for obtaining the real-time situation for the elderly at home. Some algorithms such as motion object detection, motion object tracking, posture detection, behavior analysis are used to implement elderly monitoring. For motion detection and object tracking, a method based on MHoEI(Motion History or Energy Images) is proposed to obtain the trajectory and the minimum bounding rectangle information for the elderly. The posture of the elderly is judged by the aspect ratio of the minimum bounding rectangle. And there are the different aspect ratios in accordance with the different distance between the object and ODVS. In order to obtain activity rhythm and detect variously behavioral abnormality for the elderly, a detection method is proposed using time, space, environment, posture and action to describe, analyze and judge the various behaviors of the elderly in the paper. In addition, the relationship between the panoramic image coordinates and the ground positions is acquired by using ODVS calibration. The experiment result shows that the above algorithm can meet elderly surveillance demand and has a higher recognizable rate.

Keywords: Intelligent Surveillance; Elderly People Living Alone; ODVS; MHoEI Algorithm; Pose Detection; Abnormal Behavior Recognition

1. Introduction

According to the investigation of the UN, the number of people over 65 in China will be 12.7% of the total population in 2030 [1], and the number of elderly persons who lived alone increased rapidly in recent years. As for this proliferation of the elderly, kinds of remote care services need to be provided. In 2003, GE Company made a global research on caregivers' stress of taking care of the elderly who lived alone [2], at the top of the stress list is fall. According to another report [3], after 65 years old, 30% of the person will significantly fall within a year. And after 75 years old, this proportion will reach 42%.

At present, a variety of cameras or sensors are adopted to obtain the real-time situation for the elderly at home, and elderly abnormality is judged according to the above situations. According to abnormality type and credibility, some correction measurements are advanced in order to notify the guardian or those concerned. There are different support systems depending on the different signal acquisition methods. In general, elderly home health care technology can be classified into three kinds, home monitoring technology based on image understanding, activity signal and physiological sensor.

For the home monitoring technology [4,5] based on physiological sensor, elderly physiological parameters including ECG, blood pressure, respiration, blood glucose, body temperature, and so on are acquired with using physiological sensor in real time and the condition of elderly healthy is judged. With using this method, the elderly who suffer from chronic diseases can be not only monitored effectively, but the early symptoms of the disease are also found. However, the issue of surveillance is that the elderly often forget to wear this equipment, depending on the ability and willingness of the elderly.

As for the home monitoring technology based on activity signal, the water/gas/electricity data is obtained by using human activity sensor, switch sensor or flow sensor installed in elderly home [6]. By analyzing activity data for the elderly within a period of time, the behavior pattern is established to judge abnormal activities for the elderly and to implement the health care of the elderly.

For the home monitoring technology based on image understanding, the state of the scene is guarded through the scene camera device firstly. In the following, the scene images are transmitted by the internet or other communication methods. As for the distant guardian, the scene situation of the elderly is mastered with analyzing the scene images from the distance. To reduce the workload of the remote monitoring personnel, the scene images are preprocessed with using image processing technology, data mining technology, etc.

With the development of computer vision technology, sensor technology and telecommunication, the care support system for the elderly based on computer vision gradually comes into people's vision in recent years. Some scholars obtain the condition of daily life [7,8] by using video image, and lots of results are achieved in some horizons. However, the motion object is lost in tracking easily because there is a blind area for the camera. To solve this problem, Huei-Yung Lin *et al.* proposed an intelligent surveillance system using an Omni-directional CCD Camera [9]. The research effectively carried out the problem that there is a blind area for the camera. But the system still has some short comings. For example, the tracking algorithm is so complex that a large amount of computing resources and storage resources are consumed. The fall judgment (not combine environmental factors) is so mechanized that miscarriage of justice is brought. The tracking object is lost when it expands the unwrapped edge line. The tracking data cannot be used to study the life pattern for the elderly, so that it is difficult to analyze and judge other abnormal behaviors of the elderly.

In this paper, an ODVS is adopted to provide a 360° panoramic image. According to the ODVS calibration result and Bird-View image, a one-to-one correspondence is established between the ground locations and the panoramic image coordinates. For motion detection and object tracking, we propose a method based on MHoEI to obtain the trajectory and the minimum bounding rectangle information for the elderly. The posture of the elderly (such as sitting, lying, standing, squatting, etc.) is judged by the aspect ratio of the minimum bounding rectangle. Finally, elderly abnormal behaviors are described, analyzed and judged with using time, space, environment, posture and action, etc.

2. Technical Details

2.1. Panoramic Image Acquisition and Calibration

To accurately and completely detect abnormal behaviors for the elderly, surveillance equipment should be installed in some important places such as the living room, the bedroom, the bathroom, the kitchen, etc. This strategy not only improves the monitoring cost, but also makes fall detection algorithm become relatively complex. Although the monitoring equipment is installed in many different places on indoor, it still does not work out how elderly fall is detected on outdoor. In this work, an ODVS is installed in the main place of daily life for elderly such as in the middle of the living room. This system will be able to monitor the mostly daily activities for elderly. **Figure 1** shows an ODVS used for the study and its panoramic image. The imaging principle and design are introduced in References [10].

A relationship can be conveniently established by the calibration of ODVS between the image pixels and the locations on the ground. Since the space is limited, the specific calibration algorithm references the literature [11,12].

2.2. Object Tracking

Object tracking will be a precondition for posture recognition, action recognition and behavior recognition. Recently, there are some tracking algorithms, such as Meanshift algorithm, Camshift algorithm, the algorithm based on feature matching, the algorithm based on shape and size, etc. However, the above algorithms will spend a lot of computing resources and involve a mount of calculation. In this work, an ultimate aim is to obtain the high-level behavior semantic of target object through analyzing the intelligent video image. Therefore, a rapid and efficient MHoEI algorithm is proposed.

To track the target object effectively, a key point is to hold a fast efficient algorithm. For MHI (Motion History Images) algorithm and MEI (Motion Energy Images) algorithm, the calculation is recursive. And the latest information is just saved with using the two algorithms. So the two algorithms are in accord with the above requirements.

The motion history image is obtained by using the MHI algorithm after the Inter-frame Difference processing and the Gray processing are used at a time intervals. The motion profile template of target is accurately obtained with using MHI algorithm and the MHI algorithm involves a very small calculation. Meanwhile, the MHI

Figure 1. An ODVS and its panoramic image.

algorithm can be used to create a motion gradient image by calculating the orientation and magnitude of the gradient given by the Sobel operator. The resulting gradient can be further used to estimate the direction of motion flow of the object. The motion object foreground is obtained by using the Inter-frame Difference processing and not using the background modeling. So the MHI algorithm have a high real-time and the calculation method is also extremely simple. However, the motion history image is not obtained if the motion object has stopped. In addition, when the foreground object is in temporarily stable state on the whole and some in motion, the MHI algorithm can only detect the foreground object that is in motion. For example, the arms constantly swing when the human body is in a resting state. Now the MHI algorithm can only detect the hands. The MHI updating equation is given by

$$H_\tau(x,y,t)=\begin{cases} ts\cdots\cdots \text{if } D(x,y,t)=1 \\ 0\cdots\cdots \text{if } D(x,y,t)=0 \text{ and } \\ \qquad H_\tau(x,y,t-1)<ts-dur \\ H_\tau(x,y,t-1)-1\cdots\cdots \text{otherwise} \end{cases} \tag{1}$$

where *ts* is the current time and *dur* is the duration time. For the duration time *dur*, a determining factor is a range of motion. So it is obtained through a series of dynamic search.

The motion energy image is obtained by using the MEI algorithm after the summation of Inter-frame Difference image processing is used at a time intervals. It is called binary cumulative motion energy image. The MEI updating equation is given by

$$E_\tau(x,y,t)=\bigcup_{}^{\tau-1} D(x,y,t-i) \tag{2}$$

where $I(x,y,t)$ is video image sequence, $D(x,y,t)$ is the motion region of the binary video image sequence. $D(x,y,t)$ is generated by Inter-frame Difference image in many applications.

MEI and MHI are the two different action properties of vector image coding. Since the calculation of both algorithms are recursive and the latest information is just stored with using the MHI and the MEI, the two algorithms make the calculation become fast and efficient. We note that the match is different between the MEI and the MHI in some cases. To give the difference between the match criteria, we should distinguish the movement where the movement occur and how to carry out in fact. The MEI algorithm mainly solves where the movement occur. The MHI algorithm mostly solves how to move for the foreground object.

As for the foreground object tracking, there are two states, movement state and static state. For the motion foreground object, MHI algorithm is adopted with selecting an appropriate duration *dur* and the motion object can be accurately detected. For the temporary stationary foreground object, it will gradually disappear over time. However, the temporarily stationary foreground object does not gradually disappear with using the MEI algorithm over time. Nowadays it is difficult to track the foreground object for each algorithm.

To solve this problem, a MHoEI (Motion History or Energy Images) algorithm is proposed which is fast and efficient in this work. The MHoEI updating equation is given by

$$H_\tau(x,y,t)=\begin{cases} ts\cdots\cdots \text{if } D(x,y,t)=1 \\ H_\tau(x,y,t-1)\cdots\cdots \text{if } D(x,y,t)=0 \\ \qquad \text{and } V\le\delta \\ 0\cdots\cdots \text{if } D(x,y,t)=0 \text{ and } V>\delta \text{ and} \\ \qquad H_\tau(x,y,t-1)<ts-dur \\ H_\tau(x,y,t-1)-1\cdots\cdots \text{otherwise} \end{cases} \tag{3}$$

where V is the velocity of the foreground object, *ts* is the current time and *dur* is the duration time. The duration time can be dynamically adjusted according to the foreground object velocity. In general, the faster the foreground object moves, the smaller the *dur* value is. And the slower the foreground object moves, the larger the *dur* value is. The gray value of foreground object is not subtracted one when the velocity of foreground object is less than or equal to a threshold δ. For the stationary foreground object, it will not gradually disappear over time. **Figure 2** shows a flow chart about MHoEI algorithm.

As for the motion object velocity, it is computed by the center of minimum bounding rectangle. We consider that (x_t, y_t) is the center point of minimum bounding rectangle in the *tth* frame, and (x_{t+1}, y_{t+1}) is the center point of minimum bounding rectangle in the $(t+1)th$ frame. Then the pixel distance is computed by the distance Equation (4). So the actual distance ΔS is obtained by the ODVS calibration and *S*. Finally, the motion object velocity is computed according to the equation $V=\Delta S/\Delta t$, where Δt is the running time of each frame.

$$S=\sqrt{(x_{t+1}-x_t)^2+(y_{t+1}-y_t)^2} \tag{4}$$

Since the geometric projection model of ODVS is different from the conventional CCD camera, there are some deformations for the motion object in the panoramic image. And the panoramic image cannot meet the visual habits and it is not convenient for computer processing. To solve the problem, Huei-Yung Lin *et al.* [9] proposed a approach that the motion target is tracked in 360° unwrapped image. The unwrapped algorithm is introduced in References [10]. However, the motion target

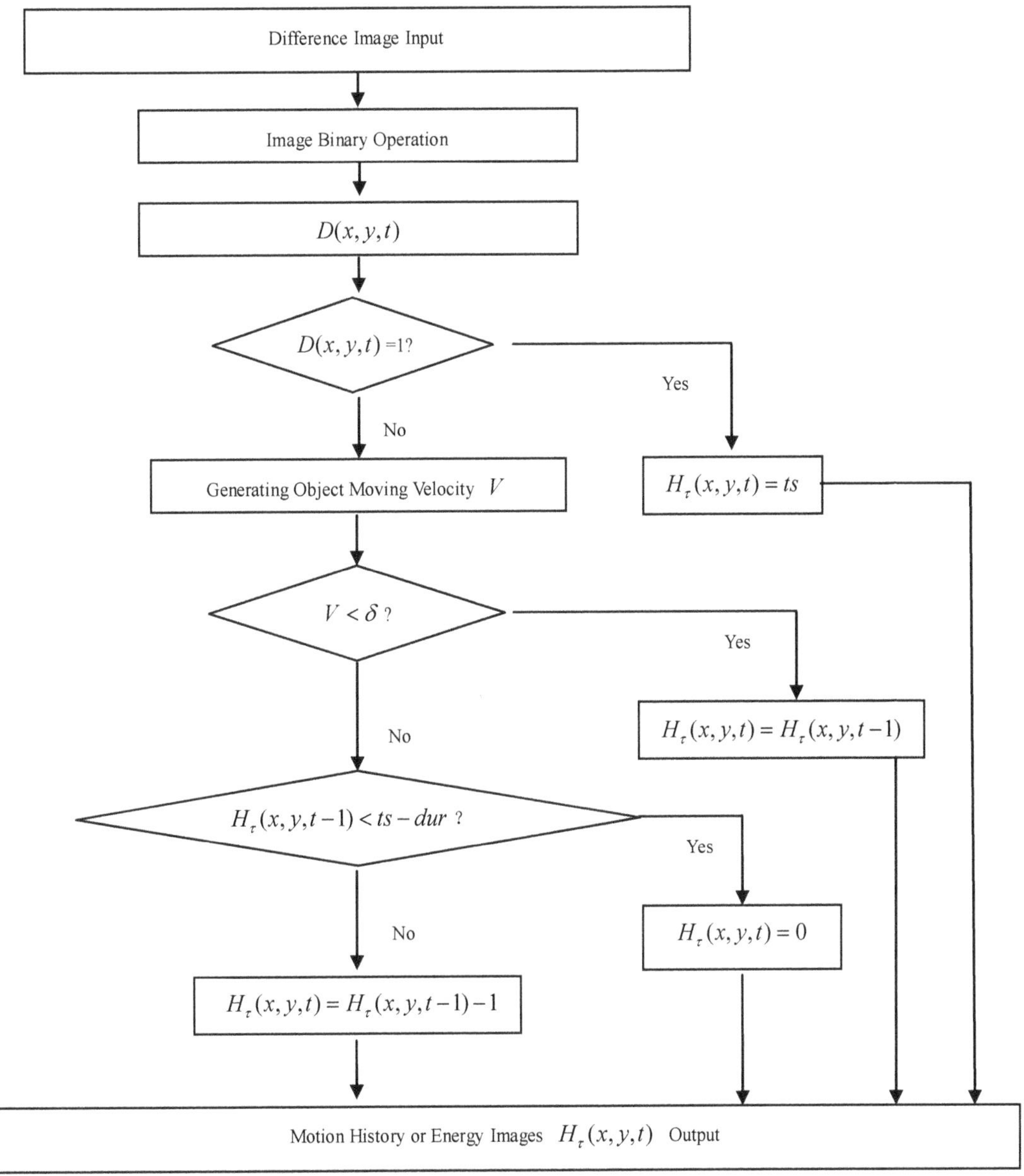

Figure 2. MHoEI algorithm flow chart.

is considered as two different targets when the motion target is near to the edge of 0° or 360°. To solve this problem and keep the integrity and continuity of tracking object, the 20° overlap region is increased in the originally unwrapped image in this paper. **Figure 3** shows a 380° unwrapped image with tracking result.

2.3. Customization for Home Environment

At the time of paying attention to the target object for human beings, the environment where the target object is located is concerned in the first place, and then the specific behavior of the object is judged. Accurate information cannot be obtained if you only rely on the human action to identify the behavior. Although the sitting during a meal and the sitting on the sofa are the same action, the behavior which is described by the action is different. It is difficult to recognize the behavior with relying on the simple action. The master purpose is easily understood if the scene where the action is taken place is used.

Almost all the environmental elements belong to static object. It is extremely difficult to use computer vision to recognize the static object. Meanwhile, there is no need to use computer vision to analyze a variety of complex environmental factors in the practical application of intelligent video surveillance. Computational resources are spent when the environmental elements will be accurately recognized, and we need a huge knowledge base. Therefore, a customization method is used for the static camera device in home environment.

As for the customization method in home environment, the physical space is divided into a number of grids in the video image in this paper. Then a one-to-one correspondence is established between the foreground objects and the environment elements. The environment element where the target object is located is judged so long as the foreground object is in a grid.

Since the panoramic image have serious distortion on the imaging plane, especially in a horizontal position, it is generally difficult to extract the geometric features from the panoramic image. To easily set up the one-to-one correspondences between the image pixels and the locations on the ground and custom all kinds of environmental elements in home, the Bird-View image is adopted to customize the environmental information in this paper. Since the space is limited, we will introduce the Bird-View transform algorithm in the other papers. Two letters are used for giving the grid a name. The first letter means the line. The second letter means the column. **Figure 4** shows the Customization method in home environment.

(a) when the object not through 360 °expansion line

(b) when the object has passed through 360 °expansion line

Figure 3. Tracking result in unwrapped image (+20°).

Figure 4. Customization method in home environment.

In the Bird-view image, AH refers to the bathroom entrance. EI refers to the room entrance. BC and BG refer to the ground in the living room. BE refers to the bathroom in the living room. BD refers to the stool in the living room. For example, the human posture is determined as the sitting when the tracking box is located on the BE number which is customized as the bathroom, then we think elderly sit on the bathroom. If the tracking box disappears on the EI number, we can judge the elderly out the door. If the tracking box disappear on the AH number, we can judge the elderly into the bathroom.

2.4. Posture Detection

As for elderly surveillance, the standing, the sitting and the lying are defined as the human basic posture in this work. P is a set of the human basic posture:

$$P = \{\text{standing}, \text{sitting}, \text{lying}\} \tag{5}$$

The human target can be detected when it is only in motion and the posture $p(t) \in P$. The human target is considered as keeping the original posture if it is not in motion. Since the human image achieved through motion detection is a high-dimensional image signal and is not recognized easily, a great deal of time has been wasted on dealing with them. To make high-dimensional image signal decrease 2-D signal, the human posture is described with using the minimum bounding rectangle of the foreground object. W is the width of the rectangle. H is the height of the rectangle. This bounding rectangle can be directly obtained from the low-level visual processing. The human posture ratio is given by $k = H/W$, as the characteristic of describing the human posture. The posture (in middle-distance region) is distinguished through compiling the different posture ratio of human daily action k, and setting the threshold by the minimum error probability criterion. **Table 1** shows the feature threshold in middle-distance region.

However, there are all sorts of human posture in fact. According to the above detection criterion, the standing will be recognized as the sitting if the arm is in expansion. To solve the above problem, comprehensive judgments are made according to tightness, solid degree, eccentricity, irregularity, etc.

Posture caused by the human unusual action misjudgement is eliminated with constructing the posture evaluation function. The posture evaluation function is given by

$$S = F/S(T) \tag{6}$$

Table 1. Feature threshold in middle-distance region.

Posture	Standing	Sitting	Lying
Threshold k	$k \geq 1.8$	$0.7 \leq k < 1.8$	$k < 0.7$

$$F = \sum_{(x,y)\in T} I(x,y) \tag{7}$$

$$S(T) = W \times H \tag{8}$$

where F is the area of the foreground object and $S(T)$ is the minimum bounding rectangle area of the foreground object. From the function, we can see that the function value varies in the range [0,1]. The evaluation function have the highest value when $S(T) = F$. While the human arm is in expansion, the evaluation function value becomes very low. For example, the posture is considered as undefined posture if evaluation function value is very low. In certain case, the human posture is not recognized. **Figure 5** shows human posture recognition results. The experimental results show that the posture can be accurately recognized in the case of the definition posture

2.5. Abnormal Behavior Detection

The detection of abnormal behavior is a core of the care support system of the elderly with using ODVS. In this work, we want to establish a low-cost abnormal behavior detecting system for the elderly and the privacy can be protected in this system. This system can automatically notify the relevant department or the guardian when the abnormal behaviors can be detected. In addition, the guardianship can monitor the activities of the agent through the web page at any time in elderly home. To implement effective automatic monitoring for the elderly, the identification of behavior is essential under different illumination conditions. To accurately identify the elderly behavior, we should describe, analyze and judge the elderly behavior by using time, space, environment, posture, action, etc.

With this in mind, the set of abnormal behaviors is a Cartesian product of the sets:

$$b = (t, a, p, e) \tag{9}$$

where t\in T, p\in P, a\in A, and e\in E. And T refers to time information. P refers to posture information that it is obtained by posture detection. A refers to action information that is acquired by action recognition. E refers to

Figure 5. Human posture recognition results.

environment information which is created by the home environment customization operation. Every human behavior can be described by *T* code, *P* code, *A* code and *E* code. *TPAE* coding system not only provides some means for decomposing, identifying and describing human behavior diversity, but also provides a coding system for computer vision analysis.

3. Experimental Results

Our system was implemented using Eclipse on a PC using Intel Core i3 2.13GHz CPU with 4GB RAM. The panoramic video sequences are with a size of 640 × 480, 25 fps, captured by an ODVS. The resolution of unwrapped image is 740 × 180 dpi. To achieve the panoramic image in elderly room, we install ODVS in the middle of the room and the height of ODVS is about 1800 mm.

In order to evaluate the system performance, We conduct an experiment in the meeting room of 80 square meters. 50 volunteers between the ages 20 and 30 years old are asked to sit the practical. At the same time, the volunteers have different weight, height and genders. They act 6 kinds of behaviors by 6 times in the elderly room. **Table 2** shows the experiment result.

From this result, we recognize that the proposed method is stable and efficient. In this table, Sum refers to number of actions, *Y* is the number of correct detection events, N is the number false detection events and R is the accurate rate.

To validate performance of the surveillance system, we make use of two well-known criteria that are universally applied to abnormal detection systems. Sensitivity is the capacity to detect an abnormal behavior and Specificity is the capacity to detect only an abnormal behavior:

$$\text{Sensitivity} = \frac{TP}{TP+FN}, \text{Specificity} = \frac{TN}{TN+FP} \quad (10)$$

The definitions of TP, FP, FN and TN are as follows:

	Abnormal behavior Occur	Abnormal behavior Not occur
System recognition positive	TP	FP
System reconition negative	FN	TN

Table 2. The experiment result of behavior recognition.

Behavior	Sum	Y	N	R
Run	135	125	10	92.59
Sit Down	135	120	15	88.89
Stand Up	135	127	12	94.07
Lie Down	135	126	9	93.33
Get Up	135	124	11	91.85
Fall	135	129	6	95.56

According to above method, we do some experiments with 1266 abnormal/normal behaviors and 386 abnormal behaviors. **Table 3** shows the evaluation of abnormal behavior recognition. According to the test data, Sensitivity and Specificity of the surveillance system will be 94.04 and 97.16 respectively.

Human object tracking is the critical technique of elderly care support. In order to testify the effectiveness of the MHoEI algorithm, the paper carried out the experiment of tracking, which showed that in comparison with ordinary methods the MHoEI algorithm is characteristics of evident effects and stable operation. **Figure 6** shows the experimental results of tracking a man.

The experimental results show that the motion target can be tracked steadily with using the MHoEI algorithm in some cases such as from motion to stationary for the target, from stationary to motion for the target, a different

Table 3. Evaluation of abnormal behavior recognition.

	Abnormal behavior Occur	Abnormal behavior Not occur
System recognition positive	363	36
System reconition negative	23	1230

(a) Tracking result in walking

(b) Tracking result in standing

(c) Tracking result in squatting

(d) Tracking result in lying

Figure 6. Experimental results of tracking a man.

posture for the target, environment brightness changes, background block, etc. And the interference caused by the similar color in the background can be overcome effectively with using the MHoEI algorithm. To give posture recognition and behavior recognition more time for the processing, the program processing speed is at a frame rate of 10 fps and can meet the requirements of real-time character. According to the trial experiment in few months, the phenomenon of tracking lost was not found. The result of study indicates that the MHoEI has a high robustness.

To improve the accuracy of posture recognition, the human minimum bounding rectangle image is saved in a JPG format, and the recognition results with time and posture are saved on a local disk storage unit. Some examples are shown in **Figure 7**.

In this work, both the sitting posture and the squatting posture are regarded as the sitting posture. As you can see from the experiment, the motion target is accurately recognized in different velocity, different direction and different state (motion and stationary). From the experiment, we can also see that the ratio of sitting is close to the ratio of lying or standing when the ODVS ray is parallel with the direction of lying or standing. In this case, the mistaken identifications are caused and judged as the sitting. Although it is a very small probability, we will eliminate the miscarriage by fusing the motion of the current frame with that of the previous frames.

4. Conclusions and Future Work

Intelligent surveillance is one of the important topics in the nursing and home-care system. In this work, we have proposed a care support system of the elderly with using ODVS. An ODVS is adopted to provide a 360˚ panoramic image in this paper. According to the ODVS calibration result and Bird-View image, a one-to-one correspondence is established between the image pixels and the locations on the ground. To achieve elderly trajectory and minimum bounding rectangle, a MHoEI algorithm is proposed. This result of study indicates that the algorithm has the advantages such as: less computation amounts, higher robustness and more effective tracking. Different posture of the elderly is determined by using the aspect ratio of the minimum bounding rectangle in the basic of effective tracking. The experiment result shows that the above algorithm can meet elderly surveillance demand and has a higher recognizable rate. In order to obtain activity rhythm and detect variously behavioral abnormality for the elderly, a detection method is proposed using time, space, environment, posture and action to describe, analyze and judge the various behaviors of the elderly in the paper.

Figure 7. Experimental results of posture recognition.

As for above proposed methods, some abnormal behaviors in the ODVS view are detected and recognized. But those abnormal behaviors are not found beyond the ODVS range of observation.

To obtain abnormal activity beyond the ODVS view, we will establish an activity rhythm model for the elderly in the future. Meanwhile, activity rhythm of the elderly is not a constant. There are different distributions of activity with the changing reasons or the increasing age. To accurately detect the abnormal activity and implement modified activity model, the reasons will be also considered. In addition, to find a deeper abnormal event and behavior and provide more effective auxiliary support for real-time monitoring, we should spend more time studying the daily life data by mining technology and neural network technology.

5. Acknowledgements

Great thanks to the support from the National Natural Science Foundation (Number: 61070134) towards this project and the assistance from elderly Surveillance Service Center in the experiment in the Tokyo Zone in Japan.

REFERENCES

[1] Y. P. Tang, W. Wang and Y. Z. Fu, "Elder Health Status Monitoring through Analysis of Activity," *Chinese Journal of Computer Engineering and Applications*, Vol. 43, No. 3, 2006, pp. 211-213.

[2] C. Paul, G. Meena, G. Catherine and W. Jenny, "Remote Monitoring and Adaptive Models for Caregiver Peace of Mind," *Proceedings of* 2003 *International Conference on Aging, Disability and Independence*, Washington DC, 4-6 December 2003, pp. 183-184.

[3] S. Andrew and J. Neil, "Smart Sensor to Detect the Falls of the Elderly," *IEEE Pervasive Computing*, Vol. 3, No. 2, 2004, pp. 42-47.

[4] M. E. Taylor, M. M. Ketels, K. Delbaere, S. R. Lord, A. S. Mikolaizak and J. C. T. Close, "Ait Impairment and Falls in Cognitively Impaired Older Adults: An Explanatory Model of Sensorimotor and Neuropsychological Mediators," *Age and Ageing*, Vol. 41, No. 5, 2012, pp. 665-669.

[5] S. H. Kim and D. W. Kim, "A Study on Real-Time Fall Detection Systems Using Acceleration Sensor and Tilt Sensor," *Sensor Letters*, Vol. 10, No. 5-6, 2012, pp. 5-6.

[6] H. Martin, H. Wang, K. Liam and M. Elean, "Monitoring of Activity Levels of the Elderly in Home and Community Environments Using Off the Shelf Cellular Handsets," *Proceedings of the* 2010 *International Conference on Consumer Electronics*, Las Vegas, 9-13 January 2010, pp. 9-10.

[7] B. T. Morris and M. M. Trivedi, "Trajectory Learning for Activity Understanding: Unsupervised, Multilevel, and Long-Term Adaptive Approach," *IEEE Transaction on Pattern Analysis and Machine Intelligence*, Vol. 33, No. 11, 2011, pp. 2287-2301.

[8] P. H. Yuan, K. F. Yang and W. H. Tsai "Real-Time Security Monitoring Around a Video Surveillance Vehicle With a Pair of Two-Camera Omni-Imaging Devices," *IEEE Transaction on Vehicular Technology*, Vol. 60, No. 8, 2011, pp. 3603-3614.

[9] H. Y. Lin, M. L Wang, C. C Huang and B. W. Tsai, "Intelligent Surveillance Using an Omnidirectional CCD Camera," *Proceedings of the Automatic Control*, Peking University Press, Taipei, 2005.

[10] Y. P. Tang, Y. J. Ye, Y. H. Zhu and X. K. Gu, "The Application Research of Intelligent Omni-Directional Vision Sensor," *Chinese Journal of Sensors and Actuators*, Vol. 20, No. 6, 2007, pp. 1316-1320.

[11] D. Scaramuzza, A. Martinelli and R. Siegwart, "A Toolbox for Easy Calibrating Omnidirectional Cameras," *Proceedings of the IEEE International Conference on Intelligent Robots and Systems*, Beijing, 9-15 October 2006.

[12] B. MicksiK, "Two-View Geometry of Omnidirectional Cameras," Ph.D. Thesis, Czech Technical University, Prague, 2004.

12

A Wireless Body Sensor Platform to Detect Progressive Deterioration in Musculoskeletal Systems

Paul Hanley, Paul Fergus, Faycal Bouhafs
School of Computing and Mathematical Sciences, Liverpool John Moores University, Liverpool, UK

ABSTRACT

Recent developments in technology have helped to reduce the physical size and weight of devices and opened up new opportunities for their application in delivering unobtrusive healthcare services. In particular, kinetic and kinematic systems, that use sensors attached to the body, are currently being used to measure and understand many different aspects of human gait and behaviour. This has been particularly useful in treating stroke patients, rehabilitation, and understanding sedentary behaviour. Nonetheless, many of these systems are only capable of providing information about rudimentary movement rather than data on the mechanics of motion itself (tendons, ligaments and so on). Therefore, the information required by healthcare professionals to treat diseases like progressive deterioration of the musculoskeletal system, *i.e.* arthritis, cannot be determined. This paper discusses some of the technologies currently used to assess movement and posits a novel approach based on strain gauge technology to measure the constituent parts of a joint and its movement. In this way, the mechanics of motion can be studied and used to help detect and treat musculoskeletal diseases. A case study is presented to demonstrate the applicability of our approach.

Keywords: Sensors; Sensor Networks; Networked Medical Devices; Networked Appliances; Home Networking; Real-Time Monitoring; Preventative Technologies; High Precision Measurement

1. Introduction

The home environment, with its range of digital services, provides an opportunity to integrate and use healthcare services beyond current practice. This has the potential to provide huge benefits to different user groups, *i.e.* consumer electronics manufacturers, healthcare facilities and more importantly people. Yet, the market is still relatively unexplored and as such, there is a unique opportunity to utilize technology in novel ways and provide care in the community. There are good reasons for doing this. Perhaps most obvious is the fact that conditions are more often than not only detected when the effects of diseases are irreversible. For example, debilitating illnesses, such as arthritis, often diagnosed in later stages of cartilage and bone damage have been found to be on the increase. In the US alone, 27 million adults are diagnosed with clinical osteoarthritis making it a high ranking degenerative or aging disease [1]. Given that this places a considerable financial burden on national health services, preventing its onset and monitoring its progress are likely to have a significant and positive impact on the healthcare provider and those suffering with such diseases.

The challenge is to harness the power of technology. In particular, to utilize those technologies that are widely available in the home, such as smart phones and wireless routers. This would allow novel wireless body sensor systems to be developed that exploit these technologies and allow individuals to be unobtrusively monitored. It may not be possible to cure such conditions. However, sensors attached to the body will empower people, promote self-care in a familiar environment by suggesting compensatory changes to individuals and help avoid or mitigate long-term damage and effects.

The motivation for this research is to develop a wireless body sensor platform that incorporates pliable sensors attached to components of the musculoskeletal system, such as tendons, muscles, ligaments and cartilage for real-time monitoring of day-to-day activities. It should be noted that the results obtained could be more robust than short-term observations in an environment alien to the patient, such as a hospital or doctor's surgery. This paper considers the difficulties and possible solutions for achieving this.

2. Wireless Healthcare

Since the inception of mobile technology, devices have evolved into small and powerful computing devices that connect directly to public networks to provide and use Internet applications and services. Wireless technologies, such as Universal Mobile Telecommunications System (UMTS-3G) and High-Speed Downlink Packet Access (HSDPA-3.5G), wireless fidelity (Wi-Fi), and Worldwide Interoperability for Microwave Access (WiMAX) [2], have converged into a common IP network [3] and this has made it much easier for devices to interconnect and interoperate with each other. One domain exploring the use of such technologies is healthcare were new medical applications are being designed to optimize and deliver better healthcare services [4]. For example, personal area communication networks are increasingly being combined with wide area networking systems to collect and transmit data about people to medical facilities for the purpose of monitoring and treating different medical conditions in the community. The following section explores some of these solutions and how they are currently being used in medical applications.

2.1. Personal Area Communications

Personal area networking has been the focus of many research initiatives over the past several years and a great deal can be learnt from existing work in this area.

Perhaps the most well-known is the 802.15.1 (Bluetooth) wireless standard (http://www.bluetooth.com). Initially designed as a cable replacement technology it allows devices to communicate over short distances (between 1 - 100 m depending on the type or class of device) and has been used to deliver *ad hoc* medical services in residential homes and medical facilities. In particular, Bluetooth has been used as an alternative to restrictive communication technologies like infrared that require line of sight before devices can communicate with each other. This has allowed devices to become more mobile. Furthermore, the use of *ad hoc* networking protocols has enabled them to form part of different networks with little or no prior configuration. Once they connect to the network, they can immediately offer and use services provided by other devices within their locale. Based on the flexibility Bluetooth provides it has been implemented in a number of different systems, *i.e.*, hands free, game controllers, biofeedback and neurology (NeXUS-10) [2], and gait analysis systems (XSens) [3], to name a few.

Nonetheless, a number of questions have been raised about Bluetooth's high power consumption and the impact that this has on medical devices [4]. The Bluetooth radio can deflate battery life very quickly and this requires constant maintenance to ensure that devices remain operational. For this reason, it is generally regarded as less viable long-term wireless solution by many medical device manufacturers. The 802.15.4 (ZigBee) specification is considered a possible alternative [5]. Like Bluetooth, ZigBee devices offer their services in an *ad hoc* fashion by continually broadcasting small packets of data about their presence. ZigBee is designed to be a general purpose, inexpensive, self-organising, mesh network that can be used by many different types of application (industrial control, embedded sensing, medical data collection, alarm systems, and automation). In terms of performance it fairs much better than Bluetooth were ZigBee takes roughly 15 milliseconds to wake from sleep mode and send a packet of data whilst Bluetooth under the same test conditions can take roughly 3 seconds. This allows ZigBee devices to sleep often and thus conserve power [6-8]. One negative aspect of ZigBee is that it has deliberately reduced data rates, designed to help conserve energy. In many instances, medical devices will only be required to transmit small control and data packets so low data rates may not be an issue. If it is, then Wibree (Bluetooth low energy) (http://www.bluetooth.com), Near Field Communications (NFC) (http://www.nfc-f orum.org/home), or 6LowPan (http://www.ietf.org), with their larger data rates and lower power consumption features could be considered as an alternative.

While many device manufactures have incorporated wireless communication standards, there still remains a problem with how to manage power consumption as demands on the device increase (*i.e.* computation) [9]. A new platform investigating this issue is the Wireless Identification and Sensing Platform (WISP) (http://seattle.intel-research.net/wisp). WISP combines the sensing capabilities provided by sensors with the operational functions used by Radio Frequency Identification (RFID) [10]. RFID readers transmit radio frequency (RF) signals and these signals are used to power up and request data from WISP sensors. Once the data has been collected, the RF signal is terminated and the sensors are powered down. The platform is new and is currently being used in several medical research projects [11,12].

2.2. Sensor Technology in Healthcare

Wireless technologies are readily available within our homes, retail outlets and the workplace and research initiatives like the Internet of Things [13] envisage a time when many objects will be internet-enabled. This presents a unique opportunity to extend the reach of healthcare services and allow people to be monitored, diagnosed and treated, as we shall see in the remainder of this section.

The wireless sensor networking community is currently investigating this idea using small computation devices designed to communicate sensed physical phenomena (temperature, gas, movement, physiological data and so on). In one example, wireless sensors have been placed in shoes to capture information about weight bearing on affected limbs [14]. Several measurements, such as time/distance by floor/foot contact, have been used to detect gait abnormalities. Information collected is accessed remotely and used to recommend small compensatory changes to increase the symmetry of gait. Adopting a more obtrusive approach, mechatronics has helped to rehabilitate patients with cerebral palsy [15]. High no-load resistance is used, that decreases with an increase in applied force dependent on the application of stretch settings and fix cast positions. The benefits of this approach have been shown by the ReWalk powered exoskeleton system that allows paralyzed patients to walk again [16]. Similar solutions have been proposed to assist the wrist and forearm motion of physically weak individuals [17]. A robotic device for neuromotor rehabilitation and upper extremity neuromuscular systems have also been developed that allow free motion when possible and provides programmable levels of therapeutic resistance when required [18]. Many of these solutions have wireless interfaces that allow data to be collected for informing assessment and for adapting treatments.

Motion capture over the past decade has also played a significant role in rehabilitation [19]. Personal area networks, in conjunction with inertial sensors, allow data to be collected from accelerometers, tri-axial gyroscopes, pedometers, and goniometers to help in the rehabilitation of functional disabilities and deviations in gait. For example, this technique has been successfully used in treating children suffering with juvenile idiopathic arthritis [20-23]. Through gait analysis, joint angles and movement can be obtained to help quantify progress and provide more detailed treatments to help minimize pain and stiffness [24].

In parallel, the fact that we are living longer is directly associated with the progressive deterioration of the musculoskeletal system. This has made diseases like rheumatoid arthritis, a chronic systemic disorder characterized by autoimmunity, infiltration of joint synovium, a high priority for a number of reasons. Firstly, effectively dealing with such diseases can help to improve the quality of life of an individual. Secondly, patients suffering from this condition often have a higher risk of premature mortality—coronary-artery disease being the most prevalent attributable cause of death which is accelerated through rheumatoid arthritis [25-29]. To date there is not general agreement as to what causes arthritis. Consequently, many believe that research needs to focus on prevention rather than cure. This will require novel solutions for data capture and processing that details the mechanics of motion. One possible area that is likely to be useful is the use of strain gauge technology.

Strain gauges have been successfully used in mechanical machineries and civil engineering structures, such as bridges, to monitor their behavior during periods of operation [30]. The medical domain has begun to explore how strain gauge technology might be used to deliver better healthcare services. One approach has placed pliable sensors in replacement joints to monitor its behavior over time were data is used to create a 3D image of the forces and torques around the replacement joints [31]. As a patient carries out a set of tasks, such as stair climbing, running and walking, the medical practitioner is able to observe and detect any particular activities that might overload the implant. This undoubtedly affects patients with replacement joints in a positive way, yet there is little research that demonstrates how strain gauges might be used to detect deterioration before a replacement joint is required.

Wireless communications and sensor technologies provide mechanisms for measuring many different aspects of human behavior and this has been useful in understanding medical conditions. However, there has been little exploitation of technology to measure the inner workings of the tendons, muscles, and ligaments used to move a joint. So while wireless communications and sensor technologies can underpin an effective approach, we must extend their capabilities to incorporate advances made—for example—in implantable pliable sensing fabrics, like strain gauges. This allows a more detailed inspection of a medical condition and its behavior to be carried out, as we shall see in the next section.

3. Wireless Strain Gauge Device

As we have seen, many approaches exist in the assessment of human movement, such as ReWalk and Inertial Measurement Units like XSens (accelerometer, gyroscopes and magnetometers). These have helped to understand and manage strategies for chronic diseases, such as, cerebral palsy, arthritis and so on [32]. Furthermore, they have allowed novel platforms to be developed to host and deploy better healthcare services. Given the success of such approaches, it is appropriate to build on the technological advances that have already been made. Using a number of existing techniques, we present an investigation detailing how a pliable strain gauge device can be used to monitor progressive deterioration in musculoskeletal systems.

The discussion describes how a generic wireless sensor can be extended to include strain gauge capabilities. This includes the design considerations for the hardware and software to prototype and run the wireless strain gauge sensor.

3.1. Approach Overview

The design goals provide the system requirements for a suitable scheme as described in this paper. The principle goals are as follows.

- *Strain Gauge*: To use a strain gauge component based on the "Foil Type" that is pliable and suitable for healthcare applications [33].
- *Wheatstone Bridge Circuit*: To improve the signal of strain gauges so that they are sensitive enough to detect slight movement [34].
- *Difference Amplifier:* To improve the condition of the output generated by the strain gauge sensor [35].
- *Non-Inverting Amplifier*: To amplify the signal output from the strain gauge sensor to a level that is acceptable to the control software [36].
- *Generic Wireless sensor*: To provide a wireless interface to the strain gauge sensor.

3.2. Strain Gauge

Strain gauges are typically "foil type" and consist of a pattern of resistive foil mounted onto a backing material that operates on the principle that if the foil is subjected to forces of compression or tension, then the electrical resistance of the foil will change in a defined way as illustrated in **Figure 1**.

The strain causes a variation in the length of the wire in the strain gauge, which responds with a change in electrical resistance. There is a linear relationship between strain in the surface of investigation and resistance variation of the strain gauge described using the "Poisson's Ratio" formula [38]. Strain gauges are comercially available with nominal resistance values. These range between 30 and 3000 ohms, with 120, 350, and 1000 ohms being the most common values. By laying and fixing the bonded strain gauge material, illustrated in **Figure 1**, over the surface of investigation in series, different areas can be measured, as the actual physical size of each bonded strain gauge is very small (3 mm by 5 mm). This effectively makes the area of the surface under investigation much larger and hence more reliable in feeding back a set of more accurate readings of the musculoskeletal components. Perhaps less obvious, is that combining smaller sensors in this way enables the surface under investigation to be more accurately modeled in terms of its size and shape.

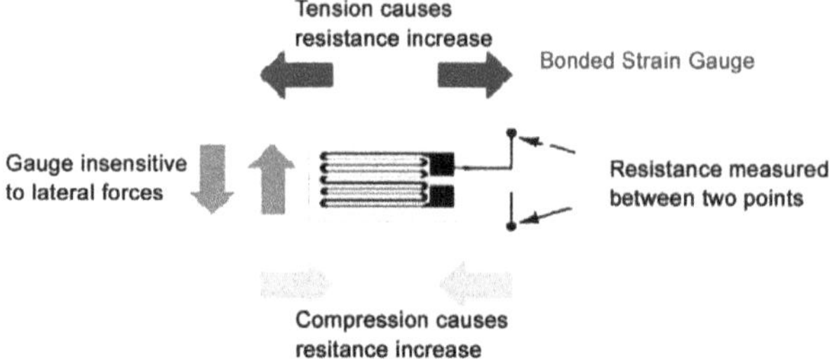

Figure 1. Source: www.circuitstoday.com. Forces of Compression and Tension.

Wiring the strain gauges in series helps cover different sized areas of investigation and helps improve the condition of the signal however, the size and quality of the signal received is too weak for data observations and capture. To overcome this problem, a further signal conditioning solution is required in the form of a "Wheatstone Bridge Circuit" [34]. The Wheatstone bridge works on the principle that, if all the resistances in each of its four arms are balanced, and it is supplied with a constant excitation voltage source across it, then the currents flowing through each arm of the bridge circuit will be balanced and hence no voltage difference will appear across its outputs.

Nonetheless, this provides a very low output value whilst the strain gauge is under a reasonable amount of tension, thus this value will be difficult to use given that it is not easy to distinguish between noise and the actual values. To address this design requirement a recognized solution is available in the form of a "Difference Amplifier" [35]. Before we consider this further, there is one last design requirement that needs to be considered when designing a Wheatstone bridge circuit.

A strain gauge applicator will never be at a zero output position when it is applied to the surface under investigation (*i.e.* ligament, tendon or the surface of the skin). This is because of the various body parts and the various patients that the applicator is likely to be fitted to. Therefore, a form of substitution is required that is built into the bridge circuit in the form of an "offset adjustment". The simplest way of doing this is to connect a series of potentiometers in series with the strain gauge sensor, one for "fine adjustment" and one for "coarse adjustment". By incorporating this facility into the circuit design, we can compensate for any slight bending of the patient applicator when it is being applied to the patient. It will be possible for the practitioner to adjust the output of the system to a "zero" level before monitoring begins. This will allow realistic results to be collected about the patient's condition.

In order to further improve the condition of the output signal received from the bridge circuit, a "Difference Amplifier" is configured using a special resistor arrangement connected to the inputs and outputs [35]. By using this resistor arrangement, the functionality of the difference amplifier can be determined and the efficiency at which it performs. The resistance amplifier is determined by the values allocated to the circuit's resistors. If all resistors are allocated the same value, then the amplifier will only have a Gain of "1"—there will be no amplification and will not be classed as an amplifier. It would however retain the advantage of performing "Common

Mode Rejection" [39], which is used to effectively filter out any noise levels present at its inputs. It can do this because when the noise is present on both of its + and – inputs the inverted and non-inverted noise waveforms have the effect of mathematically canceling each other out.

The difference amplifier provides an improved and much safer value for input into the "Non-Inverting Operational Amplifier" [36] than the noise shrouded signal level that comes straight from the bridge circuit. Nonetheless, an amplifier is required to give an increased positive output voltage from a given positive input voltage. Such an amplifier is the "Non-Inverting" type, which can be formed by utilizing the operational amplifier "building block" and a suitable resistor configuration.

The design of the "Non-Inverting Amplifier" will have a "Gain", which is determined by the value of the resistors in the voltage divider network of the feedback loop. In other words, the input is the expected maximum and the output is the required maximum. This will be discussed later in the paper.

3.3. Generic Wireless Sensor

After evaluating many sensors including MicaZ motes, SunSPOT's, Ember and Meshnetic devices, SunSPOT's were used in the prototype to process the analogue values from the strain gauge. SunSPOTS are 180 MHz 32-bit ARM920T core processors with 512 K of RAM and 4 M of flash memory. It has an onboard 2.4GHz radio with an integrated IEEE 802.15.4 radio. The battery is a 3.7 V rechargeable 750 mAh lithium-ion type that is charged through a USB port. Under normal use, the battery can last for about 7 hours. The sensor board provides several built in sensor functions, a 3-axis accelerometer, a temperature sensor, and a light sensor. Additional sensing functions can be added via the sensors six analogue inputs and analogue to digital converter, five general-purpose I/O pins and four high current output pins. In our prototype system the strain gauge is connected to the analogue inputs (A0, A1, A2, A3), which are designed to accept a 0 - 3 Vdc analogue voltage. The analogue values are converted to digital values and wirelessly transmitted to a base station.

Wireless transmission uses the IEEE 802.15.4 protocol at the 2.4 GHz transmission rate. This protocol helps prevent unwanted interference from other 2.4 GHz frequencies through multi-channel assignment and it rejects any signals that do not carry the correct authorization for connecting to its base station or free-range sensors, *i.e.* its master or its slaves. There are two types of communication possible with the SunSPOT. The first is the "radiogram" protocol, which acts like UDP, in that it, sends data out without guaranteeing delivery. This message is limited to a size of 256 bytes and is useful in delivering small broadcast messages. The second type is the "radio stream". This protocol allows for much larger data transfers as well as guaranteed delivery. The radiogram protocol is sufficient for the data rates required and given that data is not sequentially dependent, there is no need to guarantee delivery given that similar values are being constantly transmitted.

4. Detecting Deterioration in the Musculoskeletal System

In this section, we discuss how the strain gauge and SunSPOT sensor can be combined to create a system capable of monitoring the mechanics of motion in an anatomically correct knee joint. In this way, the case study can be used to:

- Test the proposed design decisions and illustrate how the collective functionality described addresses the limitations with current approaches;
- Demonstrate how fine grain motion can be measured.

In developing the prototype, a multidisciplinary approach has been adopted whereby custom hardware is used to capture sensitive movements produced by the strain gauge sensor system. A SunSPOT base station is used to provide a bridge between the sensor network and middleware services. Software has been developed and installed on free standing SunSPOT's (the sensor the strain gauge is connected to) to access and sample the data received from its analogue inputs. The middleware provides digital signal processing services for stream compositions, fact extraction, queries, inference and classification. The technical details for how the system was developed are discussed in more detail in the following subsections.

4.1. Strain Gauge Sensor

The strain gauges used in the prototype are 120 ohms each. It was necessary to connect four gauges together to create a single sensor with the overall value of 480 ohms as illustrated in **Figure 2(a)**. This Increases the physical size and the sensitivity of the sensor. It also has the added advantage of increasing the overall electrical resistance of the Wheatstone bridge circuit, which in turn reduces the current demand of the onboard battery used by the SunSPOT sensor in the prototype. This therefore allows the periods between charging the SunSPOT battery pack to be increased.

When the strain gauge is at rest, the voltage supply is 3 volts (the 3 volts supplied by the SunSPOT). Consequently, the output voltage is 0 volts at rest (3 (480/480 + 480) – (480/480 + 480). If the strain gauge is placed under tension and the resistance of the active strain gauge increases (for example to 482 ohms), then the output voltage will be 0.003v. Obviously, 0.003v is too low to be used with the SunSPOT sensors. Such low values make it difficult to distinguish between noise and actual signals. The SunSPOT's onboard Analogue to Digital Converter (ADC) requires a signal between 0 and 3 volts to be able to function correctly in outputting a readable signal to the base station. In order to achieve this a 'Difference Amplifier' is used to amplify the signal. A Gain of 10 was used to work out the resistors required. Therefore, selecting a fairly high (but standard) input resister (of 100K ohms) we get $R_f = 10/100k = 1M$ ohm (R_f is the feedback resister). Using the output voltage and the feedback resister values the signal can be amplified to a more acceptable level, *i.e.* the voltage output is (0.003v – 0v) * 1M/100K = 003 V or 30 mV. By configuring the amplifier to have a gain of "10", we can expect an output voltage of 0.03v for an expected input of 0.003v. This improves the quality of the signal and makes it a safer value for inputting into the Non-Inverting Operational Amplifier.

The correct voltage input required for the SunSPOT is 0.05v and the output voltage is 3v (SunSPOT max rated input voltage). Therefore, the required gain is 3/0.05, which is equal to 60. This can be achieved by using a minimum value of 1K ohms so as not to "ground" the Difference Amplifiers negative input, the value of the feedback resistor in K ohms is $60 - 1 = R_f/1$, which means that $R_f = 59$K ohms. The nearest standard resister is 63K ohms and this was used in the final implementation.

4.2. SunSPOT Sensor

A free-range SunSPOT sensor is used to collect data from the area of investigation. A data collection point (laptop) connects to the sensor network using a USB base station SunSPOT sensor. The base station connects to the PIE middleware as a plug-in device, which receives and processes all data received. Sensors have the ability to operate in a disconnected mode—in this instance data is written to the SunSPOT's internal flash memory—upon re-connection the data from the flash memory is streamed to the PIE middleware and processed. This allows the system to remain functional even when a person is shopping, catching a bus or taking a walk.

All SunSPOT's communicate with each other over a multi-hop network and this allows data to be transmitted over a wider range. Any number of SunSPOTs can reside between the source and sink sensors to create a network of mesh routers. Free-range SunSPOTs, *i.e.* body and environment sensors, broadcast datagram packets to their nearest SunSPOT neighbour in order to try to establish a connection with that SunSPOT. This provides support for the required multi-hop methodology. The number of hops a SunSPOT can take to relay messages can be set to a maximum of 15 hops. Each SunSPOT receives information from the surrounding environment and then relays it to an available base station (if one cannot be found the information is stored within the sensors internal data store). Free-range SunSPOT's stream data, via the base station and the implemented middleware services, and this allows data to be processed and presented to the application layer.

The strain gauge hardware is connected directly to the SunSPOT sensor. Software developed for the SunSPOT samples the analogue signal received on terminal "A0" of the ADC that is built into the SunSPOT. The sample rate is application specific and in the prototype is determined before the SunSPOT software is flashed. An easily visible bright LED on the SunSPOT has been programmed to flash when the SunSPOT is processing or sampling data. This provides information that the sensor is operational.

5. Evaluation

The prototype provides a working sensing device for the detection of movement in the individual components in the musculoskeletal system. The prototype system is illustrated in **Figure 2**. **Figure 2(a)** shows the strain gauge applicator; **Figure 2(b)** the Wheatstone Bridge, the Difference Amplifier, and the Non-Inverting Operational Amplifier; **Figure 2(c)** the strain gauge connected to the free-range SunSPOT; and finally **Figure 2(d)** shows the complete system configuration.

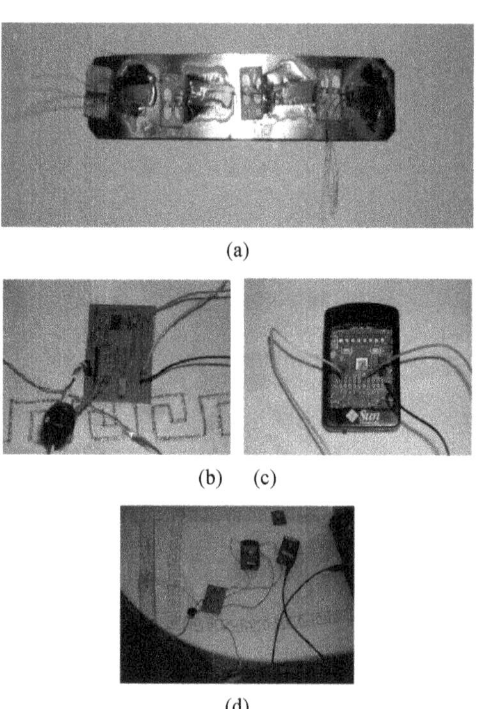

Figure 2. Prototype System. (a) Strain Gauge; (b) Circuitry; (c) Free-range SPOT; (d) Complete System.

In this section, we discuss how the wireless strain gauge sensor can be applied to various body parts for the purpose of movement analysis. In this way, the implementation can be used to:

- Test the proposed design and illustrate how highly sensitive information about movement can be obtained.
- Demonstrate how general wireless sensor technologies can be extended to include custom-made sensing functionality.
- Provide positive results to the use of strain gauge technology in progressive deterioration of the musculoskeletal system.

5.1. Artificial Knee Application

The flexible artificial knee illustrated in **Figure 3** was fitted with the strain gauge applicator to monitor the movements of the Quadriceps tendon, the Patella and the Patellar tendon (ligament).

The applicator could just as easily be applied to the Lateral collateral ligament, the Medial Collateral ligament or the anterior cruciate ligament. Using this model the knee can be flexed as a normal knee would and then allowed to return to its normal resting position. For the purpose of the demonstration the knee was flexed 5 times to show the real-time data readings collected from the strain gauge sensor. A sample of the signal produced is shown in **Figure 4** (the source of the data is from the strain gauge device attached to the analogue inputs of a SunSPOT sensor).

From the graph, it is possible to observe that the knee has managed to achieve constant bend amplitudes over a period of five consecutive exercises, with a rest period of approximately 5 seconds between each set. Although the graph is un-calibrated and uses generic values at this point, it would be possible to convert the x and y values to units of time and degrees respectively due to the linear characteristics of the strain gauges performance (we do this within the code to capture and increment 90-degree bends). The applicator is designed to fit with different body structures and capabilities. Using an offset facility (potentiometer that can be seen if **Figure 2(b)** a *null* position can be calibrated once the applicator has been fitted. This provides the therapist with a starting point of reference. The *null* or datum position can be set very easily by the therapist for each individual patient. Therefore, the same reference point can be set every time to remove the possibility of errors and inconsistencies from affecting the results.

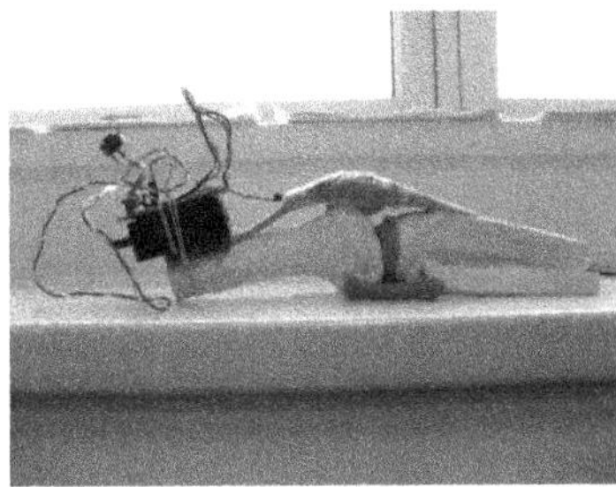

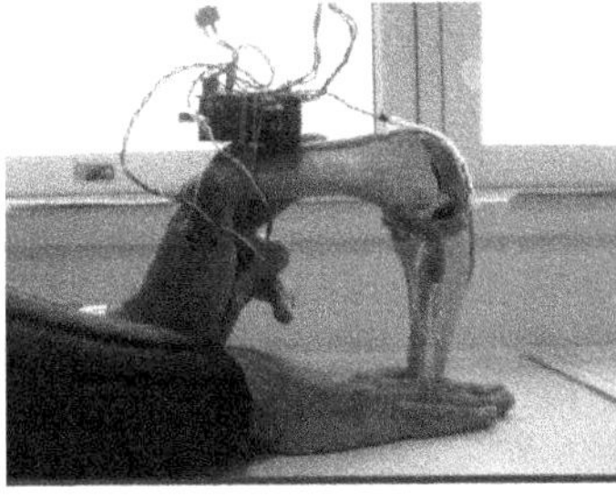

Figure 3. Strain Gauge attached to quadriceps tendon.

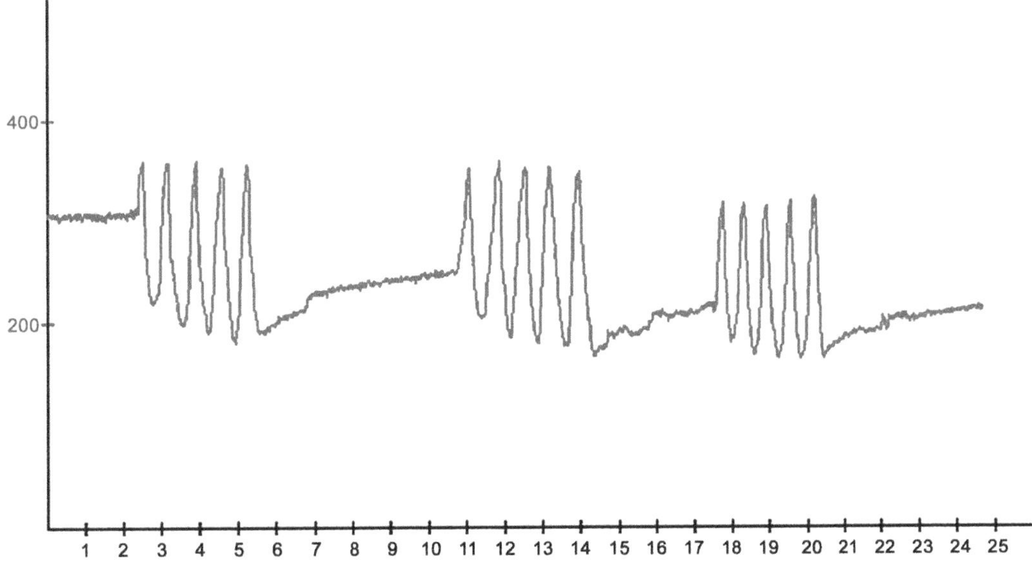

Figure 4. Real-time data stream from Artificial Knee Flexions.

5.2. The Physiotherapy Centre in Liverpool

The wireless strain gauge sensor was demonstrated at the Physiotherapy Centre located in Liverpool. Two chartered physiotherapists were presented with questionnaires, which they were asked to fill out during and after a full working demonstration of the strain gauge sensor. Some of the more notable comments that were made concerned the need to relate the readout display to units of degrees. This is because practitioners use a device called a "Goniometer". This device resembles a large adjustable protractor, which is placed against the patient's body joints to determine the extent to which that joint can bend *i.e.* its range. The demonstration proved valuable and highlighted the need to ensure that an electronic replacement, such as the one posited in this paper, should relate as closely as possible to what has been used before.

Other comments made were the possibility of displaying previous recordings on the screen and comparing them to current real-time readings. This would be useful in comparing a patient's progress during their course of therapy. Furthermore, due to the nature of body joints, the therapist felt that software would need to be devised for each body joint. Whether this is the case requires further research. Overall, the comments made by the physiotherapists were in favour of a technological solution using the strain gauge sensor.

5.3. Performance Evaluation

Data from the strain gauge sensor attached to the knee were transmitted over the air to a multi hop network consisting of several free-range SunSPOT sensors. The total number used was five to cover a distance of 35 meters (enough to cover most locations with a standard home in the UK). A base station was connected to a notebook that provided a data collection point for the strain gauge sensor.

In the first experiment, the sensor was tested with multiple data transfer rates to identify throughput and power consumption. Each packet contained a sample of data that was 105 bytes in size. When transferring a single packet to a free range sensor up to 8 meters away the results show that 0.0002 (%) of the total power available is consumed. Increasing the data rate to 10 packets per second for a period of 1 minute, the results as shown in **Figure 5** illustrate that the total power consumed is 0.0257 (%).

Increasing the distance to 16, 24, and 32 meters respectively and the time to 2, 3, and 4 minutes we find that the total power consumption used was 0.0514, 0.0815, and 0.1128 (%) when individual tests were run. **Figure 6** shows that re-running the experiment with 1000 packets per second for 1 minute and 4 minutes respectively power consumption increases from 0.6053 (%) to 2.2351 (%).

These two results show a linear correlation between distance and power consumption over time. Note that these are stress tests and the number of packets and the distance between sensors may change in a real-world solution to conserve energy.

To cover the spread of communication around the home environment between one and five sensors were used to form a mesh network. The number of nodes used has an impact on both time and power consumption. **Figure 7** shows distance verse power consumption readings. The first set of results show the power consumed over distances ranging from eight to thirty-two meters when ten packets per second were sent.

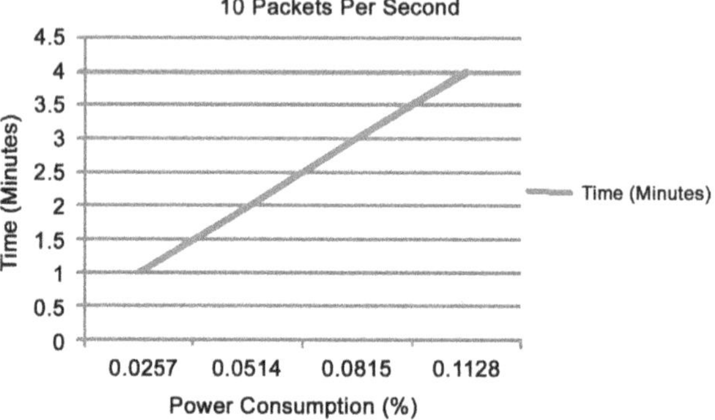

Figure 5. 10 packets of data sent per second.

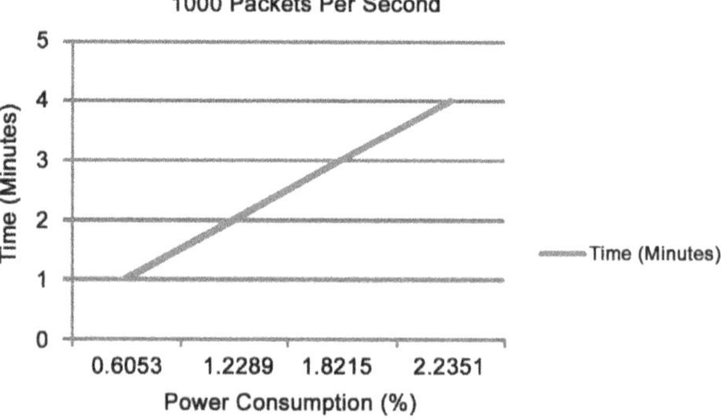

Figure 6. 1000 packets of data sent per second.

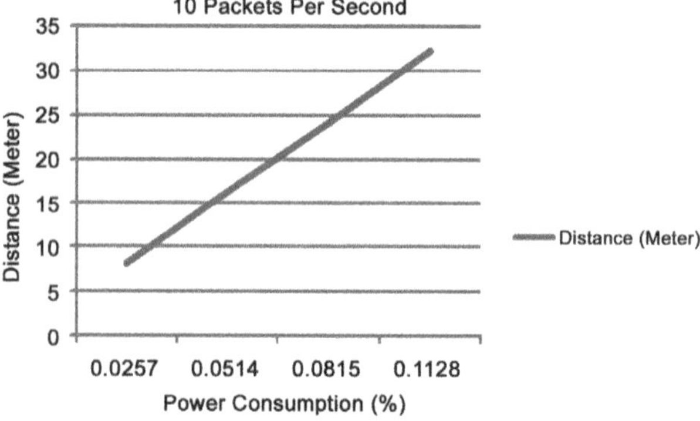

Figure 7. 10 packets of data sent per second.

Figure 8 shows the results for power consumed over distances between 10 and 40 meters when 1000 packets per second were sent.

The experiments provide valuable information for the deployment of any medical sensors and networks in body and personal area networks. They demonstrate that technology does make it possible to consider new and emerging technologies for real-time monitoring in healthcare applications and in particular those within the home.

6. Conclusions and Future Work

On-going developments in technology has helped to reduce the physical size and weight of devices and as we have seen, opened up new opportunities for their application in delivering unobtrusive healthcare services. Kinetic and kinematic systems are currently being used to measure and understand many different aspects of human gait and behaviour and this has been particularly useful in treating a number of different disease, like arthritis. Nonetheless, these systems are only capable of providing estimated information about rudimentary movement rather than detailed data on the mechanics of motion itself (tendons, ligaments and so on). This has not allowed the appropriate information to be used by healthcare professionals when making key clinical decisions. A number of interesting research initiatives that address aspects of this problem; however, we feel that our own ideas posited in this paper might provide a viable alternative that will significantly help support clinical judgement based on pliable strain gauge technology.

Nonetheless, improvements need to be made to the aesthetics of the applicator; possibly using an anti-bacterial removable outer coating. Second, embedding the sensor within the body was outside the scope of this paper; however, this issue needs to be considered in further work. Third, we did encounter some problems with the software freezing on the SunSPOTs after prolonged use—this needs to be further investigated. Fourth, the comments made by the physiotherapists during the evaluation of the system that different software versions are needed for each individual body part need to be investigated.

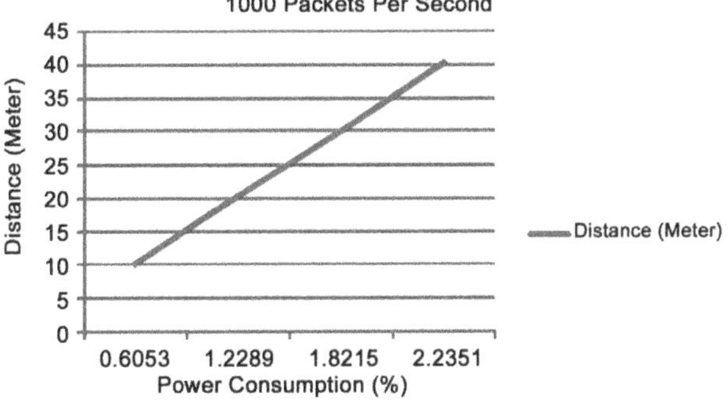

Figure 8. 1000 packets of data sent per second.

Fifth, the storage and stream reasoning middleware requires further testing on much larger data sets. Finally, we need to investigate battery-free sensor solutions for easier implantation, such as WISP sensors based on RFID technology.

7. Acknowledgements

The authors would like to thank the anonymous reviewers for providing highly constructive reviews, without which the paper would not have reached its current form. The authors would especially like to thank the Physiotherapy Centre in Liverpool for their help and constructive and positive criticism of the wireless strain gauge sensor.

REFERENCES

[1] R. C. Lawrence, *et al.*, "Estimates of the Prevalence of Arthritis and Other Rheumatic Conditions in the United States," *Athritis and Rheumatism*, Vol. 58, No. 1, 2008, pp. 26-35.

[2] H. Kwon, J. Cho and E. Lee, "EEG Asymmetry Analysis of the Left and Right Brain Activities during Simple versus Complex Arithmetic Learning," *Journal of Neurotherapy*, Vol. 13, No. 2, 2009, pp. 109-116.

[3] J. van den Noort and S. J. Harlaar, "Evaluation of Clinical Spasticity Assessment in Cerebral Palsy Using Inertial Sensors," *Gait & Posture*, Vol. 30, No. 2, 2009, pp. 138-143.

[4] N. Chevrollier and N. Golmie, "On the Use of Wireless Network Technologies in Healthcare Environments," *5th IEEE Workshop on Applications and Services in Wireless Networks*. IEEE Computer Society, Paris, 2005.

[5] D. Geer, "Users Make a Beeline for Zigbee Sensor Technology," *IEEE Computer*, Vol. 38, No. 12, 2005, pp. 16-19.

[6] P. Frehill, D. Chambers and C. Rotariu, "Using Zibee to Integrate Medical Devices," *29th IEEE International Conference on Engineering in Medicine and Biology Society*, IEEE Computer Society, Lyon, 2007.

[7] Y. M. Huang, M. Y. Hsieh and H. C. Chao, "Pervasive, Secure Access to a Hierarchical Sensor-Based Healthcare Monitoring Architecture in Wireless Heterogeneous Networks," *IEEE Journal on Selected Areas in Communications*, Vol. 27, No. 4, 2009, pp. 400-411.

[8] J. Misic and V. B. Misic, "Bridging between IEEE 802. 15.4 and IEEE 802.11b Networks for Multiparameter Healthcare Sensing," *IEEE Journal on Selected Areas in Communications*, Vol. 27, No. 4, 2009, pp. 435-449.

[9] M. A. Hanson, *et al.*, "Body Area Sensor Networks: Challenges and Opportunities," *IEEE Computer*, Vol. 42, No. 1, 2009, pp. 58-65.

[10] A. P. Sample, *et al.*, "Design of an RFID-Based Battery-

Free Programmable Sensing Platform," *IEEE Transactions on Instrumentation and Measurement*, Vol. 57, No. 11, 2008, pp. 1608-2615.

[11] U. Varshney, "Pervasive Healthcare and Wireless Health Monitoring," *Mobile Networks and Applications*, Vol. 12, No. 2-3, 2007, pp. 113-127.

[12] D. Bryant and O. Colgrave, "Knowledge and Informatics within Home Medicine (KIM): The Role of a 'Home Health Hub'," *International Journal of Healthcare Technology and Management*, Vol. 7, No. 5, 2006, pp. 335-347.

[13] G. Kortuem, *et al.*, "Smart Objects as Building Blocks for the Internet of Things," *IEEE Internet Computing*, Vol. 14, No. 1, pp. 44-51.

[14] A. Authier, *et al.*, "A Proof of Concept for a Wireless Ambulatory Weight Bearing Measurement System in Rehabilitatin and Telerehabilitation Applications," *3rd IEEE International Conference on Wireless and Mobile Computing, Networking and Communications*, IEEE Computer Society, New York, 2007.

[15] M. Bailey-Van Kuren and D. Scarborough, "Mechatronic Applications in Pediatric Therapy Devices," *IEEE International Conference on Advanced Intelligent Mechatronics*, IEEE Computer Society, Monterey, 2005.

[16] R. Bogue, "Exoskeletons and Robotic Prosthetics: A Review of Recent Developments," *Industrial Robot*, Vol. 36, No. 5, 2009, pp. 421-427.

[17] R. A. R. C. Gopura and K. Kiguchi, "EMG-Based Control of an Exoskeleton Robot for Human Forearm and Wrist Motion Assist," *IEEE International Conference on Robotics and Automation*, IEEE Computer Society, Pasadena, 2008.

[18] D. S. Anreasen, *et al.*, "Exoskeleton for Forearm Pronation and Supination Rehabilitation," *26th IEEE International Conference on Engineering in Medicine and Biology Society*, IEEE Computer Society, Turkey, 2004.

[19] B. Rosenhahn, T. Brox and H. Seidel, "Scaled Motion Dynamics for Markerless Motion Capture," *IEEE Conference on Computer Vision and Pattern Recognition*, IEEE Computer Society, Minneapolis, 2007.

[20] H. Zheng, N. D. Black and N. D. Harris, "Position-Sensing Technologies for Movement Analysis in Stroke Rehabilitation," *Medical and Biological Engineering and Computing*, Vol. 43, No. 4, 2005, pp. 413-420.

[21] H. Zhou and H. Hu, "Inertial Motion Tracking of Human Arm Movements in Stroke Rehabilitation," *IEEE International Conference on Mechatronics and Automation*, IEEE Computer Society, Niagra Falls, 2005.

[22] H. Zhou and H. Hu, "Human Motion Tracking for Rehabilitation: A Survey," *Biomedical Signal Processing and Control*, Vol. 3, No. 1, 2007, pp. 1-18.

[23] H. Zhou, *et al.*, "Use of Multiple Wearable Inerail Sensors in Upper Limb Motion Tracking," *Medical Engineering & Physics*, Vol. 30, No. 1, 2008, pp. 123-133.

[24] E. Brostrom, S. Hagelberg and Y. Haglund-Akerlind, "Effect of Joint Injections in Children with Junvenile Idiopathic Arthritis: Evaluation by 3D-Gait Analysis," *Acta Paediatrica*, Vol. 93, No. 7, 2004, pp. 906-910.

[25] T. Pincus, "Taking Mortality in Rheumatoid Arthritis Seriously—Predictive Markers," *Socioeconomic Status and Comorbidity*, Vol. 13, No. 5, 1986, pp. 841-845.

[26] C. L. J. Gonzalez-Juanatey, A. Testa, *et al*, "Increased Prevalence of Severe Subclinical Atherosclerotic Findings in Long-Term Treated Rheumatoid Arthritis Patients without Clinically Evident Atherosclerotic Disease," *Medicine*, Vol. 82, No. 6, 2003, pp. 407-413.

[27] Y. B. Park, C. H. Lee, S. H. Lee, *et al.*, "Atherosclerosis in Rheumatoid Arthritis: Morphologic Evidence Obtained by Carotid Ultrasound," *Arthritis & Rheumatism*, Vol. 46, No. 7, 2003, pp. 1714-1719.

[28] M. J. Roman, A. Davis, *et al.*, "Preclinical Carotid Atherosclerosis in Patients with Rheumatoid Arthritis," *Annuals of International Medicine*, Vol. 14, No. 4, 2006, pp. 249-256.

[29] C. P. Chung, P. Raggi, *et al.*, "Increased Coronary-Artery Atherosclerosis in Rheumatoid Arthritis: Relationship to Disease Duration and Cardiovascular Risk Factors," *Arthritis & Rheumatism*, Vol. 52, No. 10, 2005, pp. 3045-3053.

[30] S. W. Arms, *et al.*, "Wireless Strain Sensing Networks," *2nd European Workshop on Structural Health Monitoring*, Munich, 2004.

[31] S. W. Arms, "MicroStrain Wireless Sensors Measure 3-D Force and Torque Data in Live Human Knee Replacement," *MstNews*, Vol. 2, No. 7, 2007, p. 21.

[32] K. Saber-Sheikh, *et al.*, "Feasibility of Using Inertial Sensors to Assess Human Movement," *Manual Therapy*, Vol. 15, No. 1, 2010, pp. 122-125.

[33] R. A. Clark, *et al.*, "Assessment of Mechanical Strain in the Intarct Plantar Fascia," *The Foot*, Vol. 19, No. 3, 2009, pp. 161-164.

[34] T, Kakaday, *et al.*, "Advances in Telemetric Continuous Intraocular Pressure Assessment," *British Journal of Ophthalmology*, Vol. 93, No. 8, 2009, pp. 992-996.

[35] P. K. Chan, K. A. Ng and X. L. Zhang, "A CMOS Chopper-Stabilised Differential Amplifier for Biomedical Integrated Circuits," *IEEE Transactions on Circuits and Systems*, Vol. 52, No. 11, 2005, pp. 2335-2347.

[36] M. M. Bani Amer, *et al.*, "Contactless Method for Detection of Infant Apnoea," *Journal of Medical Engineering and Technology*, Vol. 34, No. 5-6, 2010, pp. 324-328.

[37] M. Merabti, *et al.*, "Managing Distributed Networked Appliances in Home Networks," *Proceedings of the IEEE Journal*, Vol. 96, No. 1, 2008, pp. 166-185.

[38] A. P. Santhanam, *et al.*, "An Inverse Hyper-Spherical

Harmonics-Based Formulation for Reconstructing 3D Volumetric Lung Deformations," *Comptes Rendus Mécanique*, Vol. 338, No. 7-8, 2010, pp. 461-473.

[39] N. Paddock and D. Behm, "The Effect of Inverted Body Position on Lower Limb Muscle Force and Activation," *Applied Physiology, Nutrition, and Metabolism*, Vol. 34, No. 4, 2009, pp. 673-680.

13

Evaluate Student Satisfaction for Social Learning Network at King Abdulaziz University

Maram A. Alshareef
Program of Educational Graduate Studies, King Abdulaziz University, Jeddah, Kingdom of Saudi Arabia

ABSTRACT

The new Web 2.0 trends have offered new tools to connect people not only to digital knowledge repositories but also to other people, in order to share ideas, collaboratively create new forms of dynamic learning content, get effective support, and learn with and from peers. Different types of collaborative content applications, such as blogs and wikis, are used by people of all ages, supporting the collaborative creation and sharing of knowledge among young and old, students and experts, inside and outside organizations and educational institutions. This research investigates the effects of Web 2.0 and social networks on students' performance in online education which uses networking as an adjunct mode for enhancing traditional education in King Abdulaziz University.

Keywords: Web 2.0; Social Learning; Student Satisfaction; Facebook; Bologs

1. Introduction

Social learning takes place in relation to four dimensions: action, reflection, communication and negotiation [1]. Each of these processes is characterized by particular tensions. Social learning therefore is about finding optimal and dynamic balances between these tensions, in accordance with the peculiar conditions and needs of concrete contexts and challenges [1]. Nowadays, students forced educational institutions to move from traditional teaching methods to social learning. Higher education students are integrating ICT completely in their everyday life and call for educational institutions to support their digital learning styles. In addition, instructors are increasingly taking up social computing applications in their work and free time. One approach is to provide support for social learning by integrating Web 2.0 tools in educational settings.

As a result, traditional teaching and learning methods in educational institutions should be adapted to provide accommodation the learning needs of the new generation of digital native students and instructors. Recently, Web 2.0 concepts have started to open new doors for more effective learning and have the potential to overcome many of the limitations of traditional learning models. Social computing tools in Web 2.0 have a potential to support both, students in higher education institutions and instructors updating their skills in new ways. In this paper, we show in which way the Web 2.0 tools, under development at the King Abdulaziz University, puts crucial success factors for Web 2.0 enhanced learning into practice, applying well known concepts like social learning.

U-learning is a learning paradigm which takes place in a ubiquitous computing environment that enables learning the right thing at the right place and time in the right way [2]. Following Ogata [3], social learning is defined as one of U-learning which is defined as follows:

- Permanency: The information remains and learners can never lose their work unless the learners purposely remove it.
- Accessibility: The information is always available whenever the learners need to use it. Learners have access to their documents, data, or videos from anywhere.
- Immediacy: The information can be retrieved immediately by the learners wherever they are.
- Interactivity: The learners can interact with peers, teachers, and experts efficiently and effectively.

We use Facebook and blogs as tools of social network learning. By browsing the nominated noble works and the comments made by peers as well as instructors on students' blogs, students are empowered to stimulate new ideas different from each other. This paper moves to additional concludes that blogging has the potential to be a transformational technology for teaching and learning.

Our survey results show that students who took the traditional courses are satisfied with blog posting, getting instructor's in-class interactions and social learning.

2. Related Work

Nowadays, Web 2.0 technology is taking part in the environment of learning and knowledge transfer by transforming the information society into a knowledge society [4]. There are several scholars doing researches on the prospective role of Web 2.0 services [5] in providing social interaction with educational values included [6]. The results of an experiment by Anderson [4] proved that the social network of Web 2.0 services are described by power laws and log normal distributions, and also proved that a small percentage of participants remain active above the threshold required for the interaction's continuance and development.

Researchers are used methods of Web 2.0 analysis [7], to study how information flows through network, how people acquire information and resources. Accordingly, they are studying for discovering densely-knit classes and looking for cohesive subclasses [8]. Wright [9] defined a blog as a website which contains posts, or text. These contents are classified to classes and categorized as stack in a chronological order.

Some researchers see that keeping in touch with social science will be just as important like technology. Ronald found that the analysis of the social network [10] helps in identifying the framework of the collaborative learning. In the same idea, Peter tries to analysis information coming from the blogs and analysis the relevance of an item [11]. Newman [12] has mentioned that social network has debatably turned into an obvious subject as regards to researchers, learning activities and collaborative learning. Oravec [13] found that the blog has a lot of extents that are suited to students' allowing them, and encouraging them to become more engaged in the class. Blogging tools are already commenced in a lot of university around the world. However, Oravec found that few of the blogs in education are used in-class [13]. Dailey [14,15] considers that the biggest advantage of blogs has more to do with traditional classroom.

This paper, quantitative analysis will be conducted to examine the effects of social learning of educational blogs in the classroom settings.

3. Methodology

Using data from a 100-student course on communication skills at a King Abdul Aziz university, we empirically tested how social networks (friendly, advising, and adversarial) related to students' performance. A study was performed for students enrolled in two sections of the course. The survey was conducted on-line using electronic questionnaires at Deanship of distance learning King Abdulaziz University. The representation of respondents by gender was 60 girls and 40 boys. The questionnaire was designed to measure the performance of the social network variables on the student collaboration. Following the work of Sparrowe *et al.* [16], advice relations could be administered to acquire a more trustworthy measure of the advice network.

This research is based as the following hypothesis: Social network performance will be positively related to the student's satisfaction. Accordingly the above hypothesis can be consisted from the following sub questioners:

H1.1: Social network using blog and Facebook provide a satisfying learning experience.

H1.2: Using social network tools I found this class is more satisfying than most other classes.

H1.3; Using social network tools, I found this class is an interesting one

H1.4: Class via social network gives me flexibility for extracurricular

H1.5: Class via social network gives me flexibility for study time

H1.6: I am feeling to getting a good education.

H1.7: The technology of social network associated with class is easy to use

H1.8: Using social network, it is easy to get feedback.

The survey included numerous scales to evaluate the constructs of interest. For that, the scales were measured using a 7-point Likert type scale anchored with the statements "Strongly Disagree" = 1, "Strongly Agree" = 7, and "Neutral" as the mid-point.

4. Results and Discussions

The result was analyzed and tested using LISREL [17]. **Table 1** shows the results with T-value and P-value.

A shown in **Table 1**, and **Figure 1**, a t-test was used to explain the value of the results of 8 questions and gives the respondents on level of satisfaction with the social network. It is clear that there is significant effect for social network satisfaction with $P < 0.011$. Students in this study are generally satisfied with course online via social network learning. As shown in T-value, the students find that the social network tools, I found this class is an interesting class.

Student found that class via social network gives them flexibility for study time with factor loading 0.934. As shown in **Figure 2**, they also found that the technology of social network associated with class is easy to use with 0.011. **Figure 2** shows that the best results get from Q4 and Q6, therefore, they found that class via social network gives students flexibility for extracurricular and

Table 1. T-value and P-value.

Item	Factor Loading	T-Value	P-value
Social network using blog and Facebook provide a satisfying learning experience.	0.954	19.11	0.010
Using social network tools I found this class is more satisfying than most other classes.	0.940	18.11	0.011
Social network tools, I found this class is an interesting one	0.934	20.65	0.012
Class via social network gives me flexibility for extracurricular	0.982	18.21	0.013
Class via social network gives me flexibility for study time	0.912	19.23	0.011
I am feeling to getting a good education	0.913	20.31	0.013
The technology of social network associated with class is easy to use	0.943	17.42	0.011
using social network, It is easy to get feedback	0.962	18.54	0.011

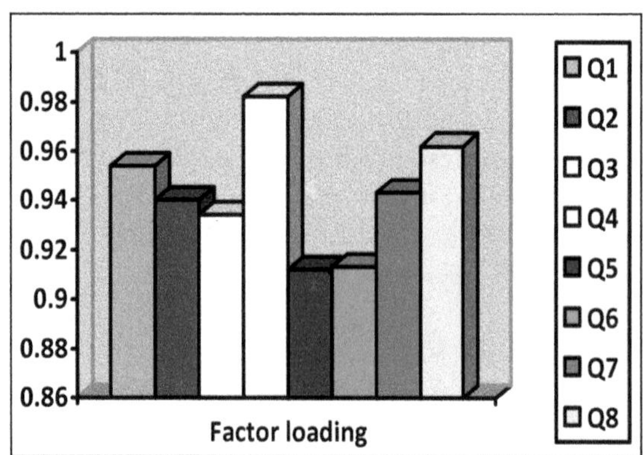

Figure 1. Factor loading results.

they are feeling to getting a good education. As shown in **Figure 1**, most of participates agree that class via social network gives me flexibility for extracurricular.

Figure 3 presents also that Q3 reflect a best question where students found that social network tools, they found this class is an interesting one.

5. Conclusion

The results of the survey on 100 students in campus, at King Abdulaziz University, Saudi Arabia, show the significant impact of social learning on the education using social networks with traditional class. This study raised some important issues in the use of social network

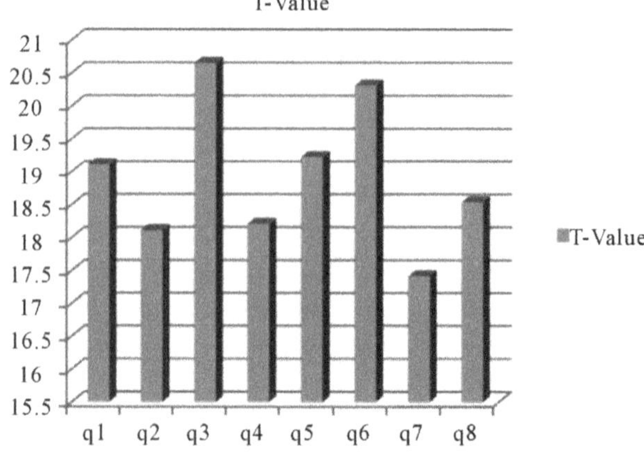

Figure 2. T-value of question.

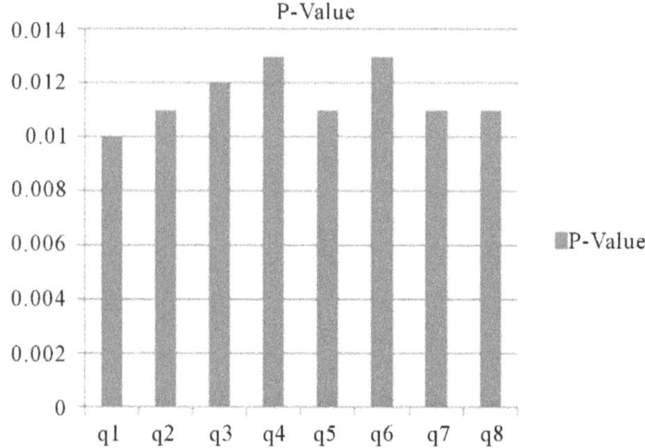

Figure 3. P-value of question.

technology and proved that the ease of use of the technology how to meet students' needs for communication. In addition, this paper shows that the social network played a major role in student satisfaction with the online course. These results also suggest that we should be evaluating social network technology use and understanding in our classrooms in King Abdulaziz University.

REFERENCES

[1] C. Janssens and D. Wildemeersch, "Social Learning in Interactive Policy Processes. The Case of City Forest Planning in Flanders," Katholieke Universiteit, Leuven, 2010.

[2] R. D. Caytiles, S.-H. Jeon and T.-H. Kim, "U-Learning Community: An Interactive Social Learning Model Based on Wireless Sensor Networks," *International Conference on Computational Intelligence and Communication Systems*, Gwalior, 2011, pp. 745-749.

[3] H. Ogata, "Features of Ubiquitous Learning from Computer Supported Ubiquitous Learning Environment for Language Learning," *Journal Transactions Processing Society of Japan*, Vol. 45, No. 10, 2003, pp. 2354-2363.

[4] P. Anderson, "What is Web 2.0? Ideas, Technologies and

Implications for Education," JISC Technical Report, 2007. http://www.jisc.ac.uk/media/documents/techwatch/tsw0701b.pdf

[5] T. O'Reilly, "What Is Web 2.0," 2005.

[6] B. Nardi, D. Schiano, M. Gumbrecht and L. Swartz, "Why We Blog," Communications of the Association for Computing Machinery, 2004.

[7] S. O'Hear, "Seconds Out, Round Two," The Guardian, 2005.

[8] P. A. Willging, "Using Social Network Analysis Techniques to Examine Online Interactions," *US-China Education Review*, Vol. 2, No. 9, 2005, pp. 46-56.

[9] J. Wright, "Blog Marketing," McGraw-Hill, Boston, 2006.

[10] R. L. Breiger, "The Analysis of Social Networks," In: M. Hardy and A. Bryman, Eds., *Handbook of Data Analysis*, Sage Publications, London, 2004, pp. 505-526.

[11] P J. Carrington, J. Scott and S. Wasserman, "Models and Methods in Social Network Analysis," Cambridge University Press, New York, 2005.

[12] M. Newman, "The Structure and Function of Complex Networks," *SIAM Review*, Vol. 45, No. 2, 2003, pp. 167-256.

[13] J. A. Oravec, "Bookmarking the World: Weblog Applications in Education," *Journal of Adolescent & Adult Literacy*, Vol. 45, No. 7, 2002, pp. 616-621.

[14] J. Dailey, "Blogging for Learning: Now Everyone Has Something to Say, Feedback," Broadcast Educators Association, 2006.

[15] A. Leene, "Web 2.0 Checklist 2.0," MicroContent Musings, 2005.

[16] R. T. Sparrowe, R. C. Liden and M. L. Kraimer, "Social Networks and the Performance of Individuals and Groups," *Academy of Management Journal*, Vol. 44, No. 2, 2001, pp. 316-325.

[17] K. G. Joreskog and D. Sorbaum, "LISREL 8: Structural Equation Modeling with SIMPLIS Command Language," Erlbaum, Hillsdale, 1993.

Electronic Commerce Technology Adoption at the Scientific and Industrial Research and Development Centre

Cosmas Rashama[1*], Wilson Mungwena[2], Tonderai Damba[1]
[1]Department of Electrical Engineering, University of Zimbabwe, Harare, Zimbabwe
[2]Department of Mechanical Engineering, University of Zimbabwe, Harare, Zimbabwe

ABSTRACT

This paper focuses on the level of adoption of E-Commerce Technology at the Scientific and Industrial Research and Development Centre (SIRDC), a Zimbabwean organization established by an act of parliament, with a mandate to develop, adopt and adapt new technologies for the benefit of Zimbabwean companies and organizations. The study was done in 2004 and the findings reviewed in 2012 with similar results. The objective of the study was to establish whether E-commerce technology adoption would result in the organization being more efficient and effective in delivering its mandate and then establish the level of adoption of the technology at the centre using abstraction and a questionnaire survey. Abstraction results showed that organizations which had fully embraced the technology were more efficient and effective while the survey revealed that the centre had partially adopted the technology. It was recommended that the centre should fully embrace the technology and market it to other organizations as per its mandate.

Keywords: Electronic Commerce; Non-Repudiation; Internet; Intranet; Extranet

1. Introduction

The Scientific and Industrial Research and Development Centre (SIRDC), Zimbabwe's Technology Centre, presents a fascinating case study due to the fact that it was established by government in 1994 with a mandate to develop, adopt and adapt new technologies that will improve the competitiveness of the Zimbabwean industries and institutions globally. Since the use of Electronic Commerce (E-Commerce) technology has resulted in industrialised countries realising great benefits nationally and globally, its adoption, adaption to the local environment and subsequent usage by the Scientific and Industrial Research and Development Centre will enhance the competitiveness of the centre in delivering its mandate. The study undertook to establish whether the centre was taking a leadership role in the adoption of E-Commerce Technology in the country as required by its mandate.

2. Objectives

In order for the study to establish whether the Scientific and Industrial Research and Development Centre was effectively and efficiently delivering its mandate, through the adoption and usage of E-Commerce Technology, the following three questions had to be answered:

- Does the adoption and usage of E-Commerce Technology result in the centre efficiently and effectively delivering its mandate?
- To what extent has the Scientific and Industrial Research and Development Centre taken a leading role in adopting E-Commerce Technology for the sake of improving its effectiveness and efficiency in delivering its mandate?
- To what extent has the centre marketed E-Commerce Technology to industry and other organizations?

3. Theory and Literature Review

E-Commerce is a modern business practice associated with the buying and selling of information, products, and services via Internet [1]. The Internet has become the fastest growing electronic technology in world history. In the United States, for example, after electricity became publicly available, 46 years passed before 30 percent of

*Corresponding author.

American homes were wired; 38 years passed before the telephone reached 30 percent of US households, and 17 years for television [2]. The Internet required only seven years reaching 30 percent of American households. E-Commerce is an integral market, with no geographical boundaries that includes all the necessary operations to carry out a transaction [3]. The rapid proliferation of Internet and the world-wide web has created a fast growing electronic channel for marketing.

E-Commerce Technology has transformed business operations into real-time transactions, conducted globally, with heightened accuracy and reduced waste. It is the technology that is driving globalisation. E-Commerce Technology has been in existence for the past 50 years and its adoption has been mainly measured by the amount of transactions that have been done using the technology and predictions of future transactions from available data. Although it is difficult to gauge the reliability of such predictions, most researchers are agreed that transactions conducted using the E-Commerce Technology surpassed US$ 6.9 trillion by the year 2005 [4,5]. Although they are founded and unfounded fears associated with the use of the technology, organisations using the technology are satisfied by the results so far.

E-Commerce is commerce for the era of globalization, an era in which networks, and in particular the Internet, make it possible to create and manage an electronic market operated through computers and at a distance, dealing in a full range of products, services, technologies and goods. It is an integral market [3], with no geographical boundaries that includes all the necessary operations to carry out a transaction. It also features the identification and selection of potential partners, assisted trade negotiations, trade reference data, access to information on support services, banks and banking transactions, attention to specific needs for special clients, handling of all the necessary documentation safely and with complete confidentiality.

E-Commerce offers multiple benefits to suppliers, clients and consumers. Public and private companies and organizations have seen enough benefits [6] with the generation of new opportunities for business, direct access to distant markets offering global presence, personalized services resulting in massive personalisation, improved competition resulting in increased competitiveness, substantial reduction in costs and time involved, shorter delivery chain, fast technology transfer, better organisational learning opportunities, relatively small investments to penetrable large markets and up to date information. Some of the benefits to consumers include global selection with purchases done from anywhere, quality of service, personalized products and services, quick response to needs, reduction in prices, new products and services.

Two models are widely used today for the development of an E-Commerce infrastructure. The first is the Information-Communication-Distribution-Transaction (ICDT) model that was first proposed by Abert Angehrn [7,8]. It takes its name from the four virtual spaces created by the Internet: Virtual information space (VIS), Virtual communication space (VCS), Virtual distribution space (VDS) and Virtual transaction space (VTS). The four spaces are treated separately because they correspond to different strategic objectives and require different types of investment and organisational adjustments. Clarke provided a five-phase model of E-Commerce that included the following stages [9]: the pre-contractual phase, the contractual phase, the ordering and logistic phase, the settlement phase and the post-processing phase. The five-phase model is basically the same as the ICDT model. The two only differ in that the ICDT model does not offer post-processing functions.

4. Methods

This was a case study research of the Scientific and Industrial Research and Development Center through a questionnaire and direct observation. The study focused on the activities of the centre to establish whether the centre was using E-Commerce Technology in the conduct of their business for the purpose of improving efficiency and effectiveness. A case study was more appropriate because it enabled a thorough investigation of the variables. However it was difficult to generalize the findings of the case study because the observations could have been situational.

The Scientific and Industrial Research and Development Centre had a staff complement of 150 employees. Due to limitations of cost, time and the need to maintain high accuracy questionnaires were distributed to 120 of the 150 staff members. In order to ensure that the results were authentic, the chosen employees included all managers, all scientists, all technicians and all secretaries because they were the ones that were supposed to use E-Commerce in their day-to-day operations. The selection of subjects who were supposed to use E-Commerce in their day-to-day operations eliminated the major weakness of judgmental sampling. This judgmental sample was also chosen because the researcher was familiar with the organization. Employees outside these categories were randomly selected so that the required number of 120 was realised. The use of judgmental sampling, which is a non-probability sampling method, had some effect on the validity of the results because the error could not be quantified.

It is important to note that some of the employees who were given questionnaires chose not to cooperate during the survey thereby causing some distortions to the established results. It is generally the practice that 5% - 15%

of the targeted participants would actually cooperate by completing the research instrument honestly and returning the instrument back in any self-administered questionnaire. It was therefore expected that at least 18 questionnaires would be returned back by the targeted participants. For this research, 86 questionnaires were returned because the questionnaires were numbered and a register for distributed questionnaires kept a situation that enabled easy follow ups. Researcher also sought the support of senior management before the study was done which also helped to increase the response rate. The register was kept without the respondents' knowledge in order to preserve a sense of confidentiality.

In conducting the survey, questionnaires and personal observations were used as research instruments. A questionnaire was designed as the main research instrument in order to solicit responses from the subjects that would enable one to answer with a high degree of accuracy the research problem. In order to ensure that the questionnaire was simple and straight forward, the majority of the questions used had single choice answers. This also served to minimise ambiguity in the questions as well as the responses. The major advantages of questionnaire that justified its use in this study included the fact that it could be implemented at low cost, it was not subjected to interviewer bias, it was good for quantifying responses and it was more convenient for respondents. The major disadvantages of the questionnaire that the study had to take into account was that it was slow to implement thereby justifying the need to number questionnaires and keeping a register for the purpose of following up respondents. A cutoff date and minimum number required was also established by the researcher to ensure that once the date was due and enough questionnaires were available, the study could proceed without worrying about the questionnaires that were not returned.

In order to ensure quality responses, draft questionnaires were sent to selected staff members with doctorate degrees in social sciences for them to check and comment on the quality of questions. The questionnaire was then pilot tested on selected subjects to determine if the instrument collected the type of information it was intended to collect. Open-ended questions were harder to implement thereby justifying keeping them to an absolutely necessary minimum in the study. There was potential for non-response bias, which justified the use of short and simple questions that were not sensitive.

The questionnaire started by looking at whether the centre had the E-Commerce tools and then further focused on whether these tools were widely distributed within the centre or whether they were found in a few critical areas, in which case the questionnaire then established whether there was an established widely shared policy over the distribution of the E-Commerce tools within the organization. Having established how the organization was equipped to use E-Commerce as a business tool, the questionnaire then focused on the usage of the tools for the intended purpose.

In terms of usage, the questionnaire mainly focused on how the centre used the four virtual spaces that were available to all E-Commerce users. The questionnaire explored usage of the virtual information space. The main area of concern in this regard was how the centre used E-Commerce Technology for internal and external information sharing. While exploring the usage of the virtual information space, the questionnaire also established whether the centre had databases for all its functional areas and whether these databases were widely accessible to internal and external stakeholders.

The questionnaire then focused on the usage of the virtual communication space. It looked at how widely the centre used the virtual communication space for internal and external communication. The major issues of concern were the effective and efficient use of E-mail and the effective and efficient use of chat. The questionnaire also focused on how effectively the centre used the virtual transaction space for internal and external transactions. The questionnaire established whether the centre used the virtual transaction space to sell their products and services to their customers through the exchange of orders and invoices. The questionnaire also established whether the centre used the virtual transaction space for payment processing.

Having looked at transaction processing, the questionnaire established whether the centre had products and services that could be digitised. If the products and services could be digitised, then it was investigated whether the centre was using the virtual distribution space for distributing the products. Having distributed the products and services, the study established whether the centre offered after sales support services using the four virtual spaces.

How the centre was marketing E-Commerce Technology to industry, government and institutions that could benefit from the technology in the country was also an issue of concern in the questionnaire. The questionnaire looked at whether the centre had a marketing program for the technology, in which case the study then established whether the centre was succeeding in marketing the technology.

Researcher's organization was housed at the Scientific and Industrial Research and Development Centre. This enabled direct personal observations to be done about the efficiency and effectiveness of the centre through the adoption and usage of E-Commerce Technology at the centre. Direct personal observation was used as a research instrument because it enabled the subjects to behave naturally without being aware that they were being observed. However, researcher did not have an opportunity to probe for reasons or to investigate further.

Direct observations were done about how the centre generated, shared and stored information within and without the organization. The researcher also looked at how the centre's employees communicated within and without the organization. Observations were also done on how the centre conducted transactions when purchasing and selling products and services. Observation method was used to establish whether E-Commerce Technology could enable the centre to be more efficient and effective in delivering its mandate.

Percentages and tables were used in the analysis of the data because the subjects returned only 71% of the questionnaires send out. The results first focused on establishing whether the center had the required tools to participate in E-Commerce. Data was also presented on the usage of the virtual communication space, the virtual information space, the virtual transaction space, the virtual distribution space, fears and concerns at the centre about using the internet for business and internet marketing usage. The results were presented in the order given above.

5. Results

The study revealed that 89% of the respondents had access to the internet, 8% did not have access to the internet while 3% did not respond to the question. Of the 89% with internet access, 56% had internet tools in their offices while 44% did not have any internet tools in their offices. Of the 44% that did not have Internet tools in their offices, 70% used the internet room that was specifically put in place by management to facilitate internet access. 12% used Internet cafes while the University of Zimbabwe, Institutes' computer labs and the directors' offices were used by 6% each. Direct observation through corporate literature revealed that the center's management had resolved that all offices within the center should have internet connection points installed just like the power points and telephone points put during construction in most office blocks. It was believed by installing internet points in every office, all members of staff would have access to the internet tools. However due to limit resources, some offices did not have the internet points nor the computers required for internet connection at the time of the study. The survey however revealed that 75% of the respondents did not have any knowledge about the policy that governed the distribution of internet tools within the organization. 20%, who could have been managers new the policy while 5% did not give a response.

All the secretaries had internet tools in their offices while 4 middle and senior managers who had donor funded projects had the internet tools in their offices. Ten scientists' offices out of the observed twenty, the accounts office and the data processing office had computers connected to the internet. The sales office and the purchasing office had computers but they were not connected to the internet. The centre had an institute called the informatics and electronics institute. In addition to carrying out research and development activities, the institute administered the centre's local area network. The local area network server was connected to Zanet, the service provider, via telephone lines as well as a radio link. The main access method was through the radio link with the telephone lines only being used when the radio link was down.

Direct personal observation revealed that for internal communication, the centre used notice boards for passing information. There were seven three-storey buildings that were operational within the centre and each of the buildings had nine corridors. Each corridor had a notice board where messages were posted. For every message that was communicated to staff, either by printing one copy and photocopying the rest or by printing all, more than sixty four copies were generated that include sixty three for the notice boards, one for the office copy and copies to senior management depending on who the message was copied to.

Internal communication also involved the use of telephone extensions as well as face-to-face direct communication to communicate urgent and important messages. Direct observation also revealed that communication with the outside world involved the use of telephones even if the other party had an E-mail address. Letters were also used for communication and most managers instructed that the letters be hand delivered by the centre's drivers if the recipients were around Harare. For recipients outside Harare, the letters were posted.

The managers who had internet tools in their offices had their E-mails opened by the secretaries who then printed them before they could read them. The managers then wrote responses where there was need to respond on papers for their secretaries to send them on their behalf. The secretary then printed the response and filed the original mail as well as the response in a physical file.

The survey revealed that 80% of the respondents had electronic mail addresses set up for them by the center, 4% did not have electronic mail addresses set up for them by the center while 8% did not respond to the question. 81% of the respondents had their own personal private E-mail addresses 10% did not have while 9% did not respond to the question. 47% of the respondents received and sent up to 5 E-mails per week, while 33% of the respondents received or sent 5 - 10 E-mails per week. 15% sent and receive 10 - 15 E-mails per week with 5% not responding to the question. Those who did not respond to the question were assumed to receive less than 5

E-mails per week.

Observations revealed that the centre had a web site where most of the centre's activities were published. The majority of the respondents, 70%, have their department's products and services on the SIRDC website while only 27% of the respondents did not have their products and services on the SIRDC web site. 3% of the respondents did not respond to the question. A visit to the web site, also clearly showed that all the centre's products and services offered to outsiders were listed on the web site. 41% of the respondents had their departments' information on the SIRDC's web sites updated monthly. This is followed by 20% of the respondents whose department's information is updated annually. 13% of the respondents reported that their department's information on the web site is never updated, while 4% did not give a response to the question. The survey revealed that 61% of the respondents' departments offer after sales support services to their customers while 22% did not. 17% did not respond to the question. Of the 61% whose departments offered after sales service to their customers, 50% used telephones to communicate with the customers while 31% each use E-mail and personal visits, 6% use the web site, while 17% use the post.

On average, 22% of the respondents stay on the internet for less than 30 minutes. 42% stay on the internet for between 30 - 60 minutes while 28% stay on the internet for 60 - 90 minutes per day. 36% of the respondents stay on the internet for more than one hour per day. Those that did not respond to the question were assumed to stay on the internet for less than 30 minutes per day.

The survey results revealed that 22% of the respondents reported that their departments had databases on the SIRDC local area network, while 65% of the respondents' department did not have any database on the local area network. 12% of the respondents did not respond to the question. Of the respondents who reported that their departments had databases on the SIRDC local area network, 16% reported that these databases were on the SIRDC web site, 70% reported that the databases were not available on the web site while 14% did not respond to the question. A visit to the web site revealed that only the finance department had a database that was on the local area network.

75% reported that they could access general information from the SIRDC web site. This was followed by 28% of the respondents who reported that they could access the SIRDC calendar from the web site. Although 14%, 11% and 17% of the respondents reported that they could access rules and regulations, in-house training materials and minutes of meetings respectively, a visit to the web site revealed that these were not available on the web site at all. What can be accessed on the web site is the SIRDC calendar that shows the coming events including seminars as well as the general information. There were no seminar presentations at all.

Abstraction results revealed that the centre had a purchasing department that processes all purchases by the centre as well as a sales office that processes all sales of the centre's products and services. For anything to be purchased by the centre, the requesting department had to look for three quotations and fill in a "Blue Form" that acted as a requisition form and attach the three quotations. The form would then be approved by the director of the department before going for approval of the Financial Controller, Deputy Director General Finance and Administration or the Director General depending on the amount.

Once the requisition had been approved, it would then go to the purchasing department where an order would be prepared. The order would have to be signed by the Financial Controller, Deputy Director General Finance and Administration or the Director General depending on whom of the three approved the requisition. The signed order would then be used by the purchasing department to purchase the required goods or services. In some cases, the order would be given to the requesting department to proceed with the purchase. The order book had three copies, that is, a white copy that would be presented to the supplier, a yellow copy that would be used by the finance department to effect payment and a pink copy that would remain in the order book for records.

Once the goods were delivered, and an invoice was received, the finance department would then effect payment. They would then write a cheque to the supplier and attach the invoice as well as the yellow copy of the order before sending the cheque to two signatories who would then sign the cheque before it is send to the supplier. Similarly, the sales office would also insist on orders for them to supply any goods or services except for cash purchases. They would then issue a receipt and invoice before any goods were delivered.

From the survey results, 15% of the respondents had their department's products and services on the web site that could be directly ordered by clients. 70% had no such facility while the other 15% did not respond to the question. A visit to the SIRDC web site revealed that none of the products offered by SIRDC could be ordered directly from the web site. 66% of the respondents had never ordered products or services on the internet, 23% ordered while 11% did not respond to the question. The average order frequency of the 23% that had ordered products and services from the internet was once in every 6 months.

Of the 23% that had ordered products or services on the internet, 30% of them used the internet to pay for the products or services ordered at an average frequency of once per year, while 56% did not use the internet for paying. 14% did not respond to the question. The low usage of the internet transaction space was as a result of deep-rooted fears in the respondents with 44% having a level of confidence below 10% with the information received or send during the ordering and payment process. 42% had a confidence level between 10% - 20%, 14% were above 20%. The few that had used the internet for ordering products and services did so about once in every 6 months and a further small percentage of these paid for the order using the internet. Although 15% of the respondents revealed that their departments' products and services could be ordered directly from the web site and visits to the web site revealed that no products could be ordered from the site. Since none of the products could be ordered directly from the web site, it therefore follows that the center cannot send, receive and confirm orders using the web site. Abstraction results revealed that the centre had the required software to enable transaction and distribution processing.

Abstraction results revealed that the centre had not established any distribution channels for its products and services. All those purchasing the centre's products or services had to physically visit the centre which is located 25 kilometers from the Harare city centre. The survey results revealed that 52% of the respondents' department products and services could be digitised, 41% could not be digitized while 7% did not respond to the question. Of the 52% of the respondents whose departments had products and services that could be digitised, 31% of them used the internet for their distribution; 56% did not use the internet for their distribution while 11% did not respond to the question.

It is important to note that 85% of the respondents believe that the centre had not marketed Electronic Commerce Technology to the Zimbabwean government, industry and organizations. 10% believed the center had marketed the technology while 5% did not respond to the question. Abstraction results show that the centre could be more efficient and effective if it used E-Commerce Technology for marketing its products and services through one-to-one marketing that was less costly and timely. The survey results show that the centre was using costly methods for marketing as revealed on **Table 1**. This could be due to the fact that traffic to the site is very low thereby not attracting advertisers.

The survey results showed that most of the computers at the centre were protected from viruses. Those who indicated that their computers were not protected from viruses could have had stand alone systems that were not threatened by virus attacks, since all the computers on the local area network were protected from viruses. The major concerns about using the internet for business seen on **Table 2** are to do with security, privacy and confidentiality.

Table 1. Table showing how the respondents market their department's products and services to potential customers (Multiple response questions).

Method	Percentage
E-mail	19.35
Internet Banners	0.00
SIRDC web site	14.52
Mail shots	0.00
Telephone	27.42
Print media	12.90
Electronic media	1.61
Other	9.68
Not involved in marketing	14.52

Table 2. Table showing respondents' concerns and fears about using the internet for business (Multiple response question).

Concerns and Fears	Percentage
Security	42.31
Privacy & Confidentiality	19.23
Server faults	11.54
No fears and concerns	11.54
Hackers	7.69
Lack of personal touch	3.85
Spam	3.85
Transaction errors	3.85
Piracy (Protection of intellectual property)	3.85
Few Zimbabweans with internet access	3.85
Risk of none payment	3.85
No security competent personal in the country	3.85
Speed of information transmission	3.85
Abuse	3.85

6. Discussion

The result on the availability of internet tools was impressive considering that only 70% of Americans 2 had internet access then. The results seem to suggest that SIRDC had the required capacity and tools to adopt Electronic Commerce as a business tool for the purpose of improving efficiency and effectiveness. The availability of a local area network, as well as a wide area network through the link to Zanet, coupled with management's desire to see internet tools in every office, was a clear indication of management's commitment to the use of internet technology for improving efficiency and effectiveness. The distribution of the internet tools within the organization was however flawed because it ignored key personal such as the purchasing office, the sales office, the scientists and the managers who should effectively utilize these tools for E-Commerce if efficiency and effectiveness was to be achieved. The results also revealed that the established policy on the distribution of internet tools was not widely shared a symptom of poor communication.

The use of Physical notice boards for communicating was not efficient and effective because it was more costly than E-mail or electronic notice boards, it took more time to generate and to reach recipient and did not give recipients an opportunity to give feedback. The use of telephones to communicate to outsiders with E-mail addresses was not efficient and effective because for local calls, although costs were almost the same for E-mails and telephones, the time required to communicate was more for telephones compared to using E-mail. For long distance communication, the cost was even more due to the time and the tariffs that were higher. The use of drivers to deliver printed mail to recipients with E-mail addresses was also costly and time consuming considering the cost of printing, paper, fuel and personal. E-mail is paperless and instantaneous. Posted letters were even worse in terms of time and costs.

Worldwide, the use of email is replacing traditional forms of communication such as telephones and postal services. The usage is also growing at a fast pace compared to other technologies that have been developed. The reason for this growth is the efficiency and effectiveness of the technology. It was therefore important that the centre use E-mail in order for the centre to be more efficient and effective in delivering its mandate. The fact that more than 80% of the respondents had both corporate and private E-mail addresses implies that most of the SIRDC staff members could use electronic mail for communication purposes. The usage of E-mail at the centre however was very low as evidenced by the number of E-mails that were send or received by the respondents. For effective usage of E-mail, it was expected that the majority of the respondents were supposed to send and receive more than 50 E-mails per week. The results showed that the facility was underutilized at the centre contrary to the theory that this was the most widely used service of the internet [2,11].

The daily usage of the internet per employee was between 30 - 60 minutes on average. Considering the functions on the internet, this was very low. This could be due to the fact that the employees were more comfortable using physical tools rather than the virtual information space for business. The results on how often the web site was updated, suggest that the centre's web site was updated regularly. However, the frequency of update was not consistent in the various departments. Although the centre offered after sales support services to customers, it was underutilizing the available internet tools for that function. If the centre would efficiently and effectively use the web, they would also achieve efficiency and effectiveness through the reduction in the costs of information sharing as well as the time required to share the information [2].

The results suggest that the centre does not have an integrated internet/intranet/extranet system nor does it have databases a key component of intranet and extranet systems. Apart from the general information that could be accessed on the intranet, the rest of the information and communication functions of the intranet and extranet are underutilized at the centre. This could be due to lack of knowledge at the centre about the effective and efficient use of the intranet and extranets. Intranets and extranets could be important tools if implemented as an integrated system. An integrated internet/intranet/extranet solution could be the best investment the centre could make to face today's globalised world [12,13].

The center was not utilizing the virtual transaction space for transaction processing. The main reason why the centre's staff did not use the internet for transaction processing could have been due to deep rooted security, privacy and confidentiality fears. This is in line with theory [13] because despite the fact that security systems are being improved regularly and internet systems are more secure than the traditional physical systems, people are still afraid to use the internet for transaction purposes. Results seem to suggest that the centre's staff were not following closely on the security and privacy technologies that were on the internet despite the education levels of the centre's employees. The whole transaction processing system could be automated if they used the virtual transaction space a situation that could result in cost and time savings [2,14]. From a strategic point of view, E-Commerce transactions are a key element for the participation of the centre in the great trade flows and in the profound changes that have taken place in the world of research, business, investment and commerce. It is the main entrance to the real Information Society.

These survey results showed that although the centre had products and services that could be distributed over the internet, the utilization of the internet tools for distribution of products and services at the centre was very low. The abstraction results reveal that the centre is using physical means for the distribution of all their products and services with no distribution channels in place. The centre could be more efficient and effective in the distribution process if they used the virtual distribution space for distributing those products that could be digitised like software and training as well as establish formal distribution channels for those products that cannot be digitised. Further, the marketing of the centre's products and services is heavily reliant on the traditional media as well as traditional methods of mass marketing, ignoring the cheaper tools available.

7. Conclusions and Recommendations

From the results of the study, the following conclusions

about the adoption of Electronic Commerce Technology at the centre can be drawn:

- The full adoption and usage of E-Commerce Technology can result in the centre being more efficient and effective in delivering its mandate as shown in the literature review.
- The centre had partially adopted Electronic Commerce Technology.
- The centre had not marketed E-Commerce Technology to industry and other organizations.
- In light of the above conclusions, it is recommended that:
- The centre implements an integrated internet/intranet/extranet system that would result in total adoption of Electronic Commerce Technology for the benefit of improving efficiency and effectiveness in delivering its mandate.
- Once the centre fully adopts the technology, it should market the technology to government, industry and organizations in the country in line with its mandate.

It will be important for an investigation to be done to establish the requirements, in terms of human and material resources, for fully adopting E-Commerce Technology since this could be the major hindrance.

8. Acknowledgements

The author would like to thank the management of SIRDC for their support during the conduct of this research and all the staff of the centre who participated in the research.

REFERENCES

[1] T. Liang and J. Huang, "A Framework for Applying Intelligent Agents to Support Electronic Trading," 2000. http://www.ecrc.nsysu.edu.tw/liang/paper/IAFramework(DSS28,4,2000).pdf

[2] J. I. Cole, "The UCLA Internet Report—Surveying the Digital Future," 2002. http://www.digitalcenter.org/pdf/InternetReportYearThree.pdf

[3] R. Lee, "Electronic Commerce: The Quest for a Global, Secure Infrastructure," Novell Developer Information, 1997. http://support.novell.com/techcenter/articles/ana19971004.html

[4] W. H. DeLone and E. R. McLean, "Measuring e-Commerce Success: Applying the DeLone & McLean Information Systems Success Model," *International Journal of Electronic Commerce*, Vol. 9, No. 1, 2004, pp. 31-47.

[5] A. Ca`Zorzi, "Electronic Commerce and Development Implications for IDB Action," 2000. http://idbdocs.iadb.org/wsdocs/getdocument.aspx?docnum=1484412

[6] A. Petri and O. Nixu, "Models of Electronic Commerce," 1995. http://www.tml.tkk.fi/Opinnot/Tik-110.501/1995/commerce.html

[7] A. Angehrn, "Designing Mature Internet Business Strategies: The ICDT Model," *European Management Journal*, Vol. 15, No. 4, 1997, pp. 361-369. http://www.calt.insead.edu/eis/icdt%20documents/icdt-emj-1.pdf

[8] A. Angehrn, "The Strategic Implications of the Internet," The European Institute of Business Administration. http://www.calt.insead.edu/Publication/ICDT/strategicImplication.htm

[9] R. Clarke, "EDI Is but One Element of Electronic Commerce," *6th International EDI Conference*, Bled, 1993. http://www.rogerclarke.com/EC/Bled93.html

[10] T. Warner, "Applied Business Statistics," 4th Edition, Juta & Co. LTD., Cape Town, 1993, pp. 168-173.

[11] D. G. Venolia, L. Dabbish, J. J. Cadiz and A. Gupta, "Supporting Email Workflow," 2001. http://www.research.microsoft.com/pubs/69881/tr-2001-88.pdf

[12] G. McGovern, "Intranet Return on Investment Case Studies," 2002. http://www.gerrymcgovern.com/nt/2002/nt_2002_11_18_intranet_roi.htm

[13] H. Lebo, "The UCLA Internet Report—Surveying the Digital Future," 2003. http://images.forbes.com/fdc/mediaresourcecenter/UCLA03.pdf

[14] A. C. Zorzi, "Electronic Commerce and Development Implications for IDB Action," 2000. http://idbdocs.iadb.org/wsdocs/getdocument.aspx?docnum=1484412

15

iPhone Independent Real Time Localization System Research and Its Healthcare Application

Xintong Lu[1], Wei Liu[2], Yongliang Guan[1]
[1]EEE, Nanyang Technological University, Singapore City, Singapore
[2]Singapore Institute of Manufacturing Technology, Singapore City, Singapore

ABSTRACT

This project studied several popular localization algorithms on iPhone and, according to the demands, specifically designed it to improve healthcare IT system in hospitals. The challenge of this project was to realize the different localization systems on iPhone and to make balance between its response time and localization accuracy. We implemented three popular localization algorithms, namely nearest neighbor (NN), K-nearest neighbor (KNN), and probability phase, and we compared their performance on iPhone. Furthermore, we also implemented a real-time localization system using the ZigBee technology on iPhone. Thus, the whole system could realize not only self-localization but also others-localization. To fulfill the healthcare needs, we developed an application, which can be used to improve the hospital IT, system. The whole project included three phases. The first phase was to localize iPhone's position using the received WiFi signal by iPhone, compare and optimize their performances. During the second phase, we implemented a ZigBee RFID localization system and combined it with the WiFi system. Finally, we combined new features of the system with a healthcare IT system. We believe that this application on iPhone can be a useful and advanced application in hospitals.

Keywords: iPhone; RTLS; WiFi; Healthcare

1. Introduction

In healthcare industry, there is a trend to decrease the doctors' workload using advanced IT technology. With the development of technology, the healthcare technology in hospitals is more and more advanced and efficient. During daily ward round of doctor, it is quite inconvenient for doctors to check every patient's cases, especially if there are lots of patients in one hospital. Traditional way to cope with it was that doctors had to memorize all cases of different patients or brought case files with themselves. Nowadays, many hospitals have used e-commerce, which will import patient cases into hospital system or even national health care system to help doctors to check patient history cases easily. By connection with this system, we can also simplify the process of ward round of doctor by our localization system. Furthermore, tracking patients' location and behavior is also useful for doctors. According to recent statistics of Midland psychiatric ward, more than 1000 mentally ill patients have escaped from the wards in the last three years, which is proved that tracking patient is a significant technology in hospitals. Finally, this localization application can also supply a function of indoor navigation to patients. No one can deny that finding a right way in an unfamiliar hospital is a tough task, especially for patients. Hence, if a mobile application can guide them to right area, it will help them save time. In our application, we developed a sub-application for patients with iPhone compass module to realize indoor navigation.

Radio frequency identification (RFID) [1] is a widely used technology in bank business field, security field and short distance communication field. The basic components of RFID system are tags, readers and application software. RFID readers can detect and read the data, which is emitted from tags through a defined radio frequency and protocol. Tags can be divided into two types: passive tags and active tags. For passive tags, they will not emit a signal by themselves. Instead, they generate a response by the power of reader's signal. It has both pros and cons. Obviously, it is energy-free, thus enabling tags to be used in a long term and making tags portable. However, the transmission range is only about 10 m to 5 meters. Alternatively, active RFID tags will transmit signal actively. They have a longer working range, which will arrive at tens of meters. In our ZigBee localization system, we use active tags. The reason of it is that not only long-range but also more accurate localization than passive tags can be achieved.

Localization system has many ways to be implemented, such as Global Positioning System (GPS), cellular (A-GPS) and etc. GPS provides information of users' location and time anywhere on earth. This system contains 24 localization satellites. Thus it can provide a satisfied service outdoors. But this above way has a limitation, though they are efficiently used in outdoors, they cannot contribute to indoors localization accuracy. Nowadays, existing methods for indoor localization are LANDMARC, RADAR, Cricket Location Support System, Angle of arrival, Time of arrival and Fingerprinting algorithm [2,3]. In this paper, because of iPhone limitation, we choose fingerprinting algorithm utilizing WiFi signal. WiFi signal indoors localization is a popular technology. For the reason that more and more mobile devices contain WiFi function, there is no extra-device needed to realize self-localization.

This paper focuses on independent indoor localization system implemented on iPhone and performance comparison of different algorithms and its healthcare application. The advantage of independent localization system is that we needn't have to connect to an AP to access a server. That means even we don't know the password of the WiFi signals, we still can use them to do localization. Section 2 discusses the implementation procedure and two systems structure. Section 3 provides the algorithm explanation and performance analysis among different algorithms and different systems. Section 4 introduces the application about healthcare and method of implementation. Finally, Section 5 concludes the paper briefly.

2. Implementation

2.1. Complete Structure of Our Prototype

Figure 1 shows the complete structure of the doctor's application. As we can see from the flow diagram, there are three main functions in this application: self-localization, patient localization, ward round application. Because this application has to use WiFi module of iPhone, it is mandatory to turn on WiFi before the application operation. There are two localization systems in this application: WiFi localization system and ZigBee localization system.

2.2. WiFi Localization System

For the WiFi system, we use SDK Xcode to program an application in iPhone to scan WiFi signal periodically. In fact, obtaining and scanning RSSI values in iPhone is proved to be a tough task [4,5]. Because Apple company

Figure 1. Overall architecture.

has stopped disclosing its public APIs for obtaining the network's information. One possible way to get current RSSI value is put all APs into monitor mode. It will send signal with RSSI strength according our programming. But the obvious drawback of this method is that all APs cannot connect to the Internet, which means that these APs just provide localization function. In our system, we have found a way to solve this problem. Instead of using monitor mode APs, we install the application in root folder of iPhone operation system, which makes it can use iPhone private API. By using this way, it simplifies the APs configuration. However the disadvantage is that this software must be setup by trained people.

Before we use the WiFi-localization, we should execute calibration phase. In calibration phase, iPhone will detect surrounding WiFi signal to record them as offline data. In online phase, according different algorithms, iPhone will execute different methods to compute the current location by comparison of recorded statistics.

2.3. ZigBee Localization System

Figure 2 shows the structure of ZigBee localization system. The main components of this system are: 1) Asset tags; 2) Sensors of fixed location; 3) Base station which will receive data from sensors; 4) Database.

It contains two parts: hardware and software.

In this project, CC2530 evaluation modules are employed as tag and readers and CC2531 USB dongle is used as base station to transmit information captured from readers to PC (**Figure 3**). Furthermore, serial port connection plays a key role in hardware part. It takes charges of transmit received statistics to database.

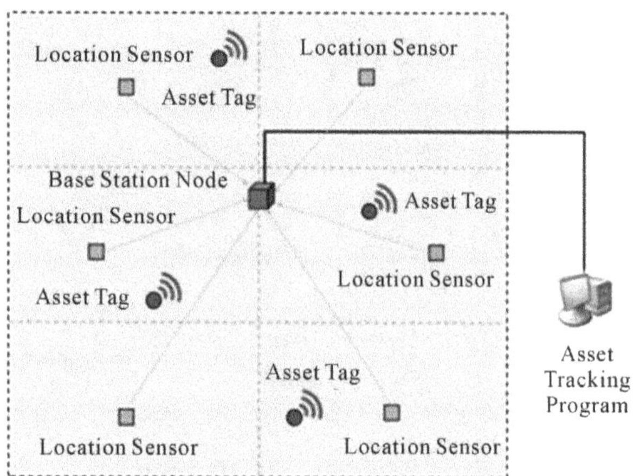

Figure 2. ZigBee system architecture.

Figure 3. CC2530.

In software part, C# and Microsoft SQL are used in programming. The localization algorithm of this system is described as follow. It is a classified as a range-free localization algorithm. The sensors with fixed location will detect whether there is a tag in their detection zone.When multiple location sensors can scan a same tag, the maximum RSSI value received by the location sensor is used to determine the detection zone.

Calibration phase, as mentioned previously, makes use of comparison between recorded map and current value. Because of unstable asset tag measured result, a probability method is adopted.

3. Algorithms and Experiment

3.1. WiFi Localization System [6,7]

Since this paper focuses on WiFi localization application on iPhone, this section will compare and analyze the performance of different localization algorithm on iPhone. We will also briefly introduce the ZigBee localization system in the second part of this section. In this project, the WiFi system uses three different algorithms: nearest neighbor, K-nearest neighbor, probability.

We did experiment in a lab. The floor plan was plotted in **Figure 4**. As we can see, there are three main APs in this lab. But we still could scan more than five WiFi signals, which also could be used to localization. For WiFi

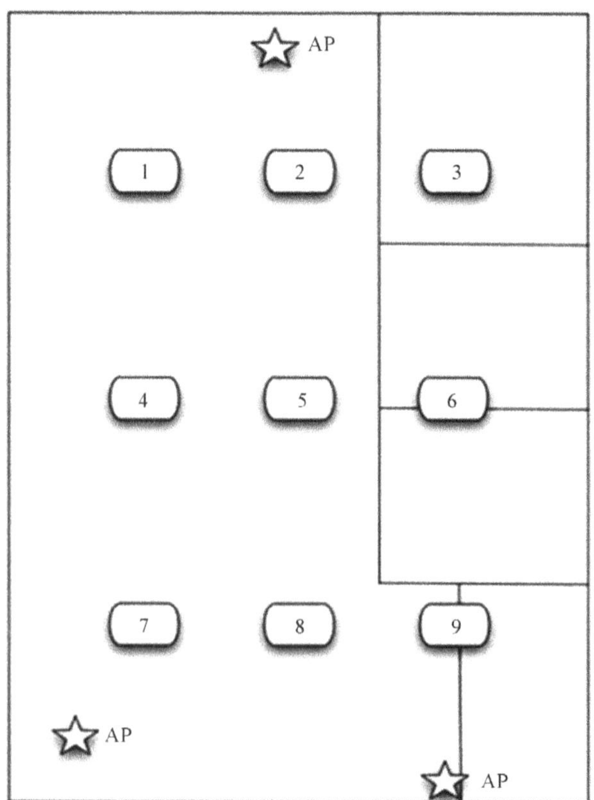

Figure 4. Floor plan.

localization phase, we don't have to know the WiFi password. As long as we can scan the signal, we can use it. According our experience, the more APs the more accurate. Hence, in WiFi phase, if we want to continue to improve the accuracy, we just simply increase the number of main APs instead of changing the algorithm.

Offline phase based on IEEE 11 channel model: In the calibration phase, a radio map of the environment is created. A radio map is a database of locations throughout the environment with RSSI value, MAC address, channel number and SSID. The process of producing a radio map based on actual measurements is not only labor-intensive and costly but also very sensitive to changes in the environment and possible effects of interference in the building. Using IEEE 802.11 channel model can be a simple alternative way to create a radio map.

To provide a better presentation of our environment, we have used IEEE 802.11 channel model in model C. The received power in IEEE 802.11 channel model is represented by (1).

$$RSS(d) = Pt - L(d) + f(d) \quad (1)$$

where, Pt is the transmitting power, d is the distance between the sender and receiver. The $f(a)$ stands for all kinds of fading. In this situation, the main fading is the shadow fading process which given by (2) and (3) respectively,

$$L(d) = L_0 + 10a_1 \log 10(d) \qquad d \le d_{BP}$$

$$L(d) = L_0 + 10a_1 \log_{10}(d) + 10a_2 \log_{10}\left(\frac{d}{d_{BP}}\right) \quad d \le d_{BP} \quad (2)$$

$$f(d) = \rho \cdot f(d-1) + \sqrt{(1-\rho^2)} \cdot N(0, \sigma) \quad (3)$$

where, L_0: the path loss at reference distance. d_{BP}: the breakpoint distance in meters (1 m). a_1: is the power-distance gradient before the breakpoint. a_2: is the power-distance gradient after the breakpoint. σ: standard deviation. ρ: a correlation coefficient.

Nearest neighbor algorithm: This is the simplest algorithm, which will release utilization of iPhone CPU. For experiment, we draw a floor plan in iPhone. Meanwhile, to execute the offline phase, we design nine points in the floor plan to record the WiFi signal strength (RSSI value), MAC address of APs, sequence number of channel and SSID of APs for calibration and story it into iPhone default database, which will automatically exist in the software when users download their software and never missing.

When the software runs the nearest neighbor algorithm, it follows below equation:

$$d = \sqrt{(ss_1 - SS_1)^2 + (ss_2 - SS_2)^2 + \cdots + (ss_n - SS_n)^2}$$

where ss_n is current RSSI value of nth AP. SS_n is calibration recorded RSSI value of nth AP.

After all of distance is computed, it will choose the highest value of Euclidian distance as its position and map it.

K-nearest neighbors algorithm: To improve the performance and accuracy of NN algorithm, the common way is using KNN. Instead of using all of RSSI value, KNN algorithm chooses K samples of Euclidian distance which are defined by follow equation:

$$E_i = \sqrt{\sum_{j=1}^{N}(ss_i - SS_i)} \quad (4)$$

After sorting the calculated E_i, K data samples with smaller Euclidian distance are picked up as K nearest neighbors. K is usually an integer number between 1 and N samples. To map the position, the position with smallest Euclidian distance will be selected as the final position.

Probability algorithm: Unlike NN and KNN, probability depends on the probability of RSSI value [8]. Because we try to complete all of calculation in iPhone, it is inconvenient to implement the probability algorithm we used in ZigBee localization system, which will increase the load of CPU of iPhone and affect the real time localization ability. In this WiFi localization system, we try to use a simple probability algorithm.

When we do the training method, we can record multiple times RSSI value for every WiFi signal. Then, when users try to use the application, it will scan current WiFi signal strength to check the probability that there is a same value in recorded data. The position with the highest sum of probability will be mapped in the screen.

Experiment measurement and result: We have done 20 times test at 9 positions for every phase. Then we calculate the error of every time and time-consumption. Then we plot the CDF (Cumulative Distribution Function).

Error:

$$\text{error}(\text{cm}) = \sqrt{(x_{\text{actual}} - x_{\text{test}})^2 + (y_{\text{actual}} - y_{\text{test}})^2} \quad (5)$$

According above **Table 1** and **Figures 5** and **6**, we can conclude:

1) NN is the simplest way to localize, but it has the worst performance.

2) KNN and probability phase have similar performance.

3) This localization system owns better accuracy in the area which is far from wall especially for KNN. Because in position 4 and 7 of KNN, the accuracy of 20 times test can reach perfection.

4) Compared with NN and KNN, the probability phase is the highest complex, which means that it needs much more time consumption.

5) Though KNN just calculate K nearest neighbor, but it still costs more time than NN phase because of the

Table 1. Error distance.

	NN	KNN	Probability
1	568.501	244.566	234.078
2	438.353	443.194	263.309
3	510	502.209	553.559
4	403.5	0	39
5	80.077	256.040	267.622
6	168	474.141	341.941
7	622.383	0	187.5
8	418.373	143.012	305.273
9	168	382.5	157.5
Average error distance	375.242	224.566	345.078
Average time consumption	1805 ms	1871 ms	3826 ms

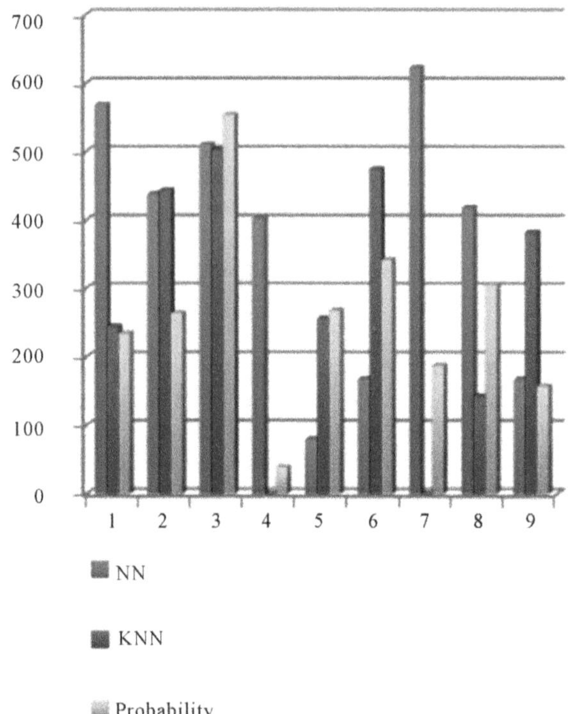

Figure 5. Position error distributions.

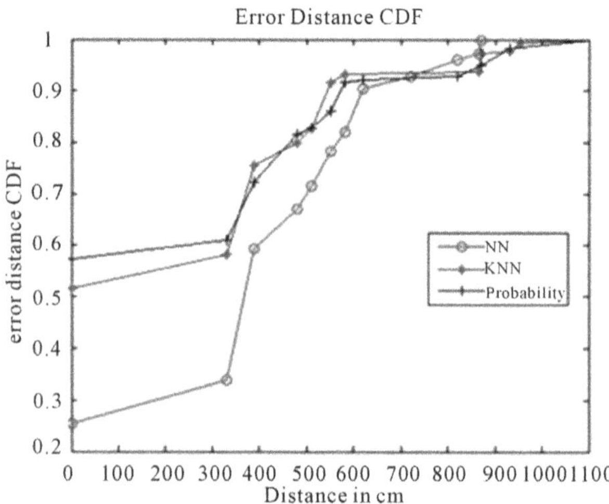

Figure 6. Error distance CDF.

sorting process.

6) According the **Figure 6**, probability phase has better performance than others. More than 50% localization points have no error. However, NN phase has the worst error statistics. More than 50% localization points have above 400 cm error distance.

7) For the health care system, since we are focusing on not only the accuracy and but real-time feature, we select KNN as our application phase.

Although the test result was good, we still can find that the position of current location may jump to other places instantaneously, which has bad performance. Thus, to improve the accuracy, we added a filter to the last result.

As the above introduction, the RSSI value may be affected by change of circumstance. For instance, if there are many people around the receiver, the RSSI value can change dramatically. According our test, the received RSSI can have 10 dB differences at a same position. Hence, to solve this problem, we store the last several times results as a reference statistics. If the final result is different from the previous data, we should make a decision whether the position should be changed. The logic of the filter is following the diagram **Figure 7**.

Furthermore, to reduce the chance that the display of the position will jump a large-scale distance, we introduced a small-scale jump phase. Instead of jumping to the destination point directly, in our system, the position will just move to the inferred point with smaller distance.Because, in our system, the calibration points in the radio map have 397.5 centimeters distance. Although walking speed is various depending on the height, weight, age, terrain, surface, load and so on. The average speed is 5 kilometers per hour, or about 1.3 meters per second. So, imagining a person is walking in our experimental circumstance, the average variation is almost one third of distance of changing.

$$\text{Inferred Position} = \text{Original Position} + \frac{\text{Distance Difference}}{3} \quad (6)$$

where, Distance Difference is the distance between last position and current measured position.

Thus, we can track the moving of inferred position. From the above analysis, we know that the probability phase has better performance for the reason that it uses more record statistics. Thus, to improve the NN, KNN performance, we change the calibration phase. Instead of recording the data directly, we adopt a method that it

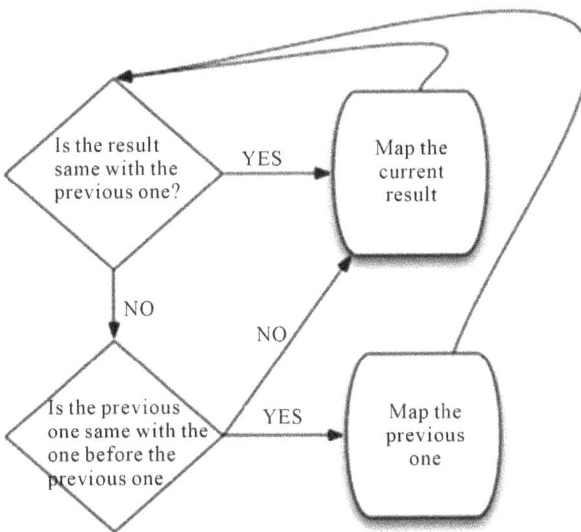

Figure 7. Logic of filter.

scans the WiFi signal n times and calculate the average RSSI value. In this way, it will avoid the break changing of RSSI value. Meanwhile, to reduce the effect of the direction of devices, we can scan the multi-direction in calibrationphase. When we do the calibration, the user should go round in the position to collect all the statistics of multi-direction.

Because we have found that the probability phase has obvious delay. Hence, we just implement above filters and phases in NN and KNN.

Then, we did the calibration phase and tested the error distance again just like the previous one. The final experimental resultis as follow:

From the final experimental result (**Table 2**, **Figures 8** and **9**), we can see that the average error distance of KNN can be reduced to 123.7 cm by mentioned filters and phases. The time consumption will increase a little from 1871 cm to 1925 ms. In addition, because the position will move small distance every time when the current position is different from the previous one, the number of small error distance increases. We can see this phenomenon from **Figure 9**. However, the performance of NN and KNN with filters gets improvement. From **Figure 9**, the performance of NN with filters is even better than the performance of probability without filters. It also shows that more than 90 percent of KNN inferred positions with filters have error distance less than 3 meters.

The reason why filters can improve the accuracy is that it filters unstable statistics in the radio map. Hence less unexpected jump happens. In addition, the step filter measures the position according human move, which can reduce the large-scale jump.

There are still two factors we can explore their relationships with performance, which are the K value of KNN and the number of sampling points.

Table 2. Error distance with filter.

Position Index	Error distance	
	NN	KNN
1	329	77
2	214	129
3	251	62
4	480	56
5	270	268
6	77	23
7	416	76
8	91	293
9	49	128
Average error distance	242	124
Average time consumption	1845 ms	1925 ms

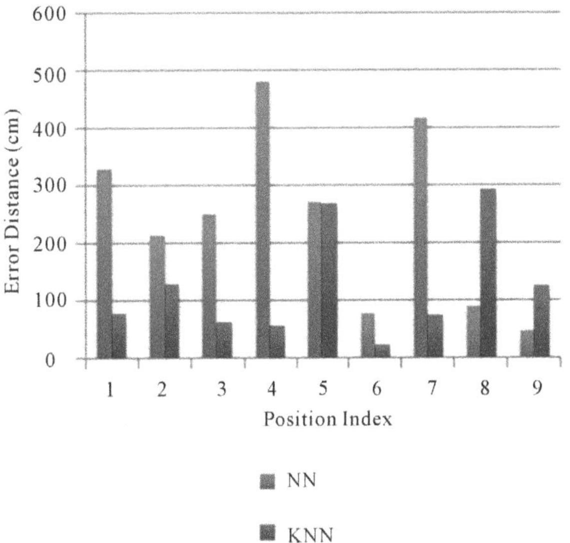

Figure 8. Position index.

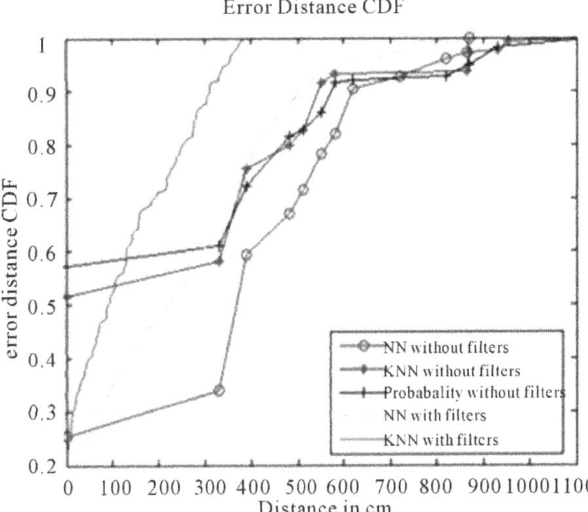

Figure 9. Error distance CDF.

We tested 9 sampling points' case, and got the statistics: From **Table 3** and **Figure 10**, we can know that the K = 4 is the best algorithm for localization in 9 sampling points' case. Furthermore we can find the average time consumption will increase with the value of K.

Next, for 16 sampling points' measurement, we got the experimental statistics as follow: From **Table 4** and **Figure 11**, we can easily find that K = 4 is more accurate than others. What's more, the time consumption still follows the law we got in 9 sampling points. And we also can find that the 16 sampling points will cost more time than 9 sampling locations case.

Finally, we tested the 25 sampling points, which is much more complex than others (**Table 5**). We plotted the average error distance at every location:

From **Figure 12** and **Table 5**, we find that the result is different from the earlier two cases. K = 5 has the best result. The reason of this is that the 5th signal is stationary at the time of the experiment. Furthermore, 25 sam pling points case will be sensitive to any small variation, so K = 4 cannot be as good as 16 sampling points case and 9 sampling points.

From all these 9 tests, we can get the following conclusions:

KNN with K = 4 has better result than others generally.

16 sampling points is the best situation.

9 sampling points' case and 25 sampling points' case have similar performance in average error distance, which are worse than 16 sampling points. Although 25 sampling points is more complex, but the statistical similarity is too high to get accurate result.

K = 3 has the least time-consumption, because after selecting k minimum error distance, it only uses the 3 minimum error distance to localize.

For time consumption, 9 sampling points < 16 sampling points < 25 sampling points. The reason for this phenomenon is that, for 9 sampling points' case, it only calculates the distance between current location and 9 recording calibration locations. But for 25 sampling points, it has to compare with 25 recording calibration

Table 3. 9 sampling test statistics.

	Error distance		
	K = 3	K = 4	K = 5
The Worst Error Distance	379	293	587
Average Error Distance	170	124	186
Average time consumption	1806 ms	1925 ms	1931 ms

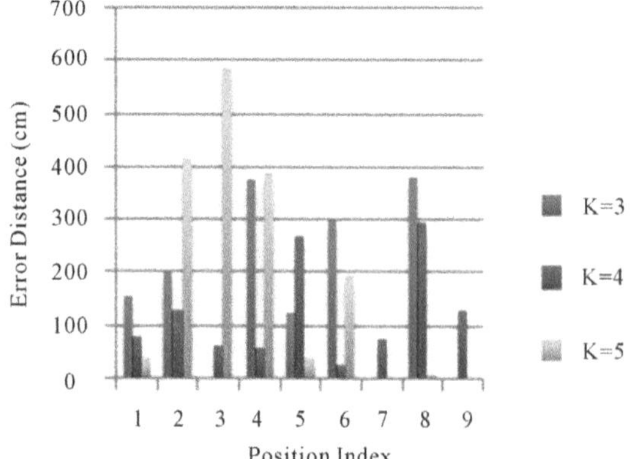

Figure 10. Average error distance at every location for 9 sampling points.

Table 4. 16 sampling points test statistics for 9 sampling points.

	Error distance		
	K = 3	K = 4	K = 5
The Worst Error Distance	304	256	244
Average Error Distance	134	107	139
Average time consumption	1810 ms	1937 ms	1944 ms

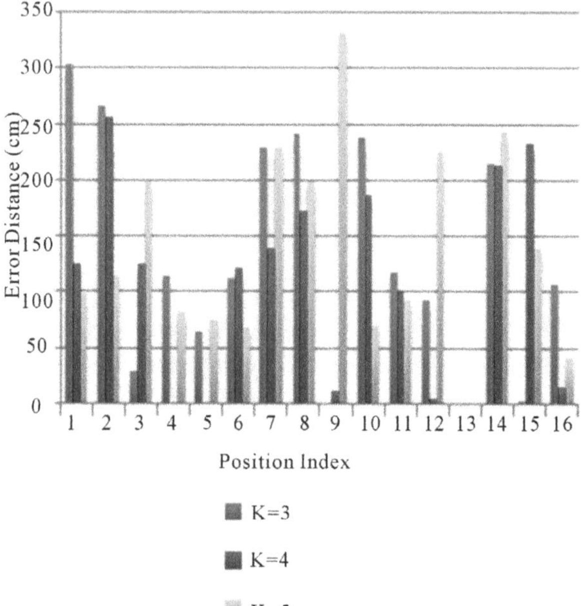

Figure 11. Average error distance at every location for 16 sampling points.

Table 5. 25 sampling test statistics.

	Error distance		
	K = 3	K = 4	K = 5
The Worst Error Distance	482	475	340
Average Error Distance	183	179	158
Average time consumption	1891 ms	1971 ms	2663 ms

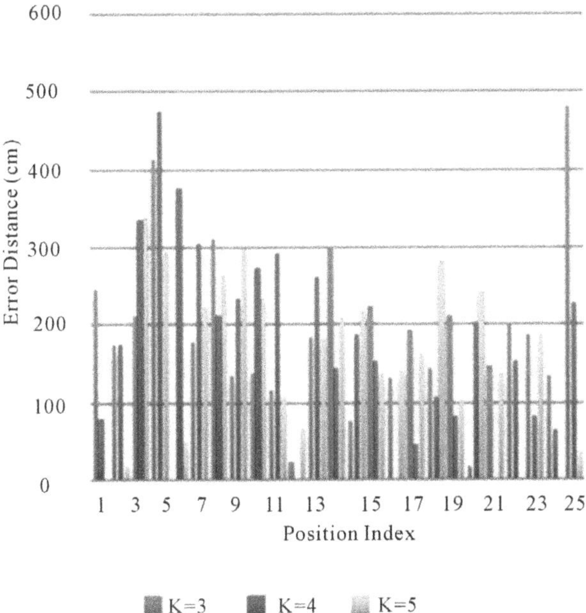

Figure 12. Average error distance at every location for 25 sampling points.

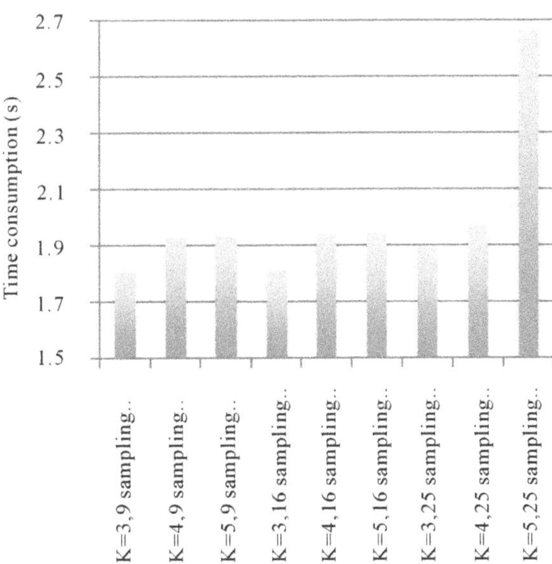

Figure 13. Time consumption of each situation.

locations (**Figure 13**).

We can also find that the bottom points have better accurate than others. The bottom points mean that the measured points near the bottom line of the floor plan. The reason of this result is that around the bottom line there are two APs, which can localize the location accurately. At the top of the floor plan there is only one AP. The system hardly finds the accurate location. To improve the accuracy of this experimental circumstance, we should add one AP at the top line of the floor plan.

16 sampling points KNN algorithm with K = 4 can achieve 107 cm error distance accuracy.

To research the relationship between the K value of KNN and its localization performance, we tested three situations with K = 3, K = 4, K = 5, and plotted their performance. According to previous literature, the K value depends on the algorithm, the measurement method and circumstance. We plotted the CDF figures of three cases (**Figures 14-16**).

From the 9 sampling points, we can know that KNN with K = 4 is the best algorithm.

From the 16 sampling points, we can know that KNN with K = 4 is the best algorithm.

From the 25 sampling points, we can know that KNN with K = 4 has outstanding performance.

According to **Figure 14-16**, we can get the conclusion:

Totally, K = 4 has better performance than others. Because, in our experimental circumstance, there are four major routers, they can provide the strong evidence for localization. For RSSI value, the closer distance between

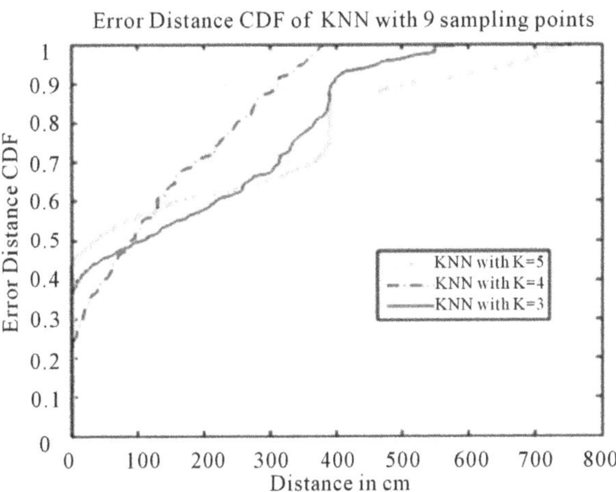

Figure 14. 9 sampling points with different K value.

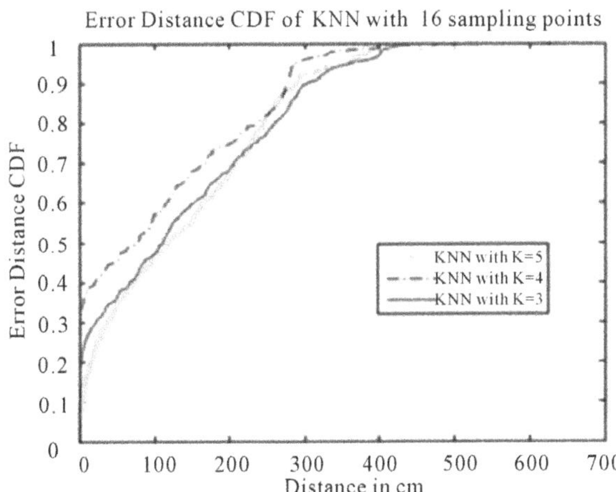

Figure 15. 16 sampling points with different K value.

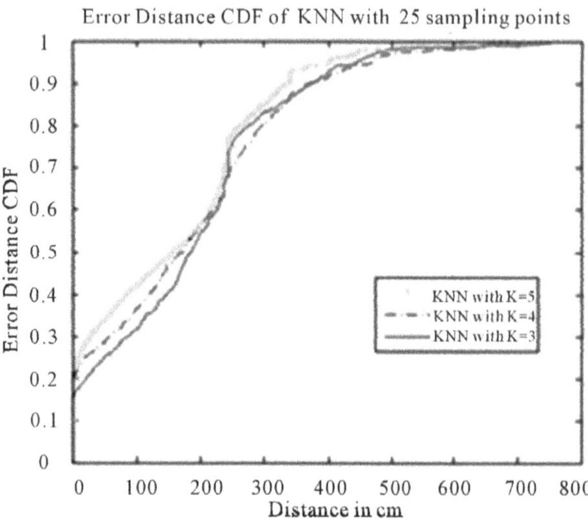

Figure 16. 25 sampling points with different K values.

APs and receivers, the better stable performance we will get.

For K = 5 cases, in 25 sampling points, it has better accuracy than 9 sampling points' case and 16 sampling points' case. Because, in 25 sampling points, neighbor distance is smaller than others, it protects against small-scale variation. For the 5th strongest signal, it is not the major signal. Hence, it will experience lots of reflection, diffraction and multipath. It also passes several walls and floors. We can use Ericsson multiple breakpoint model [9] to estimate the remote APs signal.

In 9 sampling points, the error distance for different K values is fluctuating. The reason of this phenomenon is that signal surrounding of sampling points in 9 sampling points' case are quite different. And the distance between points is large. Hence long-distance error can be happened.

To research the relationship between the sampling density and its localization accuracy, we also change the sampling density. Instead of 9 sampling points, we use 16 sampling points and 25 sampling points (**Figure 17-19**) Then we compare their performance and get the conclusion.

We measured minimum distance between two neighbors in there cases:

We plotted the above three situations in **Figure 20**. Then we compared their performance.

From **Figure 20** and **Table 6**, we can know that, for short-term distance error, 9 sampling points' case has better performance than others. For long-term distance error, 16 sampling points' case is the best one rather than 25 sampling points' case.

We can also find the result of **Figure 21** is similar with the previous one. The difference is that in short-term distance error 16 sampling points' case has similar performance with 9 sampling points' case.

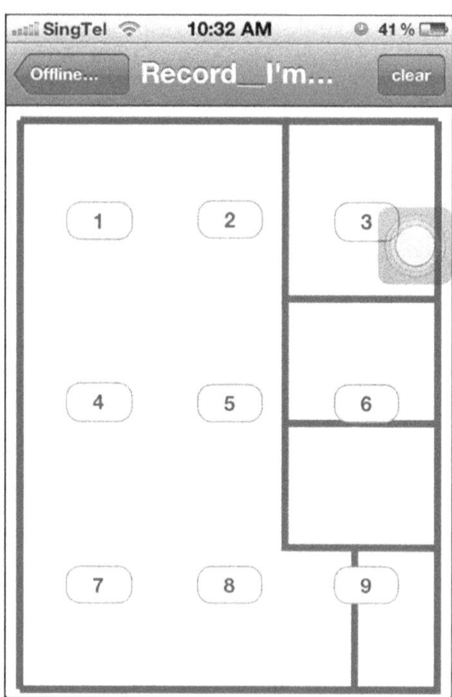

Figure 17. 9 sampling points.

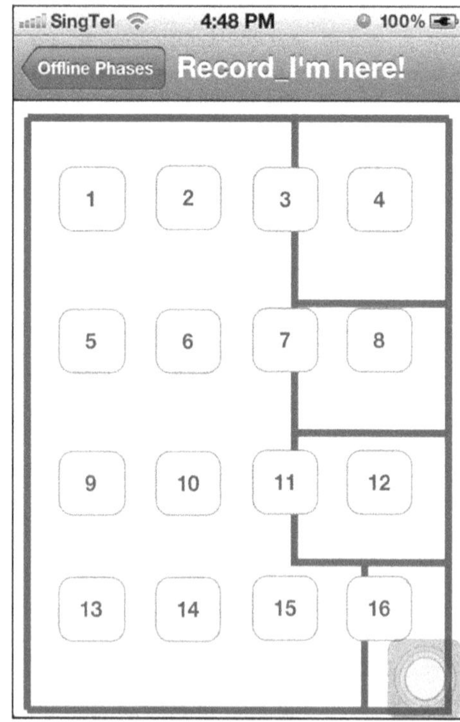

Figure 18. 16 sampling locations.

For K = 5 case, we can also find the conclusion. But the result is clearer than others. In short-term distance error almost half of result in 9 sampling points is zero error. But in long-term case, 16 sampling points is brilliant.

From **Figures 20-22**, we can get the conclusion:

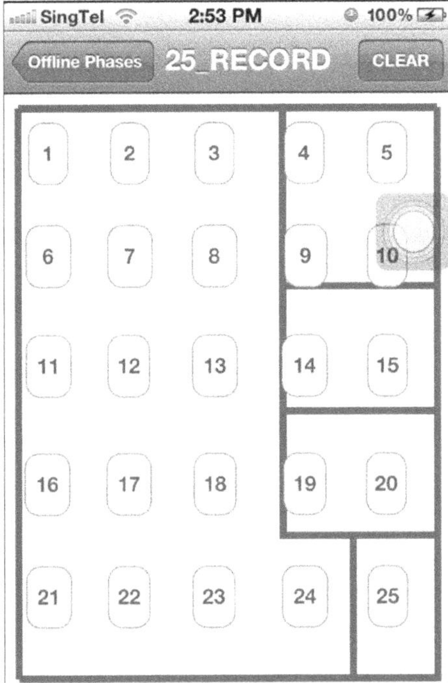

Figure 19. 32 sampling locations.

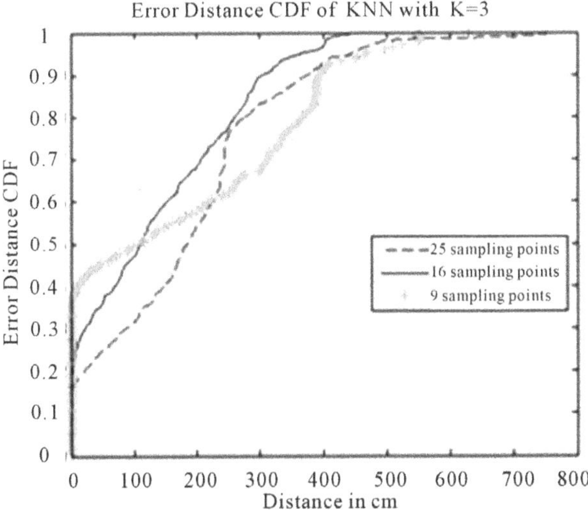

Figure 20. Different sampling points with K = 3.

Table 6. Minimum neighbors distance.

	9 sampling points	16 sampling points	25 sampling points
Minimum distance between two neighbors (cm)	330	312	260

9 sampling points has better accuracy or more zero distance in short-term distance error. As we know, 9 sampling points case has far neighbors. It has slim chance to skip to their neighbor, because their neighbors have quite different WiFi circumstance. From minimum neighbors' distance table, we have gotten the minimum distance between two neighbors. For 9 sampling points' case, the minimum distance is 330 cm, which is larger than others.

However, 16 sampling points' case and 25 sampling points' case have outstanding accuracy in long-term. For small probability error, which is long-term distance error, 16 sampling points' case and 25 sampling points case have common feature that they can protect against the happen of long-term distance error. The reason of this phenomenon is that, for these two cases, they have closer neighbor than 9 sampling points' case. Even if the measured signal strength is quite different from the calibration strength, it can also find near neighbor to localize.

16 sampling points' case is more accurate than 25 sampling points. For 25 sampling points, the minimum neighbors distance is too little to localize correctly. The relevant coherency of signal strength between neighbors

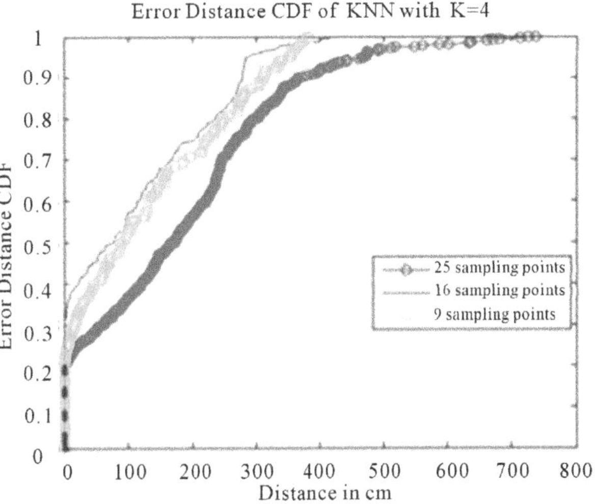

Figure 21. Different sampling points with K = 4.

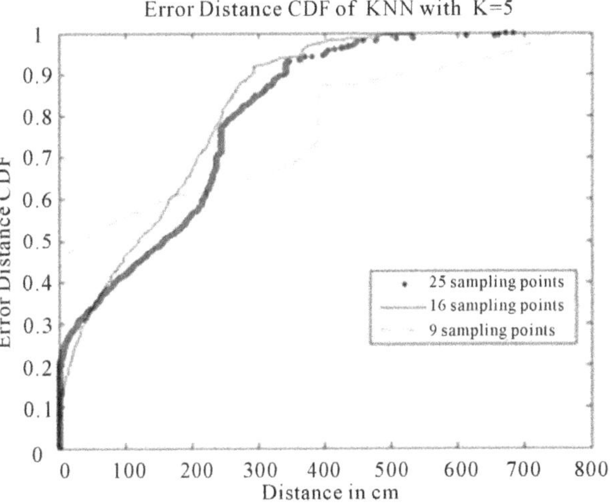

Figure 22. Different sampling points with K = 5.

affects its performance. We have already known that, even in same situation, the received strength of same signal source will be different. The range of that is ±10 dB. So for 25 sampling points, it has large probability to skip to its neighbor locations.

To find the optimization, we plotted overall CDF figure (**Figure 23**).

We can find the 16 sampling points KNN with K = 4 is the best algorithm. To find the optical number of calibration points, we can find the average area for each point.

Our experimental lab is 1560 cm × 1620 cm = 2,527,200 cm^2. Hence, for each point of 16 sampling points case, we separate the room into 16 areas. Each point covers 2,527,200 ÷ 16 = 157,950 cm^2 = 15.795 m^2. So we can get the conclusion that, to install localization system like our experimental circumstance, each separated area should cover about 16 m^2 and do calibration phase.

For value of K, we can get conclusion that the number of K value should be equal to the major APs you have.

This system has two subsystems: doctor's subsystem and patient's subsystem.

For patient's subsystem, because this system is used as self-localization and self-navigation, as users, they can clearly tell the small distance error and subjectively tell which is the correct location. We just care about long-term distance error. From **Figure 23**, we can know 16 sampling points KNN algorithm with K = 4 is the best one. We will adopt this method in our healthcare application in chapter V.

For doctor's subsystem, because it is used as ward round case filter, it should be very accurate in small-term distance and of high-resolution ratio to tell the difference form patient to patient. Thus we selected 25 sampling points with K = 4 as the algorithm.

Since there are lots of other future functions of this application, we can select different algorithm according to the requirement of the application.

3.2. ZigBee Localization System [10]

In the ZigBee localization system, we used Improved Bayesian probability radio map algorithm. Because we did this in the server, we needn't care more about the complexity of the algorithm. Thus, improving the accuracy is the target.

We assume that the value received by every location sensor belongs Gaussian Distribution. The equation for mean and deviation is shown below:

$$\mu = \frac{\sum_{i=1}^{n} x_i}{n} \tag{7}$$

$$\sigma = \sqrt{\frac{\sum_{i=1}^{n} (x_i - \mu)^2}{n}} \tag{8}$$

$$f(x) = \frac{1}{\sigma\sqrt{2\pi}} e^{\frac{(x-\mu)^2}{2\sigma^2}} \tag{9}$$

where x_i is an RSSI value; μ is the mean value of sample RSSI value σ is the standard deviation of sample RSSI value.

According the Gaussian Distribution, when the base station receives a RSSI packet, it can compute the probability of current value in each location sensor. Finally the position with highest probability will be assigned to the final position.

Improved Bayesian Probability Radio Map Algorithm [10]:

The probabilistic approach for radio map algorithm can be realized by using the concept of, conditional probability, Bayes theorem (**Figure 24**). The formula used for computing the likelihood for each position of the asset tag is shown below:

$$P(A_i|B) = \frac{P(B|A_i) \times P(A_i)}{\sum_{j}^{n} \left[P(B|A_j) \times P(A_j) \right]} \tag{10}$$

where: N is the number of location points of the radio map; $P(A_i)$ is the probability that the object is at the particular point I; $P(B|A_j)$ is the probability that the particular RSSI value B is received at a particular point I; $P(A_i|B)$ is the probability that the object is in a particular point I given the received RSSI value B.

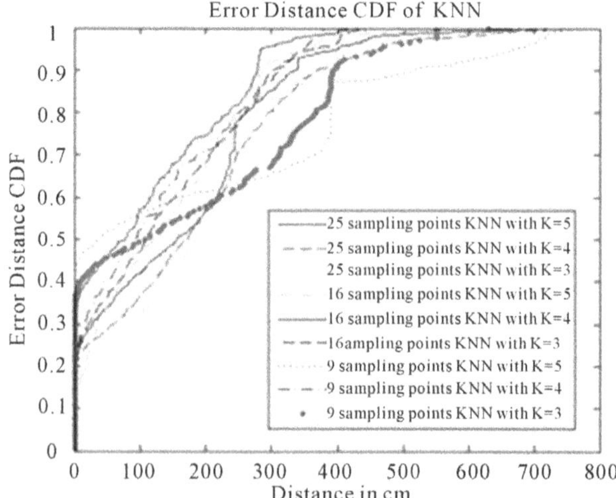

Figure 23. Overall performance.

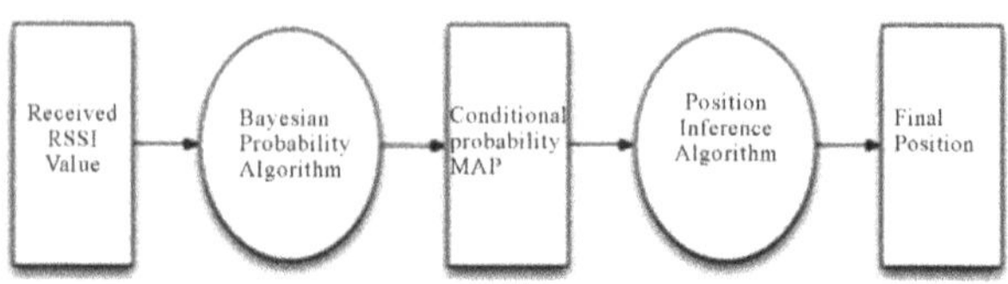

Figure 24. Block diagram of improved bayesian probability radio map algorithm.

When the reader received the RSSI value, it would first convert the values into a probability value for each calibration point using "probabilistic map". A "conditional probability map" could then be calculated by using the probability values from the previous step. A conditional probability map contained probability that the asset tag would be for each calibrated point shown below. The position of the highest probability would be deemed as the position of the object.

Position Inference Algorithm: The algorithm would take into consideration a number of calibration points that locate near the test point, instead of just the nearest calibration point, during computation shown below. It was based on the assumption that points, which were located close together, had relatively similar RSSI signature values.

The final "inferred" position was then computed in a function that involved the probability of each points and distances between the considered points.

To improve the accuracy, we combined the two algorithms. The result of the nine test points has shown in below table.

According to **Table 7**, the average error distance is 28.25cm, which is much better than the WiFi system.

Table 7. Test results of ZigBee location system.

NO#	Actual Position#	Measured Position#	Error Distance (cm)#
1#	(100,350)#	(100,350)#	0#
2#	(100,700)#	(150,760)#	78.102#
3#	(2,001,150)#	(2,001,150)#	0#
4#	(400,140)#	(400,140)#	0#
5#	(400,950)#	(470,980)#	76.158#
6#	(550,250)#	(550,250)#	0#
7#	(55,050)#	(550,550)#	0#
8#	(550,800)#	(550,700)#	100#
9#	(5,501,050)#	(5,501,050)#	0

4. Healthcare Application

To combine this system with healthcare application, we must find the demands. It is common for doctors to carry patient's case during daily ward round. So our target is to simply the work of doctors. When users click the healthcare button and switch the localization button on, it will map current self-location and all patients' location. **Figure 25** Then doctors can click nearby button to view surrounding patients' list. For instance, when the doctor stand by the patient A if he is trying to check in the diagnosis of patient A. he can press the "nearby" button and then he can easily find patient A from the nearby list, nevertheless, patient B who is far from the doctor or even in another ward will not be listed in the nearby list. (**Figure 26**) This will definitely improve the efficiency of doctors' work. Furthermore, this application can also remind doctors which patients have been checked and which one has not. If the doctor has checked the patient, the doctor can mark it. It will not display on the screen until the end of this ward round.

Further more, this application can also develop a sub-application for patients for indoor navigation. To help patients to find right direction and right way, we also use the compass in iPhone, which will help both doctors and patients to find the direction. Especially, for patient, who newly come to a hospital. It is quite difficult for them to find a right place and room to deal with the hospital issues. For instance, for patients, who should take X-ray in diagnostic imaging department. But

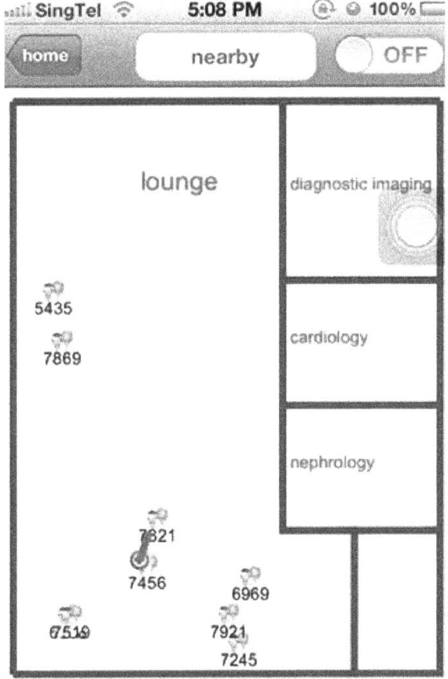

Figure 25. Doctor's application.

there are lots of departments in a hospital and there may be crowded which proves inconvenient for patients. With this application, nevertheless, patients don't have to worry about loss their way in hospitals. It can guide patients to go to right place. As we can see from the picture, the array direction is the direction that the patient is facing.

The other function of this application is to track patients (**Figure 27**). For mental disease patients, they need to be tracked to prevent accidents and escape from hospital. Hence setting some restricted zone is necessary to alert doctors to their patients' unusual locations and behaviors. In the tracking function, if a patient goes into restricted area, the application will alert.

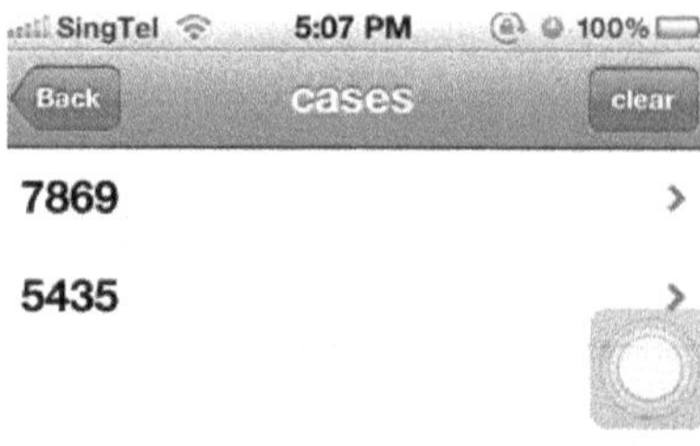

Figure 26. Nearby patient's list.

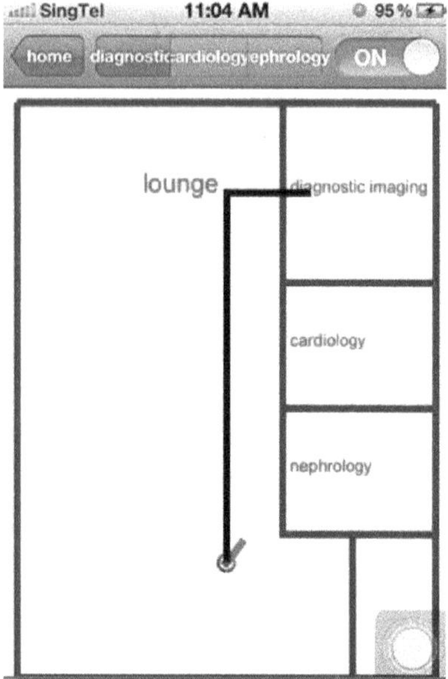

Figure 27. Navigation function.

5. Conclusion

To be more practical and efficient, the next step is to use it in hospital to verify its result. Furthermore, to improve the accuracy, adding more APs is an effective way. However, it will increase the time delay during localization, which will decrease the real-time sensitivity. So we should find a balance between the accuracy, sensitivity and complexity of a practical real-time RTLS system.

REFERENCES

[1] L. M. Ni, Y. H. Liu, Y. C. Lau and A. P. Patil, "LANDMARC: Indoor Location Sensing Using Active RFID," *Proceedings of the 1st IEEE International Conference on Pervasive Computing and Communications*, March 2003.

[2] J. Wyffels, J.-P. Goemaere, P. Verhoeve, P. Crombez, B. Nauwelaers, L. DeStrycker, K. A. H. O. Sint-Lieven, K. U. Leuven and N. V. Televic, "A Novel Indoor Localization System for Healthcare Environments," *International Symposium on Computer-Based Medical Systems* (*CBMS*), 2012.

[3] M. Pourhomayoun, Z. P. Jin and M. Fowler, "Spatial Sparsity Based Indoor Localization in Wireless Sensor Network for Assistive Healthcare," *IEEE International Conference on Engineering in Medicine and Biology Society* (*EMBC*), 2012.

[4] M. Bharanidharan, X. J. Li, Y. Y. Jin, J. S. Pathmasuntharam and G. X. Xiao, "Design and Implementation of a Real Time Locating System Utilizing WiFi Signals from iPhones," *IEEE International Conference on Networks* (*ICON*), 2012.

[5] M. Ali, "iPhone SDK Programming: Developing Mobile Applications for Apple iPhone and iPod Touch," Wiley Press, 2009.

[6] Q. X. Chen; D.-L. Lee and W.-C. Lee, "Rule-Based WiFi Localization Methods," *IEEE/IFIP International Conference on Embedded and Ubiquitous Computing*, 2008.

[7] T. Bagosi and Z. Baruch, "Indoor Localization by WiFi," *IEEE International Conference on Intelligent Computer Communication and Processing* (*ICCP*), 2011.

[8] Effelsberg, "COMPASS: A Probabilistic Indoor Positioning System Based on 802.11 and Digital Compasses," *WiNTECH '06 Proceedings of the 1st International Workshop on Wireless Network Testbeds, Experimental Evaluation & Characterization*, 2006, pp. 34-40.

[9] W.-H. Chen, H. H. Chang; T. H. Lin, P. C. Chen, L. K. Chen, S. J. Hwang, D. H. J. Yen, H. S. Yuan and W. C. Chu, "Dynamic Indoor Localization Based on Active RFID for Healthcare Applications: A Shape Constraint Approach," *International Conference on Biomedical Engineering and Informatics* (*BMEI*), 2009.

[10] L. Y. Hao, G. Y. Liang and L. Wei, "Indoor Positioning system (Middleware)," Nanyang Technological University, Nanyang, 2012.

16

Behind the Scenes with a Video Training Platform: The Challenges of Researching the Provision of Open Educational Resources

Ayse Kok
Bogazici University, Istanbul, Turkey

ABSTRACT

Video training platforms are now being implemented on a large scale in organizations. In this paper, I look at a video training platform including open educational resources available for many employees with varying patterns and motivations for use. This has provided me with a research challenge to find methods that help other practitioners in the field understand and explain such initiatives. I describe ways to model the research and identify where pressures and contradictions can be found, drawing on a reflective view of my own practice in performing the research. Open educational resources are defined as technology-enabled educational resources that are openly available for consultation, use and adaptation by users for non-commercial purposes [1]. The bank subject to this case study has been the first organisation in Turkey that provided open educational resources for all its employees. The video platform (called "For @ Tube") provides users with over 100 video lectures drawn from reputable universities around the world including Yale and Harvard. Other learning tools such as discussion forums, blogs and traditional e-learning courses have been made available to the users on the e-learning platform called "For @" since 2006. In this paper, I aim to introduce the new video training platform ("For @ Tube") and outline some of the main research issues surrounding such an initiative. I seek to explore theoretical and practical approaches that can provide suitable tools for analysis. Activity theory is seen as a suitable approach for macroanalysis and its use is illustrated in terms of the complexity of large scale research. Activity theory, besides informing research perspectives, can be turned in upon the research process itself, allowing us to consider the challenges and context of the research. By using activity theory in this way and illustrating from a range of practical approaches, I demonstrate and illustrate a useful research approach.

Keywords: E-Learning; Open Content; Video; Action Research; Activity Theory

1. Introduction

Open educational resources are defined as technology-enabled educational resources that are openly available for consultation, use and adaptation by users for non-commercial purposes (UNESCO, 2002). The internet has recently seen an increase in such initiatives, including areas such as MIT Open Course Ware, CORE (China Open Resource for Education), Wikipedia, Open Learn and Open Course Ware Universia. Key features of many of such initiatives include the provision of course content, the ability to adapt, use and develop content, the availability of social learning tools, and the introduction of other learning tools. The range of initiatives is illustrated by the membership of the Open Course Ware Consortium (http://www.ocwconsortium.org) which has members from a diverse number of countries. The impact of these resources and changes in the ability of individual users to access such educational materials is likely to impact significantly on how people learn. The confinement of knowledge to educational institutes is likely to be challenged. Alternatively, new power structures may arise as a result of "big players" dominating the open resource markets. The question arises as to how these open resources will impact on the learning of employees or groups of employees. Will these resources empower learners and how will learners' experience change? Coupled with the advent of open resources, there is also a development of new software and hardware tools such as software that supports social learning and mobile computing that may change the possible affordances of such technologies.

For @ Tube (**Figure 1**) is a video training platform provided by a Turkish banking institution and it entails open educational resources. The project was officially launched on 20 August 2012. Currently it provides over 200 video lectures for personal study. The material used in this platform is mostly derived from global universities' course materials. In addition, training videos from local providers and the global bank's (with whom the Turkish bank has established a joint venture) videos are also utilized. The conversion of all of these materials into an appropriate provision for For @ was conducted using an "integrity" model where the content is kept as close as possible to the original source material with adjustments made relating to presentation on the web, rights issues, and reshaping for a wider audience.

The entrance point for the video training platform is a website for employees called "For @". The e-platform "For @" which is a web-based application developed by a third company is divided into 2 sections (**Figure 1**):

E-learning portal: The e-learning portal called For @ includes over 350 asynchronous web-based courses, an online library and a social learning platform which provides digital collaboration tools such as blogs, forums and an internal social networking platform. This built-in social environment enables participants to share information about the training they have taken online or offline and communicate with colleagues at other branches.

The digital learning catalog (including videos) consists of four types of training:

1) Mandatory courses: These can be in the form of existing catalog courses or courses specifically developed for the bank based on the managers' needs (courses about product/process/service).

2) Regulatory mandatory courses: These are courses that need to be taken by every bank personnel due to the compliance issues within the Turkish banking industry (e.g.: information security, operational risk).

3) Elective courses: These are courses which can be selected from the existing course catalog based on one's specific interest.

Figure 1. General appearance of the online learning platform used in the bank.

4) Personal development: These are catalog courses that aim to improve one's soft skills through his/her professional life. Some of these courses can also be accessed from the online performance management tool based on the specific targeted skills of the employees.

It is also a high level management mandate to conduct frequent online exams via the LMS in order to enhance the branch personnels' information about the bank's products and sevices. From time to time, online knowledge competitions are also held within the bank based on the departmental requests.

Video Portal: This section includes video-based lessons in the categories of finance, professional development, bank-specific areas and personal development. Videos that are produced internally or announcements of higher level management are also included in this section.

The platform has also searching capabilities, tutorials, and a technical and content help desk, is targeted at nearly 9200 users of the bank. The platform is planned to be made compatible with the mobile phones (any smartphone apart from Blackberry can display the online courses.).

2. Video Training Platform—The Research Challenge

For @ Tube (**Figure 2**) is a large project with a dedicated e-learning team including also individuals involved with research and evaluation. Besides this dedicated research team others within the project have research interests including academics responsible for the transformation and development of content. The project as a whole is viewed in terms of an action research model where the results and impacts of research are fed back into project development. Within this paradigm there is also the challenge and the tension between academic research requiring high degrees of rigour and having underlying theoretical aims and that of applied research with the requirement of fast-feedback and relating more to the success of the site via such issues as marketing, usability studies, site design etc.

Researching such a large project involves examining several different areas, each of which presents its own set of challenges. The four main strands of research include; training with For @, the users' experience, project development, and sustainability. To this, we can add a meta-layer; the challenge of researching open content. This paper is chiefly concerned with this objective and aims to illustrate our own problems and dilemmas in conducting such research and by offering our insights into models of research provide a guide for others in research techniques.

An idealised approach to the research has been to:

1) Identify and develop theoretical frameworks for

Figure 2. General appearance of the video training platform used in the bank.

analysis at macro and micro levels;

2) Find tools and ways of mapping and talking about our research;

3) Develop and find appropriate methodologies to enable us to collect and process research findings.

This list may seem very logical and structured as presented here but the evolution of the framework, as we learn within an action research paradigm is more haphazard and iterative in nature. A research technique is seen not as something developed in advance but rather as something in the process of development with continual trials, implementations and reworking. For @ itself is a continually evolving construct and this presents an additional challenge to research. The three approaches listed above will be described in more detail with specific reference to research within the project and also to researching users' experience.

2.1. Developing Theoretical Frameworks of Analysis at the Macro- and Micro-Levels

2.1.1. Action Research

One possible criticism of academic research is that the impacts of such research often have little effect on organisational practice. A possible reason for this may be the divide that exists between the world of academia and the world of work. The process of academic research can be very slow with the major outputs often consisting of writings in journals for an academic audience. Research is often conducted from "afar" that is, it is separate from the object of research. An advantage of this is that research is more likely to be independent if not connected to the object of the research. This independence and objectivity is unlikely to be untainted in that research and researchers are embedded within research paradigms, personal social-cultural influences, and the influence of the grant holders who partially or wholly shape the research questions. The principles of action research call for a research process that involves change within that which is researched [2]. In a sense it is more of an experimental "trial and error" process in that it is iterative, ongoing and affects change in practice. It can therefore be seen as a process of reflection and practice, often referred to as praxis. In order to affect action research it is necessary to

1) Involve more of the organisation than simply the dedicated researchers,

2) To integrate the results of the research into decision making at managerial levels.

Dangers exist however when moving towards a culture of "self-development" where Action Research is seen as an efficiency tool as opposed to its more idealised aims of development and empowerment of workers [3]. There are also dangers when research is taken out of the hands of research savvy practitioners and placed in those of research novices. Hence, there may be many models of action research adopted according to one's perspective. Another key issue of action research is the "social-technical" view which sees the successful development of any organisation being an integration of the right social and developmental environment with the use of appropriate tools. For example, the use of tools for doing research and for enhancing interpersonal communication within the research community and others in the organisation is part of praxis resulting from the research itself. Action research can provide us with a framework of research at the level of For @ as an organisation but also as a framework of reflection and practice. In this case we see this as a way of developing ourselves as individuals and as a team allowing an exploration of ways of working and knowing.

It has been mentioned [4]:

"The self of the researcher can best be understood as intermeshed with others through webs of interpersonal and professional relationships that co-construct the researcher's identity."

In this sense action research is about both personal and professional development.

2.1.2. Activity Theory as a Way of Modelling Macro-Behaviour

For @ Tube represents one of the largest open education interventions in the financial sector in Turkey and as such the opportunity exists to understand how this operates and develops at a macro level.

Possible contenders for analysis include activity theory and actor network theory which allow potential ways of understanding macro-behaviour.

Actor Network Theory (ANT) focuses on identifying the various actors in a social organizations and examining the relationship between these actors [5]. Activity theory focuses on action as it is mediated by tools within a socio-cultural context [5]. It was used as an analytical framework in this instance because of its educational applications including learning in organisations and that ANT was felt to be less clearly structured as an analytical tool.

The foundation for Activity Theory comes from the Vygotskian view that all action is mediated by tools whether these be external or internal, concrete or psychological [6]. This has been developed into concepts such as "person plus" and cognition as a distributed activity located within a social group and the tools that they use (Perkins, 1993). Leont'ev, a prodigy of Vygotsky, explored the way in which this could be applied through emphasising the activity as the main unit of analysis (Kaptelinin and Nardi, 2006).

Engeström extended the framework and the subject-tools-object model to take into account aspects of the context within which such action was taken [6,7]. He represented the interrelationships between these contextual elements within a triangular structure each node representing some aspect of interaction. The additional contextual nodes that he added were "rules", "community" and "division of labour" [8,9]. This framework was adopted as a practical tool of analysis since it could be applied to view For @ from any number of different perspectives. These different perspectives could then be contrasted, reflected upon, or pushed against each other to force the identification of characteristics within each perspective and various "contradictions" that existed between such perspectives.

Figure 3 demonstrates the use activity theory as a way of viewing the research aspects of For @. Researching such a complex and large training initiative provides many opportunities and areas for potential study and often these are driven by project aims. These aims can be envisaged as being part of the rules in which the research is located and represent rules embedded in project design. Other rules are external to the project and include guidelines for general social research. These deal with issues such as research ethics which can sometimes create tensions in terms of the need for fast feedback and the drives for "interesting stories" that may come from other parts of the project such as marketing, or management. "Rules" may also relate to perceptions of individuals within the team (*i.e.* not formally held or shared rules) and relate to theoretical perceptions and opinions on the nature of good educational practice. Much research demands a certain standard of rigour (lower risk of error) which might create contradictions with the need for quick feedback (higher risk of error) to help move the implementation process forward. This contradiction highlights a general problem of the slowness of academic research to reach and inform its intended audience. By identifying and recognising this contradiction ways can be investigated for disseminating research internally in order to quickly feedback into the implementation and adaptation processes.

When examining **Figure 3** contradictions maybe analysed within the structure itself e.g. between the research interests, motivations, and perceived views of the team players, between individuals and rules, about the essence and nature of research itself, about the choice of methods to monitor the learning effectiveness of TEB For @. Contradictions can also be viewed of as occurring across different perspectives. For example, a contradiction may exist between the need for neutrality and a critical approach of the researchers within the research perspective and the need for promotion and publicity within a marketing perspective that is directed towards gaining the attention of users.

2.1.3. Activity Theory and Action Research

It is clear that Action Research and Activity Theory can be used effectively together. As Somekh (2006) says when talking about Action Research, "...*activity theory is particularly helpful because it gives priority to collaborative decision making on the basis of sharing*

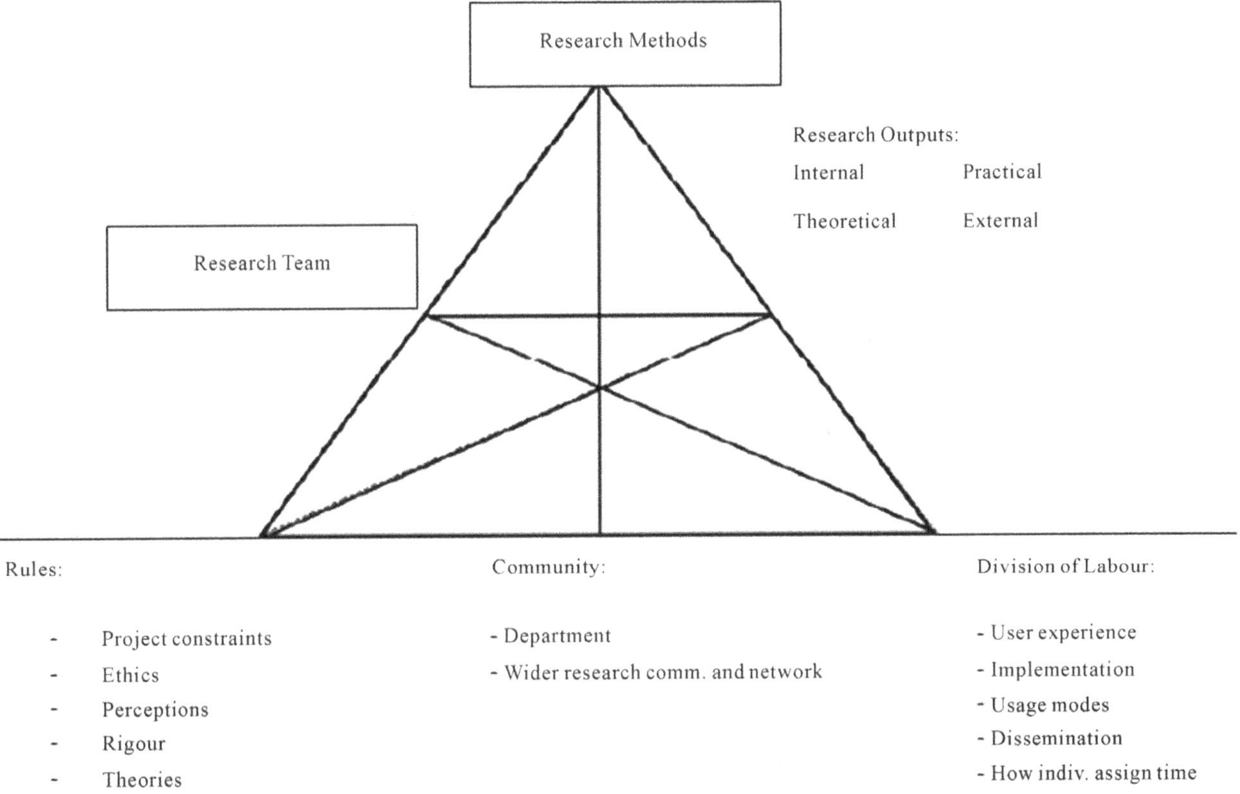

Figure 3. Using activity theory to represent the research perspective within TEB For @.

knowledge about identified 'contradictions'".

The socio-technical aspects of action theory can be related to aspects of tool mediation and the development of community. Activity Theory can be used to identify contradictions and these can be used to implement change. Such change might create new contradictions but through the iterative process of action research improvements can be made. A multi-perspective approach can be used to inform those e-learning practitioners working within the banking industry to affect change. The challenge of how this dissemination occurs is something that needs to be addressed.

2.2. Tools for Mapping and Talking about Research

Taking into account the socio-technical aspects of Action Research and the central role of tools within Activity Theory the development of various tools for thinking, analysing and describing is a key part of my research process. With such an array of available media there are difficulties in identifying the most suitable way or ways for research discussion and dissemination. The development of a research community that allows the findings of For @ to be discussed and disseminated can be seen as a good area for the application of action research. It can mean experimenting with different tools and the construction of different types of space. In discussing and disseminating research findings a number of technological options present themselves as possible platforms e.g. blogs, wikis, editable web sites and facilities which can be found in the For @ itself. Within For @, there is the opportunity to create discussion forums around research issues.

These forums can be opened up to anyone. Individual blogs in For @ can also reveal insights into research and development of For @ and open content as a whole. Linking and exploring blogs can be of value as a research activity.

2.3. Developing Appropriate Methodologies

Researching For @ is a complex phenomenon and various tensions exist internal to the research perspective in such issues as:

- Tensions between pedagogical paradigms;
- Intrusiveness of research methods;
- Nature of sampling and reaching hard to reach groups;
- Speed of research feedback;
- Choosing suitable analytical techniques;
- Dissemination methods;
- Nature of research tools used;
- Dealing with a non-homogeneous user base.

As an example we can look at one of these issues in

more depth. One of these is the fact the user base appears to be very heterogeneous and heavily skewed in terms of time spent on the site toward the low user. This pyramidal structure in terms of the time spent visiting a site is probably a common occurrence in many web sites although comparative studies are difficult because open content sites may differ greatly in form and function. Every website is in a sense competing against a large number of other sites in terms of grabbing a person's attention and part of the decision that people make in spending time on a site is their initial perception of the site's value. This can very much depend on how the home page of the site is presented and whether the site gives a clear indication of what kind of content or activity that it might contain.

A major challenge is to find out about the user experience. Questions relating to this challenge include:

1) How does the use of For @ fit into the wider context of the user's formal and informal learning context?

2) Are users learning from For @? If so how are they learning?

3) Are users engaging and using the tools? If so what are they using the tools for?

Distinctions will exist in terms of types of users. Learners may primarily study or use content but others may engage with social learning or using For @ tools. Part of the challenge is to identify the types of user. One possible means of tracing the user's experience is by using website logs. Generally one can infer whether a user was browsing, skimming, downloading or printing content, or systematically studying or reading parts of a unit. This however does not tell us about what the user is learning and with For @ it is not possible to use pre- and post-study tests since learners will often not be studying a unit as a whole. In this instance, thinking of the units as courses is inappropriate since this implies a journey from a starting point to an end point, and an externally structured pathway through the material often with some form of assessment. Identifying learning therefore depends on the unique experiences of users and needs to be process orientated. In order to get at the experience of users and the process of learning qualitative studies can provide a rich picture and thick description of users' experience. There are also several technological tools that can help the researcher in this process although there is always the problem of the degree of intrusiveness in any research exercise.

One method of examining whether learning is taking place is by in situ observation and making inferences from user activity. Getting users to think aloud and to record their thoughts can help in this although there are disadvantages to this technique. Another is by using interviews where a user's learning experience can be examined. Simple questions such as "What have you learned?" or "What have you found out that you didn't know before?" can act as the basis for more probing questions perhaps relating to a range of skills within Bloom's taxonomy [3]. A problem of such interviews is that they can become an additional form of training in that by causing the participant to recall or reconstruct their experience one is actually changing and reshaping it. Thus the research is adding to the learning experience. Remote monitoring can allow a clearer insight into the actual live experience of the learner.

3. Discussion

For @ represents one of the largest developments within the open content community in the corporate settings in Turkey and presents a challenge for research. This challenge exists within four strands: teaching with For @, the users' experience, project development, and sustainability. In this paper, I have indicated and discussed the use of action research and activity theory as tools to enable us to think and understand the dynamics of a large educational initiative. Action research can potentially allow reflection, action and change within such a project. Activity Theory represents a tool for recognising areas for action and change and communicating issues to the project team. It also allows us as researchers to inwardly analyse our own behaviour and help in our personal and professional development.

As researchers, there is a need to disseminate internally and externally the research findings to inform-change. The development of communication tools and the novel use of technology to do this are considered an evolutionary process, experiment and change by trial and error. Providing useful research networks and integrating with others are important in the social construction of knowledge and understanding about open educational resources. How to use tools such as For @ Tube effectively is a challenge and an important part of my own iterative process of development within an action research framework. Reflecting on my own research practice can be considered a meta-research process.

Some of the research challenges of finding out about users' experience have been illustrated. Possible technological tools that can help in this process have been discussed. A consideration of the use of tools as appropriated by individuals is a characteristic of the socio-technical view of action research. I have considered researching For @ Tube in terms of a number of different perspectives and themes. A three level approach has been presented. At one level, For @ Tube can be viewed using activity theory to shape various perspectives and then examine intra-nodal and extra-nodal contradictions between the perspectives. At the level of the community of researchers, there has been a consideration of the sharing and dissemination of knowledge and the tools can aid this process. At the third level, there has been a consideration of the challenge of developing research tools using the iterative processes of action research, which is illustrated in Engeström's [2] ideas: expansion, people, tools and community are in a constant state of change.

REFERENCES

[1] UNESCO, "Forum on the Impact of Open Courseware for Higher Education in Developing Countries, Final Report," 2002. http://unesdoc.unesco.org/images/0012/001285/128515e.pdf

[2] "Taxonomy of Educational Objectives. The Classification of Educational Goals," In: B. Bloom, Ed., *Handbook* 1: *Cognitive Domain*, Longmans, London, 1956.

[3] V. Kaptelinin, and B. A. Nardi, "Acting with Technology: Activity Theory and Interaction Design," MIT Press, Cambridge, 2006.

[4] J. Greenwood and M. L. Levin, "Introduction to Action Research: Social Research for Social Change," Sage, London, 2006.

[5] M. Engeström and M. Cole, "A Cultural-Historical Approach to Distributed Cognition," In: G. Salomon, Ed., Distributed Cognitions. Psychological and Educational Considerations, Cambridge University Press, Cambridge, 1993.

[6] Y. Engeström, "Developmental Work Research: Expanding Activity Theory in Practice," Lehmanns Media, Berlin, 2005.

[7] L. S. Vygotsky, "Mind and Society: Development of Higher Psychological Processes," Harvard University Press, Harvard, 1980.

[8] B. Latour, "Reassembling the Social. An Introduction to Actor-Network-Theory," Oxford University Press, Oxford, 2005.

[9] D. N. Perkins, "Person-Plus: A Distributed View of Thinking and Learning," In: G. Salomon, Ed., *Distributed Cognitions. Psychological and Educational Considerations*, Cambridge University Press, Cambridge, 1993.

[10] B. Somekh, "Action Research: A Methodology for Change and Development," Open University Press, Maidenhead, 2006.

17

Detection of Objects in Motion—A Survey of Video Surveillance

Jamal Raiyn
Computer Science Department, Alqasemi College, Baka El Gariah, Israel

ABSTRACT

Video surveillance system is the most important issue in homeland security field. It is used as a security system because of its ability to track and to detect a particular person. To overcome the lack of the conventional video surveillance system that is based on human perception, we introduce a novel cognitive video surveillance system (CVS) that is based on mobile agents. CVS offers important attributes such as suspect objects detection and smart camera cooperation for people tracking. According to many studies, an agent-based approach is appropriate for distributed systems, since mobile agents can transfer copies of themselves to other servers in the system.

Keywords: Video Surveillance; Object Detection; Image Analysis

1. Introduction

Various papers in the literature have been proposed and focused on computer vision problems in the context of multi-camera surveillance systems. The main problems highlighted in these papers are object detection and tracking, and site-wide, multi-target, multi-camera tracking. The importance of accurate detection and tracking is obvious, since the extracted tracking information can be directly used for site activity/event detection. Furthermore, tracking data is needed as a first step toward controlling a set of security cameras to acquire high-quality imageries, and toward, for example, building biometric signatures of the tracked targets automatically. The security camera is controlled to track and capture one target at a time, with the next target chosen as the nearest one to the current target. These heuristics-based algorithms provide a simple and tractable way of computing. Conventional video surveillance systems have many limitations to their capabilities. In one case, conventional video surveillance systems have difficulty in tracking a great number of people located at different positions at the same time and tracking those people automatically. In another case, the number of possible targeted people is limited by the extent of users' involvement in manually switching the view from one video camera to another. With cognitive video surveillance system, mobile agent technologies are more effective and efficient than conventional video surveillance systems, assuming that a large number of servers with video camera are installed. If one mobile agent can track one person, then multiple mobile agents can track numerous people at the same time, and the server balances the load process of the operating mobile agent on each server with a camera.

We consider the scenario that the smart camera captures two similar objects (e.g. twin), then each object selects a different path. The tracking process will be confusing. Furthermore, the smart camera is limited to cover a certain zone in public place (Indoor). Next section introduces many solutions that have been suggested to the above problem. The suggested solutions to improve the conventional video surveillance system are extended in various ways.

A part of the approaches is to use an active camera to track a person automatically, and thus the security camera moves in a synchronized motion along with the projected movement of the targeted person. These approaches are capable of locating and tracking a small number of people. Another common approach is to position the camera at strategic surveillance locations. This is not possible in some situations due to the number of cameras that would be necessary for full coverage, and in such cases, this approach is not feasible due to limited resources. A third approach is to identify and track numerous targeted people at the same time involving image processing and installation of video cameras at any designated location, since the image processing increases server load.

The limitation of human perception system in conventional video surveillance system increases the demand to develop cognitive surveillance system. Many of the proposed video surveillance systems are expensive and lack the capability of cognitive monitoring system such as no image analysis. This makes the system lack the ability to send warning signal autonomously in real-time and before the incidents happen. Furthermore, it is difficult and might take a long time for people to locate the suspects in the video after the incidents happen. The problem may get more complete on the larger scale surveillance system. The next generation video surveillance system expected not only to solve the issues of detection and tracking but also to solve the issue of human body analysis. In the literature, it can be found many references in development of sophisticated video surveillance system. In this paper, we introduce the cognitive video surveillance system (CVS). CVS aims to offer meaningful characteristics like automation, autonomy, and real-time surveillance such as face recognition, suspect objects, target detection, and use of cooperative smart cameras. Many face recognition systems have a video sequence as the input. Those systems may require being capable of not only detecting but tracking faces. Face tracking is essentially a motion estimation problem. Face tracking can be performed using many different methods, e.g., head tracking, feature tracking, image-based tracking, and model-based tracking. These are different ways to classify these algorithms.

2. Review of Human Body Analysis

This section introduces various approaches that considered the object detection and object tracking in video surveillance field [1-3]. The analysis of human body movements can be applied in a variety of application domains, such as video surveillance, video retrieval, human-computer interaction systems, and medical diagnoses. In some cases, the results of such analysis can be used to identify people acting suspiciously and other unusual events directly from videos. Many approaches have been proposed for video-based human movement analysis [4-6].

In [7] Oliver *et al.* developed a visual surveillance system that models and recognizes human behavior using hidden Markov models (HMMs) and a trajectory feature. In [8-10] proposed a probabilistic posture classification scheme to identify several types of movement, such as walking, running, squatting, or sitting. In [11] traced the negative minimum curvatures along body contours to segment body parts and then identified body postures using a modified Iterative Closest Point (ICP) algorithm. In addition [12,13] used different morphological operations to extract skeletal features from postures and then identified movements using a HMM framework. Another approach used to analyze human behavior is the Gaussian probabilistic model. In [14] has been described the real-time finder system for detecting and tracking humans. In [15] proposed a shape-based approach for classification of objects is used following background subtraction based on frame differencing. The goal is to detect the humans for threat assessment.

In [16] presented a method to detect and track a human body in a video. First, background subtraction is performed to detect the foreground object, which involves temporal differencing of the consecutive frames. In [17] presented a novel approach to detect the pedestrians, which is shown to work well in a indoor environment. They make use of a new sensing device, which gives depth information along with image information simultaneously. In [18] proposed method that deals with the direct detection of humans from static images as well as video using a classifier trained on human shape and motion features. The training dataset consists of images and videos of human and non-human examples. In [19] has been suggested to use the mobile agent for multi-node wireless video cooperation in order to reduce redundancy which will result repeated information collection in overlapping regions. In [20] introduced automatic human tracking system based on a video surveillance system enhanced with mobile agent technologies. In [21-23] has been proposed a composite approach for human detection, which uses skin color and motion information to first find the candidate foreground objects for human detection, and then uses a more sophisticated technique to classify the objects. Other approaches extract human postures or body parts (such as the head, hands, torso, or feet) to analyze human behavior.

Motion Detection

This section aims to provide the status of art of the different techniques of motion detection estimation. Various studies have been introduced on the subject and the literature is very plentiful in this province. We are trying to list some methods used methods. The idea is to give an overview of the most commonly used methods and approaches. The most used algorithms for moving objects detection are based on background subtraction. The background subtraction is based on comparing of the current video frame (foreground objects) with one from the previous frames that is called sometimes background.

3. Video Surveillance System

In this section we introduce the system model of the video surveillance system. Video surveillance system has been used for monitoring, real-time image capturing, processing, and surveillance information analyzing.

The infrastructure of the system model is divided in

three main layers: mobile agents that are used to track suspect objects, cognitive video surveillance management (CVS), and Protocol for communication as shown in **Figure 1**. Each end device, smart camera, covers a certain zone or cell. Smart camera used for collecting parameters of human face.

3.1. Communication Protocol

In the system model has been introduced two communication protocols. The first protocol used for agent-to-agent protocol. Agents used this protocol for communication. The protocol is based on messages exchange as shown in **Figure 2**. The goal of the protocol is to update the agents. The second protocol is used for communication between CVS and mobile agent.

3.2. Mobile Agent Features

Mobile agents are placed in smart camera stations. Mobile agent aims to track the suspect object from smart camera station to others. Mobile agent offers various characteristics, e.g. negotiation, making decision, roaming, and cloning.

3.3. Cognitive Video Surveillance Management

Cognitive video surveillance (CVS) managed mobile agent handoff in wireless networks. CVS provide the mobile agent with information. Based on received information mobile agents make decision when and where to move to next smart camera station.

3.4. Tracking Moving Objects

In order to track moving objects, we introduce two strategies. The first strategy is based on messaging protocol (msg_protocol). The goal of this msg_protocol is to inform the mobile agent about the position of the suspect object. The second strategy uses the protocol to help the mobile agent to roaming from point to others.

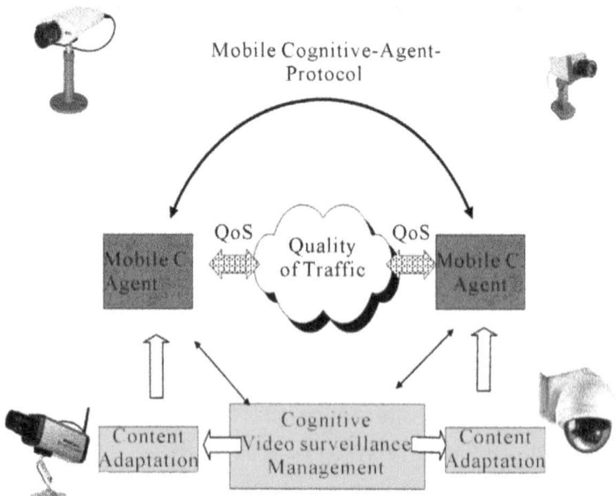

Figure 1. System model.

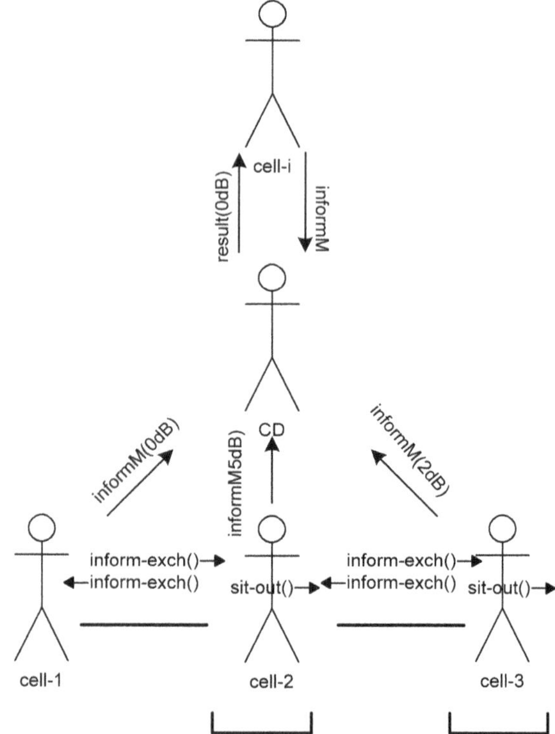

Figure 2. Agent protocol.

4. Methodology

Cognitive video surveillance (CVS) uses a data base of images. Pixels are described by a set of binary sequences. Each sequence presents certain properties (color). The database is divided into two separate sets of pixels—the training set and the test set. In both sets there are both pixels, which belong to a certain family of colors (attributes) and sequence, which do not belong.

$$TP = X = \{X_1, X_2, \cdots, X_n\}$$

$$TN = Y = \{Y_1, Y_2, \cdots, Y_n\}$$

Each image is then divided into frames, a frame being a subset of pixel from the sequence. The number of pixel in each frame is a variable and is dynamically set to obtain optimal results.

$$X_1 = \{x_1^1, x_2^1, \cdots, x_n^1\}$$

$$X_2 = \{x_1^2, x_2^2, \cdots, x_n^2\}$$

$$\cdots$$

$$X_n^m = \{x_1^m, x_2^m, \cdots, x_n^m\}$$

If for example a certain frame is comprised of 200 segments, the frames might consist of pixels 1 to 10, 2 to

11, 3 to 12, etc. Statistical methods are then applied to find correlation between a certain properties of the frame.

The basic logic of statistical differentiation of pixel is known and widely used in many prediction systems.

$$J = X \oplus Y$$

$$J = \begin{cases} 1 & \text{if } x \neq y \\ 0 & \text{otherwise} \end{cases}$$

A large number of correlating factors is defined by CVS and grouped in sets. A number is linked with each correlating factor. Each factor is then turned into a single number which represents the strength of the correlation factors for each frame with respect to the probability that this frame belongs to the certain family or not. As a result we have a large number of frames, for each pair of a frame we have a number which is correlated to the probability that this frame belongs to a certain attribute (color similarity) or does not belong.

$$J = \left\{J_1^1, J_2^2, J_3^3, J_4^4 \cdots\right\}$$

Optimization of J:

$$J_{\text{Prediction}}\left(J_1^*\right) = J_{\text{demand}} + k * (\Delta J)$$

In addition to the statistical method an innovative method of logical XOR multiplication of matrices is applied to enrich the number of frames, which are potentially contributing to the prediction model.

CVS can be implemented in a dynamic environment – when the training databases are modified the prediction mechanism is modified as well with improved prediction capabilities.

5. Smoothing EMA

In this section we introduce detection model that is based on moving average scheme. There are three types of moving average, that is, simple moving average (SMA), weight moving average (WMA), and exponential moving average (EMA). In this study, an exponential moving average is considered. An exponential moving average uses a weighting or a smoothing factor which decreases exponentially. The weighting for each older data point decreases exponentially, giving much more importance to recent observations while not discarding the older observations entirely. The detection phase focused on the collected data analysis. To increase the accuracy of the forecast model, the abnormal events in the collected data should be considered. The forecast scheme is based on the exponential moving average. The robustness and accuracy of the exponential smoothing forecast is high and impressive. The accuracy of the exponential smoothing technique depends on the weight smoothed factor alpha value of the current demand. To determine the optimal alpha factor value, fitting curve has been considered.

6. Performance Analysis

We have used the object oriented programming language C # to present the image in binary system as shown in **Figure 3**. Hence Binary vectors are implemented in WEKA platform. WEKA is stand for Waikato Environment for Knowledge Analysis. WEKA implements many machine learning and data mining algorithms. As shown

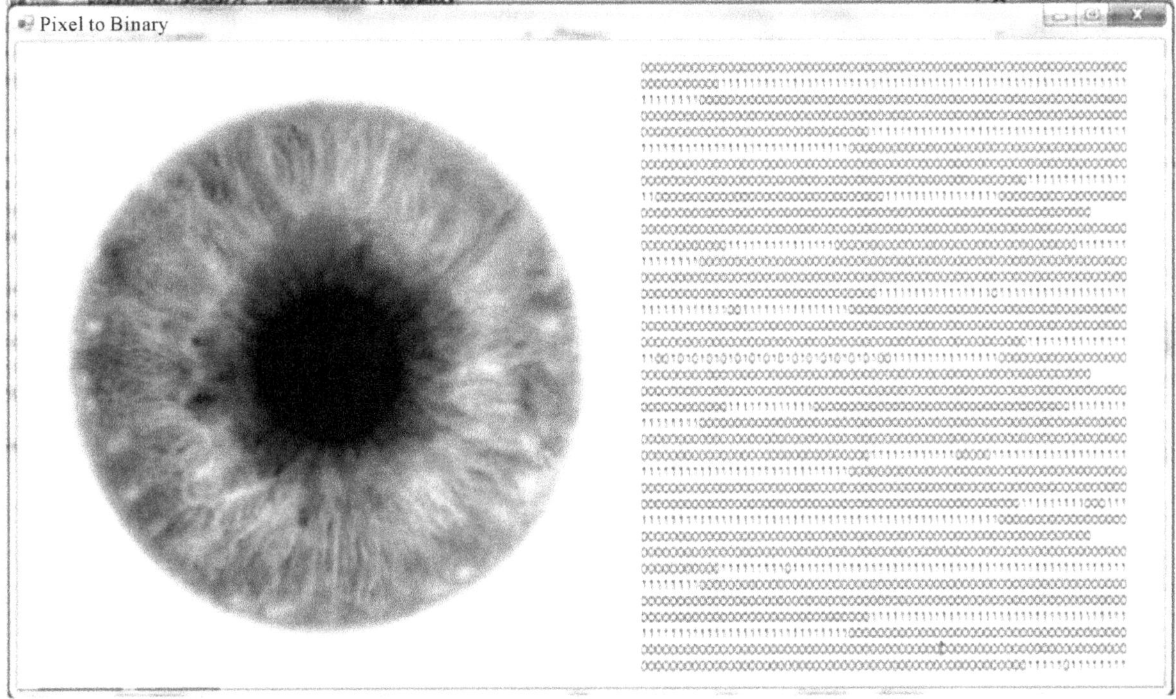

Figure 3. Image representation in binary system.

in **Figures 4(a)** and **(b)** the image analysis in visual form is based on color classification. WEKA considers the color of the image. The colors are represented in binary system. WEKA clusters the binary vectors. Each cluster represents certain attributes. As shown in **Figure 5** the comparison between simple moving average (SMA), weight moving average (WMA) and exponential moving average (EMA) is based on mean average error (MAE). Furthermore we have compared the actual observations to EMA model as shown in **Figure 6**. Results indicate that all three moving average methods have more or less similar performance in forecasting short-term times. However, as one would expect the method using optimized weights produced slightly better forecasts at a higher computational cost. Quality of forecast is diminished as the time for which forecasts are made is farther in the future. Moving average methods overestimate travel speeds in slow-downs and underestimate them when the congestion is clearing up and speeds are increasing.

7. Conclusion

In this paper, we discussed several methods in the recent literature for human detection from video. We have organized them according to techniques which use background subtraction and which operate directly on the input. In the first category, we have ordered the techniques based on the type of background subtraction used and the model used to represent a human. In the second category, we have ordered the techniques based on the human model and classifier model used. Overall, there seems to be an increasing trend in the recent literature towards robust methods which operate directly on the image rather than those which require background subtraction as a first step. The EMA model can be used for human behaviors prediction.

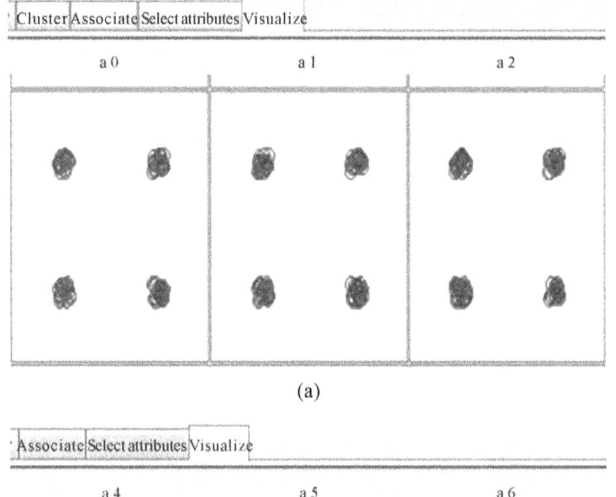

(a)

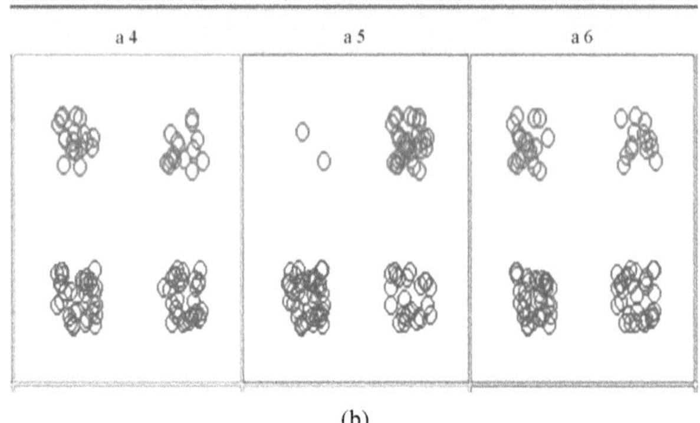

(b)

Figure 4. (a) Image analysis; (b) Color classification.

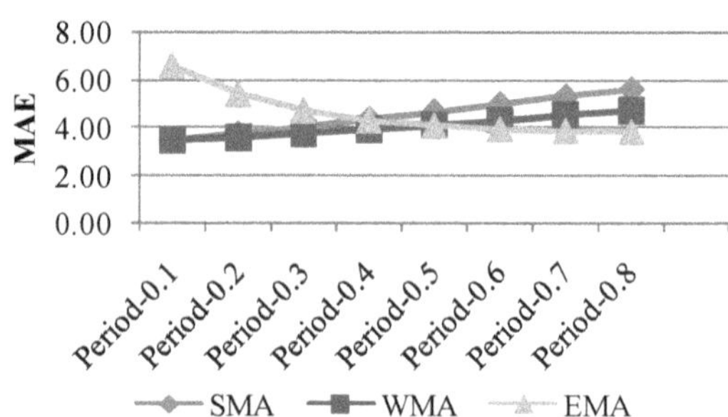

Figure 5. Comparison between MA schemes.

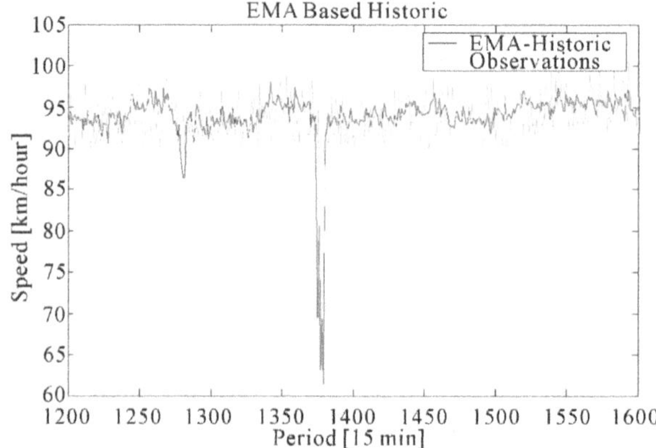

Figure 6. Actual observation vs. forecasting model.

REFERENCES

[1] R. T. Collins, A. J. Lipton, T. Kanade, H. Fujiyoshi, D. Duggins, Y. Tsin, D. Tolliver, N. Enomoto, O. Hasegawa, P. Burt and L. Wixson, "A System for Video Surveillance and Monitoring," Robotics Institute, Carnegie Mellon University, Pittsburgh, 2000.

[2] I. Haritaoglu, D. Harwood and L. S. Davis, "W^4: Real-Time Surveillance of People and Their Activities," *IEEE Transactions on Pattern Analysis and Machine Intelligence*, Vol. 22, No. 8, 2000, pp. 809-830.

[3] S. Kwak and H. Byun, "Detection of Deominant Flow and Abnormal Events in Surveillance Video," *Optical Engineering*, Vol. 50, No. 2, 2011. pp. 1-8.

[4] Z. Xu and H. R. Wu, "Smart Video Surveillance System," *Proceedings of the IEEE International Conference on Industrial Technology*, 14-17 March, pp. 285-290.

[5] S. Aramvith, *et al*., "Video Processing and Analysis for Surveillance Applications," *International Symposium on Intelligent Signal Processing and Communication Systems* (*ISPACS* 2009), 7-9 January 2009, Kanazawa, pp. 607-610.

[6] P. Bottoni, "A Dynamic Environment for Surveillance," *Proceedings of the* 12*th IFIP TC* 13 *International Conference on Human-Computer Interaction*, Uppsala, 24-28 August, 2009, pp. 892-895.

[7] N. M. Oliver, B. Rosario and A. P. Pentland, "A Bayesian Computer Vision System for Modeling Human Interactions," *IEEE Transactions on Pattern Analysis and Machine Intelligence*, Vol. 22, No. 8, 2000, pp. 831-843.

[8] D. Weinland, R. Ronfard and E. Boyer, "A Survey of Vision-Based Methods for Action Representation, Segmentation and Recognition," *Computer Vision and Image Understanding*, Vol. 115, No. 2, 2011. pp. 224-241.

[9] I. Karaulova, P. Hall and A. Marshall, "A Hierarchical Model of Dynamics for Tracking People with a Single Video Camera," *Proceedings of the British Machine Vision Conference*, 2000, pp. 262-352.

[10] Y. Ren, *et al*., "Detection and Tracking of Multiple Target Based on Video Processing," 2009 *Second International Conference on Intelligent Computation Technology and Automation*, Changsha, 10-11 October 2009, pp. 586-589.

[11] M. B. Augustin, S. Juliet and S. Palanikumar, "Motion and Feature Based Person Tracking in Surveillance Videos," *Proceedings of ICETECT* 2011, Tamil Nadu, 23-24 March 2011, pp. 605-609.

[12] T. J. Broida and R. Chellappa, "Estimation of Object Motion Parameters from Noisy Images," *IEEE Transactions on Pattern Analysis and Machine Intelligence*, Vol. 8, No. 1, 1986, pp. 90-99.

[13] Y. Su, *et al*., "Surveillance Video Sequence Segmentation Based on Moving Object Detection," 2009 *Second International Workshop on Computer Science and Engineering*, Qingdao, 28-30 October 2009, pp. 534-537.

[14] C. Wren, A. Azarbayejani, T. Darrell and A. Pentland, "Pfinder: Real-Time Tracking of the Human Body," *IEEE Transactions on Pattern Analysis and Machine Intelligence*, Vol. 19, No. 7, 1997, pp. 780-785.

[15] M. Ahmad and S.-W. Lee, "HMM-Based Human Action Recognition Using Multi View Image Sequences," *International Conference on Pattern Recognition*, Vol. 1, 2006, pp. 263-266.

[16] Y. Kuno, T. Watanabe, Y. Shimosakoda and S. Nakagawa, "Automated Detection of Human for Visual Surveillance System," *Proceedings of the* 13*th International Conference on Pattern Recognition*, Vienna, 25-29 August 1996, pp. 865-869.

[17] H. Gou, *et al*., "Implementation and Analysis of Moving Objects Detection in Video Surveillance," *Proceedings of the* 2010 *IEEE International Conference on Information and Automation*, Harbin, 20-23 June 2010, pp. 154-158.

[18] S. Wang *et al*., "A Mobile Agent Based Multi-Node Wireless Video Collaborative Monitoring System," *The* 3*rd International Conference on Advanced Computer Theory and Engineering*, Chengdu, 20-22 August 2010, pp. 35-39.

[19] H. Kakiuch, *et al*., "Detection Methods Improving Reliability of Automatic Human Tracking System," 2010 4*th International Conference on Emerging Security Information, Systems and Technologies*, Washington DC, 2010, pp. 240-246.

[20] W. Y. Zhao, R. Chellappa, P. J. Phillips and A. Rosenfeld, "Face Recognition: A Literature Survey," *ACM Computing Surveys*, Vol. 35, No. 4, 2003, pp. 399-458.

[21] T. S. Ling, L. K. Meng, L. M. Kuan, Z. Kadim and A. A. Baha Al-Deen, "Colour Based Object Tracking in Surveillance Application," *Proceedings of the International Multi-Conference of Engineers and Computer Scientists*, Hong Kong, 18-20 March 2009, pp. 459-464.

[22] B. Schiele, "Model-Free Tracking of Cars and People Based on Color Regions," *Image and Vision Computing*, Vol. 24, No. 11, 2006, pp. 1172-1178.

[23] Z. Zhang, "Head Detection for Video Surveillance Based on Categorical Hair and Skin Colour Models," *The* 16*th IEEE International Conference on Image Processing*, Cairo, 7-10 November 2009, pp.1137-1140.

18

Cloud Computing Solution and Services for RFID Based Supply Chain Management

S. M. Khalid Jamal[1*], A. Omer[1], Asiya Abdus Salam Qureshi[2]
[1]Department of Computer Science, UBIT, University of Karachi, Karachi City, Pakistan
[2]Department of Computer Science and Software Engineering, University of Hail, Hail, KSA

ABSTRACT

Deploying and Implementing RFID Systems for tracking and controlling products in supply chain management is not affordable for small and midsized companies due to its complexity, cost, and difficulties pertaining data management and maintenance. Cloud computing can be used to mitigate the risks associated with the implementation and deployment of RFID based on system in supply chain management because the complex system for data filtering, management and maintenance can be implemented on the cloud that otherwise requires the purchase of new hardware, staff and professional services.

Keywords: Cloud Computing; RFID; Tags; Readers; Barcodes

1. Introduction

Radio Frequency Identification (RFID) is a prevailing technology that uses radio waves to monitor and control the products in supply chain management. Each product has a tag affixed to it during manufacturing process which contains a unique identifier that can be used to uniquely identify a product by all supply chain participants. The deployment as well as implementation of RFID systems has been a challenging task for small and medium sized enterprises (SMEs). In this paper, we propose cloud computing solution to overcome these challenges. The supply chains can install RFID solution much faster by using the cloud implementation while avoiding many of the expensive infrastructure cost required for pre-cloud systems.

RFID technology has been introduced across a range of industries, including public sector as well as inretail and manufacturing. For example, RFID has been used by Harley-Davidson and Toyota to monitor parts for their motorcycles and automobiles, respectively. Furthermore, baggage at Las Vegas Airport is tagged to enhance and improve loading procedures as well as the tracking of passengers' baggage. The US Department of Defense and Wal-Mart hosted RFID technology a decade ago, and required their suppliers to make all supplies RFID enabled, in order to ease its inventory management. For organizations of all types, the ability to quickly locate and enumerate products may facilitate business value of supply chain management [1].

Small and midsized companies are unable to afford the costs and risks associated with the implementation and deployment of RFID systems. Therefore, we propose a cloud computing solution so that the capital investment and the return-on-investment risks associated with the new technology of RFID can be mitigated. Cloud-base services are designed in such a way as to eliminate the hardware and software infrastructure requirements whose implementation is time consuming as well as expensive. Moreover, it provides abstraction to its users by hiding all the complex details of the system. Users can only use the provided services by interacting with application software responsible for receiving inputs and providing outputs. The inner workings are completely invisible [2].

1.1. Motivation

According to an estimate, the annual savings of US leading retail Wal-Mart using RFID are $8.35 billion. This huge amount is divided as follows: it saves $600 million by meeting timely delivery of goods due to real-time and rapid information that RFID systems provide; inventory shrinkage saves $180 million; $575 million are saved by controlled tracking and monitoring of the products that

*Corresponding author.

prevents theft, mistakes and buyer fraud; pallets and the need to scan each product individually which reduces the labor cost as well as time. By implementing RFID, the total of $3 billion annual investment is made by Wal-Mart as opposed to $8.35 billion made earlier. The annual savings in different heads are represented in the Bar-**Graph 1**.

Due to its speed, accuracy and improved inventory management, RFID technology has been widely adopted and recognized as an emerging and affective technology in industry and businesses. An RFID system is made of up to following three arrangements:

- An *RF subsystem*, which uses wireless communication of RFID tags and readers to perform wirelessidentification of tagged items over a network [3].
- An *enterprise subsystem*, that stores, processes and manages the data received from the RF subsystem through software applications designed for this purpose and that makes the RFID data more powerful.
- An *inter-enterprise subsystem*, through which multiple enterprise subsystems are connected in order to share information among supply chain networks [4].

  All RFID systems have an RF subsystem where the tags are read in and almost all RFID systems also include some form of an enterprise subsystem. An inter-enterprise subsystem is used when the information needs to be shared across the enterprise boundaries.

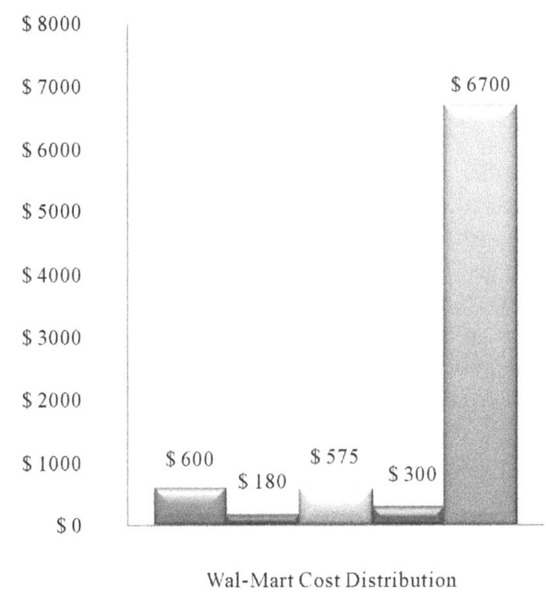

Graph 1. Annual savings by Wal-Mart in different heads.

The RF subsystem is composed of two basic components in order to identify the tagged items.

- RFID *tags* also called transponders are small electronic chips that are either attached to items or embedded within them. All tags can be uniquely identified by an identifier assigned to them. These devices may have their own storage space containing additional information about the tagged item and sensors attached to them to monitor temperature for example or other environmental and status conditions.
- RFID readers are devices that are used to retrieve the information stored on RFID tags and identify each tag uniquely by wirelessly communicating with the tags [5].

Tags can be active, having their own source for power supply or passive, depending upon the RFID reader to supply the power necessary to transmit signals. The signal can be a simple identification number, or a complex data stream stored in the tag's memory. These tags can contain information such as the expiry date, date of manufacturing, built in sensors to track temperature or other data [6].

1.2. RFID in Supply Chain Management

The most data rich and intensive RFID application is the supply chain management systems in which a tagged product is tracked from manufacture to final purchase, throughout its life cycle. In addition to process data, data information is also maintained in these systems, such as the formats in which it is stored and transmitted by the supply chain in various organizations and the database network addresses that contains data about different tagged items.

Supply chain management is also used in monitoring and product control from manufacture to retail sail including its distribution. It is typically a collection of different kind of application types, which includes asset management, process control and tracking and payment systems.

In supply chain systems, the information about the product can be stored at every phase in the supply chain. Tags are attached to products during manufacturing process or soon after it to these products in ideal situation. As the product progresses through the supply chain, the information on these tags can be altered by the supply chain participants. Moreover, larger objects such as pallets and containers can be tracked and monitored by these systems using active tags. These tags which are affixed on the pallets can store information about the items shipped in each of the container. When the products are moved out from the container the information which the tags carry are automatically upgraded to reflect the new information. An electronic history is also generated for each item in the container which ensures the buyers about the item's freshness, enabling them to identify whether it's useful, has expired or not [7].

Objects are automatically identified with the help of fully utilized EPC data. It can also be used in monitoring location and movement, and trigger events. Operational efficiencies could be gained by a near real-time view throughout the supply chain, such as improved inventory control, increasing throughput and lowering cost of the products [8].

1.3. Benefits of Using RFID

- Time spent in ordering products is minimized.
- Less number of employees required for inventory control.
- Manual entries in the inventory document might become prone to errors, whereas using RFID technology the entries are automatic and hence more accurate.
- Sales reports are created automatically.
- Overstocking in warehouses is minimized.
- Forecasting the demand for products can be performed more accurately because real time data is used for estimation of demand.
- Improved communication between suppliers and customers.
- Reduction in costs for labor needed for database management in inventory.

1.4. Electronic Product Code (EPC)

The Electronic Product Code (EPC) is a unique identifier stored on the tag that can be used to retrieve more information about the tagged item from a database. EPC is standardized by EPCglobal (a non-profit organization) and acts as a replacement to UPC (Universal Product Code) numbers when barcodes are used as identifiers on products. However, unlike UPC barcodes that refer to a class of products, EPC refer to a specific instance of product. A unique EPC serial code that is saved in the tag is transferred back to the reader when an EPC tag is read by RFID reader. The product is identified through internet using the facility of Object Naming Service (ONS). The ONS matches the specific EPC code to the corresponding entry on the internet that provides additional information about the product. EPC Information Services (EPCIS) are then used to communicate available information in real time via EPCglobal Network. The real time data that is exchanged on EPCglobal Network allows for the tracking and monitoring of products. Unlike the identification of classes of products as with barcodes, EPC allows us to uniquely identify an instance of a tagged product. A serial number embedded within the EPC is used to uniquely identify a tagged product. The set of EPCs within the domain of a person is referred to as his "EPC cloud". This EPC cloud can be used to monitor thefts within the supply chain [9].

2. Challenges Faced in RFID Implementation

One of the major challenges in RFID implementation is the high cost associated with its implementation. This includes the cost of installation of the new hardware and software as well as the hiring of new staff for professional services required for the integration of the new system. According to an estimate, an RFID-enabled warehouse would cost in excess of $2 million which makes it unsuitable, especially for Small and Medium sized Enterprises (SMEs), to implement a fully-fledged RFID system.

Another challenge is the lack of understanding of RFID technology and the approaches required to integrate the RFID technology into the current IT infrastructure. Capturing, exchanging and managing data from RFID readers and integrating the data into EPCIS and sharing data among enterprises can become a challenging task. This makes the deployment and maintenance of RFID systems a time consuming and complex operation. According to a survey, two-thirds of all respondents said they are still learning about the technology; while 26.3 percent said they have an intermediate level of knowledge. The automotive industry recorded a slightly higher level of intermediate knowledge, at 33 percent, while the transportation market, at 28 percent, was slightly higher than the average for all industries. Therefore, the low awareness and lack of understanding of RFID systems among stakeholders is a critical factor preventing its adoption [10].

Another problem in RFID implementation is the heavy volumes of data that it generates that are hard to handle. According to an estimate, Wal-Mart produces 7 terabytes of operational RFID data per day. Moreover, supply chain monitoring and real time tracking requires storing additional data that the traditionally designed databases cannot manage. This implies additional hardware costs needed to manage the large volumes of data generated by RFID systems. According to an estimate, RFID based solutions and services are expected to be adopted over the next 18 - 24 months due to the prevailing acceptance of cloud computing [11].

3. Proposed Cloud Computing Implementation

Cloud computing is a prevailing technology in which computing infrastructure, hardware, software and services are provided wherever and whenever needed. With the proposed cloud computing architecture shown in **Figure 1**, data from the scanning system is provided to the EPC Information System that is implemented on cloud as SaaS (Software as a Service). The transmitted data is stored and managed on the cloud and is made

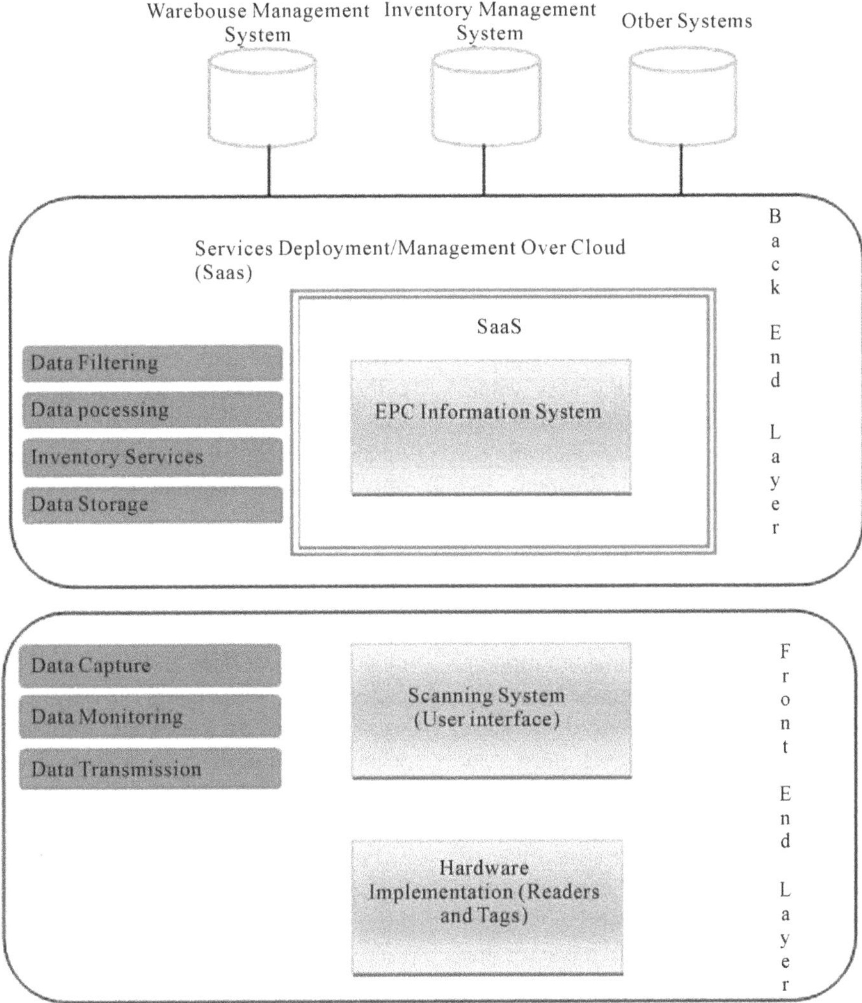

Figure 1. Cloud-based architecture.

available in a reliable manner to any application that requests it. The proposed cloud computing architecture sufficiently reduces the maintenance and support cost, which is one of the implementation barriers, while increasing overall system consistency and flexibility. Supply chains can now deploy RFID much faster while reducing the time consumption and complexity of the newly deployed system. Furthermore, the EPC Information System can also be used to implement additional functionality such as data warehousing.

3.1. Front-End Layer

The front-end portion of the proposed architecture includes the hardware implementation of RFID tags and readers over a network, the computers with sufficient capabilities for data storage and management as well as the front end software application that links the produced data with the cloud computing system. The front end begins to work when RFID tags and reader communicate over a network as a result of which RFID data is generated. Whenever an RFID tag appears within the range of RFID reader, RFID data is produced. The data that is acquired by the RFID reader is then sent to the front-end software application containing the user interface and application program connecting the front-end and the back-end layers in order to gain access to more services and information that are stored and processed on the Cloud. Since, RFID systems generate huge amount of new data specially from sensor based active tags sending data through cellular network, this data needs to filtered, stored and processed before being used. A Cloud computing backend-end layer is used in order to achieve all of these objectives that is connected to front-end layer over a network. The cloud helps supply chains to manage heavy volumes of data. In addition, there are numerous advantages achieved by supply chain operators and customers which include the reduction in IT cost, removal of the costly infrastructure necessities, elimination of the complex technology, professional services and software updates required leading to faster path to return on investment.

All the read EPCs are fed into the scanning system, that will search for those EPCs in Object Naming Service (ONS) and acquires the required information through EPCIS (EPC Information System) implemented on Cloud. The scanning system may be installed for example at a retail store's exit to scan all the products the customer purchases and the products that customer already had with him before purchase of new products. Since, EPCs are affixed within the product they need not be scanned individually as with barcodes and as EPC network stores information about individual products, these EPCs depict consumer habits and contribute to the business value. The cloud-based architecture allows the IT staff to concentrate more on other projects rather than dedicating a significant amount of time on RFID deployment and management.

3.2. Enterprise Sub-System

The enterprise subsystem provides a communication pathway for RFID readers and the computers that are running the front end application. The data obtained from RF subsystem is stored, processed and managed on these computers. For example, a retail garments store may have RFID system installed in which a unique identifier is read through RFID readers that uniquely identifies the product. The enterprise subsystem acts as a middleware that matches the identifier to the product's record stored in the database. The database records information about the product such as its price, the brand name or the manufacturing date. The proposed architecture consists of two layers the front-end layer composed of the scanning system and the hardware implementation of tags and readers, and the back-end layer containing EPCIS over Cloud [12].

3.3. Back-End Layer

The proposed cloud computing architecture (presented in **Figure 1**) contains back end layer which includes EPC Information System, data storage systems, computers and servers. The Cloud filters the data from RFID depending upon a particular application of interest. This filtered data uses the required SaaS services on the Cloud and is then stored on a specific server. The cloud computing system includes the relevant protocols and middleware that allow the networked resources, including RFID tags and readers, to communicate with each other.

The system traffic and system is managed by a server. Since RFID systems produce a huge amount of data, a lot of storage space is needed in the cloud computing system to store all the relevant information. Therefore, a copy of all RFID information is stored on the Cloud computing system. These copies are stored on backup machines and the backup data can be retrieved by the central server thus providing backup and restoration facility that was not otherwise available on traditional systems. The huge amount of data which was lost earlier at initial stages because of bearing low priority due to lack of storage space and available hardware may now be preserved and managed on the cloud to depict more intense business decisions as a result of using cloud computing. Moreover, the existing resources can be more efficiently utilized instead of demanding a need for new services and infrastructure deployment. Cloud based RFID system provides real-time data and powerful software tools. Typically the cloud offers its users additional functionalities such as warehouse and inventory management depending upon the needs of an enterprise where the client pays only for the services that are of critical importance.

3.4. Potential in the Desired Work

According to a study conducted at the end of 2012, 15,000 IT professionals have been approximated to use cloud based services and cloud computing which is estimated to increase rapidly in 2013. 61% of those queried were reported to use some form of cloud computing, whereas 39% of the respondents were not using any form of cloud services. The statistics are presented in a Pie-Chart, *i.e.* **Graph 2**.

Furthermore it is estimated that the companies spending in cloud computing will rise to $241 billion by 2020 from currently $40.7 billion. Recognizing the benefits of Software as a Service and Infrastructure as a Service, 41% of small businesses plan to invest in cloud by the end of 2014 relieving the company of the need for costly capital investment and maintenance of software thus saving the costs by up to 90%. IBM's Chief Technology Officer reports the decrease in labor cost by 50% when cloud services are used. 58% of the companies report that cloud has offered them an improved control of data. **Figure 2** shows the analysis conducted by Cisco Internet Business Solutions Group (IBSG) of the Small and Medium Businesses (SMB) total expenditure that is adoptable by cloud services (shown on the left hand side). The

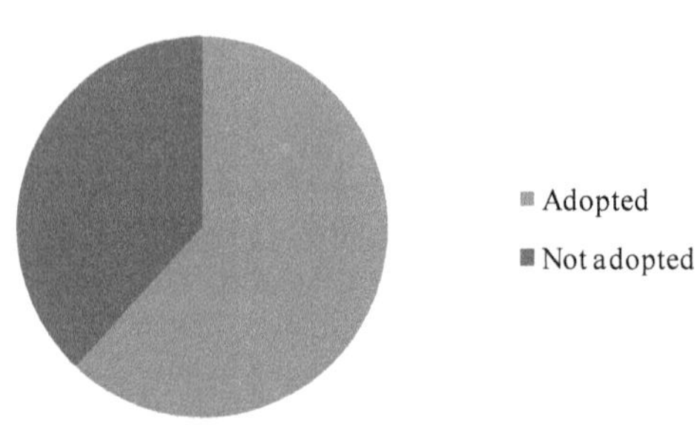

Graph 2. Pie-chart representing cloud adoption.

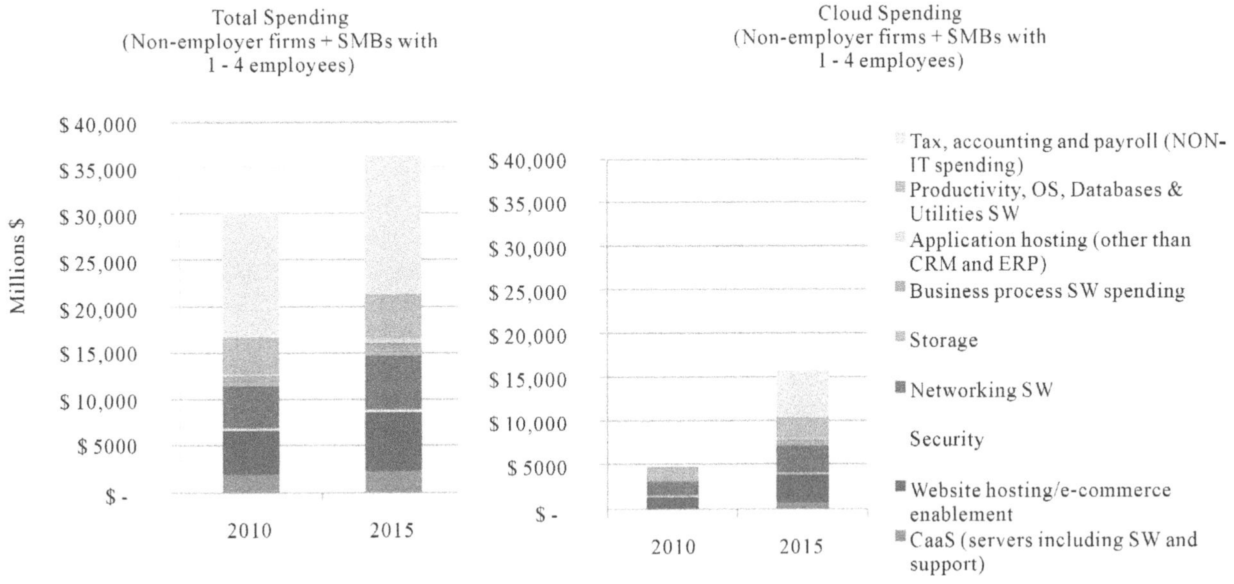

Figure 2. Between 2010 and 2015, US SMB cloud spending will increase from 16% of cloudable spending to 44%, or $16 billion, driven by tax and accounting applications and web hosting.

right hand side of the figure depicts the rates when cloud services are adapted to the spending on the left [13]. The query regarding what proportion of today's spending in IT services will ultimately move to a public cloud is unanswerable since the cloud offers on demand and flexible expenditure in contrast to the fixed contract in usual business scenario. Cisco IBSG research also depicts the high consideration of SMB towards the migration to cloud based services [14].

Analysis by Cisco IBSG shows that the total SMB expenditure on cloud adoptable services will rise from $31 billion in 2010 to $36 billion in 2015 whereas the expenditure on actual cloud based services will rise from $4 billion to $16 billion within the same period of time [15].

3.5. Benefits of Cloud Based Architecture

- One of the biggest challenges faced in RFID deployment is its associated cost. The proposed cloud computing solution provides its clients the facility to use on-demand and pay as you go services. Thus, clients will be able use RFID technology without having to make a huge investment on the fully fledged infrastructure. Small and Medium sized businesses that cannot afford the cost of deployment and implementation of new technology can benefit from cloud computing solution [16].
- The clients need not invest in the hiring of new staff or training of the current staff for the operation and maintenance of the new complex system as it will be provided as a service on cloud.
- Since, RFID produces large volumes of data that is difficult to store and manage in traditional database systems, this large volume of data can be stored and managed on the cloud on a specific server and is filtered appropriately.
- The copies of RFID data are stored on backup machines and the backup data can be retrieved by the central server thus providing backup and restoration facility that was not otherwise available on traditional systems [17].
- The vast amount of data which was lost previously at initial stages because of bearing low priority or due to lack of storage space and available hardware may now be preserved and managed on the cloud to depict more intense business decisions as a result of using cloud computing.
- Furthermore, cloud computing provides the facility of elastic capacity which means that the storage capacity and services provided are always flexible. More server resources can be allotted as and when the demand increases. When the demand decreases, there is no need to pay for the unused resources or storage space. This way the companies that are newly adopting the technology can initially demand less resources, thereby reducing the risk of return on investment on the RFID system. Then depending on the ROI, either more resources are acquired or the allotted resources are returned if the project fails [18].
- Cloud based RFID architecture is of importance to supply chains where condition based information is of

central importance as these systems provide real time, rapid and meaningful information sharing [19].

4. Conclusion

This paper discusses how cloud-based solutions can be coupled together with RFID-based sensing and monitoring systems to provide on-demand information to organizations. Supply chains can more efficiently and accurately trace products and monitor condition-based information such as expiration dates, temperature and delivery status thereby allowing the stakeholders to optimize their supply chains and use real-time information to make business decisions. The cloud computing solution can benefit small and medium sized enterprises (SMEs) because they can use RFID technology without making a major financial investment on new hardware and software purchase needed for data storage and management. Since lack of understanding is one of the biggest hurdles in RFID implementation, the proposed solution relieves its users from the complex infrastructure requirement. Cloud computing solution for RFID-based systems bears the ability to revolutionize the supply chains by cutting IT costs, overstocking and efficiently manage consumer goods.

REFERENCES

[1] GSA Smart Card Website. http://www.smart.gov/

[2] K. Finkenzeller, "RFID Handbook: Fundamentals and Applications in Contactless Smart Cards and Identification," 2nd Edition, John Wiley & Sons Ltd., Munich, 2003.

[3] Automatic Identification Technology Office. http://www.dodait.com/

[4] L. Sullivan, "RFID Implementation Challenges Persist, All This Time Later," *Information Week*, 2005. http://www.informationweek.com/rfid-implementation-challenges-persist-a/171203904?pgno=1

[5] RFID Journal. http://www.rfidjournal.com/

[6] T. Hey, S. Tansley and K. Tolle, "The Fourth Paradigm: Data-Intensive Scientific Discovery, Microsoft Research," Microsoft Corporation, 2009.

[7] Auto-ID Labs. http://www.autoidlabs.org/

[8] FCC OET Bulletins. http://www.fcc.gov/oet/info/documents/bulletins/

[9] EPC Global. http://www.epcglobalinc.org/

[10] NIST Computer Security Guideline Publications. http://csrc.nist.gov/publications/

[11] "Cisco Global Cloud Index: Forecast and Methodology, 2011-2016," Cisco, Whitepaper, 2012.

[12] D. Guinard, M. Mueller and J. Pasquier, "Giving RFID a REST: Building a Web-Enabled EPCIS," *Proceedings of the Internet of Things* 2010 *International Conference*, Tokyo, November 2010.

[13] "New Supply Chain Dynamic: Providing Actionable Data through Cloud-Based Services and Solutions," *RFID Journals*, Whitepaper, February 2013.

[14] D. P. Handler, J. Barbier and P. Schottmiller, "SMB Public Cloud Adoption: Opening a Hidden Market," Cisco Internet Business Solutions Group (IBSG), 2012.

[15] International Organization for Standardization. http://www.iso.org/

[16] S. Zhang, S. Zhang, X. Chen and X. Huo, "Cloud Computing Research and Development Trend," *Proceedings of the International Conference on Future Networks*, 2010.

[17] D. Guinard, C. Floerkemeier and S. Sarma, "Cloud Computing, REST and Mashups to Simplify RFID Application Development and Deployment," *Proceedings of the Second International Workshop on Web of Things*, New York, 2011.

[18] A. A. S. Qureshi and S. M. K. Jamal, "Taxonomy Based Data Marts," *International Journal of Computer Application*, 2012.

[19] A. A. S. Qureshi and S. M. K. Jamal, "Web Supported Query Taxonomy Classifier," *International Journal of Computer Application*, 2012.

19

Evaluation of Different Electronic Product Code Discovery Service Models

Su Mon Kywe, Jie Shi, Yingjiu Li, Raghuwanshi Kailash
School of Information Systems, Singapore Management University, Singapore City, Singapore

ABSTRACT

Electronic Product Code Discovery Service (EPCDS) is an important concept in supply chain processes and in Internet of Things (IOT). It allows supply chain participants to search for their partners, communicate with them and share product information using standardized interfaces securely. Many researchers have been proposing different EPCDS models, considering different requirements. In this paper, we describe existing architecture designs of EPCDS systems, namely Directory Service Model, Query Relay Model and Aggregating Discovery Service Model (ADS). We also briefly mention Secure Discovery Service (SecDS) Model, which is an improved version of Directory Service Model with a secure attribute-based access control mechanism. Then, we analyze the strengths and limitations of these models, by comparing based on non-functional features such as data ownership, confidentiality, business relationship independence, availability, reliability, implementation complexity, visibility, and scalability. From the analysis results, we have a better understanding of which model is more suitable in what kinds of situations or scenarios. Moreover, we suggest possible improvements and identify possible future add-on applications to SecDS model in the paper.

Keywords: EPC Discovery Service; Supply Chain; Access Control; Comparison

1. Introduction

Supply chain is a process of transforming natural resources or raw materials into finished goods, by passing through suppliers, manufacturers, wholesalers, retailers, customers and other supply chain partners [1]. When various supply chain partners work together to deliver the right amount of goods to the right customers at right time and right place, good coordination and information sharing are critical.

Lack of information sharing among supply chain partners can lead to a lot of negative consequences. For instance, when downstream retailers are not willing to share their end customer information (e.g. for security and privacy reasons), upstream suppliers and manufacturers have no idea about the customers. The manufacturers predict the customer demand from wholesalers' orders, while wholesalers predict the customer demand from the retailers' orders. This lack of information transparency can lead to "bullwhip effect" where each upstream supply chain participant observes greater demand variation and greater need for safety stocks, consequently bearing greater costs [2]. The whole supply chain can suffer as it becomes less responsive to demand fluctuations.

Therefore, in today's market where competition is very intense, it becomes increasingly important to have a structured way of fast and secure information sharing among supply chain partners. Standardized systems and communication methods, which can be used uniformly across different organizations around the globe, are required to be developed.

As such, EPCglobal organization [3], which is responsible for standardization of Electronic Product Code (EPC) technology [4], created EPCglobal Network [5] for sharing RFID information. EPCglobal Network is implemented, using standards from EPCglobal Architecture Framework [6]. It has four components, namely Object Naming Service (ONS), EPC Discovery Services (EPCDS), EPC Information Services (EPCIS) and EPC Security Services [5]. In this paper, we focus mainly on EPCDS models, since standardization of EPCDS design is still an open research question [6].

Our paper is structured as follows. Section 2 provides background information on EPCDS and EPCIS. Section 3 briefly describes existing EPCDS models which include Directory Service Model, Query Relay model and Aggregating Discover Service model. In Section 4, we describe SecDS model which is an extension of Directory Service Model. Section 5 gives comparison of the different models and Section 6 summarizes the analysis. Then, we identify possible improvements for SecDS model in

Section 6 and finally we conclude the paper in Section 7 with the role of EPCDS in future Internet of Things (IOT) [7].

2. Background

2.1. EPCDS

Electronic Product Code Discovery Service (EPCDS) is a service that allows users to find supply chain partners who possess a given product. A user just need to key in a particular EPC number, such as RFID number of the product, to search for EPC Information Services (EPCIS) provided by the related supply chain partners within the network.

EPCDS can be compared to telephone directory or search engines of the internet. To request information about a particular EPC, a supply chain participant needs to have knowledge of who are its supply chain partners and their network addresses or URLs that should be queried. This is like the need to know the phone numbers before contacting each other. Then, EPCDS acts like a telephone directory or yellow page where the contacts or addresses of EPC information providers or repositories are aggregately stored and returned to the appropriate queries accordingly, as shown in **Figure 1** [8].

Basically, EPCDS supports two operations, publishing operation and querying operation. Publishing operation is for EPCIS to publish their information on EPCIS whereas querying operation is for supply chain users, who want to find published EPCIS addresses.

2.2. EPCIS

In this context, EPC Information Service (EPCIS) can simply be viewed as a database or repository owned by a supply chain participant. It stores event information of supply chain products, where each product is uniquely identified by an EPC number. EPC event information includes product information, product location, date and time of product arrival and departure, involved business processes, and other important business information [6].

To share its critical business information with its trusted supply chain partners, EPCIS provides a querying interface for its repository. However, EPCIS may maintain access control mechanisms to ensure that only authorized users can access its sensitive information. With EPCIS querying service, any authorized users, who know the address of EPCIS service, can get access to its EPC repositories or databases easily.

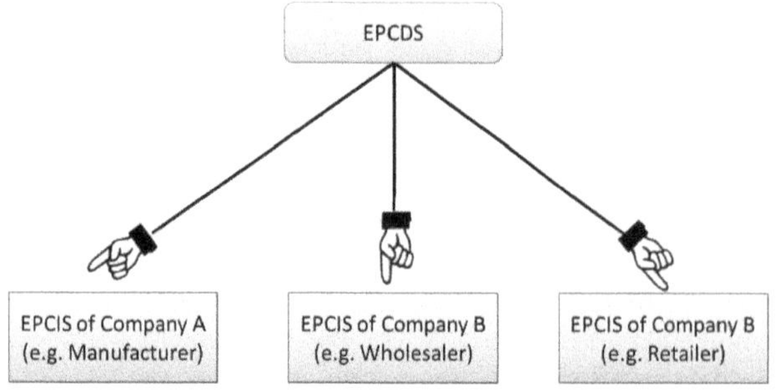

Figure 1. EPCDS as a directory of EPCIS.

2.3. Definition of Terms

In our paper, the terms "users" or "clients" is used for supply chain participants who want to get EPC event information from EPCIS. EPCIS company (owner), database and its services are collectively mentioned as "EPCIS", "resource", "EPCIS resource" "EPCIS repository" or "EPCIS company".

3. Existing Discovery Service Models

BRIDGE (Building Radio frequency identification for the Global Environment) project has modeled and analyzed eight possible high level designs of EPCDS in 2007. After considering each model's feasibility, BRIDGE selected the two models of EPCDS, called Directory Service Model and Query Relay Model [8]. Although there are a lot of variations of these two models, our paper only use basic models suggested in BRIDGE document for simplicity purpose. The third EPCDS design is Aggregating Discovery Service (ADS) Model, proposed by Hasso Plattner Institute for IT Systems Engineering in 2010 [9].

3.1. Directory Service Model

In Directory Service Model, EPCDS stores a directory of EPC numbers and corresponding EPCIS addresses. **Figure 2** illustrates the steps of this Directory Service Model.

Step 1: An owner of an EPCIS first registers at EPCDS with the details on which EPC numbers they are handling, together with its service address or URL. EPCDS stores the pairs of EPC numbers and EPCIS addresses in its lookup table.

Step 2: User sends query to EPCDS with a specific EPC number or a range of EPC numbers as parameters.

Step 3: EPCDS uses lookup table to look up queried EPC numbers, finds corresponding EPCIS addresses and returns them to the user.

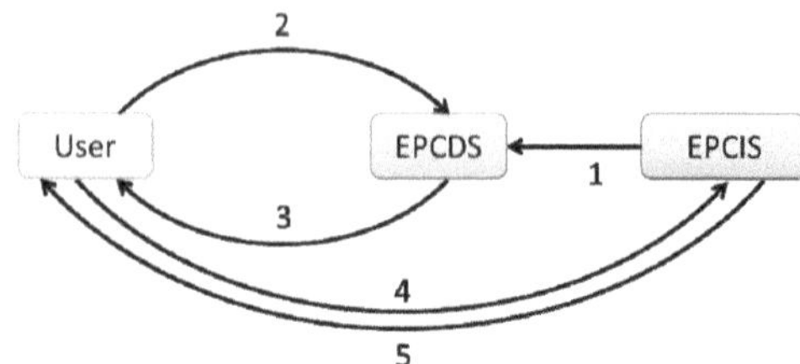

Figure 2. Steps in Directory Service Model.

Step 4: With the returned addresses, the user queries directly to EPCIS repositories to get the desired required EPC event information.

Step 5: EPCIS repositories return the required EPC event information to the user.

One of the main problems of Directory Service Model is that EPCDS returns all the related EPCIS addresses to every user who queries. Access control mechanisms are not specified in detail.

Based on the query result, every user knows exactly which EPCIS repositories are handling which EPC numbers. Availability of EPCIS addresses indicates ownership of product information in that EPCIS companies. Therefore, many companies, who consider their possession of items as confidential or sensitive information, do not want to expose their EPCIS addresses and are reluctant to publish them on EPCDS.

3.2. Query Relay Model

In the query relay model, EPCDS does not return the service addresses of EPCIS repositories immediately upon request. Instead, it redirects the query to corresponding EPCIS repositories which have their own access control mechanisms. As shown in **Figure 3**, query relay model has the following steps.

Step 1: An owner of an EPCIS first registers at EPCDS with the details on which EPC numbers they are handling, together with its service address or URL. Then, EPCDS stores the pairs of EPC numbers and EPCIS addresses in the lookup table.

Step 2: User sends query to EPCDS with a specific EPC number or a range of EPC numbers as well as user's credentials as parameters.

Step 3: EPCDS uses lookup table to look up queried EPC numbers, finds corresponding EPCIS addresses and relays user's query and credentials to those EPCIS resources.

Step 4: Each EPCIS resource checks user's credentials against its own access control database and returns the query result to the authenticated user directly.

Actually, in query relay model, user query can be of two types. The first one is a full query, directly requesting EPCIS to return the full EPC event information. The second query type is a resource query, where EPCIS returns only the service address that user should query to get required EPC event information.

3.3. Aggregating Discovery Service (ADS)

Aggregating Discovery Service (ADS) model is based on the query relay model. In this model, instead of returning EPC event information directly to user, each EPCIS returns the result back to EPCDS. Only after getting replies from different EPCIS repositories, EPCDS aggregates their information and sends them back to the user. **Figure 4** shows the steps of aggregating discovery service model.

Step 1: An owner of an EPCIS first registers at EPCDS with the details on which EPC numbers they are handling, together with its service address or URL. Then, EPCDS stores the pairs of EPC numbers and EPCIS addresses in the lookup table.

Step 2: User sends query to EPCDS with a specific EPC number or a range of EPC numbers as well as user's credentials as parameters.

Step 3: EPCDS uses lookup table to look up queried EPC numbers, finds corresponding EPCIS addresses and relays user's query and credentials to those EPCIS resources.

Step 4: Each EPCIS resource checks user's credentials against its own access control database and returns the query result to EPCDS.

Step 5: EPCDS aggregates the results and relays them back to the user.

4. Secure Discovery Service Model

Secure Discovery Service model (SecDS) is based on Directory Service Model.

As described in Section 3.1, Directory Service Model has a critical problem due to the lack of access control system in EPCDS. Sensitive business information may be leaked, since EPCDS returns related EPCIS addresses to every user query.

In SecDS model, the basic Directory Service Model is improved by implementing a secure access control mechanism inside EPCDS. Access control mechanism in EPCDS makes sure that it does not release EPCIS addresses to any unauthorized users. Confidentiality of important EPC information is preserved.

As shown in **Figure 5**, steps in SecDS model are the same as steps in Directory Service Model, except that in

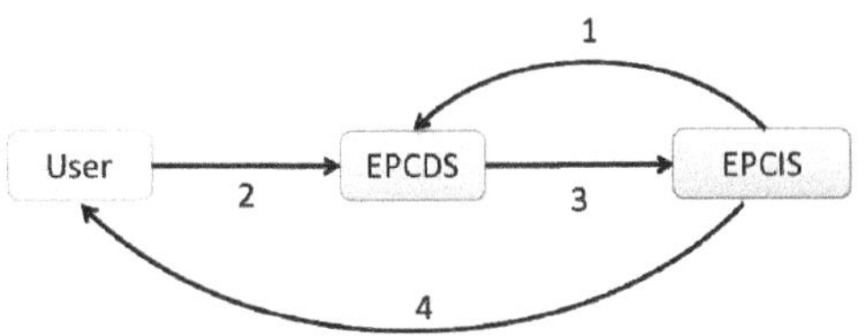

Figure 3. Steps in query relay model.

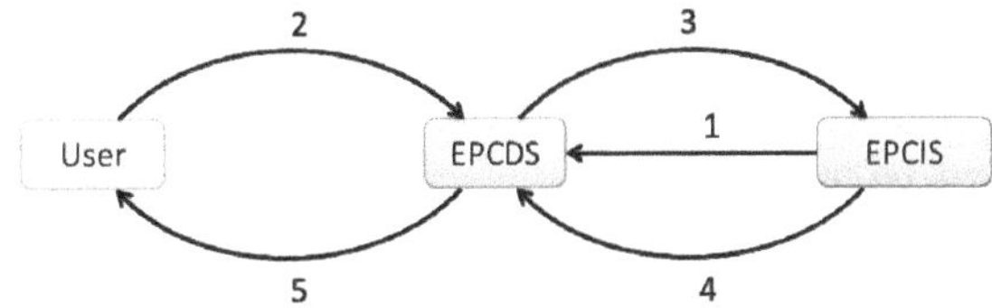

Figure 4. Steps in aggregating discovery service model.

step 1, access control policies are sent together with EPC numbers and EPCIS address from EPCIS. In addition to lookup table of EPCIS addresses, EPCDS maintain a database on access control policies in SecDS model.

Moreover, EPCDS provides interfaces for adding, deleting and modifying access control policies. EPCIS owners can use these interfaces to synchronize access control polices between EPCDS and EPCIS.

4.1. Architecture of SecDS Model

Figure 6 describes the overview EPCDS architecture of SecDS model with attribute-based access control system [10].

4.1.1. Data Storage

Data storage component contains event information related to EPC numbers. The attributes of the table are EPC number, EPCIS address, Published Date and Time, as well as other Publisher information. These attributes can be used to define access control polices in EPCDS.

4.1.2. Policy Storage

Policy storage component contains two types of access control policies for EPCDS. One is for publishing and another is for querying.

Policies for publishing determine who can publish access control policies in EPCDS and are managed by security administrators of EPCDS. On the other hand, policies for querying are defined by security administrators of each EPCIS and are used to control who is able to query its EPC event information. Complexity of SecDS model lies in managing policies for querying because attribute-based access control is needed for querying users. The policies for publishing are simple Role-Based Access Control (RBAC).

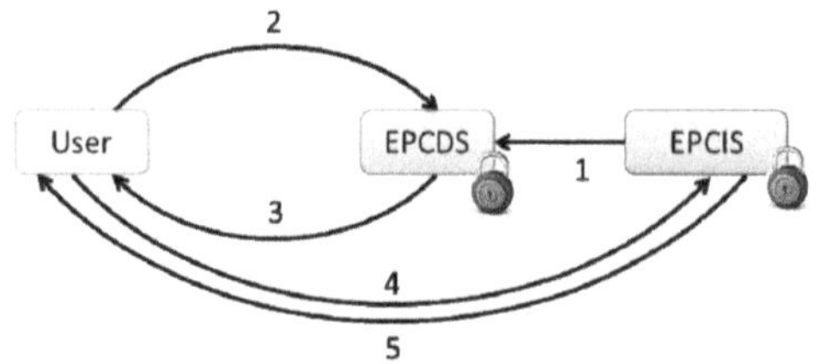

Figure 5. Steps in secure discovery service model.

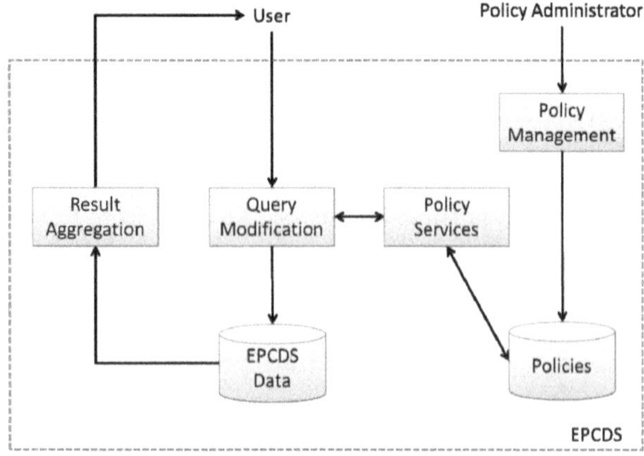

Figure 6. Architecture of EPCDS in SecDS model.

4.1.3. Policy Management

Policy management component provides an interface for EPCIS owner to publish, update or delete their policies on EPCDS. It performs syntax analysis, semantic analysis and policy transformation before saving the policies in policy storage database.

Syntax and semantic analysis checks the syntax and semantic of submitted policies while policy transformation transforms attribute-based access control policies into fine-grained access control policies. The purpose of transformation is to improve the efficiency of querying. However, the trade-off is the increased complexity of maintaining the policies.

4.1.4. Policy Services

Policy service component supports query modification component. Whenever there is a query, policy service component searches for related fine-grained access control predicates, combines them into one access control policy and returns it to query modification component.

4.1.5. Query Modification

Query modification component changes normal queries into modified queries that comply with the access control policies.

4.1.6. Result Aggregation

Result aggregation component returns the aggregated EPCIS addresses to the user. With the returned EPCIS addresses, user can then query to EPCIS companies directly to get EPC information. User may also store the EPCIS addresses and in the future, query to EPCIS repositories without the need to interact with EPCDS again.

4.2. Attribute-Based Access Control of SecDS Model

The main contribution of SecDS model lies in its secure attribute-based access control system, where each EPCIS owner can set his own access control policies based on certain attributes. Attribute-based access control (ABAC) is chosen, despite its complexity, because it is more flexible than other access control systems and fulfills the business needs and requirements of supply chain information sharing.

For instance, an EPCIS owner can define that certain EPC numbers are accessible, depending on the role attribute of the users (e.g. a manufacturer, wholesaler or retailer) and/or the time attribute of EPC events (e.g. after 5/11/2011). Generally, there are three types of attributes with which an EPCIS can define access control policies.

Subject Attribute: Subject attributes are properties related to user companies such as Company ID, Company Name, Company Role, Company Location (Country, City, etc).

Object Attribute: Object attributes are properties of EPC events such as EPC Number, Time, and Business Process.

Visibility Attribute: Three types of visibility attributes can be used, namely whole-stream, up-stream and down-stream attribute.

In whole-stream policy, information related to an EPC number can be accessed by users of any companies who also publish event information about the same EPC number. Intuitively, it means that companies which handle the same product along the whole supply chain are allowed to access information about that product.

In up-stream policy, the information related to an EPC number can be accessed by users of any companies who handle the same EPC number before the publishing EPCIS does. For example, in a supply chain of supplier, manufacturer, distributor, wholesaler and retailer, the distributor's EPC information can be accessed by the supplier and the manufacturer of the same product.

In down-stream policy, the information related to an EPC number can be accessed by users of any companies who handle the same EPC number after the publishing EPCIS does. In the above supply chain, the distributor's information can be accessed by the wholesaler and the retailer of the same product.

These attribute-based access control policies are maintained in EPCIS companies and synchronized with EPCDS all the time.

5. Comparison of Different EPCDS Models

There have been research papers on the comparisons of different EPCDS models using different requirements. In [11], basic requirements for EPCDS design are identified to compare Directory Service Model and Query Relay model. The requirement features include data ownership, security (confidentiality, reliability and availability), business relationship independent design, organic growth, scalability and quality of service.

[9] uses the same requirements from [11] but they suggested Aggregating Discovery Service model and included it in the comparison. [12] compares scalability of Direcotry Service model and Query Relay model using supply chain simulation. [13] provides a consolidated comparison of Discovery Service architecture designs of EPCglobal [6], BRIDGE project [8], Afilias [14], ID@URI naming system [15] and Distributed Hash Table DHT-based Discovery Service [16], based on the requirements from the ISO/IEC 9126 [17] standard, BRIDGE project [8] as well as [11].

Our paper reuses the basic requirements described in [11] and adds in more features to evaluate Query Relay model, Aggregating Discovery Service model and SecDS model. Since SecDS model is an improvement of Directory Service model, we do not include the latter in our comparison.

The requirements are rated as "high", "medium" or "low", indicating that the model highly fulfills, moderately fulfills or almost does not fulfill the requirements.

5.1. Data Ownership

Data ownership is defined as the right to determine data usage privileges to other companies and as the ability to track the actual usage. EPCIS companies should have complete control over its data such as EPCIS address, EPC event information, business data as well as the settings of access control rights.

In [10], it is assumed that data ownership is lost once EPCIS delegates access controls to EPCDS. However, in our analysis, we assume that EPCDS is trusted and always acts in the way that it is supposed to. It does not expose the EPCIS addresses, returned results or published policies to any unauthorized persons.

5.1.1. Right to Determine Data Usage Privileges

Query Relay Model: This requirement is highly fulfilled since EPCIS manages its own access control policies and has local control over its EPC event information. It can also determine who can access to its EPCIS address.

Aggregating Discovery Service Model: Like query relay model, this requirement is also fulfilled in ADS model because EPCIS manages its own access control policies and possesses the ability to determine who has access to its EPC event information.

Secure Discovery Service Model: In SecDS model, EPCIS needs to publish some of its data attributes on EPCDS to support attribute-based access control policies. However, EPCIS can set the access control polices in EPCDS for their data. This requirement is fulfilled, assuming that access control policies in EPCDS works perfectly and that EPCDS is completely secured and trusted, in a sense that no unauthorized persons has access to the EPC event information.

5.1.2. Ability to Track Data Usage

Query Relay Model: This requirement is completely fulfilled as EPCDS can track who queries its service address and data.

Aggregating Discovery Service Model: This requirement is completely fulfilled since every query is handled by EPCDS in ADS model.

Secure Discovery Service Model: This requirement is only partially fulfilled in SecDS model. The reason is that EPCIS can track who is querying what EPC event information but EPCIS does not know who is given its EPCIS address until the user issues a query to the resource.

Although EPCIS has published policies on who can access its EPCIS address, this only ensures the confidentiality of EPCIS address. It does not support any tractability of who is given EPCIS address.

5.2. Confidentiality

Confidentiality is defined as preventing information from unauthorized access. In the following analysis, we assume that communication channel is secure and no adversary can eavesdrop or perform traffic analysis on the network channels. The only potential adversaries are users or EPCIS resources.

5.2.1. Client Confidentiality

Client confidentiality refers to unrevealing of any user query to irrelevant resources. Client confidentiality is important because user query reflects the strategic intentions or aims of the user. Client's query for EPC event information should be treated as sensitive information.

Query Relay Model: In query relay model, EPCSD relays client queries directly to EPCIS resources. The user does not have a chance to check the EPCIS addresses. Therefore, the user' interested EPC numbers as well as query details may be released to unrelated EPCIS resources. Client confidentiality is low in this model.

Aggregating Discovery Service Model: Like query relay model, EPCDS relays user query directly to the registered EPCIS resources. Therefore, client confidentiality is also low in ADS model.

Secure Discovery Service Model: In SecDS model, the user can get the EPCIS addresses first and check if the addresses are in user's blacklist which contains addresses of competitors and dubious resources. Only if they are not in the blacklist, user can direct its queries to them. Client confidentiality of SecDS model can be rated as medium as there are still chances that client queries are leaked to irrelevant resources which are not in the blacklist.

5.2.2. Resource Confidentiality

Resource confidentiality refers to unrevealing of EPC event information and EPCIS addresses to unauthorized users. Resource confidentiality is assured in all three models since they all do not release EPCIS address and EPC event data to unauthorized users.

5.3. Availability and Reliability

Availability is defined as a system's immediate readiness for usage whereas reliability refers to continuity of service over a prolonged period of time.

Query Relay Model: When resources query is used in query relay model, EPCIS address is returned to the user. Whenever user needs to query EPCIS, user can just reuse the address from cache. User does not need any help from EPCDS to get the desired result. So, even when EPCDS is down, user's request can be fulfilled by EPCIS. Therefore, availability and reliability is high in query relay model.

Aggregating Discovery Service Model: In this model, EPCDS is a single point of failure. Once EPCDS is unavailable, users have no way of communication with EPCIS resources as users do not have any information about EPCIS addresses. So, we can conclude that availability and reliability of this model is lower than that of query relay model and SecDS model.

Secure Discovery Service Model: Since SecDS model returns EPCIS addresses to user, like query relay model, the same argument from query relay model goes for high availability and reliability in SecDS model.

5.4. Complexity

Complexity refers to difficulty of implementing and maintaining a system. It indicates time and effort that should be put in to use the services provided by the system.

5.4.1. Client Complexity

Client complexity is the implementation effort that client needs to put in to be able to get the required EPC event information.

Query Relay Model: Normally, firewall matches the returning addresses with outbound addresses. However, in query relay model, request is sent to EPCDS while a number of EPCIS replies to the user. So, client needs a proxy which allows incoming traffic from unknown addresses. Client also needs to inspect the response by checking the session identifier.

Moreover, since client has no information on the number of relevant EPCIS resources, it does not know how many responses will be. Therefore, client query needs to maintain an open connection state and waits for a certain period of time before time out. This asynchronous connection makes client complexity high in query relay model.

Aggregating Discovery Service Model: In ADS model, client complexity is low since EPCDS returns the aggregated EPC event information directly.

Secure Discovery Service Model: In SecDS model, complexity is medium as EPCDS only provides services to find the EPCIS addresses. Client itself needs to implement a system to query to EPCIS resources and aggregate the results to get the required information.

5.4.2. EPCDS Complexity

EPCDS complexity refers to the development and maintenance effort of EPCDS.

Query Relay Model: Implementation in EPCDS is less complex in query relay model. This is because EPCDS only needs to maintain a lookup table and relay any query accordingly.

Aggregating Discovery Service Model: Complexity level of EPCDS in ADS model is high. It needs to maintain a number of connections or states of queries while connecting to a number of EPCIS. Furthermore, EPCDS needs to aggregate the results before sending back to the user. The cost for query processing and maintaining a number of connections is high.

Secure Discovery Service Model: In SecDS model, complexity of maintaining fine-grained access control policy is very high. With every update, delete or publish activity, a lot of processing is needed to transform from attribute-based access control to fine-grained access control.

5.4.3. Resource Complexity

Resource complexity is the effort that EPCIS resource needs to maintain.

Query Relay Model: EPCIS resource only needs to maintain its own access control policies and returns EPC event information to authorized users. Therefore, resource complexity is medium in query relay model.

Aggregating Discovery Service Model: It is the same as query relay model.

Secure Discovery Service Model: Resource complexity is relatively high, compared to query relay model and ADS model. The reason is that in addition to maintaining its own access control database, each EPCIS resources needs to make sure that its access control policies are duplicated at the EPCDS level. Whenever there are changes in business relationship, access control polices need to be updated and synchronized in EPCDS.

5.5. Scalability

Scalability refers to the ability to handle large amount of user queries and data. EPCDS should be able to support increasing network traffic in terms of both user volume and data volume. The scalability of EPCDS is highly correlated with the complexity of managing EPCDS.

Query Relay Model: Scalability is not much of an issue in query relay model. Data volume and query processing can increase gradually with the increased number of users.

Aggregating Discovery Service Model: Scalability is one of the main problems of ADS model. As the number of user queries increases, EPCDS needs to handle a lot more increased connections to EPCIS resources and processing of the results.

Secure Discovery Service Model: Scalability is also an issue in SecDS model. With the increased EPCIS resources registering at EPCDS, a lot more fine-grained access control policies need to be stored. These policies should be retrieved and processed for each query. Moreover, as the queries need to be modified according to the access control policies, processing load will increase significantly with increased number of queries.

5.6. Independence of Business Relationship

In supply chain where business relationships and partnerships are unstable, it is important to have EPCDS mechanisms which are independent of those business relationships.

Query Relay Model: In query relay model, EPCDS is independent on the business relationships of supply chain participants. Change in business relationships affects only the local access control policies of EPCIS resources.

Aggregating Discovery Service Model: The same argument goes for ADS model.

Secure Discovery Service Model: SecDS model is dependent on business relationships. Every time there is a change in partnerships, access control policies in EPCDS should also be updated immediately.

5.7. Quality of Service

Quality of service can be measured as the completeness and correctness of the result returned to the user.

Query Relay Model: In query relay model, EPCDS does not give user any information about the total number of EPCIS resources that is relevant to the user query. Consequently, if an EPCIS does not reply due to error or unavailable service for a short period, user may just assume that that EPCIS does not exist. Therefore, completeness of query result is not assured in this model.

Aggregating Discovery Service Model: In ADS model, EPCDS replies the aggregated query result to the user, including the EPCIS resources which are relevant to user query but cannot return information to the query due to error or unavailable service. Even though user cannot get the complete result this time, user can still query again later to get complete information.

Secure Discovery Service Model: Like ADS model, SecDS model also supports completeness and correctness of the query result. Since EPCDS in SecDS model returns all the relevant EPCIS addresses, user know exactly which EPCIS does not response and query again later.

5.8. Visibility

Visibility refers to the amount of observation and assessment that an EPCDS can make on the performance of the overall system. It is important for EPCDS to make sure registered EPCIS resources are really fulfilling user's information need. High visibility on the whole system can leads to improved service fulfillment as well as quality assurance.

Query Relay Model: The visibility of EPCDS is low in query relay model because EPCDS just relays the query to EPCIS and EPCIS itself replies the results to the user directly. EPCDS has no clue on whether an EPCIS address is still working and replying to user queries or whether the service is really fulfilled.

Aggregating Discovery Service Model: In ADS model, EPCDS has high visibility as EPCDS is responsible for aggregating query results for the users. EPCDS can even track the up and down times of EPCIS resources as well as their performance and efficiency in replying user queries.

Secure Discovery Service Model: Like query relay model, SecDS model also returns the EPCIS addresses only. SecDS model does not know whether an EPCIS address is still valid and working. EPCDS cannot track if the users actually get the information that is needed. Therefore, the visibility is low in SecDS model.

6. Discussion

Table 1 below provides a summarized comparison between query relay model, aggregating discovery service (ADS) model and SecDS model.

Query relay model performs well in all areas, except its high client complexity, low client confidentiality, low EPCDS visibility and low quality of service. This model is generally good for both EPCDS and EPCIS companies because it provides less implementation complexity and high scalability for EPCDS as well as great data ownership and confidentiality for EPCIS. The only potential problem is that EPCDS may not be able to track its service fulfillment. Nonetheless, the user may be reluctant to use the service of this model since it requires user's complex system implementation but does not guarantee user's confidentiality and completeness of query result.

On contrary to query relay model, Aggregating Discovery Service (ADS) model has high quality service for user and high visibility for EPCDS. It also provides high data ownership and confidentiality of EPCIS companies. Nevertheless, client confidentiality is not assured and EPCDS is a single-point-of-failure in this model. EPCDS also needs to bear high maintenance cost and scalability is an issue for EPCDS.

SecDS model is generally good in terms of data ownership and confidentiality for all EPCIS companies and users. Like query relay model, it provides reliable service with good quality and high visibility. However, it has high complex implementation for users, EPCIS as well as EPCDS. As a result, scalability is a big issue in SecDS model.

7. Possible Future Improvements to SecDS Model

7.1. Policy Synchronization

In SecDS model, access control policies should be duplicated and synchronized perfectly between EPCIS and EPCDS.

However, in the current implementation, only the pol-

Table 1. Summary of requirement analysis.

Assessed Features	Query Relay Model	ADS Model	SecDS Model
Data Ownership: Right to Determine Data Usage Privileges	High	High	High
Data Ownership: Ability to Track the Usage	High	High	Medium
Client Confidentiality	Low	Low	Medium
Resource Confidentiality	High	High	High
Availability and Reliability	High	Low	High
Client Complexity*	High	Low	Medium
EPCDS Complexity*	Low	High	High
Resource Complexity*	Medium	Medium	High
Scalability	High	Low	Low
Independent of Business Relationship	High	High	Low
Quality of Service	Low	High	High
Visibility	Low	High	High

*Although "High" indicates positive assessment in features like data ownership and confidentiality, "High" level of implementation complexity stands for negative evaluation of the feature.

icy administrator in EPCIS can publish policies to EPCDS while normal publisher cannot. This indicates that there may be some delay in publishing EPC event data and policies. In this delayed time window, any users can query the EPC event information. The formal implementation of SecDS model will enable that every normal publisher of EPC information can also publish related policies immediately.

Moreover, as policy publishing and data publishing are two separate operations in SecDS model, there is still a risk of resource forgetting to publish access control policies after publishing data. This can also lead to exposing sensitive information to random users. SecDS model should make it mandatory for every user who publishes event data to simultaneously publish related access control policies.

7.2. Improved Tractability and Data Ownership

As mentioned in Section 5.1.2. , the current implementation of SecDS model does not provide any traceability functions for EPCIS resources to track who has queried its EPCIS address. It would be nice to have such feature, where EPCDS informs resources, every time EPCIS address is given to any authorized user.

7.3. Client Application

Current functions in EPCDS of SecDS model are mainly implemented as services. As a result, users need to implement their own systems to query EPCIS resources and aggregate the results. In order to reduce complexity for users, it would be good to develop a sample secure client application which stores EPCIS addresses, queries to EPCIS resources and aggregate the results efficiently. As such, those users, who do not implement their own system, can use this application to get the required EPC event information.

7.4. Load Balancing and Clustering

As mentioned in Section 5.5., SecDS model might have problem of supporting increased number of user queries and EPCIS resources. To solve this problem of scalability, load balancing and clustering techniques can be considered. Clustering a few servers when load-balancing between them can increase the efficiency of access control policy processing. However, co-currency control should be taken care of when there is more than one running server.

7.5. Other Security Measures

EPCDS is considered as trusted and reliable agent between user and EPCIS resources. To use EPCDS in practical business world, there are many security measures to be considered and implemented.

7.5.1. Authentication

Current SecDS model does not implement any public key based authentication schemas for users and resources. In reality, there should be a certificate authority which can verify the authenticity of publishing and querying companies and their roles in supply chain.

7.5.2. Integrity

To ensure integrity of the messages communicated, every message should be signed with the private keys of the sender.

7.5.3. Availability

Denial-of-service attacks should also be prevented by limiting the number of queries for each user and publisher.

8. Future Direction of EPCDS

In the future, it is expected that EPCDS will be used for "Internet of Things (IOT)" [7]. IOT is a network of physical objects, expected to be implemented in near future. In IOT, most physical objects in the world will have RFID or barcode tags and become uniquely identifiable and connected to the Internet via RFID, sensor, and network technology. Either they are moving in certain directions or standing still in specific places, the physical objects will be tracked by respective owners and that information may be shared with relevant individuals, business partners or even the public. In IOT, EPCDS will play a critical role as a search engine, like Google in the current Internet.

9. Acknowledgements

This work is partly supported by A*Star SERC under grant number 082 101 0022 in Singapore.

REFERENCES

[1] Wikipedia, "Supply Chain," 2011. http://en.wikipedia.org/wiki/Supply_chain

[2] Wikipedia, "Bullwhip Effect," 2011. http://en.wikipedia.org/wiki/Bullwhip_effect

[3] Wikipedia, "EPCglobal," 2010. http://en.wikipedia.org/wiki/EPCglobal

[4] Wikipedia, "Electronic Product Code," 2011. http://en.wikipedia.org/wiki/Electronic_Product_Code

[5] Wikipedia, "EPCglobal Network," 2010. http://en.wikipedia.org/wiki/EPCglobal_Network

[6] EPCGlobal, "The EPCglobal Architecture Framework," 2010. http://www.gs1.org/gsmp/kc/epcglobal/architecture/archit

ecture_1_4-framework-20101215.pdf

[7] Wikipedia, "Internet of Things," 2012. http://en.wikipedia.org/wiki/Internet_of_Things

[8] University of Cambridge, AT4 Wireless, BT Research, SAP Research (BRIDGE project), "High Level Design for Discovery Services," 15 August 2007. http://www.bridge-project.eu/data/File/BRIDGE%20WP02%20High%20level%20design%20Discovery%20Services.pdf

[9] J. Muller, J. Oberst, S. Wehrmeyer, J. Witt, A. Zeier and H. Plattner, "An Aggregating Discovery Service for the EPCglobal Network," *Proceedings of the 43rd Hawaii International Conference on System Sciences*, Hawaii, 5-8 January 2010, pp. 1-9.

[10] S. Jie, D. Sim and L. Yingjiu, "SecDS: A Secure EPC Discovery Services System in EPCglobal Network," *2nd ACM Conference on Data and Application Security and Privacy (CODASPY)*, San Antonio, 7-9 February 2012, pp. 267-274.

[11] C. Kürschner, C. Condea, O. Kasten and F. Thiesse, "Discovery Service Design in the EPCglobal Network: Towards Full Supply Chain Visibility," *Proceedings of the 1st International Conference on the Internet of Things*," Zurich, 26-28 March 2008, pp. 19-34.

[12] E. Polytarchos, S. Eliakis, D. Bochtis and K. Pramatari, "Evaluating Discovery Services Architectures in the Context of the Internet of Things," *Unique Radio Innovation for the 21st Century*, Part 3, 2010, pp. 203-227.

[13] E. Sergei, F. Benjamin, K. Steffen and S. Nina, "Comparison of Discovery Service Architectures for the Internet of Things," *Proceedings of the 2010 IEEE International Conference on Sensor Networks, Ubiquitous, and Trustworthy Computing*, Newport Beach, 7-9 June 2010, pp. 237-244.

[14] Afilias, "Finding Your Way in the Internet of Things," 2008. http://www.afilias.info/webfm_send/11

[15] K. Framling, M. Harrison and J. Brusey, "Globally Unique Product Identifiers—Requirements and Solutions to Product Lifecycle Management," *Proceedings of 12th IFAC Symposium on Information Control Problems in Manufacturing (INCOM)*, Ecole des Mines, Saint Etienne, 17-19 May 2006, pp. 17-19.

[16] B. Fabian, "Implementing Secure P2P-ONS," *Proceedings IEEE International Conference on Communications*, Dresden, 14-18 June 2009, pp. 988-992.

[17] ISO, "Software Engineering—Product Quality—Part 1: Quality Model," 2001. ISO/IEC TR 9126-1:2001

Automatic Service Discovery of IP Cameras over Wide Area Networks with NAT Traversal

Chien-Min Ou[1*], Wei-De Wu[2]
[1]Department of Electronics Engineering, Ching Yun University, Chungli, Chinese Taipei
[2]Department of Computer Science and Information Engineering, National Taiwan Normal University, Taipei, Chinese Taipei

ABSTRACT

A novel framework for remote service discovery and access of IP cameras with Network address Translation (NAT) traversal is presented in this paper. The proposed protocol, termed STDP (Service Trader Discovery Protocol), is a hybrid combination of Zeroconf and SIP (Session Initial Protocol). The Zeroconf is adopted for the discovery and/or publication of local services; whereas, the SIP is used for the delivery of local services to the remote nodes. In addition, both the SIP-ALG (Application Layer Gateway) and UPnP (Universal Plug and Play)-IGD (Internet Gateway Device) protocols are used for NAT traversal. The proposed framework is well-suited for high mobility applications where the fast deployment and low administration efforts of IP cameras are desired.

Keywords: IP Camera (IP CAM); Network Address Translation (NAT); Session Initial Protocol (SIP)

1. Introduction

An IP camera (IP CAM) [1-3] is a video camera that can be directly connected to the internet without the need for a separate computer. It contains a hardware video encoder for realtime compression of captured video sequences. It also has a built-in web server, which provides the ability for accessing digital images and configuring the camera. The camera can be easily integrated with a wide range of applications, including e-surveillance, web attractions and remote monitoring.

For applications network security is an important concern, the deployment of IP CAMs in the network address translation (NAT) [4] environments with dynamic locations are usually desired. However, without a static IP address information, accessing the web server associated with the IP CAMs will be difficult. Moreover, for a service consumer, it may not be possible to always have a complete overview over the availability of IP CAMs in an application. This is particular true when large number of IP CAMs are employed in the application. Without a protocol providing IP CAM service information, the effectiveness of IP CAMs for internet applications may be limited.

Many service discovery protocols, such as SLP (Service Location Protocol) [5], Jini [6], UPnP (Universal Plug-and-Play) [7], and Zeroconf [8,9], can be adopted for solving the problems. In the service discovery environments, IP CAMs and other devices advertise themselves, supplying details about their capabilities and the information one must know to access the service (e.g., the IP address). Nevertheless, existing service discovery protocols are limited only to local area networks (LANs). Some service discovery protocols are also not able to provide functions for NAT traversal. The goal of this paper therefore is to present a novel service discovery protocol for remote access of IP CAMs with NAT traversal.

The proposed protocol, termed STDP (Service Trader Discovery Protocol), is a hybrid combination of the SIP (Session Initiation Protocol) [10-12] and Zeroconf protocols. SIP is a protocol developed by IETF to assist in providing advanced telephony services across the internet. Basically it is a signaling protocol used for establishing sessions in an IP network. In the SIP, location of clients are maintained and updated in the registrar server. The IP address of the target node can be obtained by a query to the server. Although a direct deployment of SIP to an IP CAM is possible for accessing digital images, a number of modifications are desired. For many home network applications, costly manual pre-configurations should be avoided. However, the deployment of SIP requires the assignment of an unique pair of SIP URI and password to each IP CAM. This may result in a high manual pre-configuration cost when the number of IP CAM is large.

To reduce the pre-configuration cost, the Zeroconf

[*]Corresponding author.

protocol is employed in the STDP. The Zeroconf protocol is a light weight protocol supporting service discovery in a LAN. It operates without any kind of manual pre-configuration. As compared with other service discovery protocols, it imposes minimal implementation cost for an embedded system. The protocol therefore is well-suited for the IP CAMs.

In the proposed STDP, the SIP is required to be deployed only on a single node, termed trader, in the LAN. This assures the minimal pre-configuration cost for the system. The trader is responsible for collecting the service information provided by all the other nodes in LAN via the Zeroconf protocol. A remote access to any IP CAM in the LAN can be accomplished by first retrieving the service information from the trader using the SIP. Based on the information, the IP address of any IP CAM in the LAN can be found. A remote node can then access the web server associated with the target IP CAM based on the retrieved service information.

The employment of NAT may also be desired in STDP for network security enhancement. Nevertheless, the NAT traversal is required so that local nodes can be visible from remote nodes for service discovery. One simple way to accomplish this is by the employment of UPnP (Universal Plug and Play)-IGD (Internet Gateway Device) [13], where the gateway device will open a tunnel for each local node upon request. Although UPnP-IGD is simple to implement, the NAT mapping stored in the gateway device is subject to potential attack on internet. Since the trader in a LAN contains all the service information in the LAN, the exposure of trader is equivalent to the exposure of all nodes in the LAN.

Therefore, both UPnP-IGD and SIP-ALG (Application Layer Gateway) [14] protocols are used for NAT traversal in the STDP. All the local nodes other than trader use UPnP-IGD to open tunnels for remote access. Only the trader adopts SIP-ALG for NAT traversal. As a result, the trader is visible only to SIP servers. The security for the STDP-based network can then be effectively enhanced.

The proposed STDP protocol has been implemented in a dynamic network environment with NAT. Physical tests reveal that the IP CAMs supporting only simple Zeroconf and UPnP-IGD protocols can be easily accessed by a remote host. The proposed STDP protocol is therefore beneficial for a wide range of IP CAM applications requiring NAT and dynamic deployment.

2. Preliminaries

The proposed STDP is a hybrid combination of SIP and Zeroconf. Therefore, in this section, we give a brief description of these two protocols. The independent applications of these two protocols for accessing IP CAMs are also discussed.

2.1. SIP

SIP is a signaling protocol used for establishing sessions in an IP network. The user agents and servers are the major components of the protocol. A user agent is an end-user device. A user agent client (UAC) issues a request and a user agent server (UAS) responds to the request. When the SIP is applied for the remote access of an IP CAM, in the simplest form the UAC is a viewer and the UAS is the IP CAM, as shown in **Figure 1**. In this case, the location of the IP CAM should be fixed, and should be known to the viewer.

To support the mobility for the IP CAM, the employment of SIP servers are necessary. Commonly used SIP servers include the registrar and proxy server. A SIP registrar includes the registrar and proxy server. A SIP registrar databases (termed location server) containing user agent locations. A SIP proxy server can be viewed as the router in the SIP level that forward SIP requests and responses. In addition, it provides functions for authentication and authorization.

Figure 2 shows a simple example, which uses proxy, registrar and location servers with the INVITE message for session establishment. As shown in the Figure, an IP CAM first registers its location in the location server. A SIP proxy server then accepts an INVITE request made by a UAC and queries location server to find UAS location. Based on the address received from the server, the proxy server forwards the INVITE message to the UAS. The session will then be established after the acknowledgements from UAS are received. It can be observed from the example that the viewer does not have to know the IP CAM location prior to a connection establishment. In addition, the UAS is allowed to change its location without informing the UAC. Only a registration request

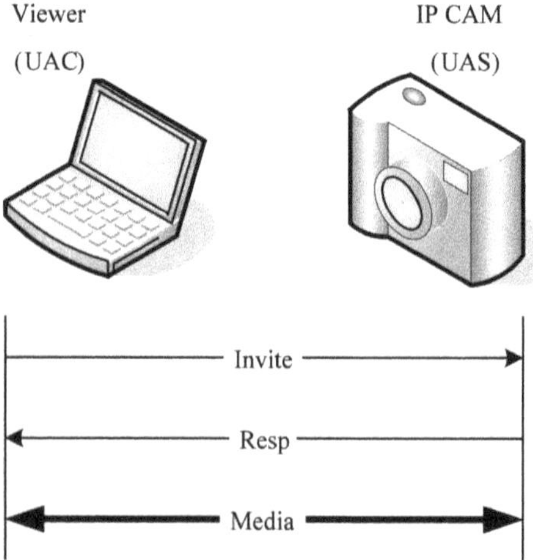

Figure 1. Basic application of SIP for IP CAM.

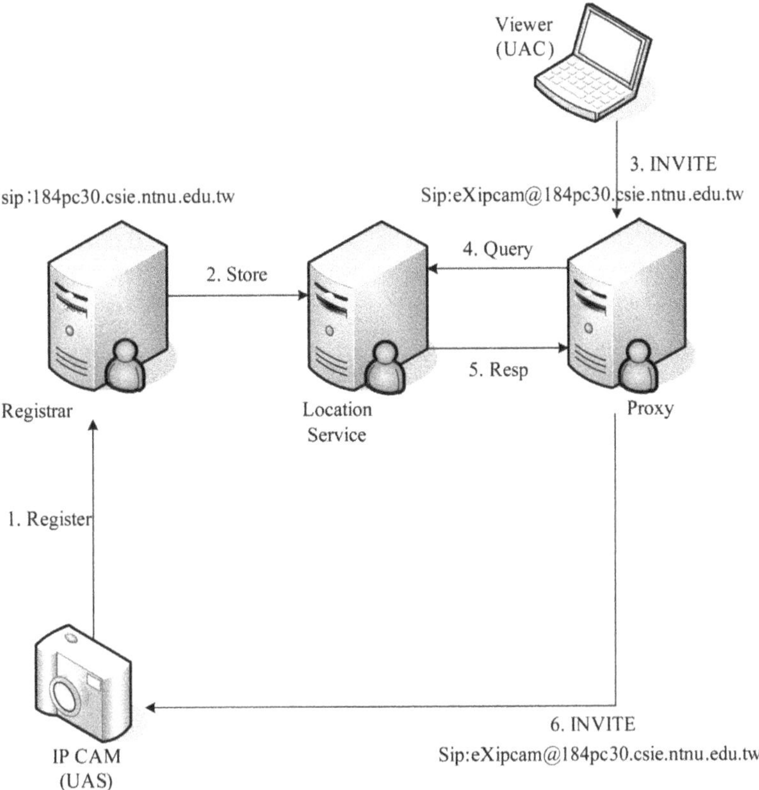

Figure 2. A simple SIP-based framework for remotely accessing IP CAM.

to the registrar server for location updating is required.

In addition to supporting the user mobility, the SIP offers the event notification framework [15,16], which uses SUBSCRIBE/NOTIFY messages for subscribing to, and receiving notifications of, SIP-related events within SIP networks. The ability to request asynchronous notification of events proves useful in many services for which cooperation between devices is required. Examples of such services for IP phone applications include automatic callback services (based on terminal state events), buddy lists (based on user presence events) and message waiting indications (based on mailbox state change events).

The SIP allows the remote access of IP CAM with mobility support and event notification. To use the SIP, however, each IP CAM should be associated with a pair of SIP URI and password. The high manual pre-configuration cost and administration efforts for the deployment of IP CAMs are therefore necessary. This is undesirable for many IP CAM applications.

2.2. Zeroconf

Zeroconf is a protocol for discovering services available in a local network. A Zeroconf network is one that can exist without a central control component, and works without any kind of manual pre-configuration.

Zeroconf can directly be adopted for discovering IP CAM in the LAN. It involves address assignment, name translation and service discovery without central servers. The address assignment for a node in Zeroconf network can simply be accomplished by randomly selecting an address in the range of 169.254.1.0 to 169.254.254.255. The node then does an ARP probe for the address. If there are any responses, the node chooses another IP address at random, and tries the ARP probe again.

The name translation in Zeroconf network is solved by the multicast DNS (mDNS) standard, which eliminates the requirement for DNS server. In the standard, all the nodes in the LAN listens to a specific IP multicast address. A node wish to publish a name will broadcast the selected name to this multicast address. Other nodes having the same name then reply to the requesting node. The name translation can be accomplished in a similar fashion. Instead of using fully qualified domain name (FQDN), a node name in the .local name space is used for mDNS.

Another standard, termed DNS Service Discovery (DNS-SD) can be used for the service discovery in Zeroconf. DNS-SD works particularly well with mDNS, since it also uses DNS records. Three basic operations are included in the DNS-SD: publication, discovery and resolution. The goal of publication is to advertise a service. The discovery operation is used to browse for available service. Based on the results of discovery operation, the resolution operation is adopted for translating service names to addresses and port numbers.

Figures 3, **4** and **5** show a simple example of these DNS-SD operations for a local network consisting of an IP CAM. The publication operations of Zeroconf are shown in **Figure 3**, which consists of address selection (**Figure 3(a)**), name selection (**Figure 3(b)**), service start up (**Figure 3(c)**) and service broadcast (**Figure 3(d)**). In **Figure 3(a)**, the IP CAM randomly selects the IP address 169.254.0.1, and announces it to the network. Because no devices respond to the announcement, the IP CAM takes the address as its own. In **Figure 3(b)**, it starts up its own multicast DNS responder, requests the host name ipcam. local, verifies its availability, and takes the name as its own. In **Figure 3(c)**, the IP CAM starts up a video service on TCP port 80. Finally, in **Figure 3(d)**, it publishes the service instance, of type _http._tcp, under the name IP CAM, in the .local domain. It should be noted that the service type (*i.e.*, _http._tcp) contains two fields: the first field (*i.e.*, _http) is service dependent, and the second

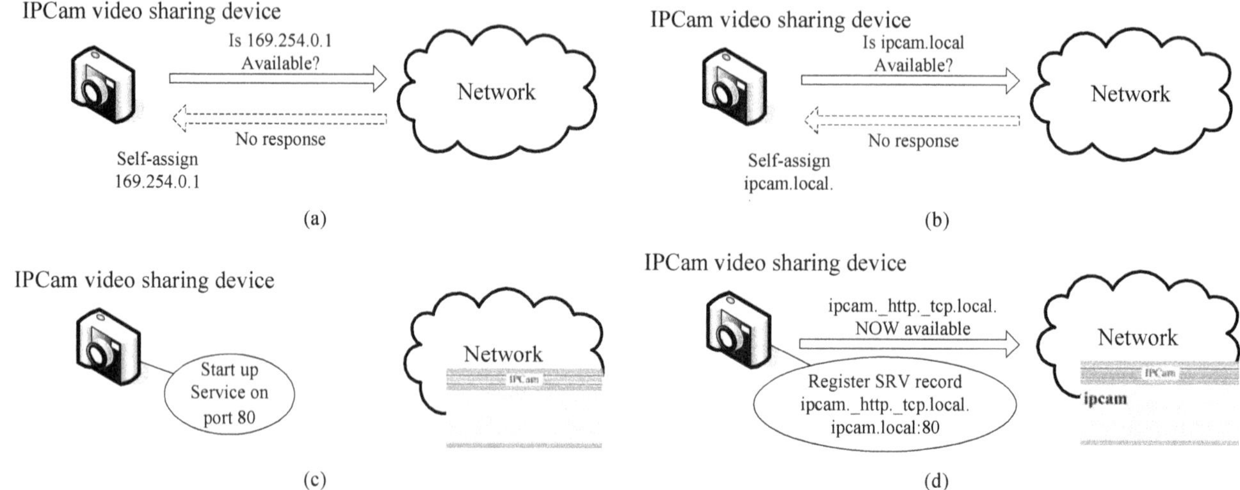

Figure 3. Publication operations of Zeroconf. (a) Address selection; (b) Name selection; (c) Service startup; (d) Service publication.

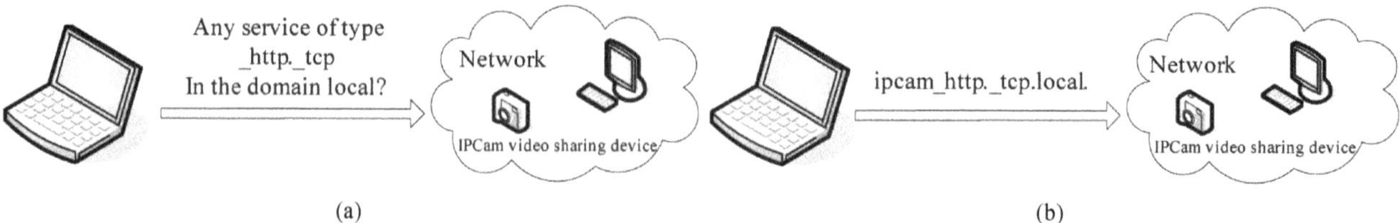

Figure 4. Service query and discovery in Zeroconf. (a) Query by service type; (b) Response.

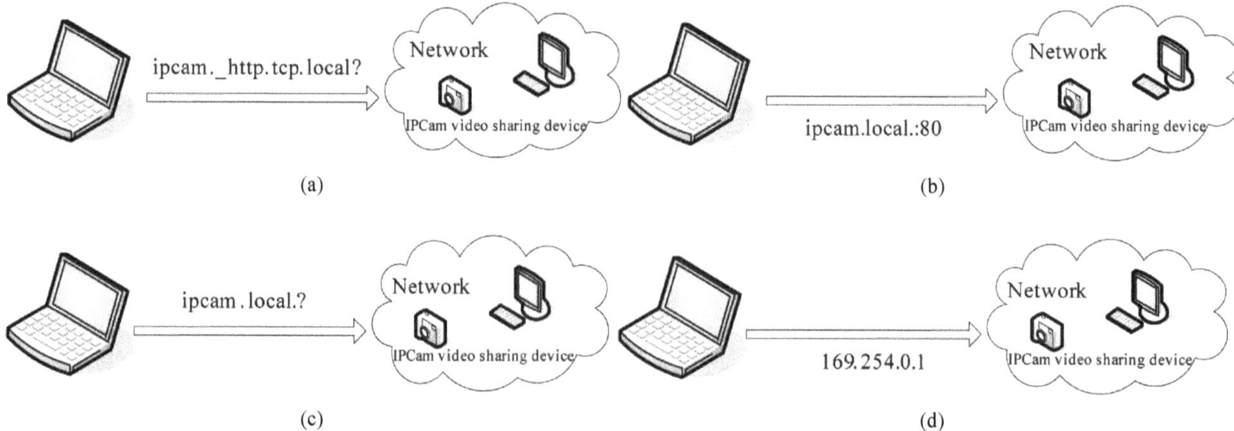

Figure 5. The query for domain name, port and IP address in Zeroconf. (a) Request domain name and port for instance name; (b) Receive domain name and port; (c) Request IP address for domain name; (d) Receive IP address.

field (*i.e.*, _tcp) indicates the transportation protocol used by the service. The service type will be used for service browsing and discovery. The instance name (*i.e.*, IP CAM) is device dependent. That is, devices sharing the same service type will have different instance names. The service instance therefore can be used for the query of port and IP address of a device.

Figure 4 depicts the service query and discovery in the Zeroconf network. In this example, the service type queried by the viewer shown in **Figure 4(a)** is _http._tcp. The service instance discovered from the network is ipcam._http._tcp.local, which represents an IP CAM. Based on the service instance, the viewer can further query for the port, domain name and IP address of the IP CAM using resolution operation, as shown in **Figure 5**.

Although Zeroconf requires no pre-configuration cost, it has the major drawback that the protocol can only be used in a local network. For IP CAM applications, however, remote accesses are usually desired.

3. STDP

The goal of STDP is to eliminate the drawbacks of accessing IP CAMs based only on SIP or Zeroconf protocols. It provides remote access of IP CAM with minimal pre-configuration cost. As shown in **Figure 6**, the STDP is an application layer control protocol that utilizes both SIP and Zeroconf. A STDP-based network contains three basic components: service provider, service requester, and service trader. In our design, the service provider and requester are an IP CAM and a viewer, respectively. Although the primary goal of the STDP is for the design of IP CAM systems, the STDP apply equally well to the broader group, where the service provider and service requester can be any networked appliances demanding low pre-configuration cost and efficient remote access.

The service traders are the nodes used for the delivery of service information over WAN. A service trader provides two functions. It can be adopted to collect/discover service information from service providers in a local network, and deliver the information to a remote node (which is also a trader) upon requests. Alternatively, it can also be used to subscribe and receive the service information from other traders in remote sites, and publish the service information to the service requesters within its local domain. A trader can be implemented in an independent device such as a computer. It can also be implemented in an IP CAM (or a viewer). In these cases, the device supports multiple roles as a trader and a service provider (or a requester).

The communications between two service traders are based on SIP protocol, as shown in **Figure 7**. Each trader can be an UAC and/or an UAS. Each local network needs only one service trader. Each of the service providers and requesters talk to its trader in the same LAN for the delivery of local service information. From **Figure 7**, we observe that the Zeroconf is adopted for the communication between a trader and a service requester (or a provider). Therefore, in our design, the service provider and requester need to support Zeroconf protocol.

To obtain information from a service provider to a service requester, both the SIP and Zeroconf protocols are used. The STDP provides a mechanism for the service information exchange between the SIP and Zeroconf. Based on the acquired service information, the viewer then can access the IP CAM using the HTTP protocol.

To discuss the STDP protocol in more detail, we divide the protocol into three parts, as depicted in **Figure 8**. The first part concerns with the communication between a trader and a service provider. It can be observed from **Figure 8(a)** that the trader will receive service information published by an IP CAM. The trader can also actively discover the service provided by an IP CAM. All the publish and discovery operations are based on Zeroconf protocol, which are illustrated in **Figures 3-5**.

The second part of the STDP protocol focuses on the interactions between traders. This part of the protocol is based on the SIP. Service traders accompanied by service providers are the UASs in the SIP. An UAS discovers/collects local services available, and delivers the service information to other UACs upon request. An UAC is the

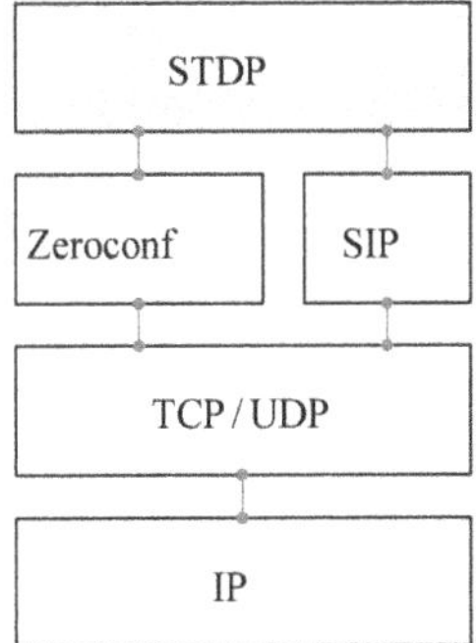

Figure 6. The protocol stack of STDP-based networks.

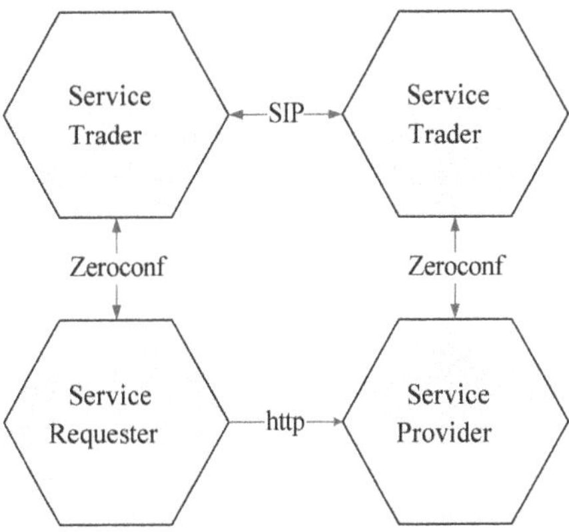

Figure 7. STDP topology.

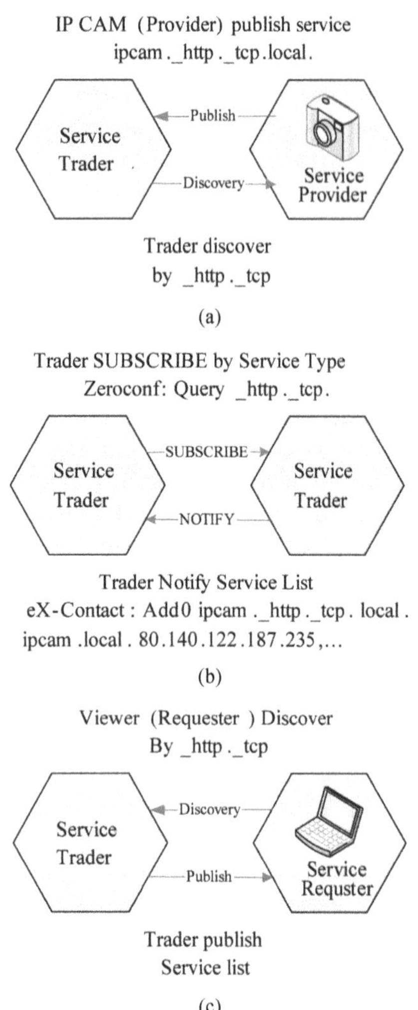

Figure 8. STDP protocol messages. (a) Communication between trader and provider; (b) Traders communication; (c) Communication between trader and requester.

service traders accompanied by service requesters. It sends subscription requests to UASs for acquiring the service information. Once the UAC obtains service notifications from UASs, it publishes the service information to its own service requesters.

In the STDP, the SIP SUBSCRIBE/NOTIFY messages are used for the service information delivery between an UAC and an UAS, as shown in **Figure 8(b)**. In the SIP, the original goal of SUBSCRIBE/NOTIFY messages is to provide the SIP related events subscriptions and notifications. The STDP extends the usage of SUBSCRIBE/NOTIFY for the service subscription and notification.

To use the SUBSCRIBE message for service subscription, the type of services desired should be specified in the message header. Here we augment a field (termed Zeroconf) in the header of SUBSCRIBE message for specifying the service type. The format of service type follows the DNS-SD format as _http._tcp, as depicted in **Figure 9(a)**.

NOTIFY messages are sent to inform traders of the service available for which the traders have a subscription. Subscriptions are established using the SUBSCRIBE method described above. Sending a NOTIFY message does not terminate the corresponding subscription. A single SUBSCRIBE request may trigger several NOTIFY messages. In each NOTIFY message, the list of services and the IP address of the corresponding service providers are carried. We also augment two fields (termed Zeroconf and eX-Contact) in the header of NOTIFY message to achieve this objective. It can be observed form **Figure 9(b)** that the Zeroconf field indicates the service type this message response to. The eXContact field contains 5 items: action, service instance, host name, port number and IP address.

The action item instructs how the service instance included in field should be handled. There are three actions: addition (denoted by Add), deletion (denoted by Del), and updating (denoted by Upd). The addition action instructs the target service trader to add the service instance to the service list. The deletion action informs the target service trader to remove the service instance. The update action directs the target trader to update the attributes of the service instance. The attributes considered here include the video coding standard adopted by the IP CAM, frame size and frame rate.

Use **Figure 9(b)** as an example, the NOTIFY message

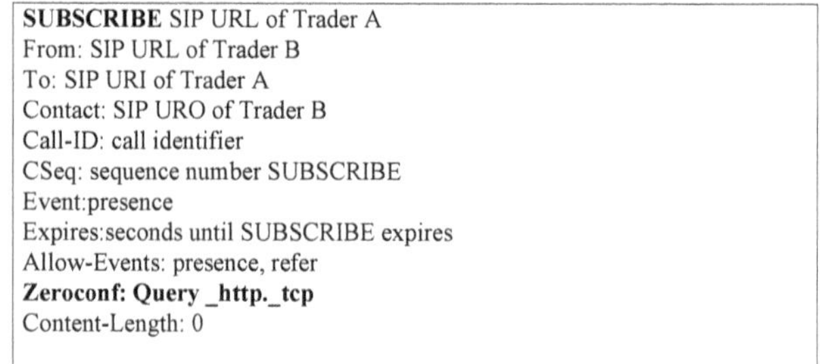
SUBSCRIBE SIP URL of Trader A
From: SIP URL of Trader B
To: SIP URI of Trader A
Contact: SIP URO of Trader B
Call-ID: call identifier
CSeq: sequence number SUBSCRIBE
Event:presence
Expires:seconds until SUBSCRIBE expires
Allow-Events: presence, refer
Zeroconf: Query _http._tcp
Content-Length: 0

(a)

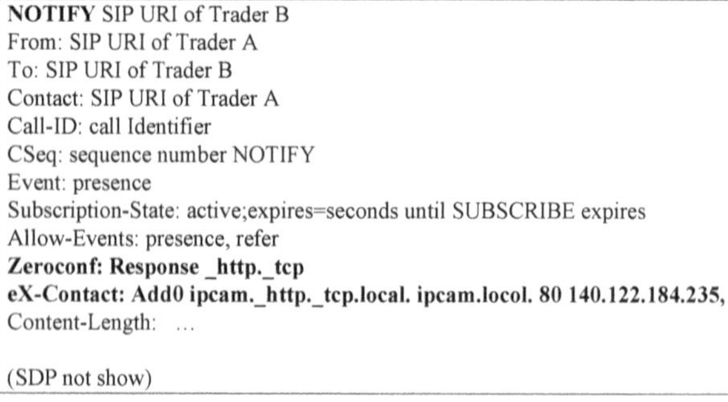
NOTIFY SIP URI of Trader B
From: SIP URI of Trader A
To: SIP URI of Trader B
Contact: SIP URI of Trader A
Call-ID: call Identifier
CSeq: sequence number NOTIFY
Event: presence
Subscription-State: active;expires=seconds until SUBSCRIBE expires
Allow-Events: presence, refer
Zeroconf: Response _http._tcp
eX-Contact: Add0 ipcam._http._tcp.local. ipcam.locol. 80 140.122.184.235,
Content-Length: ...

(SDP not show)

(b)

Figure 9. Extensions of SUBSCRIBE/NOTIFY messages for STDP service subscription and notification. (a) SUBSCRIBE message for service subscription; (b) NOTIFY message for service notification.

instructs the target trader to add the service instance ipcam._http._tcp.local, with host name ipcam.local, port number 80, and IP address 140.122.184.235, to its service list. It should be noted that the service instance and domain name should also follows the DNS-DS format in the STDP.

The final part of STDP describes the communications between a trader and a service requester, which is also based on Zeroconf. It can be observed from **Figure 8(c)** that the trader will then publish the service information collected from other traders to the service requester. The service requester may also actively discover the service information from the trader.

Three parts of the STDP protocol depicted in **Figure 8** may operate independently. That is, the SIP and Zeroconf protocols are not required to operate at a pre-specified order in the STDP. **Figure 10** shows two examples of STDP message flows. For the sake of brevity, only two LANs are considered in each example. Nevertheless, the message flows can easily be extended to the scenarios containing large number of LANs. As shown in **Figure 10**, LAN A in each example contains a service requester and a trader (termed Trader 1). LAN B consists of two service providers (termed Service Provider 1 and Service Provider 2) and a service trader (termed Trader 2).

Figure 10(a) illustrates the scenario, in which Trader 1 and Trader 2 first find their own service requester and service providers via PUBLISH/DISCOVERY messages. The service information of the service providers is then delivered from LAN B to LAN A via SUBSCRIBE/NOTIFY messages. After receiving the service information, Trader 1 then publishes this information to the Service Requester. As shown in **Figure 10(a)**, after the Service Requester received the service information, it selects the Service Provider 2 as its target device. The Service Requester then issues directly a service request via HTTP protocol to Service Provider 2. Direct video delivery from Service Provider 2 to Service Requester then follows.

For the scenario shown in **Figure 10(b)**, it is assumed that the Service Requester and Service Providers are not online at the beginning. The communication between Traders 1 and 2 is first established. This is then followed by a series of service information updating/notification when service providers and service requester become available. Similar to the case shown in **Figure 10(a)**, the Service Requester finally selects the Service Provider 2 as its target device for the IP CAM service.

As shown in **Figure** 7, the service trader plays a major role in STDP. It connects different local networks, and operates in back-to-back mode. It acts as a SIP user agent on one side, and as a Zeroconf end device on the other side. A trader has 4 operations. To further elaborate these operations, **Figure 11** depicts their flowchart in detail.

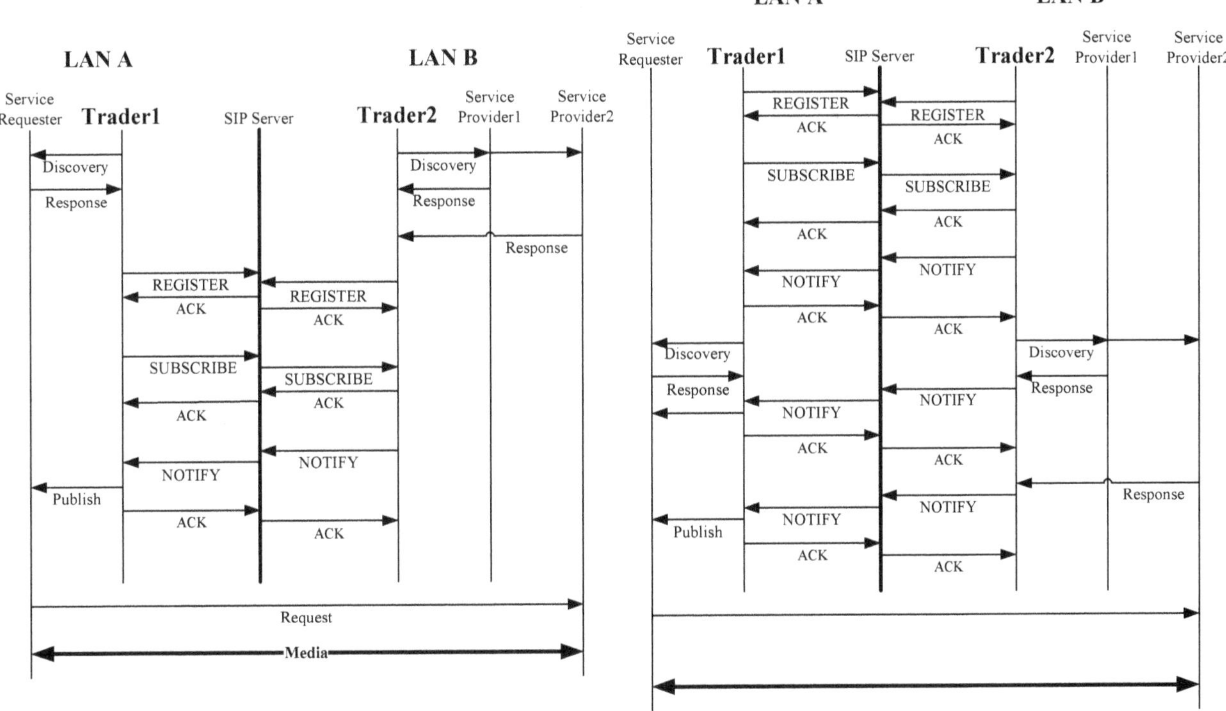

Figure 10. Two examples of STDP message flow: (a) Trader 1 and Trader 2 first find their own service requester and service providers via PUBLISH/DISCOVERY messages. (b) Trader 1 and Trader 2 first establish their connection via SUBSCRIBE/NOTIFY messages.

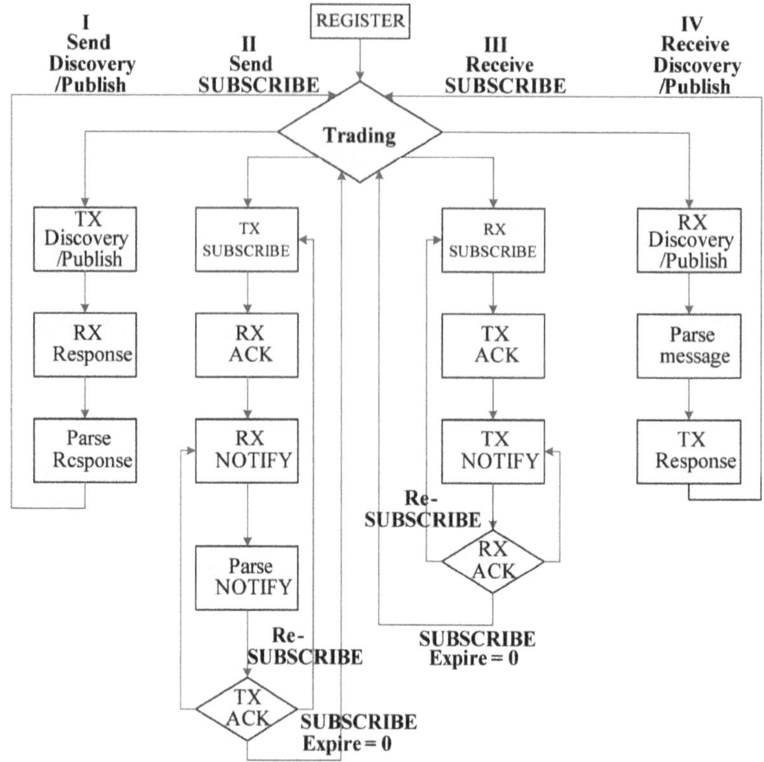

Figure 11. Operation flowchart of a trader.

The first operation is to send Discovery or Publish messages. In this operation, the trader acts as a Zeroconf end device searching or publishing the services available. In the second operation, the trader acts as a SIP UAC, and send SUBSCRIBE message for triggering the SIP event notification mechanism. After sending the SUBSCRIBE message, the trader will then waits and receives one or more NOTIFY messages for updating the service list. The trader behaves as a SIP UAS in the third operation, which receives the SIP SUBSCRIBE message. The trader will then send one or more NOTIFY messages to the subscribing node. The fourth operation receives the Discovery or Publish messages, where the trader functions again as a Zeroconf end device. This operation and the first operation are essential for a trader to acquire the service available from the service provider, or deliver the service to the service requester.

Note that the SIP is required to be installed in the service traders because of the operations of SUBSCRIBE/NOTIFY. Only one node in a local network needs to be the service trader. For the other nodes, only the implementation of Zeroconf is necessary. The employment of Zeroconf protocol can effectively reduce the pre-configuration efforts, because the protocol allows the simple plug-and-play. By contrast, the SIP devices require the assignments of SIP URI and password. For the stand alone embedded systems such as IP CAMs, the assignments may require considerable efforts especially when the number of IP CAMs is large. The STDP therefore provides an effective approach for lowering pre-configuration cost and providing remote access.

4. STDP with Nat Traversal

The employment of NAT may also be desired in STDP for network security enhancement. Nevertheless, the NAT traversal is required so that local nodes can be visible from remote nodes for service discovery. To see this fact in more detail, we first note that the proposed STDP employs HTTP/TCP for video streaming. Consequently, for a STDP-based system without NAT traversal, if a client wants to make a directly TCP connection to a IP CAM, the IP address of the IP CAM should be transmitted by service trader first. However, if the IP CAM is deployed in the residential environment behind a NAT, the information contained in STDP messages would be incorrect since the IP address of the IP CAM is private address.

To solve the problem, the UPnP-IGD protocol is adopted in our scheme. It has been found that UPnP-IGD is an effective solution for NAT traversal because of its simplicity. **Figure 12** shows that how UPnP-IGD-aware NAT works for NAT traversal. At first, the NAT joins in the multicast group 239.255.255.250 and listens on port 1900 for the request issued by a client. When the NAT receives a request, it will add the corresponding port mapping into its mapping table. The NAT subsequently returns the public IP address and the allocated port to the client. After that, the remote host in the public network can connect to the client directly through the NAT.

To integrate the UPnP-IGD with the STDP, an IP CAM will sends a port mapping request to NAT when it is in the private network (*i.e.*, behind a NAT). It then publishes its service with the port mapping information via Zeroconf. As a result, the STDP messages will have correct IP address and port number. The IP CAM is then accessible from the public networks.

Although UPnP-IGD is simple to implement, the NAT mapping stored in the gateway device is subject to potential attack on internet. Since the trader in a LAN contains all the service information in the LAN, the exposure of trader is equivalent to the exposure of all nodes in the LAN.

Therefore, both UPnP-IGD and SIP-ALG protocols are used for NAT traversal in our design. All the local nodes other than trader use UPnP-IGD to open tunnels for remote access. Because the traders are actually the UACs or UASs in the SIP, the usual SIP-ALG protocol can be effectively used for the NAT traversal. In this way, the trader is visible only to SIP servers. The security for the STDP-based network can then be effectively enhanced.

Figure 13 shows an example of STDP system with NAT traversal. The system consists of an IP CAM, and IE browsers, traders, a SIP server, and two NATs. Note that, the IP CAM and IE browser are deployed in the residential environment with NAT, as shown in the **Figure 13**.

Note that the IP CAM with private IP addresses is only available in LAN B. The IP CAM has to send the port mapping request to NAT B via UPnP-IGD to be accessible from the public networks. NAT B receives the request and subsequently adds the port mapping into its mapping table. As a result, NAT B opens tunnels for the IP CAM, and returns the information of the public address and the ports to the IP CAM. After acquiring the responses from NAT B, the IP CAM is now available for remote access.

After finishing port mapping, the IP CAM publication services with their public address and ports (e.g., IP address 140.122.184.26, port 3000) in LAN B. This information can also be actively discovered by trader B. Thus trader B will have the complete service information in LAN B. After that, trader B, as an SIP UAS, connects to the SIP server and waits for SUBSCRIBE message from trader A.

Recall that for the basic STDP, trader A sends SUB-

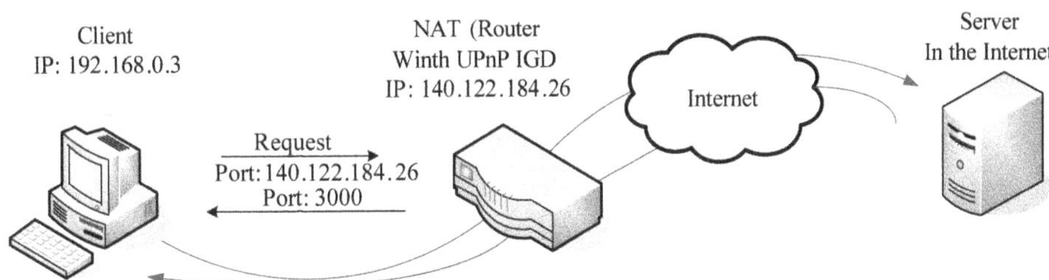

Figure 12. The NAT traversal with UPnP-IGD.

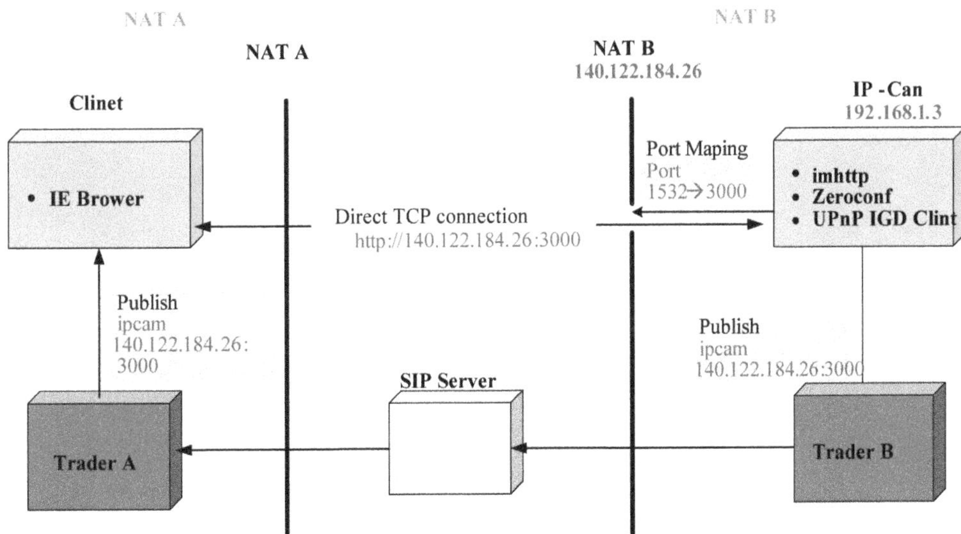

Figure 13. An example of STDP system with NAT traversal.

SCRIBE to trader B, and then trader B returns NOTIFY for the service information delivery over WAN. All the service information delivery is based on SIP protocol. Since the address information is in the packet payload in SIP, the SIP-ALG will be used for the NAT traversal of traders A and B in our design.

Consequently, for the NAT traversal, both SIP ALG and UPnP-IGD are adopted. **Figure 14** illustrates this fact in more detail. As shown in the Figure, the IP CAM first sends a port mapping request to NAT B via UPnP-IGD messages. The NAT B then opens a tunnel for TCP connection to the IP CAM, as shown in **Figure 14(a)**. In **Figure 14(b)**, trader A and trader B register themselves to SIP Server as UAC and UAS, respectively. The SIP server then activates the SIP-ALG protocol to process all the messages for NAT traversal. This allows trader A and trader B identify their own service requester and service providers via service discovery/publish operations, as shown in **Figure 14(c)**. Finally, the service information of the IP CAM is delivered from LAN B to LAN A via SUBSCRIBE/NOTIFY messages, as depicted in **Figure 14(d)**. After receiving the service information, trader A then publishes the information to the client. As shown in **Figure 14(d)**, the client acquires the service information, and it issues directly a service request via HTTP protocol to the IP CAM. Direct video delivery from the IP CAM to the client then follows.

5. Experimental Results

The STDP protocol has been implemented in a test-bed that realizes the scenario proposed in **Figure 15**. Similar to **Figure 13**, the scenario consists of two local networks (termed LAN A and LAN B in the Figure). LAN A consists of a number of laser printers, one IE browser and 2 IP CAMs. LAN B contains a number of laser printers, one personal computer and one IE browser. As shown in the Figure, personal computers serve as the

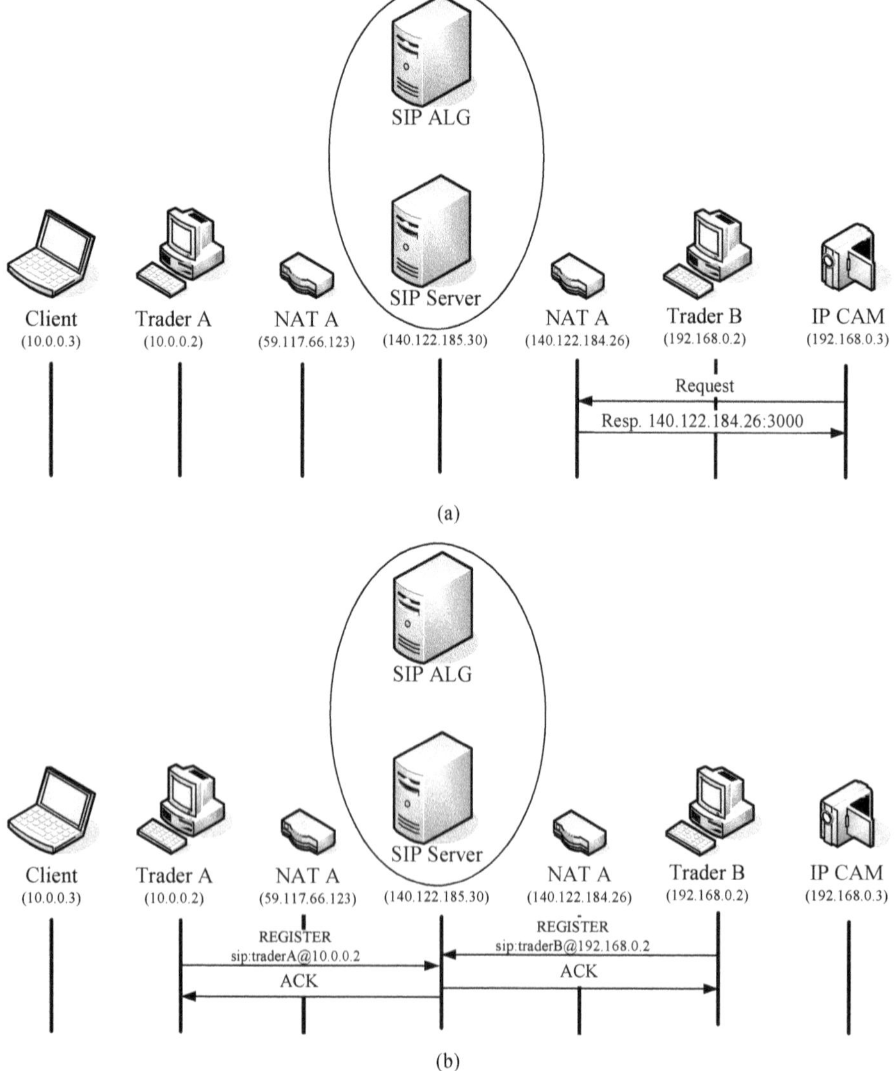

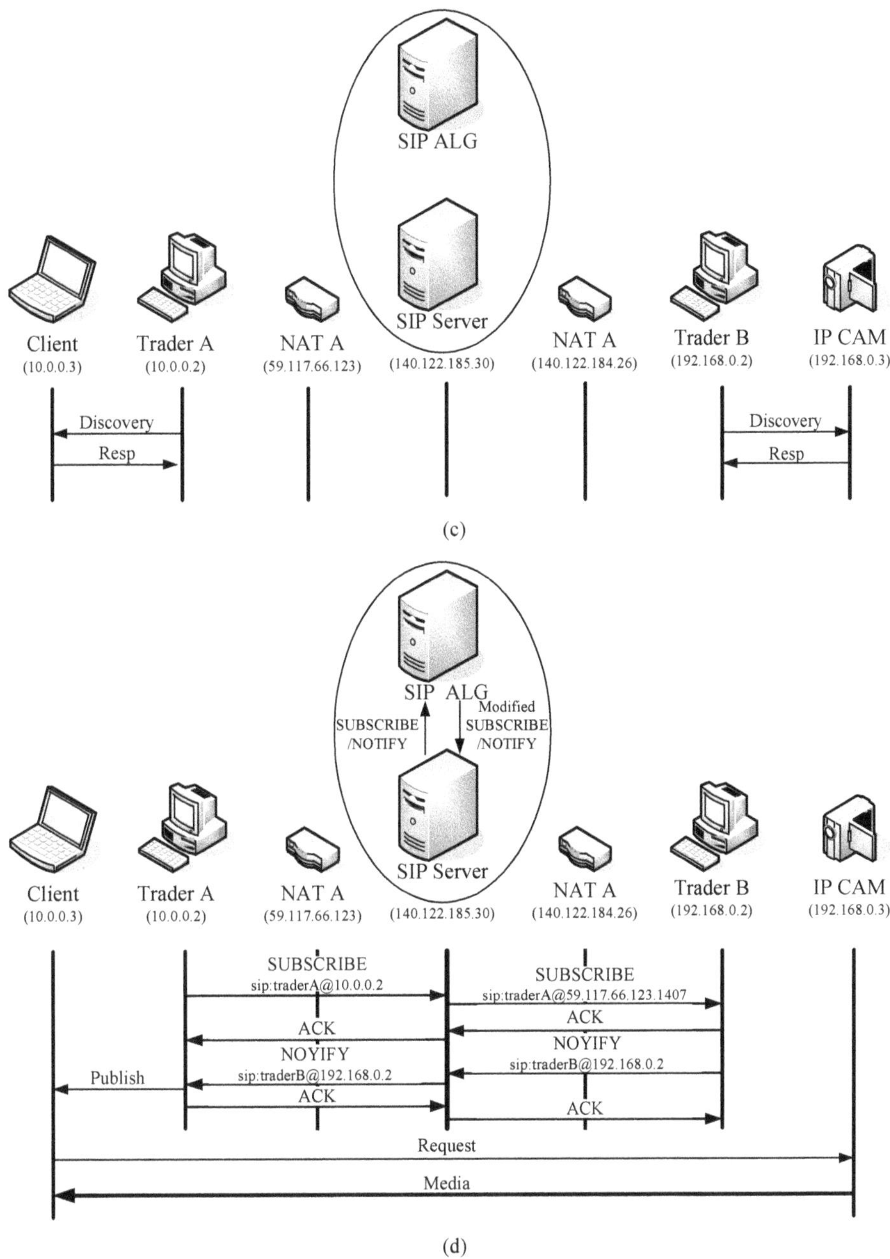

Figure 14. The message of STDP with NAT traversal: (a) IP CAM requests NAT B to open a tunnel for TCP connection; (b) Traders A and B register to SIP server with the private addresses; (c)Traders A and B find their own service providers and service requester; (d) Traders A and B establish their connection.

service trader in the LAN A and LAN B, respectively. The IE browser in each local network is the service requester in that local network. All the IP CAMs and laser printers in both LANs are the service providers. They are all of the type _http._tcp. Their IP addresses are dynamically assigned by a DHCP server. The service providers publish their service with their unique hostname. Only the traders in relative local networks require the manual pre-configuration, because the assignments of SIP URI and password are necessary to register to SIP server. Note that, in addition to the IP CAMs, the laser printers are included in this scenario. Since the laser printers supports Zeroconf, detecting the service provided by the laser printers in different local networks demonstrates the fact that the proposed protocol can be adopted for the discovery of services provided by various Zeroconf-based devices.

In our experiment, a reference design kit (RDK) based on a 200-MHz ARM 920 CPU and an MPEG4 encoder ASIC is used for the IP CAM design. The employment of MPEG4 ASIC allows the source video sequence to be encoded in real-time. Both the wired and wireless LAN interfaces (*i.e.*, 802.3 and 802.11) are also available in the IP CAMs. The operating system of the IP CAMs is Linux. The Bonjour software development kit (SDK) [17] is adopted for the Zeroconf implementation in the IP CAM. Moreover, we adopt the Bonjour SDK and PJSIP [18] library for implementing the service trader.

Customarily, the NAT functions are accomplished by a router in the residential environment. Therefdore, we choose the routers supporting UPnP-IGD protocol in our experiments. Since the IE browser is used as the service requester in each LAN, it is necessary for the browser to support the Zeroconf. In our implementation, the Bonjour plug-in is adopted, which is able to discover the services of type _http._tcp.

Figure 16 shows all the services of type _http._tcp discovered by the IE browser in LAN A without the employment of STDP. It can be observed from the Figure that these services are actually the services provided by the laser printers in LAN A. Because all the devices in LAN A and LAN B are behind the NAT, without the proper NAT traversal schemes, the IE browser in LAN A is still not able to discover the services in LAN B even the STDP is employed.

When SIP-ALG is employed, the IE browser is able to

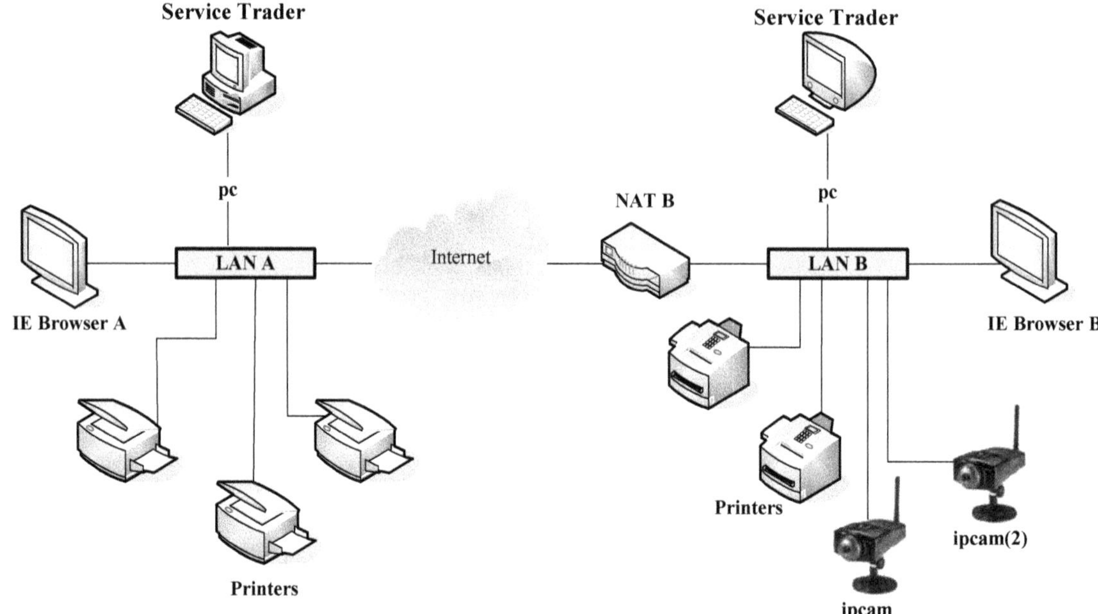

Figure 15. The scenario for our experiment.

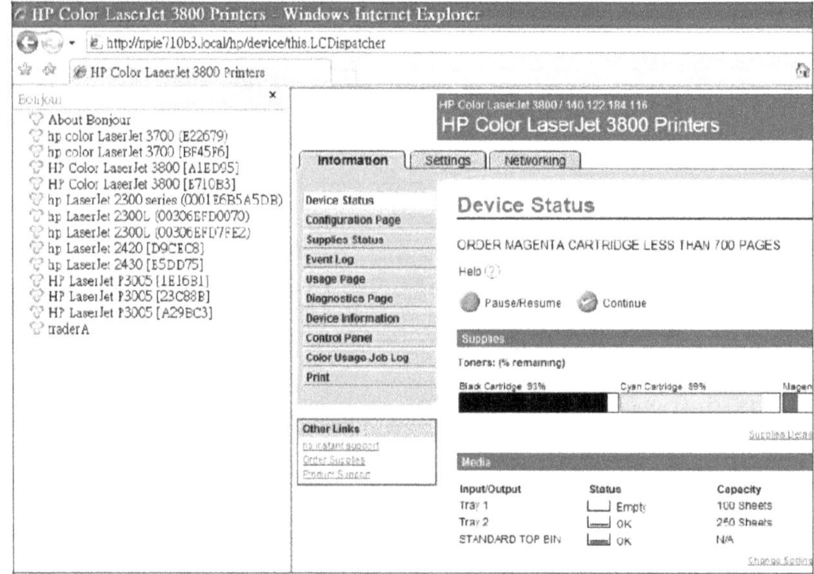

Figure 16. All the services of type _http._tcp discovered in LAN A without the employment of STDP.

discover services in LAN B, as shown in **Figure 17**. However, without the employment of UPnP-IGD, IP CAMs in LAN B still use private IP addresses. This implies the IE browser in LAN A is not able to access the IP CAMs in LAN B, as shown in **Figure 17**.

Figure 18 shows the results when the MiniUPnP-IGD [19] client is implemented in the IP CAMs in LAN B so that both SIP-ALG and UPnP-IGD are supported in our system. It can then be observed from the Figure that the IE browser is able to access the IP CAMs even when all the devices in both LANs are behind the NATs.

6. Conclusion Remarks

The proposed STDP protocol has been found to be effective for IP CAM applications. It allows both remote access and dynamic deployment of IP CAMs without the need of manual pre-configuration. In the STDP, the service lists from remote hosts are obtained by SIP SUBSCRIBE/NOTIFY event notification mechanism. The service discovery and publish in a local network are then based on Zeroconf protocol, which is also used for eliminating manual pre-configuration. When IP CAMs are deployed behind the NAT, both the UPnP-IGD and SIP-ALG protocols are adopted for NAT traversal. A test-bed verifying the STDP protocol with NAT traversal has been implemented. From the experiment, it is observed that a basic IE browser with Bonjour plug-in can be effectively used for the remote access of IP CAMs, which are installed with simple plug-and-play. All these facts demonstrate the effectiveness of the STDP.

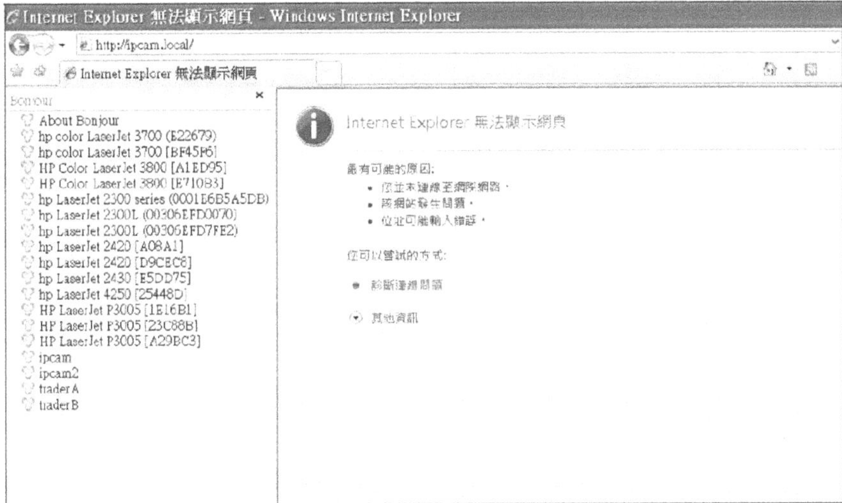

Figure 17. All the services of type _http._tcp discovered in LAN B with the employment of STDP and SIP-ALG. The UPnP-IGD, however, is not adopted.

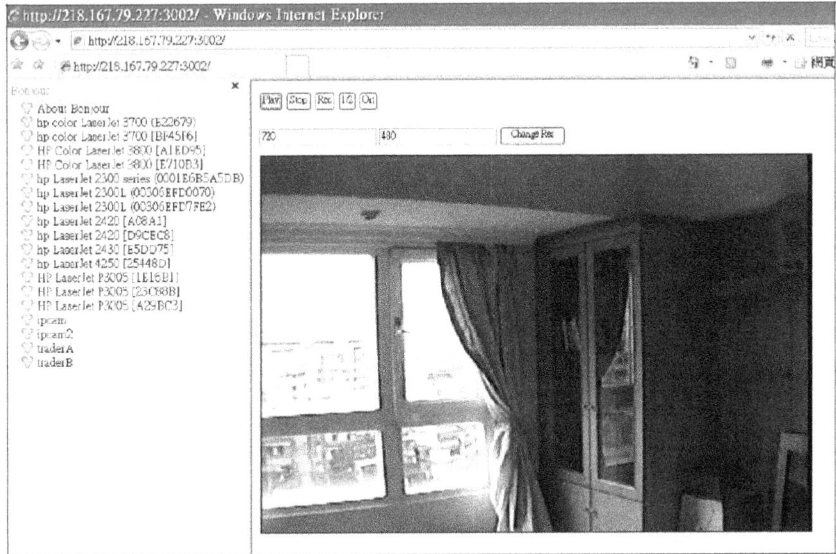

Figure 18. All the services of type _http._tcp discovered in LAN B with the employment of STDP, SIP-ALG and UPnP-IGD.

REFERENCES

[1] W. Hintermaier and E. Steinbach, "A system Architecture for IP Camera based Driver Assistance Applications," *IEEE Intelligent Vehicles Symposium* (*IV*), San Diego, 21-24 June 2010, pp. 540-547.

[2] N. A. Manap, G. Di Caterina, J. Soraghan, V. Sidharth and H. Yao, "Face Detection and Stereo Matching Algorithms for Smart Surveillance System with IP Cameras," 2010 *2nd European Workshop on Visual Information Processing European Workshop* (*EUVIP*), 2010, pp. 77-81.

[3] B. X. Li, W. H. Zhang, Z. H. Liu, M. J. Kang and S. Li, "Development and Implement of the IP Camera Based on DM6437," *IEEE Mechatronic Science, Electric Engineering and Computer International Conference* (*MEC*), Jilin, 19-22 August 2011, pp. 1961-1964.

[4] S. Guha and P. Francis, "Characterization and Measurement of TCP Traversal through NATs and Firewalls," *Internet Measurement Conference*, Berkeley, 19-21 October 2005, pp. 199-211.

[5] E. Guttman, C. Perkins, J. Veizades, "Service Location Protocol, Version 2," 1999.

[6] J. Waldo, "The Jini Specifications," 2nd Edition, Addison-Wesley Longman Publishing Co., Inc., Boston, 2000.

[7] D. S. Kim, J. M. Lee, W. H. Kwon and I. K. Yuh, "Design and Implementation of Home Network Systems Using UPnP Middleware for Networked Appliances," *IEEE Transactions on Consumer Electronics*, Vol. 48, No. 4, 2002, pp. 963-972.

[8] S. Cheshire and D. H. Steinberg, "Zero Configuration Networking: The Definite Guide," O'Reilly Media, Inc., Sebastopol, 2005.

[9] E. Guttman, "Autoconfiguration for IP Networking: Enabling Local Communication," *IEEE Internet Computing*, Vol. 5, No. 3, 2001, pp. 81-86.

[10] J. Rosenberg, H. Schulzrinne, G. Camarillo, A. Johnston, J. Peterson, R. Sparks, M. Handley and E. Schooler, "SIP: Session Initiation Protocol," 2002.

[11] W. Werapun, A. A. El Kalam, B. Paillassa and J. Fasson, "Solution Analysis for SIP Security Threats," *IEEE International Conference on Multimedia Computing and Systems* (*ICMCS*'09), Ouarzazate, 2-4 April 2009, pp. 174-180.

[12] S.-W. Hsu, K.-D. Chang, C.-Y. Chen, H.-C. Chao and J.-L. Chen, "An Efficient Path-Migration Mechanism for IP Multimedia Subsystem," *IEEE Wireless Communications and Mobile Computing Conference* (*IWCMC*), Istanbul, 4-8 July 2011, pp. 1469-1474.

[13] UPnP Forum Official Website, "UPnP—Universal Plug and Play Internet Gateway Device v1.0," 2008. http://www.UPnP.org/standardizeddcps/documents/UPnP_IGD_1.0.zip.

[14] H. Kazuhito, S. Yuichi and S. Takaho, "A Study on Call State Model in SIP Application Level Gateway (SIP-ALG)," *IEIC Technical Report*, Vol. 103, No. 121, 2003, pp. 37-40.

[15] M. Rahman, D. Braun and D. Bushmitch, "A Framework to Access Networked Appliances in Wide Area Networks," *IEEE Consumer Communications and Networking Conference*, Princeton, 3-6 January 2005, pp. 261-266.

[16] A. B. Roach, "Session Initiation Protocol (SIP)—Specific Event Notification," RFC 3265, 2002.

[17] Bonjour, "Aperture 2.1 SDK Overview," 2007. https://developer.apple.com/library/mac/#documentation/AppleApplications/Conceptual/AppleApp_Aperture_001/Overview/Overview.html#/

[18] PJSIP.ORG, "PJSIP-Open Source SIP Stack," 2008. http://www.pjsip.org/

[19] MiniUPnP Project, "MiniUPnP Project HomePage," 2008. http://miniupnp.free.fr/

21

Design and Implementation of a Low-Power Active RFID for Container Tracking at 2.4 GHz Frequency

Dawood Moeinfar, Hossein Shamsi, Fatemeh Nafar
Electrical Faculty, K. N. Toosi University of Technology, Tehran, Iran

ABSTRACT

In this paper a new active RFID system at 2.45 GHz based on the low-power system-on-chip CC2530 RF transceiver is designed and implemented. Only by using of an integrated multi-channel fast chip, both the MCU and RF operations are done which makes the RFID more reliable and reduces the complexity of the hardware and cost, vividly. This RFID system utilizes the Zig-Bee IEEE 802.15.4 standard in the ISM band. A lot amount of energy is restored by setting Tags in the sleep mode in the most of times. The maximum transmission range of 80 m at the output power of 4.5 dBm is obtained. The main application of this system is for the container identification with precise operation and high accuracy. An active Tag with unique ID is mounted on each vehicle. By enabling the AUTOCRC error detection possibility, minor errors are detected in the received frames. Receiver sensitivity of –97 dBm and current consumption of 1 μA in the sleep mode and 29.6 mA in the active mode are reported.

Keywords: Radio Frequency Identification (RFID); CC2530; RSSI; Active Tags; Collision; TDMA; IEEE 802.15.4; Sleep Mode

1. Introduction

Radio Frequency Identification technology had been widespread in recent years, and encompasses an extensive range of wireless applications such as distribution, transportation, tracing, patient monitoring, military applications and etc. RFID is an automatic real-time non-contact identification technology that deals with Identification Numbers (ID) through scattered electromagnetic waves in the air. It's more reliable, efficient, secured, inexpensive and accurate than other similar automatic identifiers such as sensor networks, imagery systems and so on. These reasons are why the RFID technology is more popular, recently [1].

An electronic label dedicates to each identifiable object, which contains main information or specification about that object. This label is named Tag and restores the data for a long time. Each Tag has a same structure and function. It consists of a microchip and antenna. Another key part of an RFID system is Reader (data collector), which collects the data stored in the Tags. A Reader includes the microprocessor, transceiver, antenna and a peripheral interface for user commands and monitoring. This two structured electronic devices which are at the heart of every RFID system, communicate with each other in the wireless manner [2]. Whenever a Tag is located at the magnetic zone of the Reader, it will be recognized by it, and afterward they enter to the relationship with each other according to the user request. Unlike some proposed RFID schemes, which have some Readers and Tags, our design is a centralized RFID with only a central Reader and numerous Tags. According to **Figure 1**, user interface (PC) is the main master of operation in RFID system. So, sub-master (Reader) commands Tags only by the request of the main master (PC). Tags only respond to the commands, whenever they have been investigated. Interrogated data from Tags are exhibited to the user with the serial interface.

One important classification in RFID is based on the method of power supply provision in Tags. Passive Tags don't have any internal power source. They extract their energy from the Reader scattered wave and only act within the magnetic domain of the Reader. This type of

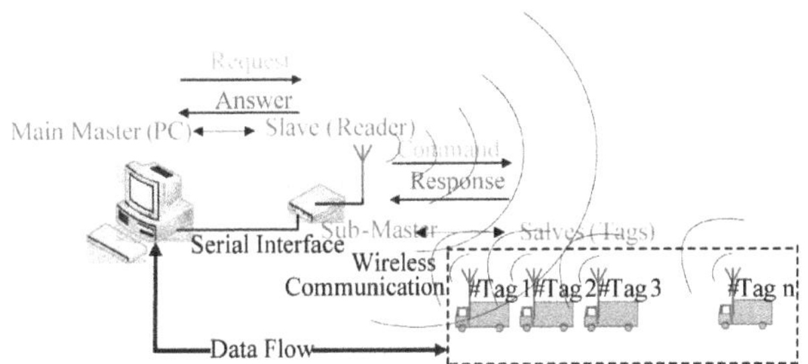

Figure 1. Centralized RFID system.

RFID is used for short-range applications such as smart cards. In addition to passive RFID Tags, active RFID Tags are designed having their own power supply, which is the basis of our work. They even act out the range of magnetic field of the Reader. RFIDs are designed at the standard frequency ranges: low-frequency (LF), high-frequency (HF), Ultra High Frequency (UHF) and Microwave. In the comparison of different types of RFIDs, lower frequencies don't penetrate or transmit around metals, handle only small amounts of data and slow the data transfer. The main advantages of microwave frequencies are smaller size, smaller antenna and higher data range than other frequencies [3].

By emerging advanced technology and improving the economy, the automation of harbors is necessary. Using RFID, a large amount of time and cost will be restored and the safer transportation method is provided. Because containers occupy a large area at the ports, the RFID interrogate zone should be large enough to cover a wide range. So active Tags at the microwave frequency should be used for these applications [2,4].

Collision phenomenon is a common problem that we have encountered at the first step of designing a multi-Tag RFID system. Whenever several Tags are presented in the interrogate zone of Reader and respond to the Reader command simultaneously, their data collide in the air. So a lot amount of energy, bandwidth and time will be wasted. Different anti-collision procedures have been designed for avoiding from the collision. Because TDMA protocols are the largest applicable group of anti-collision, hence we focus on TDMA in this paper. [3].

Power consumption is always a remarkable criterion in the design of Tags, especially in the applications where power supply is limited. One drawback of the active RFID systems is the precise synchronization requirement between the Reader and Tags. In this work, we put Tags in the sleep mode most times, which all circuitry of Tags are turned off during the sleep mode. A Tag is only activated by the Reader command in the small fraction of one reading cycle. So, in the major portion of time, Tag is inactive.

This paper is organized as below: at first the hardware is described in detail. Second, software algorithm and anti-collision protocol are described, completely. After that, experimental results are reported. Finally, we conclude our work.

2. Hardware Description

Unlike other previous similar works, which use some modules to meet the requisite of a practical RFID system, our hardware uses only a low-power high-accuracy transceiver for both Reader and Tags [4,5]. It has all capabilities of a microprocessor and RF transceiver module in an integrated chip [6]. So, it handles all the baseband and RF processing functions together. In addition to minimize the hardware size, it prevents from high frequency noise generated from connecting RF transceiver and MCU chips. This integrated chip benefits from the low power consumption, high communication range, high capacity memories, multiple channels, and high sensitivity receiver [7]. Some critical issues in the active RFID should be considered when developing the hardware [8]. The first key point of the development is the lifetime of the active RFID Tag. Because the active RFID Tag is energized by the internal battery, the lifetime of the Tag is mainly depends on the lifetime of the battery. At first, we choose the low-power components and implement a mechanism in which the processor can completely turn off the radio or simply put it in the sleep mode to save the power. The second one is the ability of the anti-collision, which is important especially in the vehicle transportation environment. To get to the high identification rate for multiple Tags, the anti-collision is carefully applied. In **Table 1**, the key parameters of the system achieved by using of CC2530 are listed [7].

2.1. Reader Structure

In **Figure 2**, the hardware of the RFID Reader is shown. The Reader acts as a sub-master in this system so it executes any command received from the PC. A personal computer is connected to the Reader through the RS-232 serial interface [9]. The block diagram of the Reader is shown in **Figure 3**. The MCU unit directly controls the RF transceiver to communicate with Tags and processes all Tags response data [5]. For precise operation of the radio part, an external oscillator with the frequency accuracy of lower than ±40 ppm is required. We used HXO-36B crystal oscillator with the frequency stability of ±25 ppm.

2.2. Tag Structure

The amount of power and area consumption is a remarkable challenge in the design of portable Tags. Decreasing the Tag's power consumption is an important factor in active RFIDs [10]. Choosing a low-power chip in hard-

Figure 2. The hardware of the reader.

Table 1. Key parameters of the system [7].

Parameters	Value (Range)	Unit
TX Output Power Range	−22 - +4.5	dBm
Receiver Sensitivity	−97	dBm
Integrated RF Chip Dimensions	6 × 6	mm^2
Current Consumption in Sleep Mode	1	µA
Maximum Current Consumption In Active Mode	29	mA
Supply Voltage	2 - 3.6	V
Programmable Flash Memory	256	kB
RX/TX Turnaround	192	µs
Radio Baud Rate	250	Kbps
Channel Spacing	5	MHz
RSSI Range	100	dB
SRAM Memory	8	kB
Radio Ram Memory	384	kB
Communication Range	80	meter
Modulation Scheme	-	OQPSK
Channel Numbers	16	numbers
Tag Size	22 × 30	mm^2

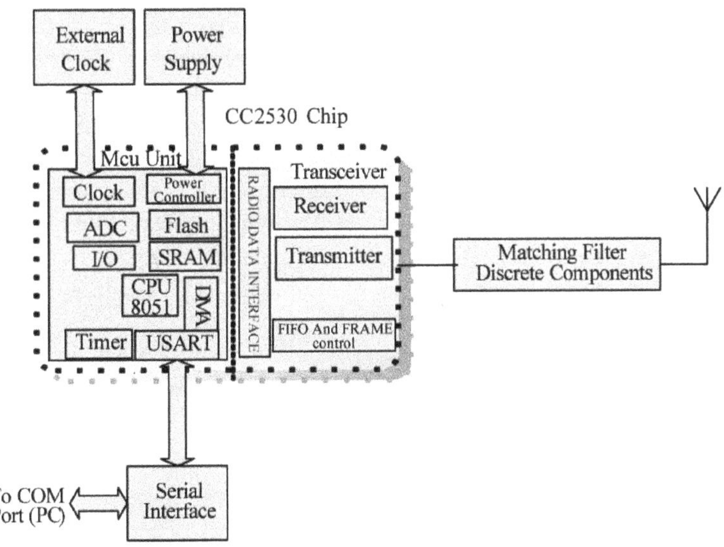

Figure 3. The block diagram of the reader hardware.

ware design is an aspect, and the software algorithm of Tags is also another key factor to decrease the power consumption. There are three kinds of states in this algorithm as follows: sleep condition, survey condition, and communication condition. The hardware of Tags is same with that shown in **Figure 2**, but it does not need any serial interface [2]. In general, in most of times, Tags are in the sleep condition. At this time all internal circuits of the Tag are inactive except the low-frequency clock. The Tag is woken up and interrupted by received data packets. Then Tag enters to the communication condition only when the received frames are from the Reader. After responding to the Reader command, Tag goes to the sleep mode. We compact the dimensions of Tags down to near 660 mm^2. The block diagram of Tags is shown in **Figure 4**.

3. Software Development

3.1. Anti-Collision Protocol

Anti-collision protocol is critical in the performance of RFID systems. Without using an anti-collision protocol,

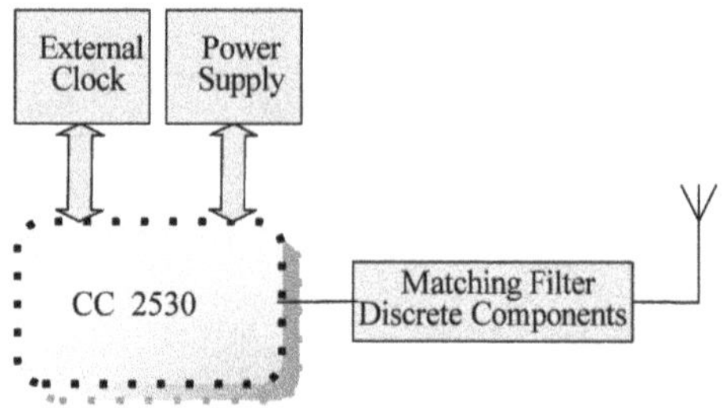

Figure 4. The block diagram of tags.

the responses from the Tags would collide together and thereby prolong the identification process. So, collision causes the bandwidth and energy wastage. There are four main types of anti-collision schemes: space division multiple access (SDMA), frequency division multiple access (FDMA), time division multiple access (TDMA), and code division multiple access (CDMA). TDMA protocols are the largest group of anti-collision algorithms. These algorithms could be classified as the Reader-driven or Tag-driven procedure. Our scheme is based on the Reader-Talk-First (RTF) protocol, in which Tags remain silent until commanded or searched by the Reader. Tag driven procedures are slower than RTF. In the Pure-ALOHA (PA) procedure, Tags respond to the Reader at random instants. So the possibility of the collision increases. In Slotted-ALOHA (SA) based RFID systems, Tags transmit their ID in synchronous time slots. Our approach is based on the SA protocol. By this method, the round time and probability of the collision decrease, greatly [3]. Here, Tags respond to the Reader commands only at certain moments. If a Tag is present in the duration of this slide, it will respond to the Reader and then go to the sleep mode at the end of this slide until the next cycle. In our algorithm, a command frame includes 20 bytes. So, at the data rate of 250 kbps, it takes 0.5 ms to be transmitted, completely. The slide duration in our protocol is about 5 ms. One Tag is active only for a short time in each cycle. The timing of SA-TDMA anti-collision protocol is shown in **Figure 5**.

3.2. Software Algorithm

As shown in **Figure 6**, we have considered three basic commands for our software. In ID allocate command, we dedicate an ID to each Tag. We search the Tag ID by the polling command and clear the Tag ID by the clearing command. This algorithm is implemented at high-level software which provides a user-interface tool on a PC. The ID allocation is performed as follows. A unique address and ID is dedicated to each Tag. The Reader receives the ID and address from the PC serial interface and then sends them to a Tag. This Tag saves ID as an identification number in the permanent memory. After receiving ID from Reader, it sends an acknowledge message to the Reader. This message confirms the successful ID allocation of the Tag. Then we allocate the ID to another Tag. This process is repeated for all Tags by the user until every Tag will have a unique identification number.

The whole flowchart of the RFID Reader is shown in **Figure 7**. The Reader waits for the user commands from the serial port. In this situation, the RF transceiver of the Reader remains in the idle state. By reception of any command from PC, the Reader interprets the command and executes it. By using the ID-Allocation command, each Tag will have a unique identification number, and subsequently the user can search Tags by their unique IDs. When we want to remove an ID, we use the clearing Tag command. By performing this command, the given Tag loses its ID and it will no longer has passing permission.

All Tags have monotonous routine in the soft protocol. They should react to the user commands that come from the Reader. In fact, Tags should be synchronous with the

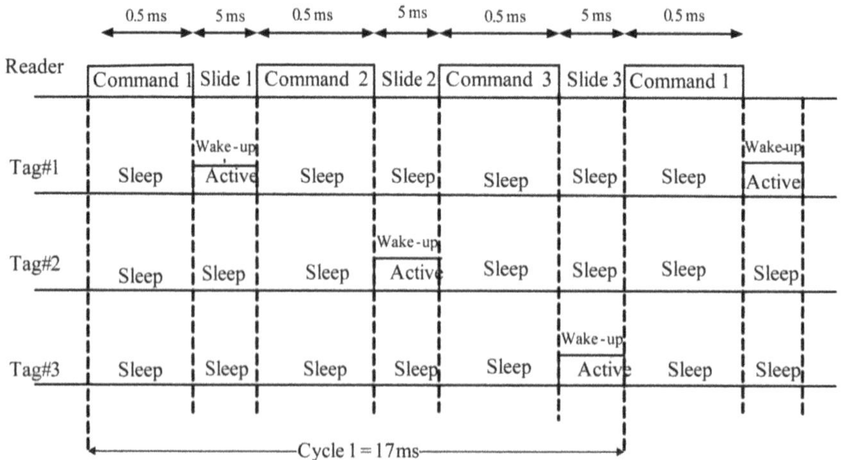

Figure 5. The timing of the anti-collision protocol.

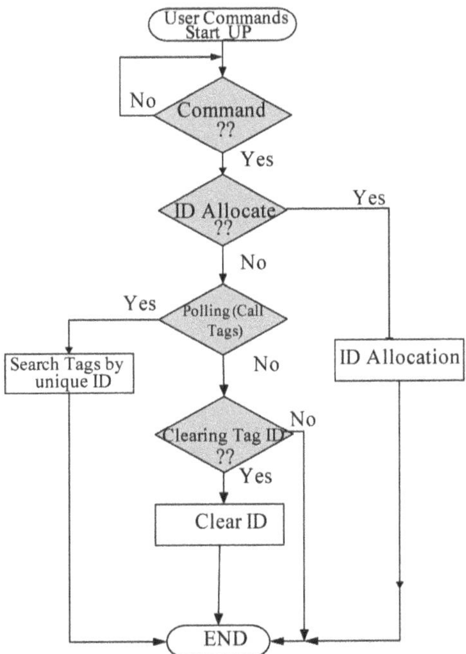

Figure 6. The flowchart of the user-interface software.

Reader. In practice, Tags are always located in inactive mode. In this mode, only internal low-power 32.768 kHz oscillator is active and all other components are dormant. In this mode, by using of the sleep timer, external events such as radio signals can be detected. Whenever SFD (Starting Frame Detector) from the received packet is detected, an interrupt will be occurred. We implement this interrupt source for synchronizing the Tags with the Reader and for reducing the power consumption in Tags. After SFD detection, Tags Wake up and go to the survey condition. Now, Tags receive whole of the frame. If the source address within the frame does not match with the Reader address, Tags do not pay attention to this frame any further and go to the sleep mode immediately. But when the source address is identical with the address of the Reader, Tags look for the type of the frame command within the frame. As shown in **Figure 8**, Tag goes to the communication condition for these three commands: ID allocation, polling, and clearing the Tag ID. When polling and clearing commands are coming from PC, at first, Tag checks the Destination address with the address of itself. Tag only acts when these two addresses are identical. After executing any of these commands, Tag goes to the sleep mode for other receptions. So, by this way, Tags always listen to the channel and after processing any event they go to the low power consumption mode, immediately.

3.3. Zig-Bee IEEE 802.15.4 Frame Format

IEEE 802.15.4 is an efficient standard for MAC protocol. There are 4 types of MAC frames in this standard. In our work, we use the data frame for communication between the Reader and Tags. In **Figure 9**, the schematics of MAC and physical layers of 802.15.4 are shown. SHR (Synchronization Header) is added at the first of any frame for synchronization between the Reader and Tag. The SHR consists of the 4-byte preamble sequence and 1-byte SFD. These two fields are set automatically by the hardware. In the PHR (Physical Header), the length of MPDU (MAC Protocol Data Unit) is written. The SHR and PHR are placed at the physical layer of 802.15.4 standard. The Radio has a FIFO memory with 128 bytes capacity. FCF (Frame Control Field), data sequence, address information, frame payload, and FCS (Frame Check Sequence) create the MAC layer. The Radio supports the automatic calculation of 2-byte FCS. By using of the source and destination addresses, each device will have a unique address, which helps us provide a precise timing in the polling process. Moreover, IEEE 802.15.4 is equipped with frame filtering and AUTOCRC protection. It rejects non-compliant frames, so decreases the packet error rate [7].

4. Experimental Results

In **Figure 10**, all the 16 channels are shown in the spectrum analyzer with a high precision. By using of a powerful RF transmitter, all out of band frequencies are filtered and the main frequency is amplified. The receiver sensitivity is a critical parameter for correct operation of RF transceivers. In CC2530, the receiver sensitivity is –97 dBm [7]. So, if the received signal strength (RSSI) becomes lower than this level, the receiver will not detect the signal properly. In **Figure 11**, the RSSI versus distance between the Reader and Tags is depicted in a practical test. For lower transmitter output power, the RSSI value is decreased. This reduction in RSSI is often more for long distances rather than short distances. As shown in **Figure 11**, the RSSI level is higher than the receiver sensitivity threshold for distances smaller than 80 meter. The PER (Packet Error Rate) is another significant parameter in RFIDs. It is expressed in the form of percentage. As shown in **Figure 12**, the PER is increased with increasing the distance, significantly. The experiments were performed for the two different TX output powers to ensure the proper operation of this system. As shown in **Figure 13**, round time for collecting 170 Tags data is near 1 second. In **Table 2**, important parameters of this system compared with similar works are shown.

5. Conclusion

In this work, a low-power high-range active RFID is implemented by using the chip CC2530. Without using any additional peripheral module, the identification process is

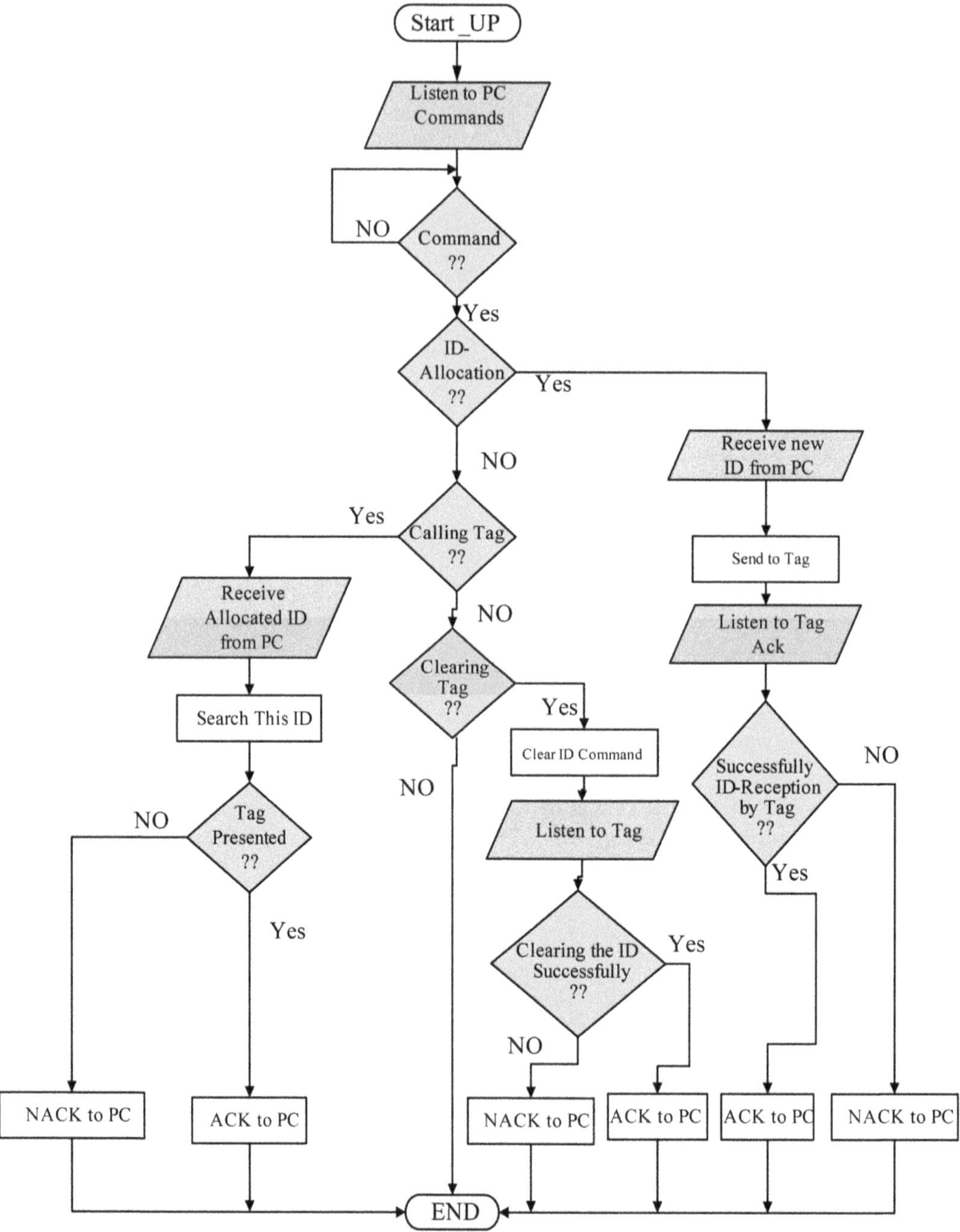

Figure 7. The reader flowchart.

Table 2. System characteristics of similar RFIDs.

Reference	Modulation Typpe	Carrie Frequency (MHZ)	Data Rate	Rang (meter)	Max Output Power (dBm)	Receiver Sensitivity (dBm)	Anti-Collision Protocol	Max Current in TX Mode (mA)
[2]	QPSK	2450	150	100	0	–95	Binary Search Algorithm	11.3 mA at 3.6 V
[4]	OQPSK	2450	250	100	1	–95	Binary Search Algorithm	15.1 mA at 3.6 V
[11]	ASK/FSK/MSK	800 - 928	500	30	+10	–110	Hybrid TDMA MAC	40 mA at 3 V
[12]	FSK	433	153	10	+5	–85	Dynamic framed Slotted-ALOHA	40 mA at 3 V
[13]	QPSK/MSK	2450	150	30	0	–90	Pure-ALOHA TDMA	13 mA at 3.6 V
This Work	OQPSK	2405 - 2485	250	80	+4.5	–97	Slotted-Aloha TDMA	29.6 mA at 3.3 V

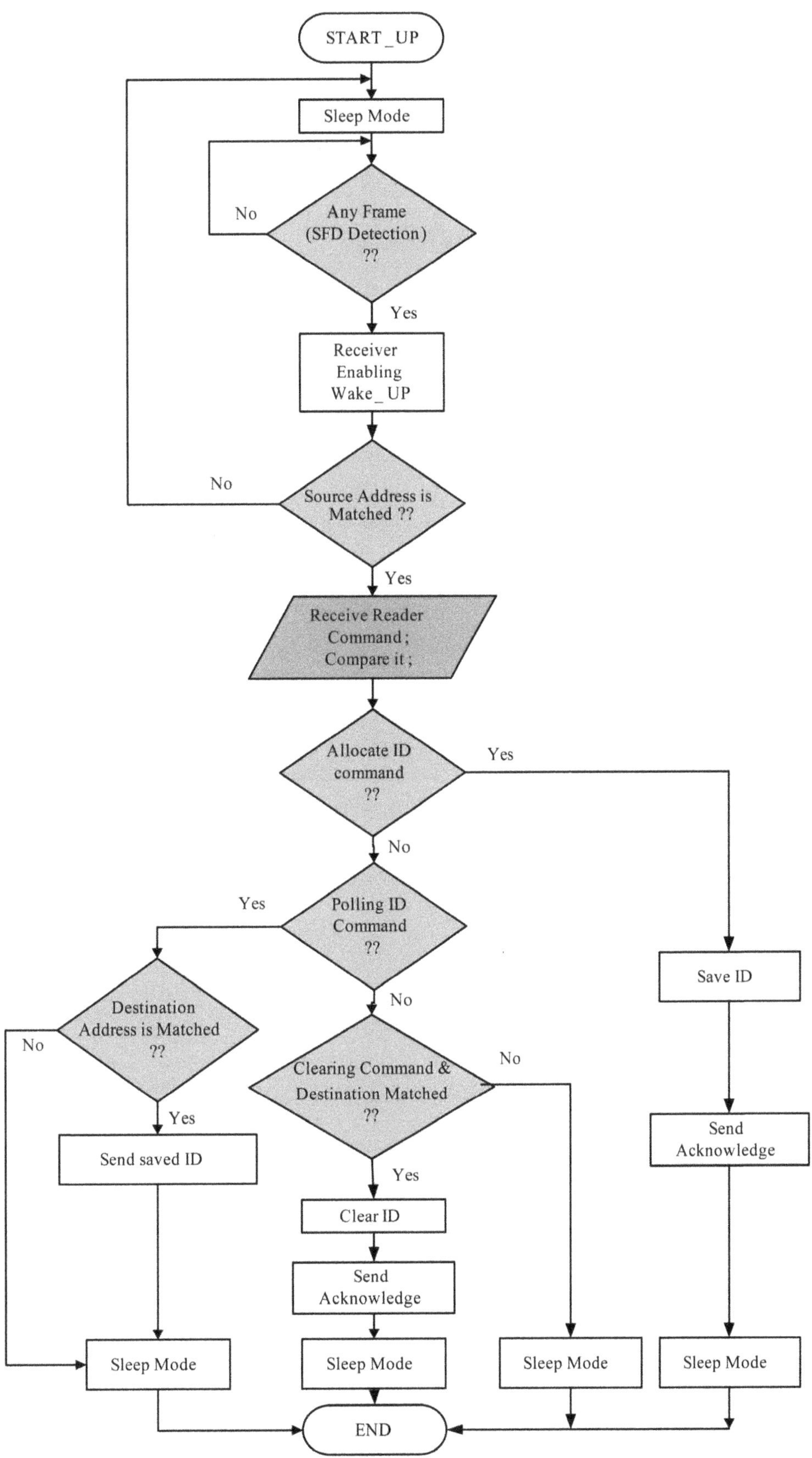

Figure 8. The flowchart of tags operation.

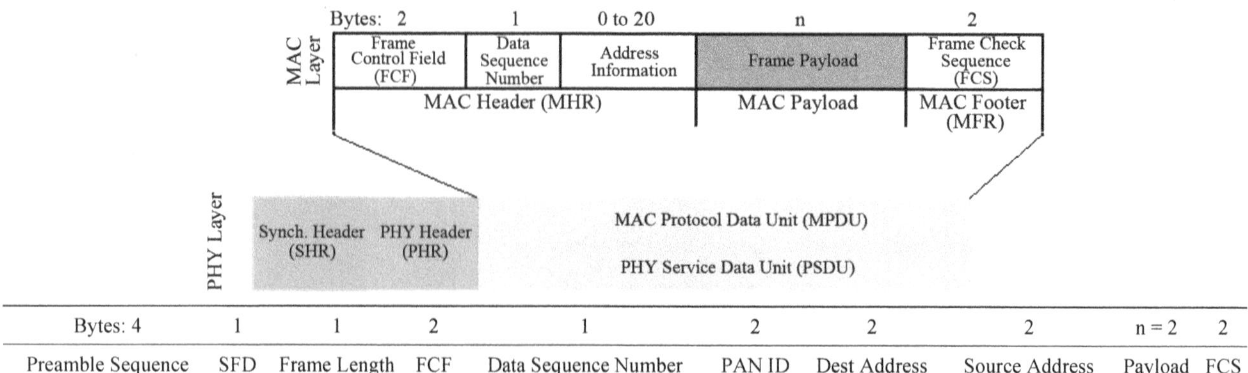

Bytes: 4	1	1	2	1	2	2	2	n = 2	2
Preamble Sequence	SFD	Frame Length	FCF	Data Sequence Number	PAN ID	Dest Address	Source Address	Payload	FCS

Figure 9. The physical and MAC layers of IEEE 802.15.4 standard frames [7].

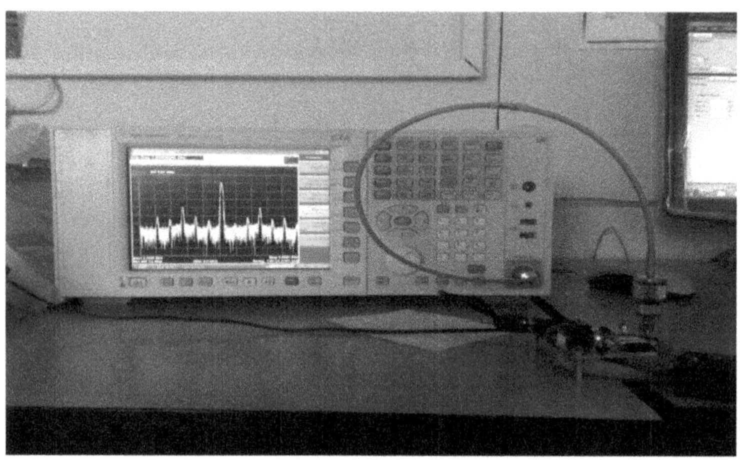

Figure 10. Frequency spectrum of the transmitting signal on spectrum analyzer.

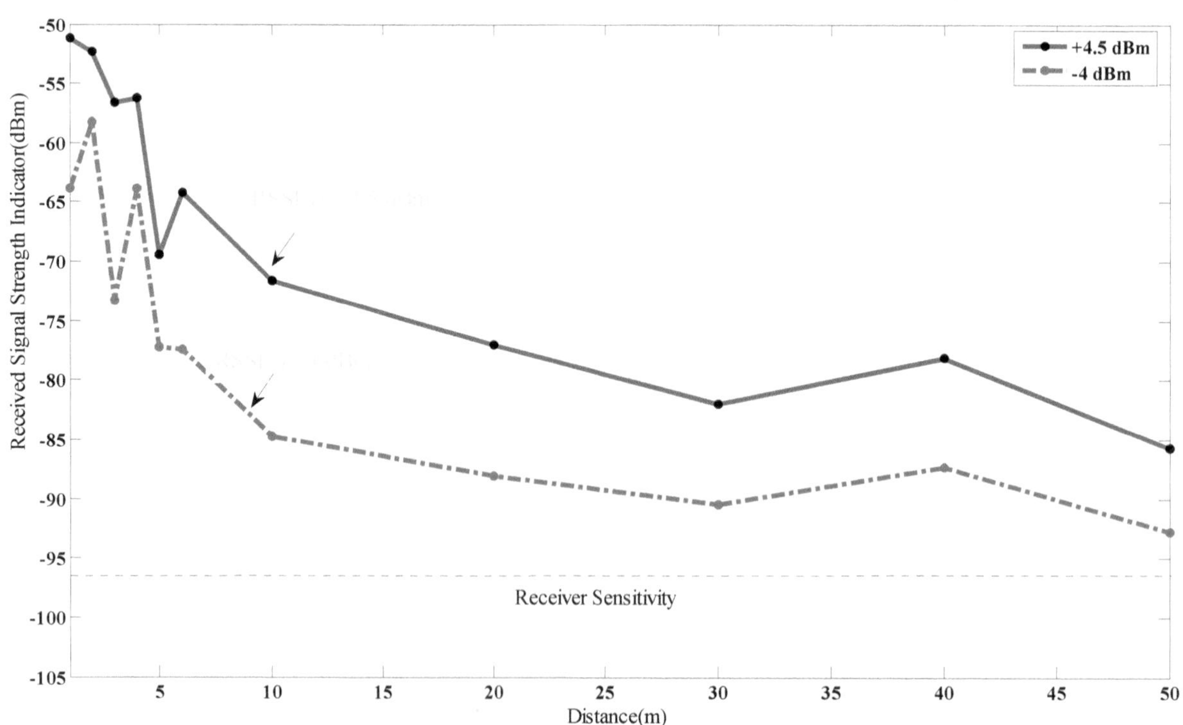

Figure 11. Received signal strength (RSSI) versus distance.

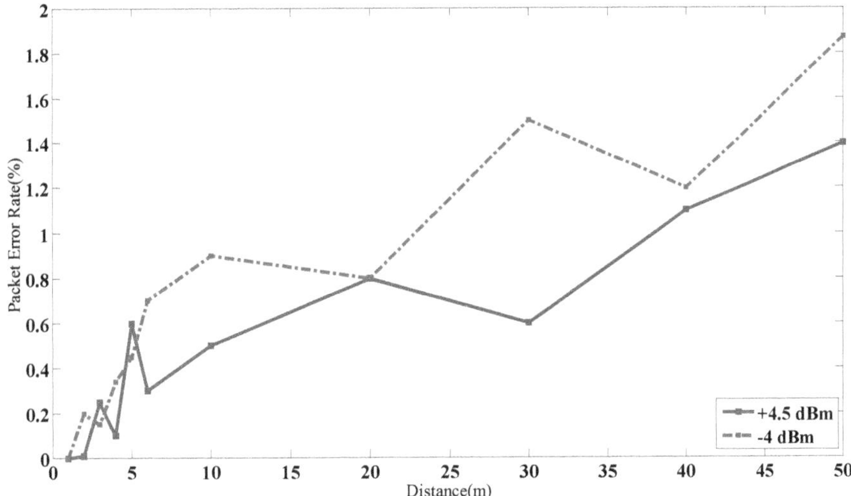

Figure 12. Packet error rate versus distance.

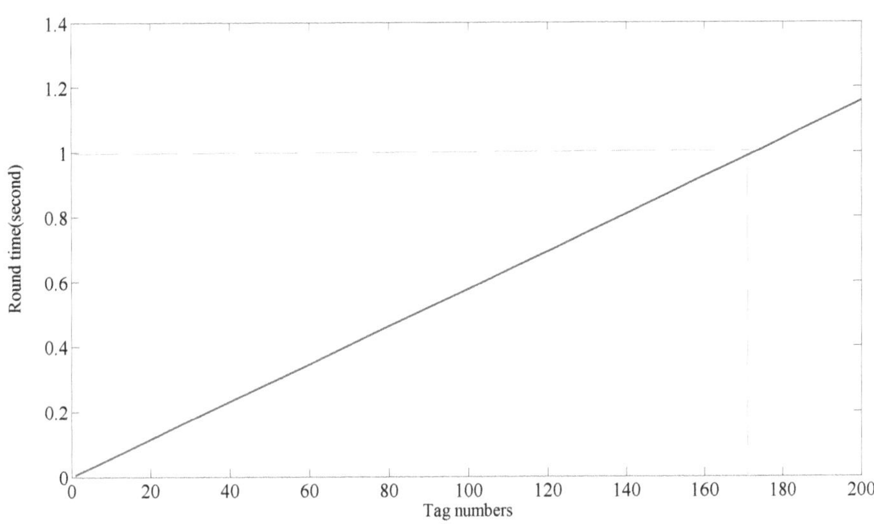

Figure 13. Round time versus tag numbers.

executed with high accuracy and minimum PER. By programming Tags in the sleep mode in most of times, a lot amount of power is restored. This system is tested and its operation is verified at outdoor environment until 80 meter distances, successfully. With a range extender device, such as CC2591, the communication range up to 300 m can be achieved. In our work, the collection time for 170 Tags is near 1 second. By using of a low-power multi-purpose Chip, small dimensions for Tags are achieved. In this architecture, compacting Tags down to near 660 mm^2 is possible, which is required in many practical environments. This system will be used for vehicle transportation and especially container tracking at commercial ports.

REFERENCES

[1] Z. Min, L. Wenfeng, W. Zhongyun, L. Bin and R. Xia, "A RFID-Based Material Tracking Information System," 2007 *IEEE International Conference on Automation and Logistics*, Jinan, 18-21 August 2007, pp. 2922-2926.

[2] Y. Sun, Y. Zhang and P. Peng, "Design and Realization of 2.45 GHz Active RFID System," *2nd International Conference on Intelligent Computation Technology and Automation*, Changsha, 11 October 2009, pp. 582-585.

[3] D. K. Klair, K.-W. Chin and R. Raad, "A Survey and Tutorial of RFID Anti-Collision Protocols," *Communications Surveys & Tutorials*, Vol. 12, No. 3, 2010, pp. 400-421.

[4] X. Huang, G. Zhang, Q. Sun and D. Qing, "Container Transportation System Using 2.45 GHz Active RFID Technology," *International Conference on Remote Sensing, Environment and Transportation Engineering*, Nanjing, 24 June 2011, pp. 3030-3033.

[5] W. J. Yoon, S. H. Chung, S. J. Lee and Y. S. Moon, "De-

sign and Implementation of an Active RFID System for Fast Tag Collection," *7th International Conference on Computer and Information Technology*, Fukushima, 16 October 2007, pp. 961-966.

[6] H. Cho and Y. Baek, "Design and Implementation of an Active RFID System Platform," *International Symposium on Applications and the Internet Workshops*, Busan, 23 January 2006, pp. 1-4.

[7] Texas Instruments, CC2530 User Guide and Datasheet, April 2009. http://www.ti.com

[8] Y. Hao and Z. Hong, "Development of a Low-Cost Active RFID Platform," *IEEE* 2007 *International Symposium on Microwave, Antenna, Propagation, and EMC Technologies for Wireless Communications*, Hangzhou, 16 August 2007, pp. 152-155.

[9] Maxim, MAX3232 Datasheet, 2007. http://www.maxim.com

[10] X.-Z. Zheng, X.-H. Cao and W.-L. Zheng, "Design of Electronic Tag in Active RFID Systems," *Port Operation*, Vol. 1, No. 2, 2008, pp. 850-853.

[11] Z. H. Xie and S. L. Lai, "Design and Implementation of an Active RFID MAC Protocol," *International Conference on Wireless Communications, Networking and Mobile Computing*, Shanghai, 21 September 2007, pp. 2113-2116.

[12] H. Cho, H. Choi, W. Lee, Y. Jung and Y. Baek, "LITeTag: Design and Implementation of an RFID System for IT-Based Port Logistics," *Journal of Communications*, Vol. 1, No. 4, 2006, pp. 48-57.

[13] U. Bilstrup and P.-A. Wiberg, "An Architecture Comparison between a Wireless Sensor Network and an Active RFID System," 29*th Annual IEEE International Conference on Local Computer Networks*, Tampa, 16 November 2004, pp. 583-584.

22

A Semantic Model for Socially Aware Objects

Giulia Biamino
Department of Computer Science, University of Turin, Torino, Italy

ABSTRACT

The Internet of Things (IoT) assumes that things interact and exchange information thus defining the future of pervasive computing environments. The integration between people and interconnected objects realizes a new physical and social space and opens new frontiers in context awareness and objects adaptation. In this paper we investigate the possibility of creating socially aware objects able to interact not only among themselves but also with human beings sharing the same environment. The main contribution of this work is to provide a knowledge model for social context-awareness and reasoning using an ontology-based context modeling, a user model and exploiting of social networks. This model is part of a larger framework called *So Smart* that aims at empowering networks of interconnected objects with social context awareness in order to improve their social interaction with people.

Keywords: Social-Context Awareness; Smart Objects; User Model; Semantic Models; Social Networks

1. Introduction

The Internet of Things (IoT) defines a shared social environment where objects are integrated into people's everyday life, identifying a new social ground of communication. The future of pervasive computing rises some questions about how objects can properly adapt to social spaces. For these reasons the notion of context awareness and context modeling has become fundamental in pervasive computing applications in order to ensure adaptation and contextual services. Most of the research in the area of context aware computing has been mainly concerned in location, time, activity and identity recognition. Intelligent objects or applications seem to be largely *a-social*, lacking in dealing with people social needs. On the contrary we believe that taking into account variables that are user-related and that socially influence the whole context is important to enhance agents' intelligence. Moreover social-awareness about users can significantly improve adaptation and human-object interaction by providing a better behavior that takes into account social features so far unexplored. In computer science an accepted definition of context is [1]:

"[...] any information that can be used to characterize the situation of an entity. An entity is a person, place or object that is considered relevant to the interaction between a user and an application, including the user and the application themselves."

According to this definition, the information useful for defining a context is not only given by the environment and its features, but also from people interacting with that environment. This paper presents a knowledge model developed for *So Smart*, a framework supporting social-context awareness in the Internet of Things and that relies on users relationships, preferences and demographic data. We consider social context awareness as the recognition of surrounding real-time social interactions and structures, with a particular attention to users preferences and features inside the network. The contributions of this work consists in 1) introducing a model for social-context awareness which is based on users features and social relationships, 2) using social data from the web and in particular from online social networks to build the social context and 3) exploiting semantic web ontologies for social context modeling and reasoning.

2. State of the Art

The Internet of Things (IoT) shows potentialities that make possible the development of a huge number of applications that involves different domains and environments. Atzori *et al.* [2] grouped four domains where IoT applications can be deployed: transportation and logistic, healthcare, smart environment, personal and social applications. The social potentialities of the Internet of things relate to the automatic update of information about users' social activities supported by online social networks such as Facebook or Twitter. One apporach in this direction has been made by [3] Julian Bleeker who coined the term *blogjects* to describe objects that blog. *Blogject* is a neologism which is meant to focus attention on the participation of objects and things in the sphere of networked social discourse variously called the blogosphere, or social web. Xia and Ma [4] envision that the convergence of CPS and social networking allows the emerging of a new paradigm that they call *smart community.* A smart community is defined by both humans and physical things delivering ubiquitous services by exploring cyber-physical and social intelligence. Social Network Analysis have emerged in sociology and recently gained significant success in computer science along with the growing of online social networks. Specific measures and metrics have been defined to describe topology and evolution of social networks [5]. We use some of these metrics to describe our social context structure (see Section 4.2). We exploit ontology to represent the social models and to reasoning to them, since they have been evaluated as most promising assets for context modeling in pervasive computing environments [6], since they are useful for specifying concepts and complex interrelations among them, and allow for reasoning on concepts relation. An ontology representation of social aspects has been provided by Hoekstra [7] but it is mainly social roles oriented and does not address social contexts in our meaning. In our project we strongly rely in the effectiveness of using ontology models and we believe that semantically enhanced objects can play a key role in context-aware applications. Our aim therefore is to use ontologies to build our smart objects knowledge-base by representing social contexts and their features.

3. A Semantic Model for *So Smart*

In this paper we will address the semantic model used in *So Smart* that represents the knowledge base responsible of providing social intelligence to smart objects in ubiquitous environments. Our semantic model is framed in two modules: the *OnSocial* Ontology (see Section 5) and the user model that includes basic user's data, such as demographic data and user's interests. The goal of *So Smart* is to give social intelligence to interconnected things in order to improve their capability to interact with users and thus better address users' needs. We plan to organize the *So Smart* framework in three layers (see **Figure 1**). The first layer is where smart objects gathers information from the environment. The second layer is responsible of the whole reasoning. The third layer, *Semantic Layer*, will be addressed in this paper.

In this paper we assume the following requirements:

User awareness. The most important requirement to make the approach possible is that the objects should be able to detect users. To do, this many solutions can be used, such as using RFID.

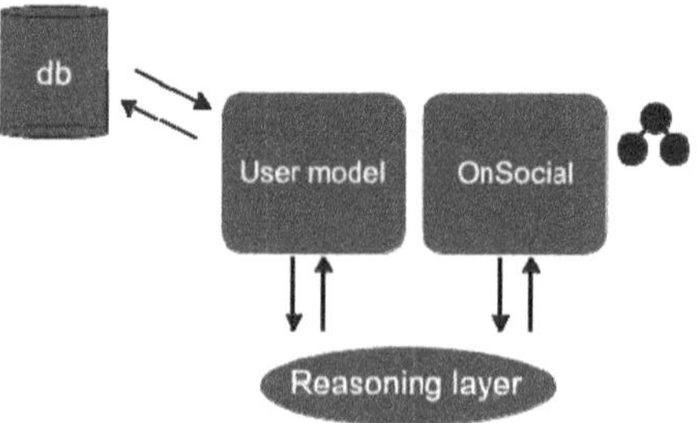

Figure 1. The Semantic layer in *So Smart*.

Users preferences detection. Another requirement is that objects should have a mechanism to gather users preferences. These can be gathered accessing users' basic information and interests by using existing technologies such as API provided by Google + 1[1], Facebook 2[2], LinkedIn 3[3]. Notice that we do not consider semantic differences in user information representation, but in this work we use only homogeneous information.

4. Core Definitions

In order to understand the importance of bringing social awareness to pervasive environments, we now define what we mean for what we mean for smart object, context and goal. With respect of previous work [8] we want to propose an improvementof our definition of social context by adding variables about users' and group's preferences and features. We also give a description of our vision of smart objects illustrating their features and their expected behavior.

4.1. Smart Object

We call *smart* any physical object connected to the web with some sensing capabilities. Its main abilities are: 1) detect users and the social connections between them, 2) access users' data, 3) infer the social context according to users' networks topology, preferences and features, 4) infer social goals according to the social context and the user model, 5) coordinate their behavior, and 6) provide a context-driven output.

4.2. Social Context

According to the sociological approach instead a social context is synonym of social environment, and it is considered as the culture, the persons and the institutions with which people interact. We started from such a definition to gradually narrow it down to a more specific interpretation that met the point of view of ubiquitous computing [1].

In our vision, social contexts can be assimilated to social groups, identified as a number of nodes (people) in a given location, linked by some kind of ties (relations), that determine their nature, and characterized by specific

[1]http://plus.google.com.
[2]http://facebook.com.
[3]http://linkedin.com.

features such as sex, age or preferences. We refine our previous definition of social context [8], identifying a tuple with two sets of variables: *cxt* = <*NT*, *UM*> where *NT*, Network Topology, is the set of network types depending on the number of nodes (*Size*), the number of connections between them (*Density*) and the nature of such connections (*Type of Connection*), whereas *UM*, User Model, is the set containing the user model variables, e.g., average age, prevalent gender, common interests. According to this definition, a possible context representation in the framework could be:

cxt = <{*Size*, *Density*, *Type of Connection*}, {*Age*, *Gender*, *Interest*}>.

Network Structure. As previously stated in our vision social contexts can be seen as social aggregation of people that share particular kind of relationship between each other: they can be friends, colleagues or they simply do not know each other. According to this definition a strong similarity exists between social contexts and social networks structures studied by social networks analysis. In social networks analysis a network is represented by a labeled graph where people are nodes and their connections are the arcs connecting two nodes. We therefore believe that social contexts can be derived from social networks structures and topology. Many important properties can be derived from such structures, but we distinct three main elements useful to describe the context: the number of people, their relationship and how well they know each other. We now present the variables set that, according to our model, describes the network structure:

<*Size*, *Density*, *Type of Ties*>

where *Size* is given by the number of nodes, *Density* by the number of connections between them and *Type of Ties* is defined by the nature of the relations between the nodes of the network. The correlation of these three variables provides a good approximation of a number of social contexts.

1) **Size** depends on the number of nodes in a defined location. We isolate four configurations going from very small to very large networks.

Private ($n < 4$): a network with a small number of nodes;

Small ($5 < n < 10$): a network with a few nodes;

Open ($20 < n < 50$): a relatively large network;

Wide ($n > 50$): a network with a very large number of nodes.

2) **Density** indicates the number of links between the nodes of the network. Starting from the definition of a *sociometric clique* [9], we count the number of triangles in the graph to classify networks with a large number of triangles, networks with easy to close triangles and networks with many isolated nodes and hard to close triangles. As an example, we provide the following basic classification where we distinguish three types of density values:

Clique: a fully connected graph;

Dense: a graph with easy to close triangles;

Sparse: a graph with many isolated nodes and hard to close triangles.

3) Each arc of the network needs to be labeled with possible values that give information about the type of ties between two nodes. Types of ties can be:

Relatives: two nodes sharing the same class or superclass in the ontology;

Relationship: two nodes in a romantic relationship with each other;

Friends: two nodes with a friendship-kind of relation;

Partners: two nodes with a partnership-kind of relation;

Unknown: no relation exists between two nodes.

To gather type of relation values we propose to crawl users social web applications anonymous graph, such as Facebook, LinekedIn or Delicious. Facebook for example can bring useful data about users friends or family members while LinkedIn could be a reliable source for finding partnership kind of relations.

User Model. As previously stated, users networks are not the only variables influencing reasoning and consequent objects behavior. We also suggest to consider users features and preferences. The age, the sex and the number of interests that people share in a group determine its level of homogeneity and change people's behavior and expectations. For this reason, through the definition of appropriate user models we should be able to improve social context modeling by inspecting users data. In particular we now illustrate how we model the variables expressed in this 3-tuple:

<*Age*, *Sex*, *Interests*>

A User Model is a knowledge structure which contains all the features the system knows about users (from demographic features such as age, gender, profession to interest and knowledge in some domain category). For adaptation purpose, the user model included 1) demographic data and 2) users preferences. Demographic data we consider are: *age* and *sex*.

1) **Age** is an important variable for defining the type of group: teen or adult, mixed or unmixed types of group and therefore the related social goals. For this reason we identify three particular values:

Average age: it determines the personality and the behavior of a group. Groups of teens for example show emotions, feelings and priorities rather different from adult or elderly groups.

Age variance: it measures how the set of ages is spread out and how far age values are from the mean. Small tight groups tend to show a low age variance while big open networks have a high value of age variance. Equation (1) shows how we calculate *AgeVariance*.

$$AgeVariance = \frac{1}{N}\sum_{n=1}^{N}\left(a-\overline{a}\right)^{2} \quad (1)$$

where a is a single age value and $\overline{a}$ is the average age value.

Underage: this boolean variable is useful to know if there is at least one child in the group.

2) **Sex** is a sensible variable in describing attitudes, interests and social behavior of a group. Gender studies [10] show that the social and cultural constructions of masculinities and femininities strongly influences social activities, goals and relations. We are interested in determine the *dominant sex* and *sex variance of* a group.

Dominant sex: this variables indicates the main sex in a group.

Sex variability: it is the ratio between number of men and number of women in a group. It measures the frequency of occurrences and gives values between 0% and 100%. We use a univariate descriptive statistics index: Gini I. Interests indicates users' preferences about movies, music, books and so on. They are expressed as a couple *category-value,* where category is the domain category the user is interested in, and value is the numerical level of this interest (overlay user model). We collect such data from Social Web applications (e.g. Facebook) that make them available by means of API (e.g. using OpenSocial4 or Facebook Graph API5).

Interest ratio: this is a variable that concur in defining the homogeneity of a group and it indicates the ratio between the number of common items and the total number of items of interest in within a group.

4.3. Social Goal

Social goals are guessed about what users might need in a certain context. According to social influence theory [10], two kinds of goals can be identified within groups: individual goals and group goals. The former are related to specific users' objectives, while the latter encourage group cohesiveness such as working together to complete a task or imitating members behavior to stick together in the group. Some contexts tend to preserve a strong individuality, while others favor group collaboration, privileging group goals rather than individual ones as in the scenario. According to this perspective the set of social goals can be represented as $G = f(cxt)$, where Context cxt has a set G of possible social goals. Common social goals have to do with desired social rewards or with the roles agents can play in specific contexts such as being accepted, entertain, making friends, pleasing someone etc. In our vision social goals are guesses about what users might need in a certain situation, or a context.

5. Defining *OnSocial*

In order to fully understand the importance of building a social ontology, we give a description of what we signify as a social context according to our research approach. Since we work with smart objects in ambient intelligence, we started from the definition of context from the point of view of pervasive and ubiquitous computing and we call it *social* to distinguish it from its general characterization. Since we want to use this ontology to improve agents adaptations to the social environment, we propose to model the social reality not only using a set of properties but also identifying possible social goals in a given context. This solution makes this knowledge base strongly recommendation oriented, but it also emphasizes the dynamism of a social context as a human organization made of interactions, social desires, possible rewards and punishments. For a proper ontology design we cooperate with domain experts such as sociologists and psychologists who give us a complete understanding of the notions of context, goal, group and their relations. In order to keep simple the development and to formally separate the static description of the social context from the concept of social goal, we develop two ontologies: a *Social Context Ontology* and a *Social Goal Ontology*. We also develop a domain ontology, the *Objects Ontology* to represent smart objects, organizing them in a taxonomy and identifying their basic actions in relation with social goals. We then merge all these ontologies together into a upper ontology called *OnSocial* that fully describe social contexts. In order to formalize the social context information we chose OWL (Web Ontology Language[4]) that uses a standardized syntax from Description Logics (DL), a subset of First-Order Logic (FOL). The advantages of DL reasoning are subsumption reasoning, consistency checking and classification on taxonomies. We used OWL 2 because we wanted to exploit some of its extensions with respect of OWL 1 and in particular the possibility to support datatypes with ranges. We built the ontology with Protegee, Top Braid Composer and using Pellet reasoner engine.

5.1. Social Context Ontology

The *Social Context Ontology* is the center of the context modeling. It is responsible for representing all the information about a social context according to the features that define it. Our *Social Context Ontology* must be able to properly represent all the elements that have to be take into account when describing a social context. Given the variables previously described, we identify two top categories: *SocialContext* and *ContextProperty*. Since we

[4]W3C: Ontology Web Language Overview. http://www.w3c.org/TR/owl-features/.

look at a social context more as at nodes clustered in a social group, the class *SocialContext* includes a predefined number of contexts following the classifications provided by group sociology. Typical examples of groups and social networks are: tribe, community, family, peer, club, household etc. Our ontology currently shows only a short list of all the possible context. We use classes to represent the contexts in order to keep our model at a high level to guarantee flexibility and reuse.

ContextProperty class describes all the variables that define the social context. Subclasses of *ContextProperty* are: network structure properties: *Number*, *Density*, *Type OfTies* (object properties) and user properties: *Age*, *Sex*, *Interest* (datatype properties). These classes have as their subclasses the values that we have listed in section IV-A. Therefore we have *small*, *private*, *open* and *wide* for *Numbers*, *clique*, *dense* and *sparse* for *Density* and *friendship*, *unknown*, *relatives*, *partners* and *relationship* for *TypeOfTies*. The representation of the class *Number* and its subclasses requires the use of datatype properties in order to define a numeric range for each subclass.

The *Social Context Ontology* includes a predefined number of contexts following group sociology: *tribe* (a group of people that has many of the same interests and commonly found in a high school/college setting), *community* (a group of people with a commonality often, but not always, in proximity with one another with some degree of continuity over time), *family* (a group of people related by blood or marriage), *work* (colleagues), *public* (unknown people), *romantic* (two people in a relationship), *club* (a group with members dedicated to particular activities), *team* (small group collaborating to reach a goal), *peers* (members of approximately the same age, social status, and interests and equal in terms of power). The property *DescribedBy* associates the domain *Social-Context* with the range *ContextProperty*. Intuitively, subproperties of *DescribedBy* are *hasDensity* (with range *Density*), *hasNumber* (with range *Number*), *hasType* (with range *Type-OfTies*). Furthermore, each social context is properly described by the definition of class restrictions over the subproperties of *DescribedBy*.

In OWL restrictions use existential ($\exists$) universal quantifier ($\forall$) or cardinality restrictions on specific values. See the following example for existential and universal restrictions that represent the class *community*.

Table 1 shows the main restrictions for the class *community*. The first two restrictions mean that the context *community* can take some values from the class *small* and some values from the class *open*. The third imposes that a *community* must only take all values from clique on the property *hasDensity*.

5.2. Social Goal Ontology

The *Social Goal Ontology* aims at representing social pur-

Table 1. Restriction to represent the context "community".

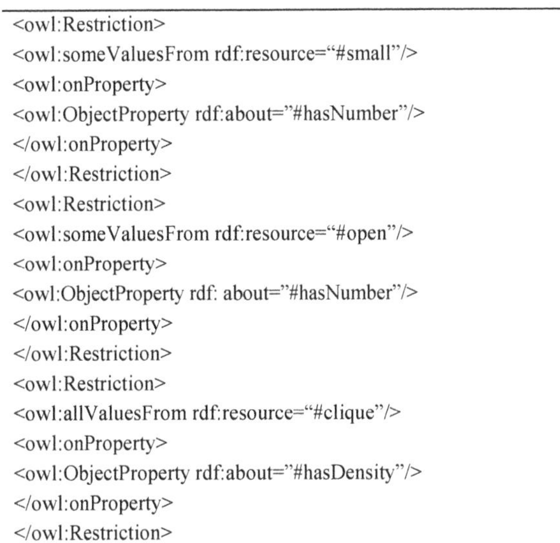

```
<owl:Restriction>
<owl:someValuesFrom rdf:resource="#small"/>
<owl:onProperty>
<owl:ObjectProperty rdf:about="#hasNumber"/>
</owl:onProperty>
</owl:Restriction>
<owl:Restriction>
<owl:someValuesFrom rdf:resource="#open"/>
<owl:onProperty>
<owl:ObjectProperty rdf: about="#hasNumber"/>
</owl:onProperty>
</owl:Restriction>
<owl:Restriction>
<owl:allValuesFrom rdf:resource="#clique"/>
<owl:onProperty>
<owl:ObjectProperty rdf:about="#hasDensity"/>
</owl:onProperty>
</owl:Restriction>
```

poses of individuals or of an entire group according to different contexts. Social goals lie at a very high level of representation and they have to do with general desires such as the need of cohesiveness, collaboration or getting in power. However our ontology must be able to represent these goals at different levels of abstraction in order to be understandable and performable by smart objects. For these reasons a social goal must be associated with subgoals and with lower level goals, organized into a taxonomy where leaves are associated to smart objects' basic actions expressed in the objects' ontology. From the ontological point of view, a very interesting point is the division between individual needs and hence individual goals, and group or network needs and goals. Some contexts tend to preserve a strong individuality while others enable group behaviors and collaboration privileging group goals rather than individual ones.

Individual vs Group: Social science states that in groups two kinds of goals can be identified: goals of an individual inside the group and goals of the group as a whole. The *Social Goals Ontology* has two main classes: *IndividualGoal* and *GroupGoal*. Individual goals are goals of single users within the network, whereas group goals are goals of the group as one entity. Individual goals concern self achievement and more self-centered needs and desires. Group goals encourage group cohesiveness. We want to model different goals and subgoals starting form theories about classification of users' main desires and objectives. Classification and definition of the classes follows small group sociology [11], social psychology of group dynamics and teamwork research [12]. Once again we decided to use classes to model social goals in order to keep the ontology as flexible as possible. This choice give us the chance to add new instances formulated as actions and further interpreted by objects to trigger specific primary goals. The *Context Ontology* and the *Goal Ontology* must be merged for goal-context association. To reasonably associate goals to contexts, social groups and social identities theories have been taken into consideration [13].

5.3. Objects Ontology

Let us now briefly introduce a third ontology, the *Objects Ontology*, that is the representation of the domain of interest and that serves the purpose to complete the semantic model of our project *So Smart.* This ontology is not directly connected with the description of social contexts, but it is fundamental for the logical chaining of the three ontologies and therefore for a proper reasoning of smart objects. For these reasons the *Objects Ontology* organizes objects of the domain into a taxonomy and relates basic actions of single objects with social goals illustrated into the *Social Goal Ontology*. For example a DVD player has action *Play Movie* that is connected to the social goal *entertainment. So Smart* relies in this ontology to assure that smart objects are able to provide a contextual output after social context and social goals have been identified.

5.4. *OnSocial*: The Social Ontology

This section illustrates our high level ontology that we call *OnSocial* and that aims at being a starting point for a future standard ontology to represent social contexts and more generally social reality. The proposed design of this ontology enables specializations to the social domain but it allows interoperability with external ontologies. The light-weight ontologies *Social Context Ontology*, *Social Goal* and *Objects Ontology* are imported into the upper ontology that represents social contexts, social goals, objects and their relationships. In particular this is the place where the ranges of all the social goals are connected with specific social contexts and where objects' basic actions find a relation with social goals. As reflected by its name, *OnSocial* has a clear sociological bias. In this sense it captures ontological categories that underline the sociological properties of being in a group and interacting with it, trying to be rewarded or avoiding punishments. Indeed, the fundamental ontological distinction is between *ContextProperty* and *Goal* it can be seen as the distinction between statics and dynamics. Both categories are used to describe one ore more social contexts but they do it from a different sociological sense: properties describe the structure of the group, goals describe the aim of a group or of a single individual within that group. Another important aspect of this ontology is the understanding of the indissoluble link between the single person and the social context or the social group he belongs to. Even if individual goals address singular desires, they exist only to solve a need of an individual inside a specific social context. Collective attitudes and intersubjectivity are therefore key concepts that we derived from social science [14] in order to represent social reality. As we previously stated, in *OnSocial* the two lower lever ontologies are mapped linking each social context to one or more social goals. The association of social goals and social contexts is derived from behavioral science and sociological theories previously cited. We started from the assumption that strongly connected groups and therefore context such as tribes, communities or families, are more attached to the conservation of a high level of social identity, belongings and dominance. On the other hand contexts with only few connections are more interested in personal achievement or need of cooperation. As an example we describe the main objects property *hasGoal* that has *SocialContext* as domain and Goal, which contains the *subclassesIndividualGoal* and *GroupGoal*, as range. In particular we illustrate which goals we assigned to the context *community*. A community is a group of friends sharing particular interests. Main goals of people in a community are having fun, connect with each other and being accepted by the other members. Therefore, looking at our *Social Goal* ontology, we can assume that *Identity*, *SharedCommunication* and *Interdependence* can be appropriate social goals for *community*. To do this we simply use the property *hasGoal* that, as previously stated, links the class *SocialContexts* with the class *Goal*. Moreover we also want to specify whether we are considering individual goals or group goals. The property *hasGoal* has therefore two subproperties: *has IndividualGoal* and *hasGroupGoal*. We define restrictions over these properties exactly how we did for contexts features (see Section 5.1). This solution gives us the possibility to associate specific individual or group goals to our class *community*. The following **Figure 2** shows *OnSocial* main categories and some of its subclasses. The main restrictions and datatype properties are also shown.

6. Evaluation

To test our knowledge base and in particular the *Semantic Layer* of *So Smart*, we developed a web-based application prototype, exploiting Servlets and JSP as main technologies, with the Jena framework[5] along with Pellet reasoner. Semantic Layer (Section 5) is composed by the context ontologies, by a music domain ontology and by a database for user data. Users are asked to register through their Facebook account, which the system uses to collect their public profiles using *Facebook Social Graph API* through *RestFb library*[6]. In order to gather users' network and demographic information we ask every

[5]http://jena.sourceforge.net.

[6]http://restfb.com.

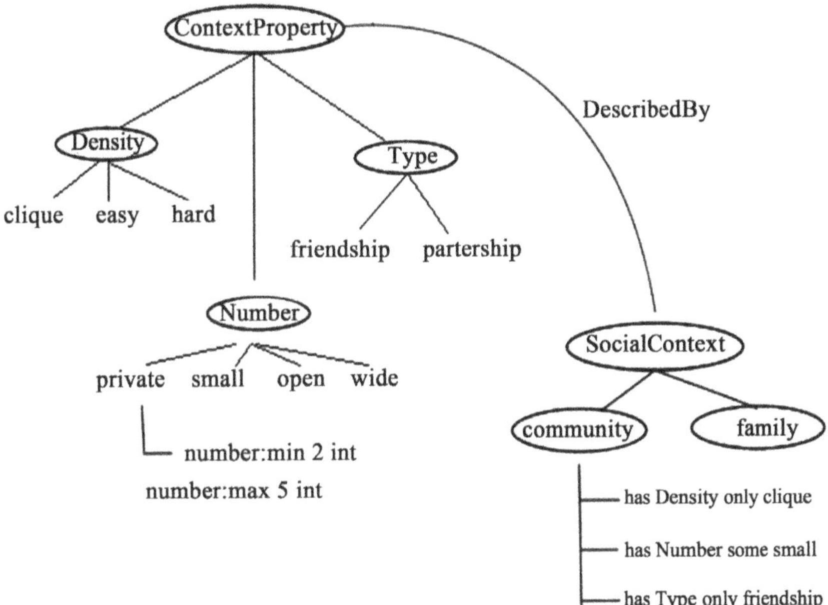

Figure 2. Social context ontology.

single user to explicitly identify herself and provide the name of the people she is with. In this first version of the prototype[7], we gather users' interests by asking every single user to fill a short form with her preferences about about music, sport, cinema and their subcategories. For each group detected, our prototype gives an output of $0 < n < 3$ social contexts, each one associated to a set of goals. Each social context inferred is ranked according to a weight associated during the inference process. This weight w is based on network topology and it is calculated by multiplying values of the following properties: *Size*, *Density* and *Type of connection*. Values of each property have been associated to a numerical range going from 1 to N following a scale going from small to large for *size*, clique to sparse for *Density*, relative to unknown for *Type of connection*. Our ranking prioritizes small clustered social networks therefore contexts with a small value of w figure the top of the output list.

6.1. The Experiment

This section describes the experiment that we conducted for the evaluation.

1) **Hypothesis**. We assumed that our social context model can positively infer a social context in a shared environment of people and objects. To validate this hypothesis, we tested the accuracy of the social context inference.

2) **Subjects**. The sample included 33 subjects, 25 - 60 years old, recruited according to a judgmental sampling strategy[8] so that we could control the correctness of social context inference. Users have been divided into pre-defined social contexts (see Section 3.1): 2 *communities*, 1 *tribe*, 2 *work*, 2 *families*, 2 *public* and 1 *romantic*.

3) **Experiment set up**. We installed our prototype on a laptop in two different locations: a living room and an office. Right before starting members have been asked to nominate a group "leader" who performed the actions required by the system. Each member was asked to participate to the whole experience looking at the laptop. The leader needed to log into the system and to indicate the users she/he was with.

4) **Measures**. To test social context inference accuracy we compare the lists of social contexts and social goals generated by our framework with groups defined for the experimental setting. First we looked at the whole set of contexts inferred for each group. We used a boolean variable $x = 1, 0$ to define whether or not the social context expected was in the output set. We then calculated the inference accuracy by using two measures: *Precision* and *Recall.* The first is defined as the ratio of correct contexts inferred to total number of contexts inferred as shown in Equation (2).

$$P = \frac{N_{rc}}{N_{ic}} \tag{2}$$

Since our prototype infers up to three different contexts for each group detected the *Precision* expected cannot be close to one. We therefore calculate it by considering only the first context of the set list inferred.

Recall is defined as the ratio of correct context inferred to total number of relevant context available. Equation (3)

[7] In the future we are willing to use automatic preference detection.

[8] Judgmental sampling is a non-probability sampling technique where the researcher selects units to be sampled based on their knowledge and professional judgment.

shows its equation.

$$R = \frac{N_{rc}}{N_c} \quad (3)$$

We then looked at the whole set of social context inferred and in particular at their ranking. We associated to each context an absolute values according to its own ranking.

0 if the right context is not in the set;

0.1 if the right context is in the last position of the set list;

0.3 if the right context is in the second position of the set list;

0.5 if the right context is in the first position of the set list.

In order to evaluate the correctness of our ranking we calculated the Mean Absolute Error (MAE) as shown by Equation (4).

$$\mathrm{MAE} = \frac{1}{N}\sum_{i=1}^{N}(f_i - y_i) \quad (4)$$

where f_i is the expected value, y_i is the absolute value and N is the total number of observation, in this case $N = 10$. In statistics, the mean absolute error (MAE) is a quantity used to measure how close forecasts or predictions are to the eventual outcomes and can assume values from 0 to 1.

6.2. Results

During the evaluation our prototype inferred a total of 30 social contexts and their related social goals. Since we knew the type of contexts we were testing, it was easy to compare results. The *Precision* ratio is 0.8 and the *Recall* is 0.9 with only one case where the expected context was not in the output list. *Precision* represents the probability that a inferred context is correct and *Recall* represents the probability that a correct context will be inferred. Their values affirm the positive behavior of our prototype that was able to correctly infer a large number of contexts according to our expectations. Finally the calculated value of the Mean Absolute Error is 0.2. This data confirm that our knowledge model is able to make good prediction of social contexts with a not significant error. Since we wanted to test if our social context model was able positively infer a social context in a shared environment of people and objects, we can conclude that the evaluation validated out hypothesis considering also the approximations we made for *Precision* and values of ranking position.

7. Discussion and Future Work

This paper introduced a model for empowering networked objects with social context awareness. We illustrated our formalization of social contexts and we presented *OnSocial* an ontology that represents users' social contexts and social goals and that serves as a semantic model for context-aware agents. Our social oriented approach for modeling contexts relies on the idea of looking at on social network structures and user data for context classification and reasoning. We gave an overview of our semantic model structure and of the main categories of our ontology. The preliminary test described above aimed at evaluating the effectiveness of our framework with respect to social context inference. The evaluation used a web-based application proto-type and a small sample. We focused only on a reduced set of contexts (community, family, tribe, work, public, romantic). Despite of these limitations, the results are promising. For a great number of the cases we were able to generate the expected social context and users' and group' ratings were high and almost every user showed that the recommendation proposed was correct. This work represents the backbone of a wider project that aims at providing social context awareness to network.

REFERENCES

[1] A. Dey, "Understanding and Using Context," *Personal and Ubiquitous Computing Journal*, Vol. 5, No. 1, 2001, pp. 4-7.

[2] L. Atzori, A. Iera and G. Morabito, "The Internet of Things: A Survey," *Computer Networks*, Vol. 54, No. 15, 2010, pp. 2787-2805.

[3] J. Bleecker, "A Manifesto for Networked Objects Cohabiting with Pigeons, Arphids and Aibos in the Internet of Things (Why Things Matter)", 2006. http://research.techkwondo.com/blog/julian/185

[4] J. Xia and J. H. Ma, "Building Smart Communities with Cyber-Physical Systems," *ACM UBICOMP Symposium on Social and Community Intelligence* (*SCI*), Beijing, September 2011, arXiv:1201.0216v1.

[5] J. Kleinberg, S. Kumar, P. Raghavan, S. Rajagopalan and A. Tomkins, "The Web as a Graph: Measurements, Models and Methods," *International Conference on Combinatorics and Computing*, Vol. 1672, 1999, pp. 1-17.

[6] T. Strang and C. Linnhoff-Popien, "Context Modeling Survey," *UbiComp—International Conference on Ubiquitous Computing*, September 2004.

[7] R. Hoekstra, "Representing Social Reality in Owl 2," *International Workshop on OWL*: *Experiences and Directions OWLED*, 2010. http://ceur-ws.org/Vol-614/owled2010_submission_29.pdf

[8] G. Biamino, "Modeling Social Contexts for Pervasive Computing Environments," *IEEE International Conference on Pervasive Computing and Communications Workshop*, Torino, 21-25 March 2011, pp. 415-420.

[9] R. D. Alba, "A Graph-Theoretic Definition of a Sociometric Clique," *Journal of Mathematical Sociology*, Vol. 3, 1973, pp. 3-113.

[10] R. B. Cialdini, "Influence: Science and Practice," 4th Edition, Allyn & Bacon, Boston, 2001.

[11] R. F. Bales, "A Set of Categories for the Analysis of Small Group Interaction," *American Sociological Review*, Vol. 15, No. 2, 1950, pp. 257-263.

[12] C. E. Larson and F. M. J. LaFasto, "Team Work: What Must Go Right," Sage Publications, Newbury Park, 1989.

[13] H. Tajfel and J. C. Turner, "An Integrative Theory of Intergroup Conflict. In the Social Psychology of Intergroup Relations," Brooks/Cole, Monterey, 1979.

[14] J. Searle, "Speech Acts: An Essay in the Philosophy of Language," Cambridge University Press, Cambridge, 1969.

23

The Influence of Memetic Primers in Online Comments in Video Game Blogs

Ibrahim Yucel
State University of New York Institute of Technology, Utica, USA

ABSTRACT

Through investigating a particular blog, several factors were found which have significant influence on reader actions. This study uses the term "memetic primers" for those styles that most often cause readers to take notice of a particular comment, remember information included in it, and take action. The memetic primers were derived in a discourse analysis. The study discovered the memetic primers using logic-of-inquire approach to the online comments. While evidence indicated that the usefulness of some primers was low, it emerged those negatively written comments where the most common impact on a comment's volume.

Keywords: Computer-Mediated Communication; Social Networking Site Design and Use; Virtual Worlds/Avatars/Proxies; Community Analysis and Support; Virtual or Physical; Entertainment/Games

1. Introduction

In today's digitally driven and fast paced media landscape, blogs have emerged as a powerful and growing media outlet. This new media is at once a noun and verb, both as the site and the uploading of new information. Blogs evolved from Web 2.0 technologies which allow for content creation without the need of hypertext scripting or programming ability. Instead, through simple interfaces on the website themselves, these sites can quickly grow with entire communities contributing to their content. With further development, most blogs incorporate the best the Web 2.0 has to offer-video feeds from YouTube and profile management for all their devoted readers. Such websites are connecting individuals with similar interests into communities. Many blogs often focus on one or two topics, tightening community bonds and increasing member investment by providing insights from both experts and amateurs in a shared space.

These messages that are more prevalent and easy to read within online communities are referred to in this study as "shouts". The idea of shouts grew from a PricewaterhouseCoopers white paper, which was aimed at gauging a client's reputation on the Internet, as well as from various studies analyzing popular opinion as expressed on blogs [1-4]. The white paper suggested that whispers of customer interaction gradually grew in volume into shouts as they proliferated across blogs and other forms of media [4]. This concept can be applied on a smaller scale. The mixture of popular opinion, memes, and shouts combine to create what this study will refer to as "memetic primers". When a particular comment acts as a memetic primer, it gains attention and causes those reading the comment to remember the conversation.

While examples of powerful comments are be found readily on the Internet, it's beyond the scope of this study to consider all commented pages and blogs, since each community has a commenting style of its own with its own nuances. Therefore, as is explained in detail below, the focus of the study will be special-interest blogs, specifically blogs that cover news of the video game industry. This focus on blogs with community identities allows us to gain more insight into their behavior, through methods established in socio-technical fields. Special-topic blogs show some evidence to support the view that their members, due to shared interests, are inclined to "bandwagoning" heuristics [5,6]. "Bandwagoning" is a component of the MAIN Model, a mental model of media consumption [7]. This heuristic governs a trust decision on part of the reader, making the reader more likely to agree with the major opinion in the community. This phenomenon, in addition to other heuristics within the MAIN Model, may give insight into the "volume" or "loudness" of a given comment.

Memetic primers also are potentially useful for providing new insights into both analyzing web discussions and forecasting trends in web communities. Interest in the examining discourse that happens in online spaces is increasing in both academia and industry [1-3,8]. This analysis provides a way to gauge the opinions of large, interested collectives of experts, in order to predict outcomes in various fields. Adamic and Glance's study of the predictions of bloggers during the 2004 presidential campaign is an important example of this technique [1]. Many predicted a very insular and divided election, and the study of the blogging community confirmed that cross-posting between liberal and conservative blogs was very uncommon, indicating that both groups were "mini echo chambers". In essence, people tended to comment on and link to evidence on sites they agreed with [1].

Formation of a consensus within a community is only one way a shout can increase in volume. While consensus in online communities does develop over time, arguments and differences in opinion can also call attention to comments and be a predictor of shouts. A community without dissenters is unlikely. A single story may draw hundreds of comments, and that story may then be copied in another community drawing hundreds of that community's own comments. Each one of these comments may contain subtleties that make any comment difficult to classify as positive or negative, as opposed to sarcastic. This nesting of meaning and context creates huge problems for those examining trends in communities in hope of predicting consensus. However, if in fact most readers notice only the comments with the most volume, it is possible that a smaller set of comments could be used to gain insight into a community.

This paper first reviews the literature regarding blogs and memes, and the frameworks used to create the term memetic primers. Then, possible primers are identified on the video game blog "Kotaku". An analysis and implication for the consideration of memetic primers in online community design follows.

2. Literature Review

2.1. Blogs

There are many of definitions of "blog" available that include varying amounts of detail on the word's first use and coinage, but Blood's history of the origin of blogs is most often cited. She provides a large number of sources and studies both the creation of the term "blog" and the authors who created those definitions. Blood identifies the first use of the term "weblog" by Jorn Barger, a frequent web surfer who began to log websites he visited and found interesting by publishing the list on his own website [9]. The term "blog" evolved from this first site as others began to create similar logs on their own sites. One of these was Jesse James Garrett's site that started to compile a list of similar sites. Garrett's list eventually came into the hands of Cameron Barrett, who published it on his own site, Camworld. Garrett's list of twenty-three "only weblog" pages soon grew until much of the web was following the style of updates which began with these "weblogs". The term "weblog" was shortened to "blog" and the activity of updating the page began to be referred to as "blogging" [9-11].

As the nascent blog community grew, readers began to add their own blogs to Garrett's list and to expand the definition of "blog". Blood mentions starting her own blog within this community in April of 1999. As the blogger community grew, it became increasingly difficult to read through the output of the entire community regularly. The founders of this community began to limit their listings of blogs to those they themselves frequented on a daily basis. At this point, Brigitte Eaton's Eatonweb Portal attempted to provide a directory of all blogs, the only criterion for listing being inclusion of a series of dated posts [12]. Eatonweb Portal grew in popularity as tools became available for automatically creating blog spaces. Blood cites Pitas.com as the first of these tools. Soon the web was flooded with other tools such as Blogger and Groksoup. Later web community pages such as Myspace, Livejournal, and Facebook made creating personal spaces with dated entries almost universal web culture. Soon sites like Reddit, Slashdot, and Fark brought their own communities into the picture, linking to blogs and news stories on the web, and creating a form of meta-community of those who read blogs and in turn became part of the definition themselves [10,11,13,14].

Blog Classification

The term "blog" is used to cover a variety of styles. The primary function of a blog helps define it further by subtype. Blogs, which started out mostly as communities recording day-to-day events, have evolved into many different types of blog subgenres [11]. These subtypes can in turn be divided according to the number of authors writing on a particular blog, as seen in **Table 1**.

Blogs with a single author are often personal in nature, serving as diaries visible to the web [13]. A number of services are offered on the web to help authors automatically create such personal blogs. These services include Blogger, Livejournal, Myspace, Twitter, and Facebook. Most personal blog services act as community boards, encouraging interactions between members with similar interests. Individual blogs, while mostly of a personal nature, can vary in their content. For example, while one member of Livejournal may use his or her blog to keep in

Table 1. Blog classification.

	Single Author	Multiple Authors/ Contributors
Diverse Topics	Personal blogs, Blogger, Twitter	Fark, Reddit, Digg
Specific Topics	Professional blogs (producers, directors, lawyer, etc…)	Slashdot, Kotaku

touch with family and friends, another member may use a blog in a professional capacity to discuss a new project and communicate with a professional readership [14,15].

Blogs with multiple contributors, such as Slashdot, usually are either formed by contributions from a community or have a number of editors, as in the case of Kotaku. These contributors act as reporters for the blog, finding links to suggest to their readership. Many of these sites focus on a specific topic [11]. Such topics are usually associated with already established communities. Science and technology news is the focus of Slashdot, while Kotaku has a more specific focus on video games and Japanese culture. More general blogging communities have fewer restrictions on what posts are worthy. Sites like Fark, Reddit, and Digg receive submissions from their readers and post them for other readers to comment on. These communities discuss current news and provide commenters with tools such as image and HTML links to help enhance discussions [11]. Understanding all of these blog communities and mining their discussions is an area researched by authors in socio-technical fields.

Blogs with multiple authors and specific topic classifications were chosen as the most useful for this study, since they include the largest number of users, all centered on one particular subject. While individual blogs (such as those on Blogger) may also have communities and comments, comments on these sites are usually addressed to the blog's author rather than to a community. On large, multi-author blogs without a central focus, the great number of posts and diversity of topics encourages commenters to simply make statements rather than to discuss topics. On such sites, popular topics also tend to be on polarizing political or social issues. In these cases, trolling (posting comments aimed at inciting anger) and "echo chamber" responses are very common [1].

2.2. Memes

Use of the term "meme" is expanding and slowly changing due to its use in describing Internet culture, but the term's roots are in the book *The Selfish Gene* by Richard Dawkins [16]. The book describes the evolutionary process as competition between genes that are not working toward the "good of the whole species", but rather acting "selfishly" to preserve themselves [17]. Furthermore, genes are one of many "replicators" which transfer information down generations via "vehicles" that protect data [17]. From this comes the use of "meme" to mean a unit of cultural transmission, or as Blackmore puts it, a unit of imitation from the Greek "mimeme" for something imitated [16]. Dawkin's examples of memes include a description of how a scientific idea jumps from the mind of one scientist to another, replicating itself until it is eventually accepted by the entire scientific community. Brodie takes this concept further, asserting that memes form the basis of the "paradigm shift" first proposed by Kuhn during the transition from Newtonian physics to Einstein's new theories on relativity [18]. Following this train of thought further, Brodie proposes that not only do memes replicate, but they do so aggressively like a virus [18]. Brodie's "meme" is comes closest to the terms popular usage on the Internet.

Memetic primers, as described in this paper, build from the original, academic definition of memes. The definition of memetic primers falls into a very specific context and implementation much in the way "Internet memes" fit a narrow subset of the broader academic use of the term meme [18]. Memetic primers are guidelines that prepare the user to treat the concept presented as a meme, rendering the concept memorable and increasing the volume of the comment. For example, inflammatory comments may cause a number of effects that make them stick out in the reader's memory and incites them to reply, increasing the visibility of the comment for future readers. Shouts, very loud comments, are not always memes, but most memes receive shout-like levels of attention and could possibly be used to attract more attention to a comment on a blog. Another distinction between a meme and a shout, as described in this study, is that a meme has won an established following while a shout may still be growing in outreach or "volume". Various websites, such as Reddit, Fark, and Slashdot act as growth media, spreading and amending a particular meme until it is "heard" by all in the community [19]. As Ohanian points out in his TED talk, the goals of the community are not very predicable, so it is hard to say what the members will elevate to meme status and what will remain whispers on a website [19]. In his example, whale hunting by Japan was not a major concern of the Reddit community until the goofy idea of naming the mascot of Greenpeace's anti-whaling initiative, "Mr. Splashy Pants", motivated the community to take action [19].

Definition of Memetic Priming and Memetic Primers

Memetic priming is an element of communication that snares the reader's attention and prods them to repeat and spread the meme. Memetic primers are the guidelines that, if they exist, can be keys to understanding how to attract attention and more readily spread information virally on the Internet. Depending on the context of the message and the audience, it is possible that these primers are very complex. Cultural differences may be an even larger hurdle, as one not familiar with the culture of the community will possibly overlook its memetic primers. I theorize that memetic primers would not be transferable between cultures for the most part. A meme based in humor in one culture could fall flat in a culture that did not find it funny.

An example highlights what memetic primers are and how they differ between communities. Let us take two Internet communities, Reddit and Fark, for example. Both of these communities have sections in which politics are discussed. If one were to use a negative memetic primer—say, using slanderous untrue remarks about a candidate—the reaction and eventual volume of the comment would differ between the communities due to differences in the social norms and moderation styles. If the candidate was particularly liked in the Reddit community, the community would use "down votes" (a negative form of moderation) to move the comment down and further from view. In Fark, comments are always presented in the chronological order in which they were posted, so users tend to repeat comments using italics to form a reply to something they either agree or disagree with. Regardless of the situation, agreement or disagreement, within the Fark community the negative primer gains volume and attention.

The deeper our understanding of the effect of memetic primers on consumption of media, the more effectively we build defenses against those who would abuse them. For example, negative language should play a significant role in memetic priming. Much of our current understanding of media, as stated earlier in this chapter, shows the influence negative media has on people. This, in turn, has created an influx of negative media to broadcast and print news. In a market where audience size is paramount, any sensational hook will be used to grab attention. This abundance of negative information has caused significant damage to public understanding of the world. Recent studies at Georgia State University [20] show evidence that, even when corrected with hard facts, individuals' tend to believe what they are first told, and that corrections may even further cement their faith in incorrect information. With a better understanding of how memes work to spread information, steps could be taken to lessen the impact of false information, exposing the abuse of memes.

2.3. Source

Source is a concept that is central to communication theory [21]. It is a concept that changes meaning with new technology. It is a mental understanding of the reader where they receive their information. Source requires careful study when applied to new forms of computer based communication, since a clear and concise definition is not available even in traditional media [21]. In Sundar and Nass's article "Conceptualizing Sources in Online News" the authors found that online news creates new sources not found in other forms of media, (such as the computer itself and the website's audience). This realization brings new insight into how all new media, including blogs, are conceptualized by their readers. New media holds a large number of sources not considered in more traditional forms of communication. Readers must manage these new sources to transform the article into knowledge that they can act upon. There are a number of models which can be used to as a framework to for the consumption of online media, one of which is the MAIN Model.

2.4. MAIN Model

The MAIN Model (**Figure 1**) provides a framework for analyzing how readers perceive information from new media, such as blogs, and makes judgments of the media's credibility. This framework can be focused on credibility judgments about comments, which influence any actions the readers may take. This, in turn, affects the comment's volume on the blog. Of particular interest is the second layer of the MAIN Model, in which heuristics are used by readers to make credibility judgments on online media. These heuristics are organized by the affordances that accommodate them. Utilizing a number of these heuristics, the reader makes credibility judgments, consciously or unconsciously. Although each of these levels is quite complex, it is possible to isolate a few of these heuristics and examine how they apply to a specific form of new media [7].

Within the MAIN Model one can see a heuristic that is central to the blog affordance of agency, the Bandwagon Effect. While blogs are a great place for those interested in certain topics to read up on the latest news, they are most frequented by those enthusiastic on the subject

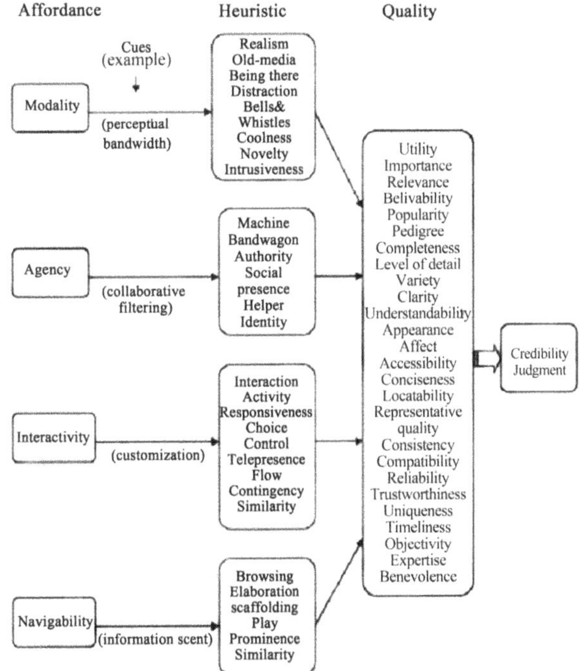

Figure 1. The MAIN Model [6].

matter. Through comments, these users interact and in turn affect new readers, creating a consensus in the community via these heuristics. "The Bandwagon Effect of Collaborative Filtering Technology" is a study that looks at the use of the Bandwagon heuristic in purchasing items on sites like Amazon, where comments can sway buyers [6]. In that study, commenters are the primary source of information, however when looking at blogs one has two sources of information, the author and the commenters. This study looks at the interaction between the commenter source and the readers of these blogs. Memetic primers are the means in which a commenter may possible cue a reader to act, in the effort to create a meme.

Proposed Framework

The following figure (**Figure 2**) describes how this study poses the interaction between the blog and reader creates a shout.

Blogs have many affordances that may lead to a credibility judgment. These credibility judgments influence volume of the comment. The new framework focuses on this volume and how a memetic primer can initialize interest. The original flow does not model any decisions to take action, either in the form of replying to a comment or taking other forms of action on the comment. By allowing the reader to then take action, these actions may then increase the interest other have in the comment, thus increasing the comment's volume. This loop continues until a comment becomes a shout or meme.

3. Method

An in-depth examination of online discourse provides a solid foundation for understanding possible memetic primers. This required the identification of a web community with a commenting system that encourages members to write popular comments. Since the term "discourse analysis" is very common and used interchangeably with many different forms of research, it requires a more detailed explanation. First, this study will not fall into the subcategory of "critical" discourse analysis as the study does not presume that any group has a position of power which perpetuates the condition over others in the case of these blogs. While blogs may address critical issues, the form of the research question does not address anything that would require a critical perspective [22]. This study will instead use a discourse analysis that examines the Logic-of-Inquiry approach of discourse analysis used often in education [23] while also having intercoder verification to protect against bias. The Logic-of-Inquiry discourse analysis takes a look at the conversation of students, taking apart the meaning in their discourse to discern the student's intention and logical process [23]. I believe that with the application of this style of open coding discourse analysis I would better understand if the user was attempting to be sarcastic or trolling by identifying their thought process.

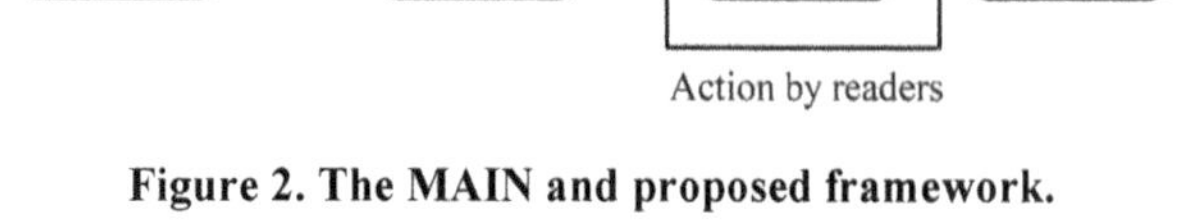

The first requirements of a Logic-of-Inquiry and intercoder verification entails there will be two coders performing the discourse analysis. The coders will read each comment, inductively creating the codes from the content of the discussion as opposed to using a preset deductive set of codes. Using such a preset coding scheme would hurt the investigative nature of this study phase and may hide unexpected elements in the comments. The codes made by each researcher are then compared to find inconsistencies that could occur from bias. While Logic-of-Inquiry was originally intended for educational settings, Gee and Green state that discourse analysis "provided new insights into the complex and dynamic relationships among discourse, social practices, and learning" which indicated it would be suited for use in online social spaces [23]. The reason for this is the closeness of the theoretical underpinnings of Gee and Green's approach that links language and community to knowledge. This method also discusses in detail the use of situated meanings, cultural models, and reflexivity needed in understanding knowledge generated from discourse. Many of the online discussions, in particular special interests discussions, are dense with cultural connotations and meaning. The Logic-of-Inquiry methodology has an understanding of community and situated meanings that match well to the online discussions found within web communities. Both coders of the data set were familiar with video game culture and current events so they could understand the context of each comment. Utilizing this method, the comments from a blog summary with the most replies or highest community score were coded to identify possible memetic primers. After coding had been completed, the power of possible memetic primers were identified by a quantitative analysis between the codes and responses and percentage of comments devoted to the comment. The two primary metrics to determine the "volume" or "loudness" of the comment were the number of replies the comment received and the percentage

Figure 2. The MAIN and proposed framework.

of all the comments on a topic that were replies to the comment. This thread percentage value indicates how capable a comment was in controlling the conversation and is referred to as loudness.

Codes

Two code sets were inducted from the comments by a pair of researchers. These sets where then compared to each other to determine intercoder reliability. Each set was analyzed independently to find any significant correlations of the codes to the metrics mentioned above. Loudness, once again, is the percentage of all comments in the post that were replies to the shout. For example, if the most popular comment in a thread has 35 replies, and the total number of comments to the subject is 100, then loudness of the comment would be 35/100 or 35%.

The following **Table 2** lists the codes created from the analysis of comments by both coders. They are listed in order of possible significance (anecdotally, from codes that appeared in both sets and occurred most often). Those marked with an asterisk were found by both coders independently.

As one can see there is much overlap between the two code sets. Positive, Negative Tangential, Inflammatory, Question, Explanatory and Humor are all identified as elements in the comments that need illumination. This is in addition to other pairs of codes that share similar meaning like Exp for Expansion and Story codes. The

Table 2. Raw codes.

Code	Meaning
Negative*	The comment is negative toward the article subject matter.
Positive*	The comment is positive toward the article subject matter.
Explanatory*	Provides more insight into a specific point.
Tangential*	The comment offers a new subject to discuss.
Humor*	An attempt at being funny or ironic.
Inflammatory*	A remark that possibly tries to encourage angry replies, possible "trolling".
Question*	The comment is a question requesting more information.
-*	Not codeable, usually a censored comment, but also includes comments whose intent is not clear.
Pop	The comments makes note of another trend, icon, or person.
List	Lists a number of examples.
Plea	Asks for action on part of the audience, author.
Story	The comments makes note of another story from within the community.
Null	Makes a comment on an indefinite pro-noun that is not clear. "They", "people", "he", "she".
Console	Makes a comment that shows preference for, or against, one of the major video game console manufactures.
Fact	Makes note of an outside fact (no link).
Caps	The author uses capital letters on some words to emphasize them.
Emotive	Using expressions such as HAHA, lol, ROFL. WTF, OMG.
Post	References the article the comment appears in.
Anecdotal	Provides evidence from own experience.
Txt	Using common testing shortcuts. ! = (not equal), ITT (in this thread). These are not emotional (see Emotive).
Design	Makes a comment on the design or content in a game.
Expletive	Used an expletive.
Critical	Critical of the author of the post. Grammar, factual, or any other mistake found in the post.
Insightful	Comment takes notice of an element in the post and brings it to light.
Community	A reference to Kotaku and/or its authors or popular commenters.
Video	Comment embedded a flash video.
Informative	Provided more information.
Per	Personal, front page comment is expressing a personal viewpoint or personal feelings.
Cor	Correction, front page comment is correcting some apparent misinformation in the topic.
Cla	Clarification, front page comment is asking for clarification on the topic.

number of codes per comment however was different for each coder, as one coder tended to only attribute one or two codes per comment while the other coder was more detailed in the content of each shout.

4. Analysis

Qualitative codes from each set are listed in **Table 3**. They had their distribution analyzed to see if the number of occurrences would be sufficient for variance tests. A number of the codes did not have enough instances to be properly analyzed. These included List, Story, Null, Fact, Txt, Vowel, Critical, Community, Video, Informative, QA, Exp, and Cor.

4.1. Negative Comments

Negative comments were associated with a number of significant findings as seen in **Figures 3** and **4**. First, as shown on the chart of occurrences, they have a large number of occurrences in both coding sets. This gave an indication that negative commenting on stories was important. Further investigation brings to light statistically significant relationships between negative comments and volume.

Table 3. Coder analysis.

Coder 1:

Code	# of Occurrences
Negative	94
Anecdotal	51
Question	40
Positive	39
Humor	38
Design	33
Emotive	32
Post	31
Explanatory	27
Pop	26
Console	22
Inflammatory	18
Plea	17
Expletive	14
Caps	10
Tangential	10
Insightful	10
Story	8
Community	7
Informative	5
Txt	3
Null	2
Fact	2
Video	2
List	1
Vowel	1
Critical	1

Coder 2:

Code	# of Occurrences
Tan	64
Neg	34
Per	30
Cla	21
-	17
Pos	14
Inf	13
Com	13
QA	5
Exp	4
Cor	2

t Test and Analysis of Variance for Thread Percentage by Negative Comments, Code Set 1.

Difference	0.045795	**t Ratio**	3.785124
Std Err Dif	0.012099	**DF**	203
Upper CL Dif	0.069650	**Prob > |t|**	0.0002
Lower CL Dif	0.021940	**Prob > t**	0.0001
Confidence	0.95	**Prob < t**	0.9999

Source	DF	Sum of Squares	Mean Square	F Ratio	Prob > F
Has_Negative	1	0.1067406	0.106741	14.3272	0.0002
Error	203	1.5123953	0.007450		
C. Total	204	1.6191359			

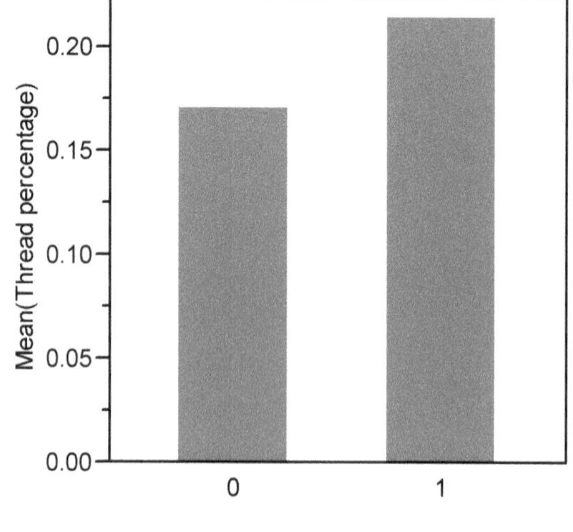

Figure 3. Mean thread percentage by negative comments, code set 1.

t Test and Analysis of Variance for Thread Percentage by Negative Comments, Code Set 1.

Difference	0.045795	**t Ratio**	3.785124
Std Err Dif	0.012099	**DF**	203
Upper CL Dif	0.069650	**Prob > |t|**	0.0002
Lower CL Dif	0.021940	**Prob > t**	0.0001
Confidence	0.95	**Prob < t**	0.9999

Source	DF	Sum of Squares	Mean Square	F Ratio	Prob > F
Has_Negative	1	0.1067406	0.106741	14.3272	0.0002
Error	203	1.5123953	0.007450		
C. Total	204	1.6191359			

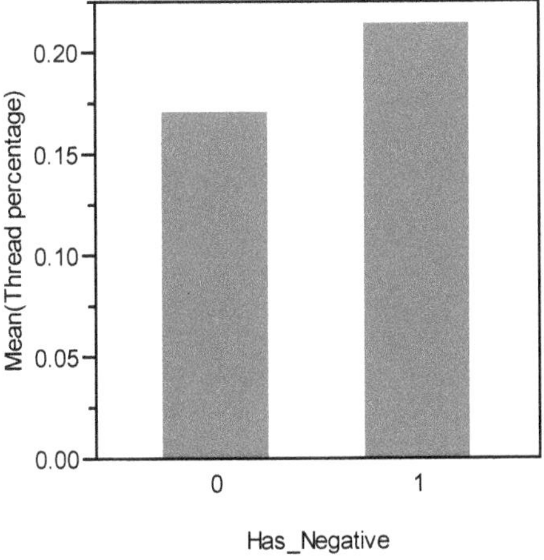

Figure 4. Mean thread percentage by negative comments, code set 2.

t Test and Analysis of Variance Front page Responses by Console Comments, Code Set 1.

Difference	8.4391	**t Ratio**	2.854792
Std Err Dif	2.9561	**DF**	202
Upper CL Dif	14.2678	**Prob > |t|**	0.0048
Lower CL Dif	2.6103	**Prob > t**	0.0024
Confidence	0.95	**Prob < t**	0.9976

Source	DF	Sum of Squares	Mean Square	F Ratio	Prob > F
Has_Console	1	1395.713	1395.71	8.1772	0.0047
Error	203	34648.726	170.68		
C. Total	204	36044.439			

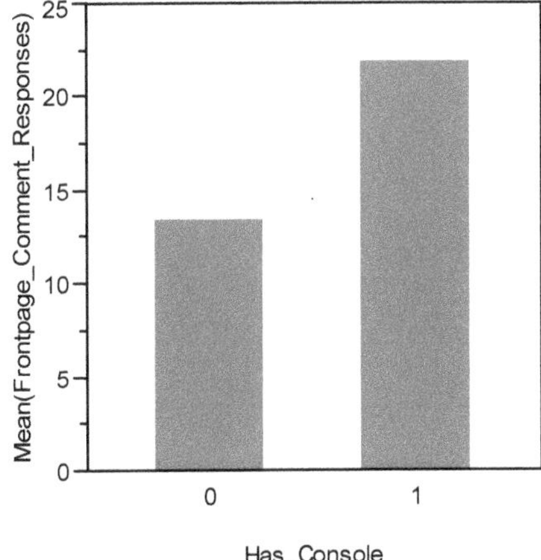

Figure 5. Number of front page responses by console comments, code set 1.

The above figures show an analysis of the variance of the code sets on negative comments. The bars indicate the mean thread percentage of the category. While the second set required the exclusion of one outlier, both sets show a significant relationship between the percentage of comments as replies to shout and if a comment was negative in nature. One scenario to explain this relationship is that a commenter responding negatively then causes an argument consuming much of the conversation on the topic. Alternatively, a large group of the readers replied to agree with the negative comment, eager to also make their stance known. In either case, this significant factor is one that will be further tested during the experimental phase of the study.

Related to negative comments, though not necessarily negative, were comments referring a preference for a particular video game console as seen in **Figure 5**. This code was only recognized by one of the coders, so data supporting this finding only came from one set.

Arguments for why this would be a significant guideline are similar to that of the negative code. Showing favoritism or distaste for a particular console is a way to cause an argument by those not sharing that opinion. This argument is so common that many who bring it up are thought to be "trolls", those looking to start an argument for personal satisfaction. While trolling may be viewed as a negative social action, its goals are similar to the goals of anyone trying to gain volume or attention in an online discussion. This combined with the difficultly of determining the commenter's true intent, so no distinction was made between comments that may or may not have been trolling attempts.

4.2. Positive Comments

While there is an old saying, "You catch more flies with honey then you do with vinegar", only one piece of evidence was found to support this popular phrase. While the first set of codes do not show a significant relationship between these two variables, the second set of qualitative codes does show this relationship. A correlation was found between positive comments and the number of replies the comments received. Since this is only present in one code set bias can be a factor in showing this relationship. Therefore testing positive comments was a primary goal within the second phase of the study.

As one can see in **Figure 6**, the positive front page comments received more replies, however in both code

t Test and Analysis of Variance Front Page Replies by Positive Comments, Code Set 2.

<table>
<tr><td>Difference</td><td>10.8865</td><td>t Ratio</td><td>3.008068</td></tr>
<tr><td>Std Err Dif</td><td>3.6191</td><td>DF</td><td>202</td></tr>
<tr><td>Upper CL Dif</td><td>18.0225</td><td>Prob > |t|</td><td>0.0030</td></tr>
<tr><td>Lower CL Dif</td><td>3.7504</td><td>Prob > t</td><td>0.0015</td></tr>
<tr><td>Confidence</td><td>0.95</td><td>Prob < t</td><td>0.9985</td></tr>
</table>

Source	DF	Sum of Squares	Mean Square	F Ratio	Prob > F
Has Positive	1	1543.733	1543.73	9.0832	0.0029
Error	203	34500.706	169.95		
C. Total	204	36044.439			

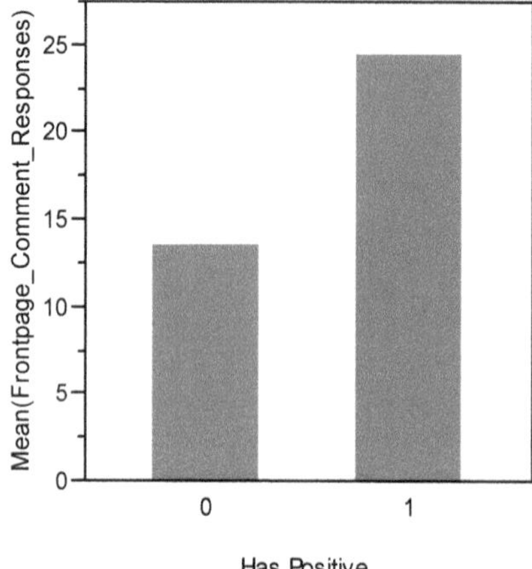

Figure 6. Front page replies by positive comments, code set 2.

t Test and Analysis of Variance Front Page Replies by Question Comments, Code Set 1.

<table>
<tr><td>Difference</td><td>−4.6823</td><td>t Ratio</td><td>−2.00746</td></tr>
<tr><td>Std Err Dif</td><td>2.3325</td><td>DF</td><td>202</td></tr>
<tr><td>Upper CL Dif</td><td>−0.0832</td><td>Prob > |t|</td><td>0.0460</td></tr>
<tr><td>Lower CL Dif</td><td>−9.2814</td><td>Prob > t</td><td>0.9770</td></tr>
<tr><td>Confidence</td><td>0.95</td><td>Prob < t</td><td>0.0230</td></tr>
</table>

Source	DF	Sum of Squares	Mean Square	F Ratio	Prob > F
Has_Question	1	705.470	705.470	4.0525	0.0454
Error	203	35338.969	174.084		
C. Total	204	36044.439			

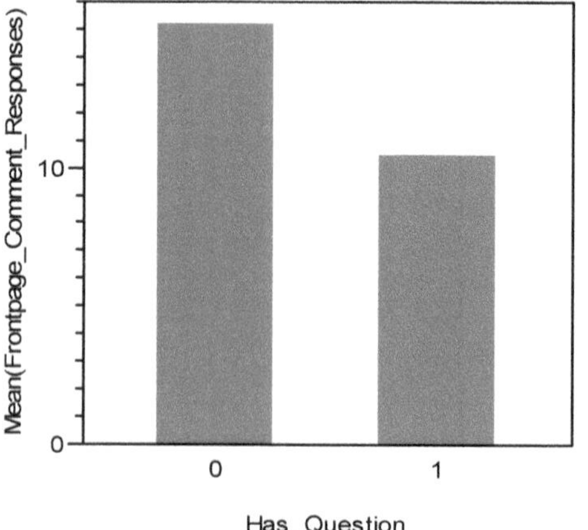

Figure 7. Front page replies by question comments, code set 1.

sets there was no relationship between the positive comments and thread percentage, indicating that positive comments are not able to monopolize the conversation to the extent negative comments can.

4.3. Question Comments

The first set of qualitative codes only showed a single code that indicated a significantly lower chance of increasing volume, posting questions.

Figure 7 shows that shouts in the form of a question had a significantly lower number of replies that those which were not. This can be explained as the answer was quickly provided and the discussion did not continue as the answer was quickly accepted. This is not to say that questions did not have the same chance to become the shout in the thread, just that from these statistics they do so without a large number of replies, hence a lower volume. Further discussion of this finding and its implications on a question's relationship with volume on a comment thread can be found in the conclusions chapter.

5. Discussion and Implication

The discourse analysis discovered a number of possible memetic primers. These primers were then analyzed to find any significant relationships between these memetic primers and measures of volume, thread percentage and number of replies. Negative comments showed a relationship with thread percentage in both coder sets. Positive and question comments showed significant relationship with number of replies in individual coder sets.

The use of blogs as trusted primary, sources of information has become a reality, and the people that comment on such blogs have the power to sway public policy through activism and discourse. The results found in this dissertation are important to understand the way these large communities can be influenced and possibly controlled. Information is abundant and at times overwhelming in the web, and we rely on our trusted online communities to help turn this data into knowledge. If there are disadvantages to trusting these online communities, they need to be exposed now so that these communities can continue to foster open discussion and interest into their various subjects. While the example of a gaming community is used within this study, I believe that the results can be generalized to other online interest groups.

Examples of online communities making an impact are numerous, bringing urgency to understanding them now. One example is that of the recent "Tea Party" groups in the United States calling for fiscal responsibility of the federal government. Regardless of the origins or motivations of this group, they have become a factor in the American political landscape. Online discussion helps build the social ties the Tea Party uses to grow [20,24,25]. Another example is the one mentioned in the literature review, of Reddit's campaign to name the Greenpeace spokes-whale "Mr. Splashy Pants" [19]. While the community was nonsensical in its approach, the goals and impact they created is real. Understanding memetic primers will give individuals, corporations, and academia the perspectives they need to rationally analyze social movements.

The introduction of memetic primers as a concept is the primary contribution of this study. Understanding this aspect of online communication is important to the future of online communities as they continue to grow as major, and some cases, primary form of human to human engagement around the world. This chapter will explore the possible implications of memetic primers, what this study does to provide evidence for their existence and what actions might need to be taken in future studies of this form of communication and in the design of online communities.

Design Implications

This study has implications for the design of future blog sites. Blog geared to discussion may wish to implement comment systems that encourage differences in opinion and hide those which do not add new evidence to the discussion. Similar systems exist in a number of special interest blogs, such as Slashdot.org which focuses on science and computer news. A comparison of a blog with these systems and one without would also be an area of future work.

Sites such as Kotaku, Slashdot, Fark, and Reddit continue to change even during the course of writing this dissertation. As of the writing of this dissertation, Kotaku has incorporated Facebook logins for their commenting system, but has also kept the original, stand-alone, anonymous login system. This allows Kotaku community members to choose to have their comments seen by offline contacts or to be anonymous so that they can be as blunt and forthcoming as they please. A study on the use of memetic primers within a community dependent on a user's known or anonymous status would shed some light into the social implications of particular memetic primers. While negative primers would be more effective at garnering attention to the author's post, the possibility of the comment being seen in a poor light in the users' local community could prevent their use.

As communities of special-topic blogs grow, these communities will also have to deal with their members aging and changing tastes, adjusting to new needs. This study focused on a gamer community, a demographic of people who played electronic games as children is now having its own children. As the community grows older, its stands to reason that the time available to allocate to online communities is shorter. This might make shouts and memes their primary connection to the community. Future work can be done to see how individuals remain active in blog communities as their contact with the communities shortens. It is possible that memetic primers will play an even more important role for these individuals seeking to quickly and easily keep up with the development of the community while dealing with day-to-day life.

REFERENCES

[1] L. A. Adamic and N. Glance, "The Political Blogosphere and the 2004 US Election: Divided They Blog," *Proceedings of the* 3*rd international Workshop on Link Discovery*, Chicago, 21-24 August 2005.

[2] Y. Chi, B. L. Tseng and J. Tatemura, "Eigen-Trend: Trend Analysis in the Blogosphere Based on Singular Value Decompositions," *Proceedings of the* 15*th ACM International Conference on Information and Knowledge Management*, Arlington, 5-10 November 2006.

[3] J. G. Conrad and F. Schilder, "Opinion Mining in Legal Blogs," *Proceedings of the* 11*th International Conference on Artificial Intelligence and Law*, Stanford, 4-8 June 2007.

[4] PricewaterhouseCoopers, "How Consumer Conversation Will Transform Business," Pricewaterhouse Coopers, London, 2008.

[5] I. Yucel, "Understanding the Sources and Bandwagon Effects in Blog Communities," 2007. http://www.psu.edu/dept/medialab/researchpage/newabstracts/blog.html

[6] S. S. Sundar, A. Oeldorf-Hirsch and Q. Xu, "The Bandwagon Effect of Collaborative Filtering Technology," *CHI'*08 *Extended Abstracts on Human Factors in Computing Systems*, Florence, 2008, pp. 3453-3458.

[7] S. S. Sundar, "The MAIN Model: A Heuristic Approach to Understanding Technology Effects on Credibility," In: M. J. Metzger and A. J. Flanagin, Eds., *Digital Media and Learning*, 2007, pp. 73-100.

[8] R. McArthur, "Uncovering Deep User Context from Blogs," *Proceedings of the Second Workshop on Analytics for Noisy Unstructured Text Data*, Singapore, 24 July 2008.

[9] P. Boutin, "Robot Wisdom on the Street," 2005. http://www.wired.com/wired/archive/13.07/posts.html?pg=6

[10] R. Blood, "Weblogs: A History and Perspective," 2000. http://www.rebeccablood.net/essays/weblog_history.html

[11] J. Bar-Ilan, "An Outsider's View on 'Topic-Oriented Blogging'," *Proceedings of the* 13*th International World Wide Web Conference on Alternate Track Papers & Posters*, New York, 17-20 May 2004, pp. 28-34.

[12] B. Eatonweb, "The Blog Directory," 2008.

http://portal.eatonweb.com/

[13] R. Blood, "How Blogging Software Reshapes the Online Community," *Communications of ACM*, Vol. 47, No. 12, 2004, pp. 53-55.

[14] K. R. Cohen, "A Welcome for Blogs. Continuum," *Journal of Media & Cultural Studies*, Vol. 20, No. 2, 2006, pp. 161-173.

[15] M. Chymes, "An Incomplete Annotated History of Weblogs," 2001. http://web.archive.org/web/20031119025356/

[16] http://www.chymes.org/hyper/weblogs.html

[17] S. J. Blackmore, "The Meme Machine," Oxford University Press, New York, 1999.

[18] R. Dawkins, "The Selfish Gene," Oxford University Press, Oxford, 1976.

[19] R. Brodie, "Virus of the Mind: The New Science of the Meme," Integral Press, Seattle, 2004.

www.youtube.com/watch?v=tPgQsv2KPwc

[20] A. Ohanian, "Alexis Ohanian: How to Make a Splash in Social Media," 2009.

[21] B. Nyhan and J. Reifler, "When Corrections Fail: The Persistence of Political Misperceptions," *Political Behavior*, Vol. 32, No. 2, 2010, pp. 303-330.

[22] S. S. Sundar and C. Nass, "Conceptualizing Sources in Online News," *Journal of Communication Research*, Vol. 27, No. 6, 2001, pp. 683-703.

[23] N. Fairclough, "Critical Discourse Analysis and the Marketization of Public Discourse: The Universities," *Discourse & Society*, Vol. 4, No. 2, 1993, pp. 133-168.

[24] J. P. Gee and J. L. Green, "Discourse Analysis, Learning, and Social Practice: A Methodological Study," *Review of Research in Education*, Vol. 23, 1998, pp. 119-169.

[25] L. V. Braekel, "The Impact of Blogging on Society and Politics," 2007. http://lvb.net/item/5470

Permissions

The contributors of this book come from diverse backgrounds, making this book a truly international effort. This book will bring forth new frontiers with its revolutionizing research information and detailed analysis of the nascent developments around the world.

We would like to thank all the contributing authors for lending their expertise to make the book truly unique. They have played a crucial role in the development of this book. Without their invaluable contributions this book wouldn't have been possible. They have made vital efforts to compile up to date information on the varied aspects of this subject to make this book a valuable addition to the collection of many professionals and students.

This book was conceptualized with the vision of imparting up-to-date information and advanced data in this field. To ensure the same, a matchless editorial board was set up. Every individual on the board went through rigorous rounds of assessment to prove their worth. After which they invested a large part of their time researching and compiling the most relevant data for our readers. Conferences and sessions were held from time to time between the editorial board and the contributing authors to present the data in the most comprehensible form. The editorial team has worked tirelessly to provide valuable and valid information to help people across the globe.

Every chapter published in this book has been scrutinized by our experts. Their significance has been extensively debated. The topics covered herein carry significant findings which will fuel the growth of the discipline. They may even be implemented as practical applications or may be referred to as a beginning point for another development. Chapters in this book were first published by Scientific Research Publishing Inc.; hereby published with permission under the Creative Commons Attribution License or equivalent.

The editorial board has been involved in producing this book since its inception. They have spent rigorous hours researching and exploring the diverse topics which have resulted in the successful publishing of this book. They have passed on their knowledge of decades through this book. To expedite this challenging task, the publisher supported the team at every step. A small team of assistant editors was also appointed to further simplify the editing procedure and attain best results for the readers.

Our editorial team has been hand-picked from every corner of the world. Their multi-ethnicity adds dynamic inputs to the discussions which result in innovative outcomes. These outcomes are then further discussed with the researchers and contributors who give their valuable feedback and opinion regarding the same. The feedback is then collaborated with the researches and they are edited in a comprehensive manner to aid the understanding of the subject.

Apart from the editorial board, the designing team has also invested a significant amount of their time in understanding the subject and creating the most relevant covers. They scrutinized every image to scout for the most suitable representation of the subject and create an appropriate cover for the book.

The publishing team has been involved in this book since its early stages. They were actively engaged in every process, be it collecting the data, connecting with the contributors or procuring relevant information. The team has been an ardent support to the editorial, designing and production team. Their endless efforts to recruit the best for this project, has resulted in the accomplishment of this book. They are a veteran in the field of academics and their pool of knowledge is as vast as their experience in printing. Their expertise and guidance has proved useful at every step. Their uncompromising quality standards have made this book an exceptional effort. Their encouragement from time to time has been an inspiration for everyone.

The publisher and the editorial board hope that this book will prove to be a valuable piece of knowledge for researchers, students, practitioners and scholars across the globe.

List of Contributors

Shoichiro Tomii and Tomoaki Ohtsuki
Graduate School of Science and Technology, Keio University, Yokohama, Japan

Zain Abbas, Nadeem Mahmood and Qamar-ul Arifeen
Department of Computer Science, University of Karachi, Karachi, Pakistan

Aqil Burney
Institute of Business Management, College of Computer Science and Information Systems, Karachi, Pakistan

Nitya Ahilandam Kamalanathan, Alan Eardley, Caroline Chibelushi and Tim Collins
Faculty of Computing Engineering and Sciences, Staffordshire University, Stafford, UK

Haoru Su and Zhiliang Wang
School of Computer and Communication Engineering, University of Science and Technology, Beijing, China

Sunshin An
Department of Electrical Engineering, Korea University, Seoul, Korea

Tung-Hung Lu, Hsing-Chen Lin, Rong-Rong Chen and Ya-Ling Chen
Service Systems Technology Center, Industrial Technology Research Institute, Hsinchu, Taiwan

Lijuan Huang and Yeming Xiong
School of Economics and Management, Xidian University, Xi'an, China

Peter Darcy, Steven Tucker and Bela Stantic
School of Information and Communication Technology, Griffith University, Gold Coast, Australia

Johanna Virkki
Department of Electronics and Communications Engineering, Tampere University of Technology, Tampere, Finland

Liquan Chen
School of Information Science and Engineering, Southeast University, Nanjing, China

Muzammil Khan
Department of Computer Science and Software Engineering, University of Swat, Saidu Sharif, Pakistan

Khushdil
Institute of Business and Computer Mgt Sciences, Department of Computer Science, Agriculture University, Peshawar, Pakistan

Chung-Ming Own
Department of Computer and Communication Engineering, St. John's University, New Taipei City, Chinese Taipei

Haw-Yun Shin
Department of Computer Science and Engineering, National Taiwan Ocean University, Keelung City, Chinese Taipei

Chen-Ya Teng
Department of Computer Science and Information Engineering, Tamkang University, New Taipei City, Chinese Taipei

Yiping Tang, Baoqing Ma and Hangchen Yan
Zhejiang University of Technology, Hangzhou, China

Paul Hanley, Paul Fergus and Faycal Bouhafs
School of Computing and Mathematical Sciences, Liverpool John Moores University, Liverpool, UK

Maram A. Alshareef
Program of Educational Graduate Studies, King Abdulaziz University, Jeddah, Kingdom of Saudi Arabia

Cosmas Rashama and Tonderai Damba
Department of Electrical Engineering, University of Zimbabwe, Harare, Zimbabwe

Wilson Mungwena
Department of Mechanical Engineering, University of Zimbabwe, Harare, Zimbabwe

Xintong Lu and Yongliang Guan
EEE, Nanyang Technological University, Singapore City, Singapore

Wei Liu
Singapore Institute of Manufacturing Technology, Singapore City, Singapore

Ayse Kok
Bogazici University, Istanbul, Turkey

Jamal Raiyn
Computer Science Department, Alqasemi College, Baka El Gariah, Israel

S. M. Khalid Jamal and A. Omer
Department of Computer Science, UBIT, University of Karachi, Karachi City, Pakistan

Asiya Abdus Salam Qureshi
Department of Computer Science and Software Engineering, University of Hail, Hail, KSA

Su Mon Kywe, Jie Shi, Yingjiu Li and Raghuwanshi Kailash
School of Information Systems, Singapore Management University, Singapore City, Singapore

Chien-Min Ou
Department of Electronics Engineering, Ching Yun University, Chungli, Chinese Taipei

Wei-De Wu
Department of Computer Science and Information Engineering, National Taiwan Normal University, Taipei, Chinese Taipei

Dawood Moeinfar, Hossein Shamsi and Fatemeh Nafar
Electrical Faculty, K. N. Toosi University of Technology, Tehran, Iran

Giulia Biamino
Department of Computer Science, University of Turin, Torino, Italy

Ibrahim Yucel
State University of New York Institute of Technology, Utica, USA

Printed in the USA
CPSIA information can be obtained
at www.ICGtesting.com
JSHW051440221024
72173JS00006B/1535